Cognitive Technologies

Managing Editors: D. M. Gabbay   J. Siekmann

Editorial Board: A. Bundy   J. G. Carbonell
M. Pinkal   H. Uszkoreit   M. Veloso   W. Wahlster
M. J. Wooldridge

Advisory Board:

For further volumes:
http://www.springer.com/series/5216

Toru Ishida

Editor

The Language Grid

Service-Oriented Collective Intelligence
for Language Resource Interoperability

 Springer

Editor
Prof. Toru Ishida
Department of Social Informatics
Kyoto University
Yoshida-Honmachi
606-8501 Kyoto
Japan
ishida@i.kyoto-u.ac.jp

Managing Editors
Prof. Dov M. Gabbay
Augustus De Morgan Professor of Logic
Department of Computer Science
King's College London
Strand, London WC2R 2LS, UK

Prof. Dr. Jörg Siekmann
Forschungsbereich Deduktions- und
Multiagentensysteme, DFKI
Stuhlsatzenweg 3, Geb. 43
66123 Saarbrücken, Germany

Cognitive Technologies ISSN 1611-2482
ISBN 978-3-642-27046-8   ISBN 978-3-642-21178-2 (eBook)
DOI 10.1007/978-3-642-21178-2
Springer Heidelberg Dordrecht London New York

ACM Codes: I.2.7, J.5, H.3

Cover design: deblik, Berlin

Printed on acid-free paper

Springer is part of Springer Science+Business Media (www.springer.com)

Preface

The idea of *the Language Grid* was born from the long term research initiative of *intercultural collaboration* in Kyoto University as follows. The concept of intercultural collaboration was invented after 9.11 in 2001 to establish the practical research goal of cross-cultural study: measuring the progress made in this study is feasible if we focus on collaborative work rather than general communication. We targeted machine translation as a key technology for intercultural collaboration, because only machine translators can overcome language barriers.

We took the approach of creating innovation from studies in the field. In 2002, we conducted a one year experiment called the *Intercultural Collaboration Experiment (ICE2002)* with Chinese, Korean, and Malaysian colleagues. They used their mother tongues to jointly develop open source software. After trying to collect and customize machine translators to cover five languages, we realized that the Internet needed a language infrastructure. Though there are language resource associations scattered throughout the world, their missions are to provide language resources to researchers, not to end users. We need an infrastructure for end users that provides unhindered access to language resources worldwide and that allows them to be combined to create customized multilingual environments.

In 2005, we designed a service-oriented language infrastructure, and submitted a research proposal to the National Institute of Information and Communications Technology. Our idea is to shift *from language resources to language services*. The research goal is not to collect language resources but to interconnect them as Web services. Since language is used everywhere in our daily life, delivering general technologies is not enough to cope with language barriers: we need to encourage end users to create their own customized multilingual environments to cover the situations they face. We think that the language barriers created by billions of people will be overcome by the very same people. The research proposal was accepted and the Language Grid Project commenced in 2006.

This book includes eighteen chapters in six parts that summarize various research results and associated development activities on the Language Grid. The first part describes the framework of the Language Grid, *service-oriented collective intelligence*, to bridge service providers, service users, and service grid operators. Two kinds of software are newly introduced: the *service grid server software* and the *Language Grid Toolbox*. The former is able to form any kind of service grid such as language services, e-learning services, and agricultural knowledge services. The Language Grid has been created based on this software and various language services. The latter is client software to create customized multilingual environments for end users. Both source codes are available with open source licenses. The second part provides technologies for *service workflows* that compose atomic language services. Since there can be different language services with the same functionalities, *horizontal service composition* to select the optimal atomic services for a given workflow is proposed based on constraint optimization algorithms. To this end, *language service ontology* has been studied to specify the semantics of various language services. To monitor and control the execution of composed workflows, the notion of *service supervision* was introduced.

The third part reports research work and activities on sharing and using language resources. Pivot translation is often applied, for example, when Asian languages are translated into European languages via English. Context-aware supervision has been proposed to prevent the decrease in translation accuracy that has, up to now, been inevitable with cascading translation services. Researchers whose background is not natural language processing also started using language resources: cultural differences in pictograms drawn by kids were analyzed by using a concept dictionary. NPO staff developed a system by which volunteer interpreters could collectively create questions and answers in different languages to support foreign patients at hospital receptions. The fourth part provides various applications of language services as applicable to intercultural collaboration. International NPOs have been using translation services for daily communication among their volunteer members worldwide. The accuracy of translation has been improved by developing their own dictionaries to be used in conjunction with translators. Researchers created a language-barrier-free room in the Second Life virtual space to naturally observe informal communication using machine translators. In parallel, controlled experiments have been conducted to understand the *inconsistency*, *asymmetry* and *intransitivity* of machine translations.

The fifth part collects reports on applying the Language Grid for translation activities including localization of industrial documents and Wikipedia articles. Protocols for *collaborative translation* have been studied to guarantee the effectiveness of group activities for translation. The sixth part illustrates how the Language Grid can be connected to other service grids. The Language Grid has already been combined with *Heart of Gold*, which was developed by DFKI in Germany for pipelining language processing software. The Language Grid has been also connected with smart classroom services in Tsinghua University in China. Furthermore, the two operation centers of the Language Grid in Kyoto University and NECTEC have been federated for joint operation.

We hope this book will strongly support and encourage researchers who are willing to utilize various language resources worldwide to create customized multilingual environments to overcome local language barriers. We are grateful to the many people who have worked on, collaborated with, and supported the Language Grid Project. This project will continue to guarantee the free exchange of ideas in different languages to prevent serious cultural conflicts in the future.

Toru Ishida
March, 2011 in Kyoto

Contents

Part I Language Grid Framework

Part II Composing Language Services

Part III Language Grid for Using Language Resources

Part IV Language Grid for Communication

Part V Language Grid for Translation

Part VI Towards Federation of Service Grids

Part I

Language Grid Framework

Chapter 1
The Language Grid: Service-Oriented Approach to Sharing Language Resources

Toru Ishida[1], Yohei Murakami[2], and Donghui Lin[2]

1 Department of Social Informatics, Kyoto University, Yoshida Honmachi, Sakyoku, Kyoto 606-8501 Japan, e-mail: ishida@i.kyoto-u.ac.jp

2 Language Grid Project, NICT, 3-5 Hikaridai, Seikacho, Sorakugun, Kyoto 619-0289, e-mail: {yohei, lindh}@nict.go.jp

Abstract Since various communities, which use multiple languages, now want to interact in daily life, tools that can effectively support multilingual communication are necessary. However, we often observe that the success of a multilingual tool in one situation does not guarantee its success in another. To develop a multilingual environment that can handle various situations in various communities, existing language resources (dictionaries, parallel texts, part-of-speech taggers, machine translators, etc.) should be easily shared and customized. Therefore, we designed our proposal, the Language Grid, as service-oriented collective intelligence; it allows users to freely create language services from existing language resources and combine those language services to develop new services to meet their own requirements. This chapter explains the design concept and service architecture of the Language Grid, and the approach of user involvement in the collective intelligence activities.

1.1 Introduction

Though the Internet allows people to be linked together regardless of location, language remains the biggest barrier: only 35% of the Internet population speaks English (Paolillo et al. 2003). The remainder is divided between other European languages and Asian languages. In fact, it is not possible for anyone to learn the languages needed to access all possible information on the Internet. In particular, Asian people are not taught neighboring languages. Few Japanese understand Chinese or Korean and vice versa. People learn English to collaborate, but often cannot think in English: serious barriers to intercultural collaboration exist, because the collaboration often requires elaborating new ideas in the native language. As there is no simple way to solve this problem, it is necessary to combine different ideas. Teaching English is one way, but learning another's language and respecting another's culture are also important. Since one cannot master all languages, the use of machine translation systems is a viable solution.

The above background drove us to conduct the *Intercultural Collaboration Experiment 2002 (ICE2002)* with Chinese, Korean and Malaysian colleagues (Nomura et al. 2003). We thought that machine translation would be useful in facilitating intercultural exchanges. We gathered machine translators to cover five languages: Chinese, Japanese, Korean, Malay and English. More than forty students and faculty members from five universities joined this experiment. The goal of the experiment was to develop open source software using the participants' first languages: Japanese participants used the Japanese language, Chinese participants used the Chinese language, and so on. The experiment started in April 2002 and ended in December 2002. During this experiment, the following problems were found in using language resources. Note that language resources include dictionaries, parallel texts, part-of-speech taggers, machine translators and so on.

- *Language resources are often not accessible* because of intellectual property rights and prices. We can now see many new language services on the Internet. We tend to think that effective language infrastructures have been developed, since we can use machine translations to view Web pages. However, if one tries to create new services by combining existing language resources, he/she is soon forced to face the realities: the language resources available come with different contracts and prices. Contracts tend to be complex because of concern over intellectual property rights. Explanations of the pricing structure are often incomplete or confusing even if the price is high.
- *Language resources are often not usable,* because of nonstandard interfaces and low service quality. For application interfaces, users have to develop different wrappers for different language resources. There is no quality assurance for language processing software including machine translators. Users have to estimate their quality of services, when selecting one. Moreover, language resources are often not customizable. Machine translators seldom allow users to modify them; it is hard to add new words to their dictionaries.

To increase the accessibility and usability of language resources, we proposed the *Language Grid* as *service-oriented collective intelligence*, i.e., it wraps existing language resources as atomic services and enables users to compose new services by combining atomic services. To realize the Language Grid, however, we must deal with the following issues.

- *Service architecture*: The service platform should allow users to create services and share them. Based on various atomic services with standard interfaces, an infrastructure for service composition should be provided. The service architecture should also allow users to develop application systems for supporting multilingual activities in their communities based on the provided language services.
- *User involvement*: Collective intelligence platforms can grow only through the voluntary efforts of users (Weiss 2005). The more users provide resources, the

more they can utilize the benefits of the resources. Therefore, it is necessary to encourage the participation of both users and communities.

Researchers in several organizations including Kyoto University and National Institute of Information and Communications Technology (NICT) started working on the Language Grid in April 2006 (Ishida 2006). This project is based on collaboration between industry, government, universities and non-profit organizations (NPO/ NGOs). The remaining parts of this chapter are organized as follows. First, Section 1.2 explains the necessity of shifting from language resources to language services. Section 1.3 shows the design concept and the service architecture, and Section 1.4 introduces how the Language Grid is operated for user involvement.

1.2 From Language Resources to Language Services

This section describes why the service-oriented approach is promising for sharing language resources. To illustrate this, let us look at what would happen in a Japanese school, where the number of Brazilian, Chinese and Korean students is increasing. We use machine translators in this example.

Suppose the teacher says "You have cleanup duty today" in Japanese, it means "It is your turn to clean the classroom today," and foreign students cannot understand this. Puzzled students are invited to a multilingual room in the school. Sitting in front of a computer connected to the Internet, the teacher types these words in Japanese on the screen: "You have cleanup duty today." Then the translation of this sentence appears: "今天是你负责打扫卫生" in Chinese, "오늘은 네가 청소 당번이야" in Korean, and "Hoje é seu plantão de linpeza" in Portuguese. "Aha!" say the kids with excited faces. One of them types in their language "I got it" and translation appears in Japanese on the screen.

Is it that simple to use machine translation? Several portal sites already offer translation services. Let's try to use them. First, enter "You have cleanup duty today" in Japanese and translate it into Korean. The sentence "오늘은 너가 청소 당번이야" appears on the screen. The Japanese teachers do not understand Korean, so they are not sure if the translation is correct. They use *back-translation* which translates the Korean translation into Japanese again. This yields "You should clean the classroom today!" It seems a little rude to hear, but may be acceptable, if accompanied with a smile. Let's translate it into Chinese in the same way. The Chinese sentence "今天你是扫除值日哟" appears on the screen. The Japanese teachers back-translate this Chinese sentence into Japanese and find the very strange sentence "Today, you remove something to do your duty." It seems the Japanese word "掃除当番," which means duty to clean the classroom, was not registered in the dictionary of this machine translator.

It appears that we need to customize machine translators with local dictionaries. For schoolteachers, it is necessary to compile a multilingual dictionary of words frequently used in schools. Suppose the available multilingual dictionaries are adequate. To combine those local resources and machine translators, however, we need to negotiate with the companies that provide the machine translators, and make contracts with them. Let's assume all contracts are signed successfully. It is still not easy to combine machine translators and dictionaries, because the APIs and data formats are not standardized.

The service-oriented approach allows users to create and share standardized dictionary services while protecting the intellectual property rights of language resources. Fig. 1.1 shows how to create atomic language services from corresponding language resources. Data like multilingual dictionaries and parallel texts can be wrapped to create atomic language services to provide a translation of words or sentences. However, those atomic services do not have to be a simple retrieval function: a parallel text service can return the translation of a sentence that is similar to the input sentence. Wrapping software like machine translators is straightforward. Even human interpreters can be wrapped as translation services. Users do not have to distinguish machine from human translation services other than by their quality of services: machine translators can provide faster services while human interpreters return higher quality translations.

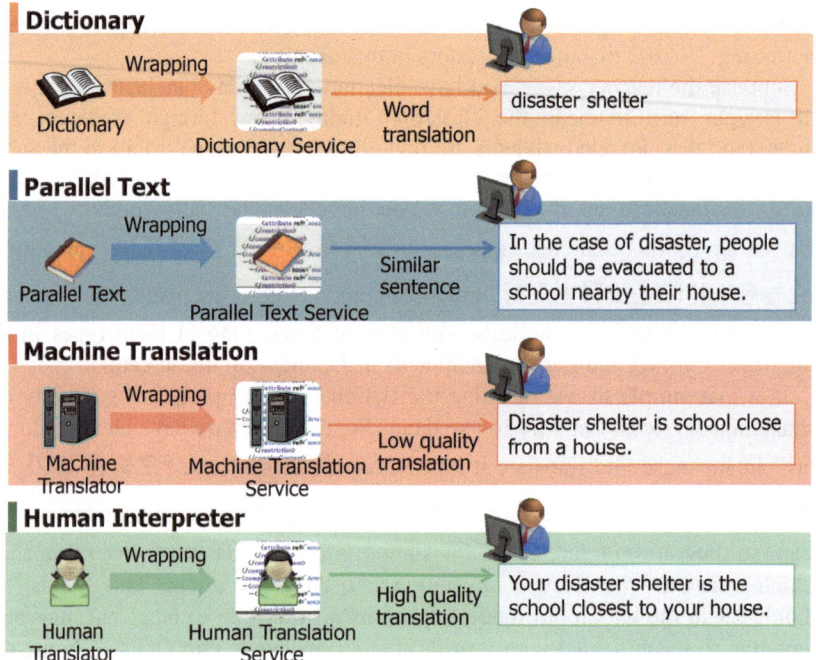

Fig. 1.1 Language service (atomic)

The next step is to compose atomic language services to create a new service. Fig. 1.2 illustrates the process of composing a variety of atomic language services for Japanese teachers to translate their announcements for Brazilian parents. To translate Japanese sentences into Portuguese, we first need to cascade Japanese-English and English-Portuguese translators, because there is no available direct translator handling Japanese to Portuguese. To replace words output by machine translators with the words in multilingual dictionaries for schools, part-of-speech taggers are necessary to divide the input sentences into parts. We can train *example-based machine translators* with Japanese-Portuguese parallel texts. We then have different types of translators including example-based machine translators and will face the problem of determining which one is best: example-based machine translators can create high quality translation only when they trained with similar sentences. We may use back-translation, say Japanese-Portuguese-Japanese translation, to compare original and back-translated Japanese sentences, and select the translator that can produce back-translated sentences most similar to the original ones. If the quality of translation is still not enough for the Brazilian parents to understand, however, Japanese teachers may use human translation services to create an announcement in Portuguese.

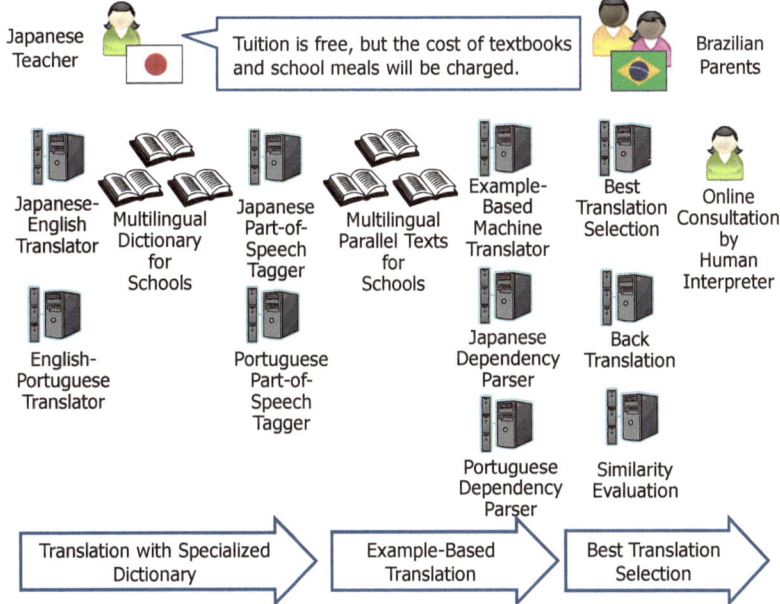

Fig. 1.2 Language service (composite)

By the way, part-of-speech taggers are often developed in research institutes or universities, and are provided only for research purposes. Their Web sites do not state that they can be used in schools, hospitals and so on. If an elementary school wants to use them, the school needs to ask those providers for permission by a letter or e-mail. One of the important roles of the Language Grid is to reduce such negotiation costs related to intellectual property rights.

1.3 The Language Grid

1.3.1 Design Concept of the Language Grid

As discussed in the previous sections, language resources already exist online. However, difficulties often arise when people try to use those language resources in their intercultural activities; complex contracts, intellectual property rights, and non-standard application interfaces make it difficult for users to create customized language services that support intercultural activities. To improve the accessibility and usability of existing language resources, we need to allow users to easily create new language services by combining existing ones. As shown in Fig. 1.3, the Language Grid should provide an environment where users can share language resources developed by both professionals and end users in various application fields. The word *grid* is defined as "a system or structure for combining distributed resources; an open standard protocol is generally used to create high quality services." Our approach, applying the grid concept to ensure the collaboration of language services, has not been tried before.

Fig. 1.3 Role of the Language Grid

To realize the Language Grid, *collective intelligence* is a promising solution, since it involves connecting people and computers so that collectively they act more intelligently than any individual or computer (Levy 1999) (Gruber 2008). Recent systems like Wikipedia are successful examples of content-based collective intelligence on the Web. For the Language Grid, however, we propose the *service-oriented collective intelligence* approach. Although the Language Grid lies in the domain of language services, it actually reveals some general problems in open service environments: how to collect and share services, and produce new services on the Internet. In content-based collective intelligence, contents are always provided by either discarding the intellectual rights or accepting common licenses for the contents. However, the service-oriented approach should handle intellectual property rights issues so as to support service providers to protect their contents and provide services based on their own policies.

Fig. 1.4 illustrates the design concept of the Language Grid. The platform allows users to register services and share them. Major stakeholders of the Language Grid fall into three categories: *service grid operator*, *service provider* and *service user*. Service grid operator manages the Language Grid and controls language resources and services. Service provider provides language services such as machine translations, part-of-speech taggers, dependency parsers, dictionaries, and parallel texts and registers them in the Language Grid. Service user invokes registered language services for their intercultural activities. Note that stakeholders are not individuals but groups like research units in universities, and that a single group can act as two different stakeholders: service provider and service user.

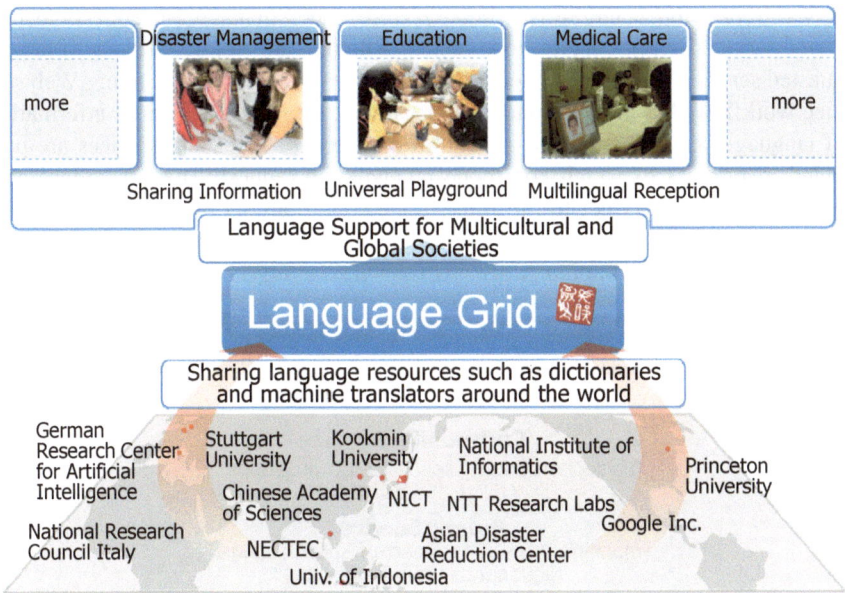

Fig. 1.4 Design concept of the Language Grid

Conceptually, the Language Grid has two main structures: a *horizontal grid* and a *vertical grid*. The horizontal grid concerns the combination of existing bilingual dictionaries or machine translation systems for various languages. The vertical grid concerns specific scenarios of intercultural collaboration activities, which require customized language services including jargon handling.

Among published studies, EuroWordNet (Vossen 1998) and Global WordNet Grid (Fellbaum and Vossen 2007) are pioneers in using word semantics to connect dictionaries in different languages. However, the Language Grid is an attempt to build a platform that can combine language services provided by stakeholders with different incentives. Therefore, standardization of language services becomes quite important (Calzolari et al. 2002). There also exist several efforts to pipeline language processing programs: *Heart of Gold* (Callmeier et al. 2004) and *UIMA* (Ferrucci and Lally 2004). They aim at pipelining various language processing programs efficiently, but the Language Grid is more application-oriented and focuses on managing the intellectual property rights associated with language resources. Since the motivations are orthogonal, we have bridged Heart of Gold and the Language Grid (Bramantoro et al. 2008), and will apply the results to UIMA.

1.3.2 Service Layers of the Language Grid

As shown in Fig. 1.5, the Language Grid consists of the following four service layers. The bottom layer, called *P2P Grid Layer,* aims at connecting two kinds of servers (*core nodes* and *service nodes*). Core nodes manage all requests to language services, while service nodes actually invoke the atomic services. If the requested service is a composite one, core nodes invoke the corresponding Web service workflow that includes one or more atomic services. Registered information of language services is shared among all core nodes. The same services are provided, regardless of which core node receives the request. The core nodes also control access to services to fulfill the usage conditions set by the service providers. Service providers can access the usage statistics of the services they provide using a system called the *Language Grid Service Manager*.

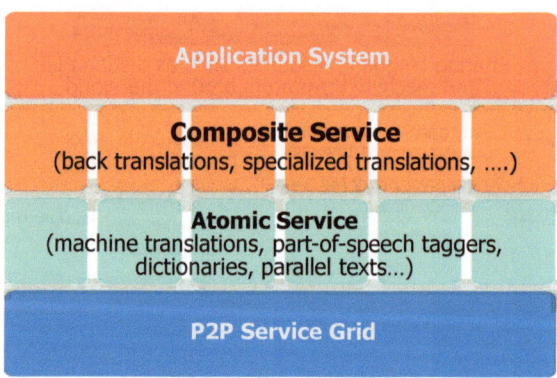

Fig. 1.5 Service layers

The second layer is called the *Atomic Service Layer*. In this layer, any user can add new language resources to the Language Grid. A Web service that corresponds to a language resource is called an *atomic service*. Each language resource is *wrapped* to develop an atomic service. The third layer is the *Composite Service Layer*. Atomic language services can be composed by Web service workflows. A service described by a workflow is called a *composite service*. Various composite services have been made available up to now, including back-translations and specialized translations. For example, specialized translation can be realized using several atomic services, such as machine translators, part-of-speech taggers, and domain-specific dictionaries. BPEL4WS and Java-based scenarios are used to describe workflows. Currently, more than 90 atomic and composite language services are being shared via the Language Grid with standard interfaces. Table 1.1 lists all types of language services currently available in the Language Grid.

Table 1.1 Language services provided by the Language Grid

Service Category	Service Type	Number of Services
Translation	Translation Service	21
	Domain-Specific Translation Service	2
	Multilingual Mixed Document Translation Service*	0
	Back Translation Service	1
	Multi-hop Translation Service	2
Paraphrase	Paraphrasing Service*	0
	Transliteration Service*	0
Dictionary	Multilingual Dictionary Service	7
	Multilingual Dictionary Service with Longest Match	22
	Concept Dictionary Service	4
	Pictogram Dictionary Service	1
	Multimedia Dictionary Service*	0
	Multilingual Glossary Service*	0
	Dictionary Creation Support Service*	0
Corpus	Parallel Corpus Service	20
	Dialog Parallel Corpus Service	1
	Template Parallel Corpus Service*	0
Analysis	Morphological Analysis Service	7
	Dependency Parsing Service	2
	Similarity Calculation Service*	0
	Language Identification Service*	0
Speech	Text To Speech Service	1
	Speech Recognition Service*	0
Other	Structural Alignment Creation Service*	0
Meta Service	Service Management Service	1

Service types marked with * are currently under development.

To realize the second and third layers of the Language Grid, Web service technologies including *language service ontology*, *horizontal service composition* and *service supervision* have been developed to enable the collaboration needed among language services. Language service ontology is a technology to define standard language service APIs in a hierarchical way so that end users are provided with simple interfaces while professionals can access more complex interfaces (Hayashi et al. 2008). For horizontal service composition, we apply constraint optimization algorithms to select the appropriate services and thus satisfy QoS requirements (Ben Hassine et al. 2006). To compose machine translators working on the same document or conversation, *context-aware service composition* is proposed: multiple translations are coordinated to determine the meanings of words consistently (Tanaka R et al. 2009). Service supervision, on the other hand, is a runtime technology to monitor and modify the process of composite services (Tanaka M et al. 2009).

Different types of *Application Systems* including collaboration tools have been developed on the top layer. *Language Grid Playground* provides easy access through a Web browser to the Language Grid to try a variety of registered language services. Examples of real-world challenges, such as the creation of community dictionaries, or real-world application of the Language Grid technologies, are also introduced through this website. *Language Grid Toolbox*, on the other hand, is a collection of modules to support multilingual communication in a community. Users can install this software on their servers to offer services, such as multilingual BBS and multilingual dictionary creation. Toolbox is provided as open source software. Therefore, the functions of Toolbox can be extended to meet the requirements of user communities. Furthermore, by using registered language services, existing communication tools can introduce multilingual functions easily. For instance, popular collaboration tools including LiquidThreads and NOTA have been successfully multilingualized.

1.4 User Involvement for Customization

1.4.1 Power of Customization

Computer scientists help to overcome language barriers by creating technologies as language services based on *generalization* of various language phenomena; user communities can then customize and use those technologies to fit their own context by composing language services. There are two reasons why *customization* is a major goal for the Language Grid.

First, machine translators are half-products. The obvious customization step is to combine multilingual dictionaries with machine translators. The provider of those dictionaries does not have to be a research institute or a university. Organizations that are conducting intercultural activities can also register their own multilingual dictionaries. The major difference between machine translation on the Language Grid and a conventional translation system on the Internet is that the users themselves can improve the quality of translation. For example, users can use the registered parallel texts in the translation process. When a user enters a sentence, examples with meanings similar to the entered sentence will appear automatically. If the user is unable to find the intended expression, machine translation is then executed. In this case, a dictionary registered by the user also helps to improve the quality of translation. If the quality of translation is not good enough, however, another user in the multilingual community might manually correct the translation results. The corrected parallel texts are accumulated so that the machine translator can learn from them. This becomes possible when the multilingual community members share their context. In this way, machine-translation-mediated communication might work better in high-context multicultural communities, such as an NPO/NGO working on particular international issues.

Fig. 1.6 Shared screen multilingual chat system for junior high school

Second, we often observe that the success of a multilingual tool in one situation does not guarantee its success in another. Let us examine an example of customized environment for intercultural collaboration. Japan now has an increasing number of students who are non-native Japanese speakers, and most teachers have a problem in communicating with the foreign students and their parents. We provided a multilingual chat system for a distance meeting as a quick solution, but the system does not work well in face-to-face meetings. Therefore, we developed the service in which users can chat on the same screen. The support site, called a *shared screen multilingual chat system* (see Fig. 1.6), was designed specifically for this situation; students, parents and teachers can chat while looking at the same display. They can input text in their mother tongue, translate the sentence, check the back translation, and post it to the log area at the top of the page. In addition, users can register terms used in the school into the user dictionary, which makes the translation result more correct. This service also provides auto-completion using the parallel texts provided by the city office in charge of the school.

Though extensive dictionaries will help us to find the correct translations of given words, we seldom see people use dictionaries in a conversation. Since language is used everywhere in our daily life, we need customized tools for various situations. You may think that it is not possible to develop such tools customized for different user communities, and may claim that this is the reason that computer scientists provide a generalized solution to cover many different situations. However, the approach taken by the Language Grid is totally opposite. We try to create an environment that allows users to easily develop their own multilingual environments: *the language barrier created by billions of people can be overcome by those billions of people.* For example, the site in Fig. 1.6 was developed in two weeks by three master students. The example shows how quickly a customized multilingual environment can be created by using the language services provided via the Language Grid.

1.4.2 Participatory Design Project

To realize user involvement for customization, we organized a participatory design project that stressed collaboration among researchers, operators and users. At the beginning of the project, in parallel with forming the research project, we established the *Language Grid Association*, a user group of the Language Grid, to conduct multilingual activities on intercultural collaboration. The association is a loosely coupled organization formed by collaboration among industry, government, academia, and citizens with the goal of guiding the development of the Language Grid. Sixteen organizations including laboratories of universities, research institutes, and NPO/NGOs participated in the association. After development of the server software, operation of the Language Grid was commenced. Fig. 1.7 shows the three related organizations. NICT is working on R&D and provides software to the Operation Center run by Kyoto University. Language Grid Association uses the resulting language services and provides feedback to R&D.

The association consists of various SIGs (Special Interest Groups) such as research groups or projects, each of which aims to accumulate use cases and best practices. SIGs can be classified as *creating language services*, *creating collaboration tools* and *supporting multicultural activities* (Sakai et al 2008). Each SIG creates and shares technologies for using language services registered with the Language Grid. NPO/NGOs, schools and other nonprofit sectors have started to play a central role in breaking down the language barriers. Their activities cover a broad range of fields, including disaster management, education, and medical care (Ishida 2010).

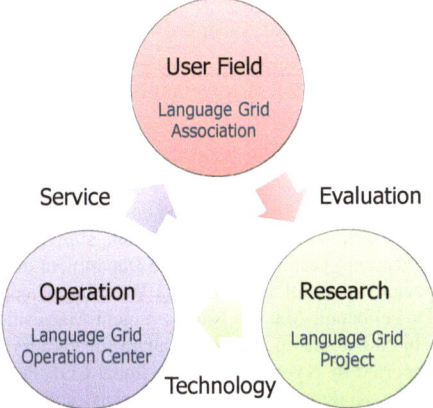

Fig. 1.7 Participatory design project

1.5 Conclusion

The Language Grid is an infrastructure that allows end-users to create new language services for their intercultural collaboration activities. This chapter explained how the Language Grid increases the accessibility and usability of online language resources. Using the Language Grid, various kinds of intercultural activities have begun at hospital receptions, local schools, shopping streets and so on (Ishida et al. 2007) (Fussell et al. 2009).

In general, this chapter proposed the approach of using service-oriented collective intelligence to support the collection, sharing, and production of new services on the Internet while dealing with the issues of intellectual property rights. The main contributions of the proposed approach include the following two aspects.

- *Service architecture*: We developed the service architecture for the Language Grid, including layers of P2P grid infrastructure, atomic services, composite services, and application systems. The proposed architecture applies the service-oriented collective intelligence approach, where language resources including data and software are wrapped as Web services so that users can easily share and combine language resources for creating their own multilingual environment.
- *User involvement*: We proposed a participatory design approach for the formation of service-oriented collective intelligence by bringing the researchers, operators and end users together. Customization of the application systems based

on the Language Grid enables various users and communities to participate in the creation of new multilingual environments.

Our proposed service architecture can be applied to far more than just the language domain. In other domains, the proposed service architecture has been used or is being considered for use in the pervasive computing domain, e-learning domain and so on. In the pervasive computing domain, the open smart classroom has been developed (Suo et al. 2009). In the e-learning domain, open courseware services developed by different organizations can be provided and shared. To provide free usage in various domains, the Language Grid has been released as open source software.

Acknowledgments   The project was carried out based on the collaboration between many people in various organizations. We acknowledge the considerable support of the National Institute of Information and Communications Technology, and the Department of Social Informatics, Kyoto University. We are especially grateful to Wolfgang Wahlster, Nicoletta Calzolari Zamorani, Nancy Ide, Christiane D. Fellbaum, Makoto Nagao, Yuichi Matsushima, Takashi Matsuyama, Hiromitu Wakana, Satoshi Nakamura and Hitoshi Isahara for giving advice and encouragement to us. This work was supported by Kyoto University Global COE Program: Informatics Education and Research Center for Knowledge-Circulating Society, and a Grant-in-Aid for Scientific Research (A) (21240014, 2009-2011) from Japan Society for the Promotion of Science.

References

Ben Hassine A, Matsubara S, Ishida T (2006) A constraint-based approach to horizontal web service composition. International Semantic Web Conference (ISWC-06), Lecture Notes in Computer Science 4273, Springer: 130-143

Bramantoro A, Tanaka M, Murakami Y, Schäfer U, Ishida T (2008) A hybrid integrated architecture for language service composition. 2008 IEEE International Conference on Web Services: 345-352

Callmeier U, Eisele A, Schafer U, Siegel M (2004) The deep thought core architecture framework. LREC2004: 1205-1208

Calzolari N, Zampolli A, Lenci A (2002) Towards a standard for a multilingual lexical entry: the EAGLES/ISLE initiative. CICLing2002, Lecture Notes in Computer Science 2276, Springer: 264-279

Fellbaum C, Vossen P (2007) Connecting the universal to the specific: towards the global grid. International Workshop on Intercultural Collaboration, Lecture Notes in Computer Science 4568, Springer: 1-16

Ferrucci D, Lally A (2004) UIMA: an architectural approach to unstructured information processing in the corporate research environment. Natural Language Engineering 10: 327-348

Fussell S, Hinds P, Ishida T, Eds. (2009) Proceedings of the Second International Workshop on Intercultural Collaboration

Gruber T (2008) Collective knowledge systems: where the social web meets the semantic web. Journal of Web Semantics 6(1): 4-13

Hayashi Y, Declerck T, Buitelaar P, Monachini M (2008) Ontologies for a global language infrastructure. International Conference on Global Interoperability for Language Resources: 105-112

Ishida T (2006) Language Grid: an infrastructure for intercultural collaboration. 2006 IEEE/IPSJ Symposium on Applications and the Internet: 96-100

Ishida T, Fussell SR, Vossen PTJM, Eds. (2007) Proceedings of the First International Workshop on Intercultural Collaboration, Lecture Notes in Computer Science 4568, Springer

Ishida T (2010) Intercultural collaboration using machine translation. IEEE Internet Computing 14(1): 30-32

Levy P (1999) Collective intelligence: mankind's emerging world in cyberspace. Basic Books

Nomura S, Ishida T, Yamashita N, Yasuoka M, Funakoshi K (2003) Open source software development with your mother language: intercultural collaboration experiment 2002. 2003 International Conference on Human-Computer Interaction: 1163-1167

Paolillo J, Pimienta D, Prado D (2003) Measuring linguistic diversity on the Internet. UNESCO Institute for Statistics, Montreal, Canada

Sakai S, Gotou M, Tanaka M, Inaba R, Murakami Y, Yoshino T, Hayashi Y, Kitamura Y, Mori Y, Takasaki T, Naya Y, Shigeno A, Matsubara S, Ishida T (2008) Language Grid Association: action research on supporting the multicultural society. 2008 International Conference on Informatics Education and Research for Knowledge-Circulating Society: 55-60

Suo Y, Miyata N, Morikawa H, Ishida T, Shi Y (2009) Open smart classroom: extensible and scalable learning system in smart space using web service technology. IEEE Transactions on Knowledge and Data Engineering 21(6): 814-828

Tanaka M, Ishida T, Murakami Y, Morimoto S (2009) Service supervision: coordinating web services in open environment. 2009 IEEE International Conference on Web Services: 238-245

Tanaka R, Murakami Y, Ishida T (2009) Context-based approach for pivot translation services. International Joint Conference on Artificial Intelligence (IJCAI-09): 1555-1561

Vossen P (1998) Introduction to eurowordnet. Computers and the Humanities 32(2-3): 73-89

Weiss A (2005) The power of collective intelligence. netWorker 9(3): 16-23

Chapter 2
Service Grid Architecture

Yohei Murakami[1], Donghui Lin[1], Masahiro Tanaka[1], Takao Nakaguchi[2], and Toru Ishida[3]

1 National Institute of Information and Communications Technology (NICT), Language Grid Project, 3-5 Hikaridai, Seika-Cho, Soraku-Gun, Kyoto, 619-0289, Japan, e-mail: {yohei, lindh, mtnk}@nict.go.jp

2 NTT Advanced Technology Corporation, 12-1 Ekimae-Honmachi, Kawasaki-Ku, Kanagawa, 210-0007, Japan, e-mail: takao.nakaguchi@ntt-at.co.jp

3 Department of Social Informatics, Kyoto University, Yoshida Honmachi, Sakyoku, Kyoto 606-8501 Japan, e-mail: ishida@i.kyoto-u.ac.jp

Abstract The Language Grid is an infrastructure for enabling users to share language services developed by language specialists and end user communities. Users can also create new services to support their intercultural/multilingual activities by composing language services from a range of providers. Since the Language Grid takes the service-oriented collective intelligence approach, the platform requires the services management to satisfy stakeholders' needs: access control for service providers, dynamic service composition for service users, and service grid composition and system configurability for service grid operators. To realize the Language Grid, this chapter describes the design concept and the system architecture of the platform based on the service grid.

2.1 Introduction

Although there are many language resources (both data and programs) on the Internet (Choukri 2004), most intercultural collaboration activities still lack multilingual support. To overcome language barriers, we aim to construct a novel language infrastructure to improve accessibility and usability of language resources on the Internet. To this end, the Language Grid has been proposed (Ishida 2006). The Language Grid takes a service-oriented collective intelligence approach to sharing language resources and creating new services to support their intercultural/multilingual activities by combining language resources.

In previous works, many efforts have been made to combine language resources, such as UIMA (Ferrucci and Lally 2004), GATE (Cunningham et al. 2002), D-Spin (Boehlke 2009), Hart of Gold (Callmeier et al. 2004), and CLARIN (Varadi et al. 2008). Their purpose is to analyze a large amount of text data by linguistic processing pipelines. These pipelines consist of language resources, most of which are provided as open sources by universities and research institutes. Users can thus collect language resources and freely combine them on those frameworks without considering other stakeholders.

Different from the above frameworks, the purpose of the Language Grid is to multilingualize texts for supporting intercultural collaboration by service workflows. A workflow combines language resources associated with complex intellectual property issues, such as machine translators, parallel corpora, and bilingual dictionaries. These resources are provided by service providers who want to protect their ownership, and used by service users who need a part of the resources. Therefore, the Language Grid must coordinate these stakeholders' motivations. That is, it requires language service management to satisfy the following stakeholders' needs as well as language service composition for service users.

- Protecting intellectual properties of resources: Some service providers can agree on providing their services if they can retain ownership of their resources and specify the extent that service users utilize the services. For detecting fraudulent usage, they also want to know what their service is used for.
- Utilizing necessary services when needed: Service users want to utilize necessary services when needed, but not own the resources. Moreover, they may want to customize composite services for their goals by freely combining services.
- Configuring platform according to operation models: Operators create various operation models to meet stakeholders' needs. To fit their platforms to their operation models, they need to optimize system configuration. In addition, by connecting their platforms, they want to allow service users to share and invoke services on other platforms.

The above requirements are not only inherent in the Language Grid and language resources, but in any system composing services provided by others. Here we call the platform to share and compose services provided by different providers as the *service grid*, and design the service grid architecture. The service grid is a general platform independent of specific service domains so that it can be applied to a specific domain by defining services specific to the domain. For example, the Language Grid is a service grid specific to the language resource domain. Firstly, based on these requirements, this chapter clarifies functions that the service grid should provide, and explains its design concept and system architecture. Furthermore, we validate the service grid architecture by using it as basis for constructing the Language Grid.

2.2 Design Concept

The purpose of the service grid is to accumulate services and compose them. To realize the service grid, system architecture should be designed to satisfy different requirements from the stakeholders. Therefore, this section summarizes requirements of each of the stakeholders, and clarifies the required functions of the service grid.

2.2.1 Requirements

Service providers demand prevention of data leaks and fraudulent usage of resources because the resources represent intellectual properties. Specifically, the service providers want to deploy their services on their servers and provide their services following their provision policies, but not publish their resources under a common license, like Wikipedia. Furthermore, to check whether service users employ their services properly, they may want to know when their services are accessed and who accesses them.

On the other hand, service users prefer flexibility in customizing services and convenience in invoking the services to acquiring ownership of the resources. This is because they want to concentrate on developing application systems by reducing the resource maintenance cost. Specifically, they need to access the services through standard Web service technologies over HTTP. Moreover, they also need to create composite services freely and change service combinations.

Finally, service grid operators require flexibility of system configuration so that they can adapt the configuration to stakeholders' incentives. For example, the operators operate the service grid on a single cluster of machines by collecting services if the provision policies of the services are relaxed. Meanwhile, they operate the service grid in a distributed environment by deploying services on each provider's server if the provision policies of the services are too strict. In the former case, the operators place high priority on performance of services. In the latter case, they put priority on resource security. Further, they may want to expand available services by allowing their users to access services on other service grids.

2.2.2 Functions

The service grid platform should provide the following functions extracted from the stakeholders' requirements in the previous subsection.

(1) Service access control and monitoring: Service providers can set out their provision policies defining the terms of service use, and the platform controls access to the services according to these policies. For instance, restrictions on users who may be licensed to use the service, on the purpose for which the service may be used, and on the number of times the service may be accessed, the amount of data that may be transferred from the service, and so on. Furthermore, the platform accumulates service request messages and service response messages as access logs, and enables service providers to monitor service invocation histories and the status of

their services. Service monitoring involves monitoring events or information produced by the services; viewing services' statistics, including the number of accesses; viewing the status, or a summary, of selected services; and suspending, resuming, or terminating selected services.

(2) Service workflow execution and service dynamic binding: Service users can invoke a composite service consisting of several services on the service grid according to a service workflow. By employing standard workflow technologies such as WS-BPEL, the service grid platform allows service users to independently create and register service workflows. Besides, by standardizing service interfaces, the service grid platform enables service users to freely change the alternative services with a dynamic service binding function. This leads to various composite service invocations.

(3) Service grid composition: Service grid operators can compose several service grids in order to increase the number of services in the same domain and different domains. The service grid platform realizes information sharing among service grids, and service invocation across service grids.

(4) Modularization of system components: Service grid operators can change implementations of each component in the service grid platform in order to build their own service grids compliant with their operation models. In particular, switching communication components is necessary to operate the platform both in a centralized environment and a distributed environment. The platform combines implementations of each component based on a configuration file defined by the operator.

In designing the service grid architecture that provides the above functions, there are several technical constraints. For example, the architecture should be independent of domains because service profiles and service interfaces vary depending on domains. In addition, the architecture should be independent of specifications of service invocations because there are several such specifications over HTTP, such as SOAP, REST, JSON, and Protocol Buffers. Moreover, it is necessary to distribute the platform to handle physically distributed services if the services are deployed on their providers' severs. In the next section, we explain the system architecture of the service grid platform considering these constraints.

2.3 System Architecture

2.3.1 Overview

The service grid architecture consists of six parts: *Service Manager, Service Supervisor, Grid Composer, Service Database, Composite Service Container,* and *Atomic Service Container.* Fig. 2.1 (a) focuses on the first four parts, and Fig. 2.1 (b) focuses on the last two parts.

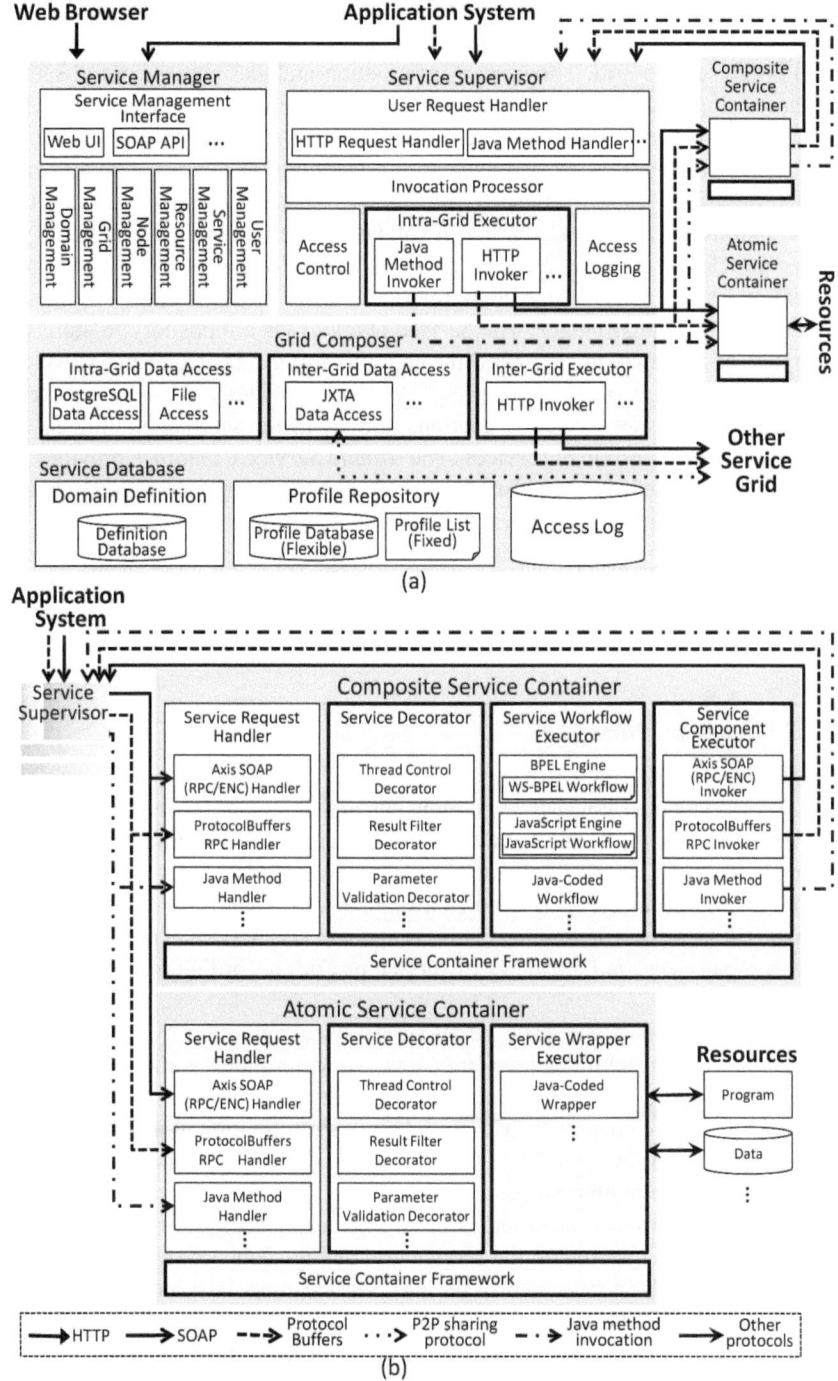

Fig. 2.1 Service grid architecture

The *Service Manager* manages domain definition, grid information, node information, user information, service information and resource information registered in the service grid. The service information includes access control settings and access logs. Since the information is registered through the *Service Manager*, it plays a front-end role for any functions other than service invocation. The *Service Supervisor* controls service invocations according to the requirements of the service providers. Before invoking the services on the *Composite Service Container* and *Atomic Service Container*, it validates whether the request satisfies providers' policies. The *Grid Composer* connects its service grid to other service grids to realize service grid composition for operators. The connection target is set through the *Service Manager*. The *Service Database* is a repository to store various types of information registered through the *Service Manager* and service invocation logs. The *Composite Service Container* provides composite service deployment, composite service execution, and dynamic service binding so that service users can customize services. The *Atomic Service Container* provides several utilities that service providers need in deploying atomic services. By using a SOAP message handler, providers can deploy their services on their servers.

In the remaining parts of this section, we provide the details of the *Service Manager*, *Service Supervisor*, *Grid Composer*, and *Composite/Atomic Service Container*, such as configuration of components.

2.3.2 Service Manager

The *Service Manager* consists of components managing various types of information necessary for the service grid, such as domain definition, and grid, node, resource, service, and user information.

The *Domain Management* handles a domain definition that applies a general service grid to a specific domain. This component sets service types, standard interfaces of services, and attributes of service profiles according to domain definitions.

The *Grid Management* sets a target service grid connected by the *Grid Composer*. Based on the settings, the *Grid Composer* determines available services on other service grids. The *Node Management* handles node information of its service grid and the connected service grid. Based on this information, the *Grid Composer* decides whether to save information registered on other nodes, and whether to distribute information to other nodes.

The *Resource Management* and *Service Management* handle resource and service information registered on the service grid and the connected service grid. The information includes access control settings, service endpoints, intellectual properties associated with the resources, and access logs. Based on this information, the *Service Supervisor* validates service invocation, locates service endpoints, and attaches intellectual property information to service responses.

Finally, the *User Management* manages user information registered on the service grid. Based on this information, the *Service Supervisor* authenticates users' service requests.

2.3.3 Service Supervisor

The *Service Supervisor* controls service invocation by service users. The control covers access control, endpoint locating, load balancing, and access logging. To realize architecture independent of service specifications such as SOAP and REST, the *Service Supervisor* conducts such service invocation control based on an HTTP header.

The *User Request Handler* extracts information necessary to invoke a service from the service request over HTTP, and then authenticates the user who sends the request. The extracted information is sent to the *Invocation Processor*. Using the information, the *Invocation Processor* executes a sequence of pre-process, service invocation, post-process, and logging process. The access control defined as the system requirements is implemented as the pre-process, or the post-process.

After passing the access control, the *Intra-Grid Executor* invokes the service within its service grid. To invoke the service, the *Intra-Grid Executor* locates the service endpoint using the service ID. If there are multiple endpoints associated with the service ID, it chooses the endpoint with the lowest load. Finally, it invokes the service using *Java Method Invoker* implementation or *HTTP Invoker* implementation, which are selected according to the endpoint location.

2.3.4 Grid Composer

The *Grid Composer* not only creates a P2P grid network within its service grid, but also connects to other service grids. The former is needed to improve latency if the services are physically distributed. The latter is necessary to realize service grid composition defined in the system requirements.

The *Intra-Grid Data Access* provides read/write interfaces for the *Service Database* in its service grid. In writing data, the *Intra-Grid Data Access* broadcasts the data to other nodes using a P2P network framework so that it can share the data with other nodes in the same service grid. As a result service users can improve latency by sending their requests to a node located near the service. In this way, usage of the P2P network framework contributes to scalability of the service grid while keeping data consistency.

On the other hand, the *Inter-Grid Data Access* shares various types of information with other service grids. The *Inter-Grid Data Access* also uses the P2P network to share information with other nodes across service grids. However, based on grid information registered through the *Service Manager*, the *Inter-Grid Data Access* saves only information related to the connected service grids.

The *Inter-Grid Executor* invokes services registered on a different service grid. To invoke a service across service grids, it replaces a requester's ID with the operator's user ID because the different service grid does not store user information of the requester, but rather of the operator as a service grid user. In addition, to control access to the services on a different service grid, the *Inter-Grid Executor* inserts the user ID of the requester into the request in invoking the service. By separating the service grid that performs user authentication from the different service grid that performs access control, the two service grids do not have to share users' passwords.

2.3.5 Service Container

The *Service Container* executes composite services and atomic services. The *Composite Service Container* that executes composite services provides service workflow deployment and execution, and dynamic service binding defined as system requirements. The *Atomic Service Container* that executes atomic services wraps resources of service providers as services with standard interfaces.

The *Service Request Handler* has multiple implementations according to the types of service invocation protocols. If the *Service Container* is deployed on the same server as the *Service Supervisor*, the *Java Method Handler* implementation can be selected. When receiving a service request, the *Service Request Handler* receives from the *Service Container Framework* a chain of *Service Decorator*, *Service Workflow/Wrapper Executor*, and *Service Component Executor*, and executes the chain.

In invoking a component service of a composite service, the *Service Workflow Executor* can select a concrete service based on binding information included in a service request. This dynamic service binding is realized because resources are wrapped as services with standard interfaces in the *Atomic Service Container*.

2.4 Open Source Customization

The operation model of the service grid varies depending on the target stakeholders. If service providers demand intellectual property protection, services are deployed on their servers and the service grid platform has to provide access control. That is, priority is placed on security of resources. On the other hand, if service providers publish their resources under an open source license, services are aggregated and deployed on a cluster of machines, and the service grid platform does not provide user authentication and access control. That is, priority is placed on service performance.

The types of stakeholders assumed rely on service grid operators. This implies that it is impossible to develop a general platform dealing with various types of operation models beforehand. Therefore, we selected open-source style customization so that each operator can adapt the platform to his/her operation model.

We have published the source codes of the service grid platform under an LGPL license and begun an open source project wherein each operator can freely customize the platform. In the project, the source codes are classified into a core component and optional component with different development policies because unregulated derivatives prevent interoperability of service grids. The specifications of core components are decided by core members in the open source community. On the other hand, the specifications of optional components can be freely changed by developers in the open source project, and derivatives can be created. This classification is done to improve the interoperability of service grids. As shown in Fig. 2.1, the core components are thick-frame rectangles, and optional components thin-frame ones. In nested rectangles, outside ones are APIs and inside ones are their implementations. These implementations can be changed. Implementations with gray labels have yet to be implemented.

The *Intra-Grid Data Access*, *Inter-Grid Data Access*, *Intra-grid Service Executor*, and *Inter-Grid Service Executor* are core components because they are used to communicate with other service grids, and they share information with other service grids. In addition to this, *Service Decorator*, *Service Workflow/Wrapper Executor*, *Service Component Executor*, and *Service Container Framework* in *Composite/Atomic Service Container* are also core components because the implementations of the components are interleaved in atomic services or composite services by the *Service Container Framework*. On the other hand, the *Service Supervisor* and *Service Manager* are optional components so that operators can extend them according to their operation model, because their functions are used only within the service grid.

2.5 Realization of the Language Grid

In this section, we validate the service grid architecture by using it as basis for constructing the Language Grid. In particular, we focus on language service composition for language service users, language service management for language service providers, and system configurability for the Language Grid operators.

2.5.1 Language Service Composition

Among the existing research, EuroWordNet (Vossen 2004) and Global WordNet Grid (Fellbaum and Vossen 2007) are pioneering works on connecting dictionaries in different languages based on word semantics. The Language Grid, however, aims to build an infrastructure where users can share and combine various language services. The following two types of language services are available in the Language Grid:

- Atomic service: A Web service with a standard interface that corresponds to an individual language resource. Examples include bilingual dictionaries, parallel texts, morphological analyzers, machine translators, and so on.
- Composite service: An advanced service described by a workflow that combines several atomic services. Examples include domain-specialized translation and multilingual back translation.

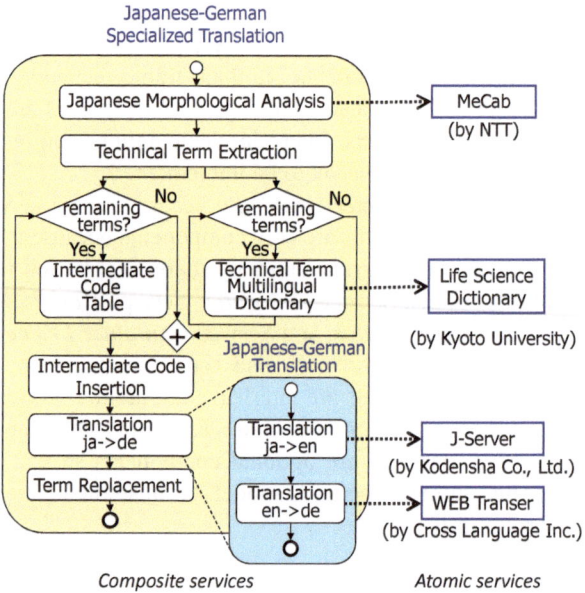

Fig. 2.2 Example of composite services

Fig. 2.2 shows a domain specialized translation workflow for improving the translation quality of technical sentences. The Language Grid uses Java-coded workflows, JavaScript, BPEL4WS (Khalaf et al. 2003), and WS-BPEL to describe the workflow. Domain specialized translation workflow consists of several component services: morphological analysis, multilingual dictionary, and translation. To invoke the composite service, service users have to bind a concrete atomic service to each component service, such as MeCab to the morphological analysis service, Life Science Dictionary to the multilingual dictionary service, and a two-hop translation service consisting of J-Server (machine translator) and WEB-Transer (machine translator) to the translation service. Service users can also invoke other combinations of concrete atomic services by changing the service bindings.

In the case of invoking composite services, the request will be sent to the Service Workflow Executor in the service grid architecture. After receiving the request, the Service Workflow Executor invokes the atomic services defined in service binding information through the Service Component Executor. If SOAP communication is used between the Service Supervisor and Composite Service Container in the service grid architecture, we can employ not only a BPEL engine but also Web service-based language resource coordination frameworks as the Service Workflow Executor, such as Heart of Gold, UIMA, and D-Spin. We have bridged Heart of Gold and the Language Grid (Bramantoro et al. 2008) and will apply the results to combine UIMA and the Language Grid.

2.5.2 Language Service Management

Language Grid Service Manager[1] is a Web application-based implementation of the service management interface in the service grid architecture. This enables Language Grid users to access various types of management functions provided by the Language Grid. In the current Language Grid, three types of access control component are implemented: access right control, access count control, and data transfer size control.

The access control function allows service providers to set access rights for each language service. Service providers who find that service users are accessing the service excessively can prohibit them from accessing the service. Moreover, service providers have two choices in publishing their services: "public mode," which permits every user by default, and "members only mode," which prohibits every user by default. Using the "members only" mode, a service provider who sells a language resource can permit a service user who purchased the language resource or its license to access the resource.

The access control function provides access constraint settings as well as access right settings. Access constraints include total access count per month, week, and day, and data transfer size (KB) per month, week, day, and request. This function enables a service provider who sells a language resource to provide limited service as a trial to service users who have not purchased it, and provide various types of service according to the fees.

In the Language Grid operated by Department of Social Informatics in Kyoto University, service providers who sell their resources realize various ways of providing their services by effectively employing the language service management (Murakami et al. 2010).

National Institute of Information and Communications Technology (called NICT hereafter) for a fee offers a concept dictionary and a bilingual dictionary, called EDR, as a whole. That is why NICT has difficulty in allowing language service users to freely employ EDR. Therefore, NICT provides a trial service of

---

[1] http://langrid.org/operation/service_manager/

EDR to every user by setting maximum access counts per month at 1000 counts and maximum data transfer size per request at 15 KB for the concept dictionary, and maximum access counts per month at 1000 counts and maximum data transfer size per request at 5KB for the bilingual dictionary, respectively. These constraints are configured so as to take about one year to extract all the data of the EDR. Moreover, NICT has registered the concept dictionary and the bilingual dictionary of EDR with no restrictions in the "members only mode". In this way, NICT provides unlimited EDR services only to users who purchase the EDR license.

KODENSHA Co., Ltd. (called KODENSHA hereafter) allows us to provide translation service based on J-Server, a machine translator, to third parties, if the application area of the Language Grid does not conflict with an already existing business market. Kyoto University and NICT have now purchased J-Server software to provide a translation service to other language service users. If the application area of the Language Grid conflicts with the existing market, NICT and Kyoto University prohibit the conflicting users from accessing J-Server. Furthermore, KODENSHA has registered the J-Server ASP service operated by KODENSHA in the "members only mode". This lets KODENSHA provide the latest J-Server service to only those users who purchase a J-Server ASP license. KODENSHA has registered Japanese and Simplified Chinese, Japanese and Traditional Chinese, Japanese and Korean, and Japanese and English translation separately in order to increase service variations. This enables users to purchase the language pairs that they need to use.

Kyoto University provides language service users with various language services based on machine translation software, translation ASP service, and a text-to-speech engine that Kyoto University purchased from several companies; KODENSHA Co., Ltd., Cross Language Inc., Translution, and HOYA Corporation. Since Kyoto University concluded an agreement that establishes the provision of a language resource for only non-profit use with each language resource developer, Kyoto University has to monitor for any potential abuse of the language resource. In fact, by monitoring access to the language resources, Kyoto University detected that a user accessed J-Server excessively from a specific IP address. It then obtained a contact address from the user profile and contacted the user to confirm whether it was being employed for non-profit use.

2.5.3 System Configuration of the Language Grid

In the Language Grid operated by Department of Social Informatics in Kyoto University, service providers have several provision policies to protect their language resources as described in the previous subsection. Therefore, the Language Grid prefers security of language resources to performance of language services. For this reason, the Language Grid enables service providers to protect their resources on their servers, and must coordinate the resources deployed on the providers' servers. To equip the Language Grid with such a function, we construct it with two different types of server nodes: the service node and core node (Mura-kami et al. 2006).

The service node provides only atomic services by deploying service wrappers to standardize interfaces of language resources. The service nodes are distributed to their service providers. On the other hand, the core node controls access to services and composes services. Moreover, it communicates with other core nodes in other Language Grids to realize federated operation of the Language Grid.

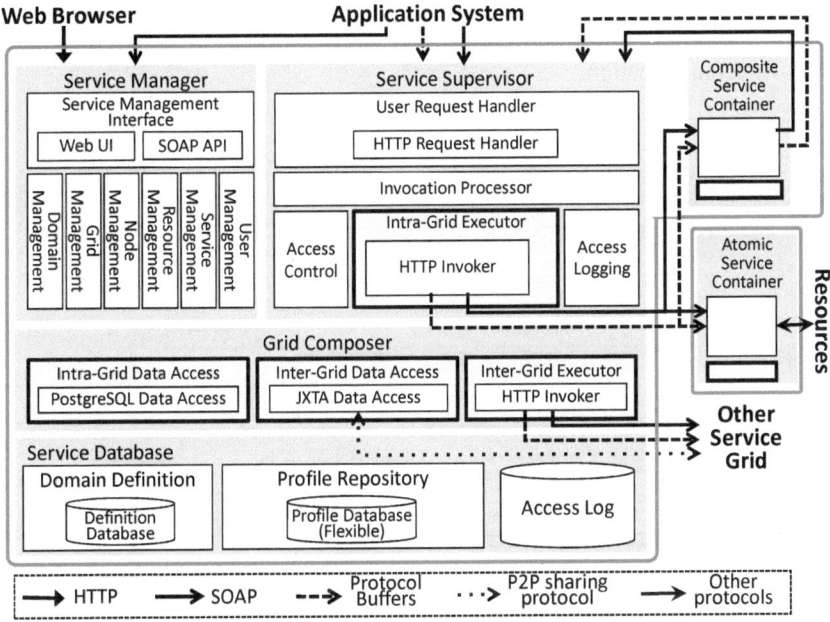

Fig. 2.3 System configuration of the Language Grid

To instantiate the service node and core node, the Language Grid is configured as shown in Fig. 2.3. The components surrounded by gray lines in the figure are deployed on the same server. The server on which the *Service Manager, Service Supervisor, Composite Service Container, Grid Composer,* and *Service Database* are deployed is called the core node, while that on which the *Atomic Service Container* is deployed is called the service node. This system configuration employs an HTTP invoker as the *Intra-Grid Executor* to distribute the *Atomic Service Container* as service nodes. Furthermore, the core node includes the *Inter-Grid Data Access* to share language services with other Language Grids and the *Inter-Grid Executor* to invoke language services on other Language Grids.

Unlike the above system configuration, a Language Grid prioritizing performance of language services is sometimes required. For example, in the case of employing the Language Grid to multilingualize Wikipedia articles, the performance of language services should be given higher priority due to the huge amount of articles and users. Furthermore, the smaller the code size of the platform is, the more the Wikipedia operator likes it.

Fig. 2.4 shows the other system configuration to satisfy the operator preferring performance and simplicity. The system configuration does not include the *Service Manager, Access Control*, and *Access Logging* components because the Language Grid handles only language services associated with simple licenses. The *Inter-Grid Data Access* and *Inter-Grid Executor* are also removed because necessary language services will be aggregated into a single location. Moreover, the system configuration employs Java method invocation for communication between the *Service Supervisor* and *Composite/Atomic Service Container* to improve the latency of communication.

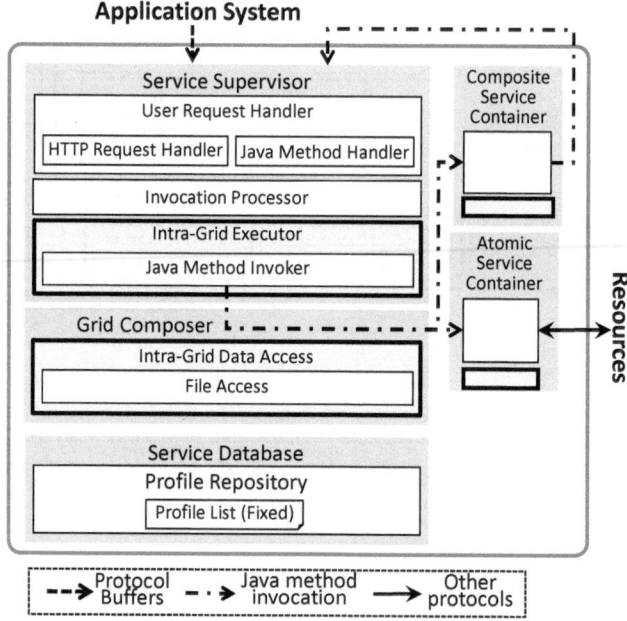

Fig. 2.4 System configuration of the Language Grid for Wikimedia

2.6 Conclusion

In this chapter, we have proposed a service grid architecture to share and compose services while satisfying stakeholders' needs. The main contributions of the proposed architecture include the following aspects.

- Protecting intellectual properties of resources: We have developed the Service Supervisor, which controls service invocations from service users. It extracts the user ID, the purpose, and so on from a service request before invoking the service, and then checks whether the user can satisfy the provision policy of the service. In this way, service providers can provide their services within their provision policies.

- Utilizing necessary services when needed: We have developed the Composite Service Container, which binds services with service workflows at run-time. Based on service binding information in service requests, the Composite Service Container can select a concrete atomic service to invoke as a component service.

- Configuring platform according to operation models: We have developed the Grid Composer, which communicates with other service grids. It enables service providers to share their services with service users of other service grids, and service users to invoke services across service grids. Moreover, the service grid architecture allows the service grid operator to select any implementation of each main component for his/her system configuration because the main components of the service grid architecture are modularized.

We have already applied the proposed architecture to the Language Grid operated by Kyoto University. To encourage service users and providers to share and compose language services on the Internet, we need not only the proposed service grid architecture but also institutional design considering incentives among stakeholders (Ishida et al. 2008). This institutional design will be introduced in the Chapter 18.

Acknowledgments   We are grateful to Nicoletta Calzolari Zamorani, Riccardo Del Gratta, Luca Dini, Alessio Bosca, Nancy Ide, and Erik Moeller for giving advice and encouragement to us. We acknowledge the considerable support of National Institute of Information and Communications Technology, and Department of Social Informatics, Kyoto University. A part of this work was supported by Strategic Information and Communications R&D Promotion Programme from Ministry of Internal Affairs.

References

Boehlke V (2009) A prototype infrastructure for D-spin-services based on a flexible multilayer architecture. 2009 Text Mining Services Conference (TMS'09)

Bramantoro A, Tanaka M, Murakami Y, Schäfer U, Ishida T (2008) A hybrid integrated architecture for language service composition. The Sixth International Conference on Web Services (ICWS'08): 345-352

Callmeier U, Eisele A, Schäfer U, Siegel M (2004) The Deep Thought core architecture framework. The Fourth International Conference on Language Resources and Evaluation (LREC'04): 1205-1208

Choukri K (2004) European Language Resources Association history and recent developments. SCALLA Working Conference KC 14/20

Cunningham H, Maynard D, Bontecheva K, Tablan V (2002) GATE: an architecture for development of robust HLT applications. The Fortieth Annual Meeting of the Association for Computational Linguistics (ACL'02): 168-175

Fellbaum C, Vossen P (2007) Connecting the universal to the specific: towards the global grid. Intercultural Collaboration, LNCS 4568, Springer-Verlag

Ferrucci D, Lally A (2004) UIMA: an architectural approach to unstructured information processing in the corporate research environment. Journal of Natural Language Engineering 10: 327-348

Ishida T (2006) Language Grid: an infrastructure for intercultural collaboration. The IEEE/IPSJ Symposium on Applications and the Internet (SAINT'06): 96-100

Ishida T, Nadamoto A, Murakami Y, Inaba R, Shigenobu T, Matsubara S, Hattori H, Kubota Y, Nakaguchi T, Tsunokawa E (2008) A non-profit operation model for the language grid. The First International Conference on Global Interoperability for Language Resources (ICGL'08): 114-121

Khalaf R, Mukhi N, Weerawarana S (2003) Service-oriented composition in BPEL4WS. The World Wide Web Conference (WWW'03)

Murakami Y, Ishida T, Nakaguchi T (2006) Infrastructure for language service composition. The Second International Conference on Semantics, Knowledge, and Grid (SKG'06)

Murakami Y, Lin D, Tanaka M, Nakaguchi T, Ishida T (2010) Language service management with the language grid. The International Conference on Language Resources and Evaluation (LREC'10): 3526-3531

Varadi T, Krauwer S,Wittenburg P, Wynne M, Koskenniemi K (2008) CLARIN: common language resources and technology infrastructure. The Sixth International Conference on Language Resources and Evaluation (LREC'08): 1244-1248

Vossen P (2004) EuroWordNet: a multilingual database of autonomous and language-specific wordnets connected via an inter-lingual index. International Journal of Lexicography 17(2): 161-173

Chapter 3
Intercultural Collaboration Tools Based on the Language Grid

Masahiro Tanaka[1], Rieko Inaba[2], Akiyo Nadamoto[3], and Tomohiro Shigenobu[1]

1 National Institute of Information and Communications Technology, Hikaridai 3-5, Seika-cho, Soraku-gun, Kyoto, Japan, email: {mtnk, shigenobu}@nict.go.jp

2 Center for Promotion of Informatics Education, Graduate School of Informatics, Kyoto University, Yoshida-Honmachi, Kyoto, Japan, email: rieko@i.kyoto-u.ac.jp

3 Department of Intelligence and Informatics, Konan University, Okamoto, Higashinada-ku, Kobe, Japan, email: nadamoto@konan-u.ac.jp

Abstract As the number of online machine translation tools continues to expand, the importance of utilizing machine translation in multilingual communities is also increasing. Yet several problems exist when using the existing machine translation tools with intercultural communication in a multilingual community. 1) Translation of community-specific terms or sentences within communities is always of low quality. 2) Machine translation tools lack a view of how a multilingual community's activities should include the improving of low-quality translation. 3) They do not provide a means for customization based on the requirements unique to a community. To address these issues, we developed Language Grid Toolbox. Language Grid Toolbox aims to support intercultural collaboration using the Language Grid and provides various functions such as creation of community-specific dictionaries combined with a machine translator and multilingual BBS where translated language can be corrected collectively by community members. Moreover, since Toolbox is developed as open source software and provides APIs of basic functions, customized functions for each community can easily be developed. Several customized communication tools extended from Toolbox's basic modules have already been implemented by universities and local governments.

3.1 Introduction

In intercultural collaboration, when those of various nationalities and with different languages and cultures share a common goal, English may not always be the common language for communication (Aiken et al. 1994). This makes machine translation an alternative medium for communication. With the number of online machine translation tools (such as Google Translate) continuing to expand, the importance of exploiting machine translation in multilingual communities has been increasing (Nomura et al. 2003). Also on the Language Grid, several machine translators are available.

However, simply translating a document into another language is not enough due to a number of aspects of machine translation and multilingual communities. First, intercultural collaboration requires communication that aims to satisfy a goal in a specific domain. This may reduce the translation quality because a target document often contains community-specific terms that a machine translator cannot appropriately translate. Next, since the result of machine translation is not always of good enough quality, an intercultural communication support tool must be designed to help users communicate to detect errors and correct results of machine translators (Yamashita and Ishida 2006a, Yamashita and Ishida 2006b). Third, different situations using intercultural collaboration tools have different requirements, though most multilingual communities have translation as a common requirement.

Most of the existing translation tools relying on machine translators aim to support general translation tasks and do not consider means of supporting intercultural collaboration via communication in a multilingual community. To solve these issues, we developed the Language Grid Toolbox (or simply Toolbox), which provides basic functions for intercultural collaboration, such as language resource creation, translation, and multilingual BBS. As shown in Chapter 1, the service layers of the Language Grid consist of four layers: P2P Service Grid, Atomic Service, Composite Service and Application System. Toolbox is one of the Application Systems and exploits atomic/composite services on the Language Grid.

To appropriately translate community-specific terms, Toolbox allows multilingual community members to create their own language resources. For instance, combining customized dictionaries containing community-specific terms with a machine translation service on the Language Grid helps improve the translation quality (Inaba et al. 2007). Moreover, Toolbox provides a way for community members to correct results of machine translation. On the multilingual BBS, where messages can be exchanged and users can post and read them in their own languages, users proficient in multiple languages can correct the translation to help other users understand the message. Toolbox's functions can easily be extended because the source code is open and APIs of fundamental functions are provided. A community wishing to extend or customize existing functions according to its requirements can develop a personalized function that utilizes features of existing functions.

3.2 Communication Patterns

Forms of communication for intercultural collaboration are strongly linked to the goals and nature of each communication. In this section, we identify three communication patterns of intercultural collaboration and propose how these patterns should be supported.

First, we discuss communication in an established community. In a community whose members are highly motivated to achieve a clear and common goal, the members are expected to strive to improve their inter-communication. They therefore need to be equipped with a way to make one of their efforts the improvement of translation quality. Such communities benefit from combining a community dictionary with a machine translator, and correction of machine translation results. A community dictionary is a multilingual dictionary containing translation of community-specific terms. By combining such a dictionary with a machine translator, the dictionary, rather than the translator, serves to translate only the community-specific terms within an input document. This results in higher quality translation for documents containing such terminology. Correction of machine translation results allows a community member who understands both the source and target language to help others understand the translation.

Next, we consider a community which focuses on publishing multilingual contents. Multilingual communities commonly have the goal of translating documents into various languages. Translated documents are published outside the community to assist those who have difficulty acquiring information in their own environments. A typical scenario is a website publishing multilingual contents. For instance, it is important for municipalities to create multilingual documents for foreign residents. Another scenario is when inquiries about multilingual communities come from outside of a community, such as when a student seeking to study in another country wants school information in his/her native language. Generally speaking, published information should be much more accurate than information exchanged through face-to-face communication. Translated contents therefore should be shared and reviewed by community members. Answers to inquiries given by external parties should also be created via discussion among community members, as well as translation.

Finally we examine on-site communication. The previous two communication patterns assume communication among people in different areas. Yet some communities focus more on face-to-face communication. A typical scenario is customer support in a store or at a reception desk at a hospital or museum. In these situations, it is essential to adapt the user interface of the intercultural collaboration tool to specific requirements because the users have no time to learn how to use the tool. Therefore the tools need to be easily customizable. To effectively develop a customized user interface, tool components should be clearly separated into parts that should be customized and parts that provide reusable and black-box functions at the back end.

3.3 Language Grid Toolbox

Based on the communication patterns and requirements described in the previous section, we developed the Language Grid Toolbox, an intercultural collaboration support tool using the Language Grid. Toolbox is a Web application based on XOOPS, an open-source content management system (CMS). Fig. 3.1 shows the top page of Toolbox.

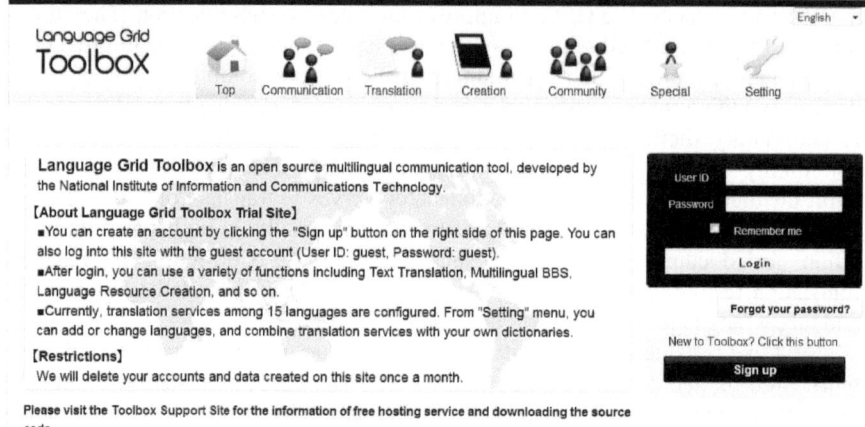

Fig. 3.1 Top page of Language Grid Toolbox.

This section describes the architecture of Toolbox, basic functions for supporting intercultural collaboration, and APIs for customization by extending/combining the basic modules.

3.3.1 Architecture

As fundamental functionality for supporting intercultural collaboration, Toolbox offers the following features to satisfy the requirements described in Section 3.2.

As described in Section 3.2, requirements of intercultural collaboration depend on communities. Toolbox therefore consists of several standalone tools called Toolbox modules. The community administrator can activate only the Toolbox modules that are required for that community, and install new Toolbox modules customized for the community. Community members communicate with each other via the Toolbox modules. The default modules are called basic modules, while those modified for a specific community are called customized modules.

User Management

In a multilingual community for intercultural collaboration, users need to be identified during communication; therefore they are required to first log in to Toolbox for authentication. Logged-in users can access almost all the Toolbox modules. This enables identification of who makes contributions by creating community dictionaries or posting messages on the BBS.

Supporting Multilingual User Interface

For a more comfortable experience for members of a multilingual community, Toolbox enables members to select the language of the user interface. When

Toolbox does not support the languages a community requires, community members can add a language by creating text resources for the user interface.

Translation Settings

Since most Toolbox modules rely on machine translation and dictionary services to support communication in a multilingual community, Toolbox modules are equipped with an easy means of accessing services on the Language Grid. Toolbox is also responsible for management of the service settings by providing an interface for selecting a machine translator and dictionaries for each translation path.

Fig. 3.2 briefly details the architecture including the above major components. Community members access Toolbox via the modules, and only the administrator can install a new module. Each module utilizes user management and service invocation as the fundamental function of the intercultural collaboration support tool. The UI resource management is invoked when a Toolbox module displays the user interface and returns text resources for the interface in the specified language.

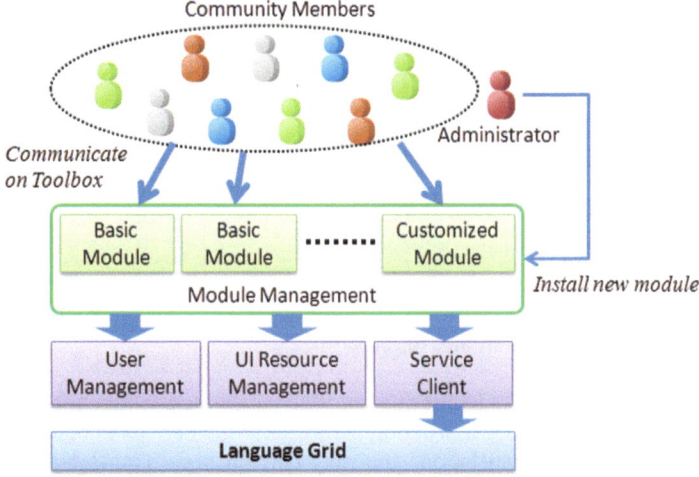

Fig. 3.2 Major components of Toolbox.

3.3.2 Basic Modules

A basic module is one that works as a standalone application for supporting intercultural collaboration and provides APIs that help a community develop personalized customized modules.

The primary basic modules are described below.

Resource Creation

This function allows users to create multilingual dictionaries, parallel texts, Q&As, and glossaries. Fig. 3.3 shows a multilingual dictionary created on Toolbox. As described in Section 3.2, community members can improve translation quality by creating a community dictionary and combining it with a machine translator. Community users also benefit from features like deployment of language resources as language services. For example, deployed community dictionary services can be shared and used as local dictionary services on Toolbox, which can be combined with machine translation services as well as the global dictionary services provided by the Language Grid. In this way users can use an increasing number of alternative language services created by communities.

Multilingual Q&As and glossaries, which are accumulated and shared by community users, also assist a multilingual community's activities. APIs for the types of resources are also provided and other modules can easily access the resources.

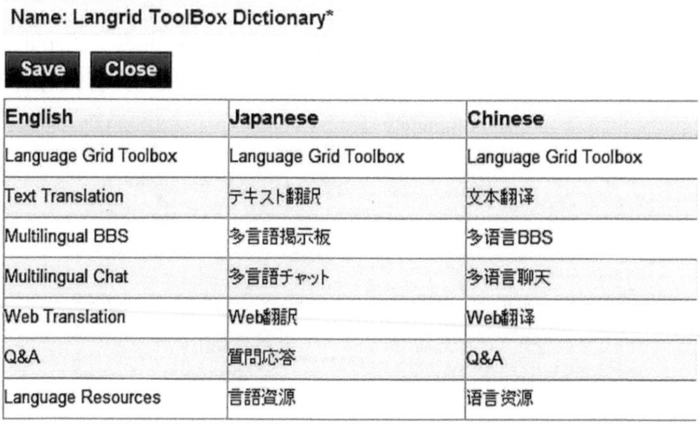

Name: Langrid ToolBox Dictionary*

| Save | Close |

English	Japanese	Chinese
Language Grid Toolbox	Language Grid Toolbox	Language Grid Toolbox
Text Translation	テキスト翻訳	文本翻译
Multilingual BBS	多言語掲示板	多语言BBS
Multilingual Chat	多言語チャット	多语言聊天
Web Translation	Web翻訳	Web翻译
Q&A	質問応答	Q&A
Language Resources	言語資源	语言资源

Fig. 3.3 Language resource creation (dictionary).

Toolbox also features a multilingual Web page creation function for community members, which provides translation templates, which are pairs of an expression on a Web page and its translation, and may contain tags. Translation templates are stored in the Toolbox file store to be accessed by community members. For translating Web contents, the user can apply a translation template and a part matching the template is translated as specified by the user. Fig. 3.4 shows a screenshot of the Web creation function.

| English | ▼ | > | Japanese | ▼ | | Translate |

From: English	↕ ↕	To: Japanese	↕ ↕
How to join		□ 参加するには	
Procedure to use Language Grid		□ 言語グリッドを使うための手続き	
Agreement		□ 覚書	

| Display | Save HTML | Download HTML | Display | Save HTML | Download HTML |

□Select all □Show html tag

Fig. 3.4 Web creation.

Translation

Toolbox provides a text translation tool equipped with back-translation and combined with its native multilingual dictionaries (Fig. 3.5). Community members can use the tool to easily check how the community dictionary affects the translation quality.

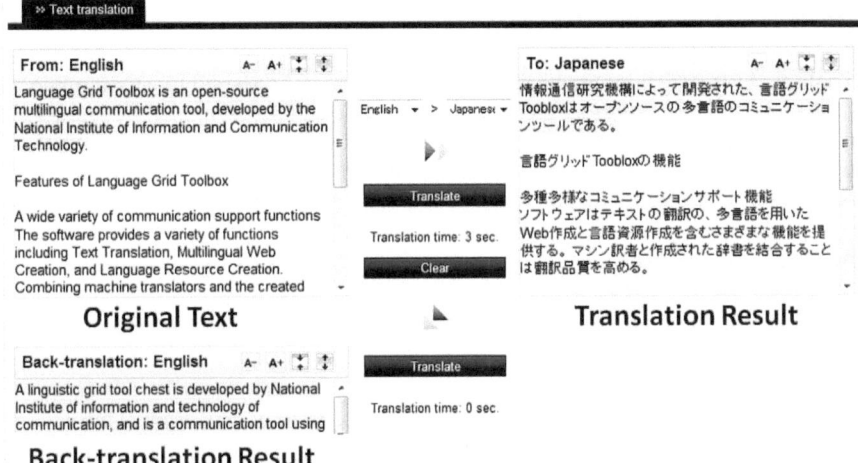

Fig. 3.5 Text translation.

Multilingual BBS

The multilingual BBS lets community members communicate with each other in their native language since its contents are translated multilingually by language services on the Language Grid.

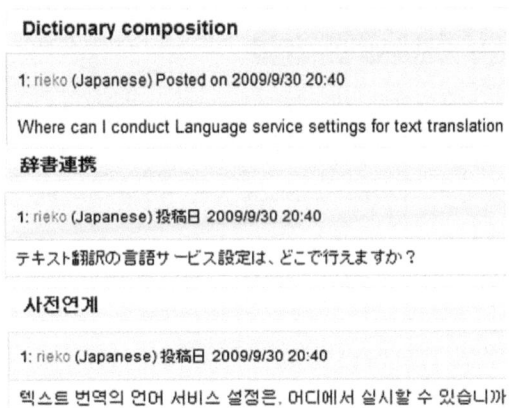

Fig. 3.6 Multilingual BBS.

An important feature of the multilingual BBS is that users can modify the machine translation results. As described in Section 3.2, this function works when certain community members are highly motivated to help other members' communication. Fig. 3.6 is a screenshot of the multilingual BBS.

3.3.3 Module Customization

Toolbox APIs called by the backend components can be shared by any module, as shown in Fig. 3.2. Therefore a customized module can be developed by creating or modifying the user interface components and business logic. Here we provide some examples of module customization, classified into three categories: adding new features, specializing user interfaces, and accessing data from outside.

Adding new features

In a scenario such as a seminar that hosts speakers of different languages, as described in Section 3.2, discussants during the presentation have no time to create a new community dictionary or to correct machine translator translation. Therefore we need another way to cover the insufficient quality of machine translators.

One solution is to show content related to the presentation and link messages to that content. Kyoto University realized this concept for improving communication between Japanese and overseas students by extending the multilingual BBS. Fig. 3.7 shows a screenshot of this discussion function.

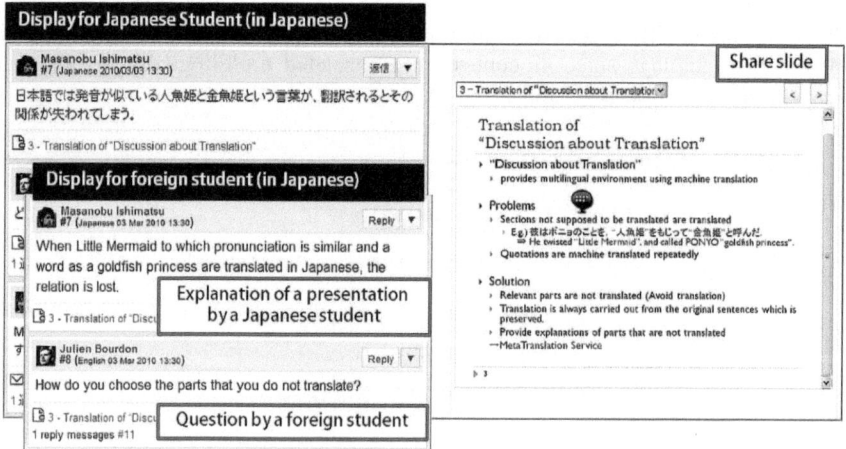

Fig. 3.7 Customization of multilingual BBS.

A slide of the presentation is shown on the right. Users posting a message can link it to a slide. The user can also put a pointer which clarifies the context for other participants who read the machine translation of the message.

Specializing the user interface in each community

In face-to-face multilingual communication, the user interface should be specialized for each community, as described in Section 3.2. A developer can easily customize the user interface of Toolbox modules because it clearly separates the user interface components and components at the back end.

The city of Kyoto developed a Toolbox module with a specialized user interface that utilizes this feature. The module shows Q&As created via the resource-creation functions. This module is intended for assisting foreigners in stores. It is assumed to operate via a touch panel and allows users to search for Q&As simply by clicking buttons that represent the Q&A category. Fig. 3.8 provides a screenshot of this function.

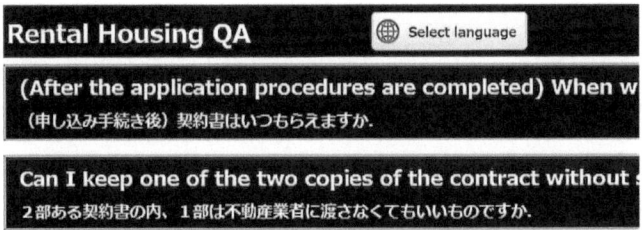

Fig. 3.8 Extending multilingual Q&A to assist foreigners in stores.

Resource creation functions were reused in order to realize this functionality, which also allows administrators to associate the multilingual glossary on Toolbox with Q&As. When a word contained in the associated glossary is found in a question or answer, the user can look up the definition.

Providing data access to users outside the community

As described in 3.2, users outside the multilingual community may need information accumulated within it. A multilingual Q&A site was developed to satisfy this requirement. Questions posted to the site by users are first translated into various languages, then posted on the multilingual BBS and registered multilingual Q&As on Toolbox. Community members discuss the question to come up with an answer, and register the answer to the multilingual Q&As. Finally, a user outside the community can obtain the answer on the Q&A site. Since Q&As created on Toolbox become available on the Q&A site, users outside the community can also search for them.

3.4 Open Source Customization

Although requirements of intercultural collaboration tools depend on the community, individual communities usually have little energy to spare for developing software. Therefore the design of the architecture and basic functions are insufficient for satisfying the requirements. One solution to this issue is to include users and developers in numerous multilingual communities in the software development cycle. This leads to quick feedback and more effective development.

To achieve the goal, the entire source code of Toolbox is open under a GPL license. An open source project was started to manage the source code as well as other software related to the Language Grid, including the Service Grid Server Software and language services. The project has a community site built based on Toolbox. Users from various multilingual communities can join and post requests and feedback in their own language. As the open source community itself is a multilingual community, users are expected to share their goals and cooperate to develop new basic functions.

This section shows how the source code of Toolbox is managed under the policies of the open source project, and then explains the project's development process.

3.4.1 Source Code Management

As shown in Fig. 3.9, Toolbox consists of three layers: Toolbox modules, Toolbox APIs, and XOOPS Core. Rectangles containing further rectangles represent a Toolbox module. A module provides functions for supporting multilingual communication as an independent application, and is designed to satisfy a specific communication requirement in a multilingual community. Since modules are configured for XOOPS administrators can easily install/uninstall them using XOOPS features. Toolbox provides some default basic modules such as language resource creation, text translation, and multilingual BBS.

Toolbox APIs are interfaces of fundamental functions of Toolbox and its modules. As shown in Fig. 3.9, basic modules provide APIs that allow other modules to use their functions. On the other hand, the discussion module does not have its own APIs since it is an extended version of the multilingual BBS and developed utilizing multilingual BBS functions. Most APIs of the currently available basic modules provide a way to access persistent data managed by basic modules. For example, a module can read/write messages on the multilingual BBS using multilingual BBS APIs.

Language Grid APIs, however, do not belong to a basic module on Toolbox. It is designed to provide other modules with an easy access to language services on the Language Grid. Since information on such services is retrieved and stored in Toolbox, the APIs refer to the information when receiving a request for service invocation.

In the open source project, software components are classified into two categories: core component and optional component as described in Chapter 2. As for Toolbox, Toolbox APIs and XOOPS core are considered as core components, and Toolbox modules are considered as optional components.

Toolbox relies on functions originated from XOOPS for authentication and user management. This part is shown as XOOPS Core in Fig. 3.2 and remains as close to XOOPS as possible. This makes it easy to update XOOPS Core by replacing the part with a new released version. Toolbox modules except for basic ones are expected to be designed according to the requirements of each community.

Therefore the whole source code of a module developed by a community directly contributes to the open source community. On the other hand, APIs of the module may be reused by other modules as well as the most fundamental functions such as authentication and user management.

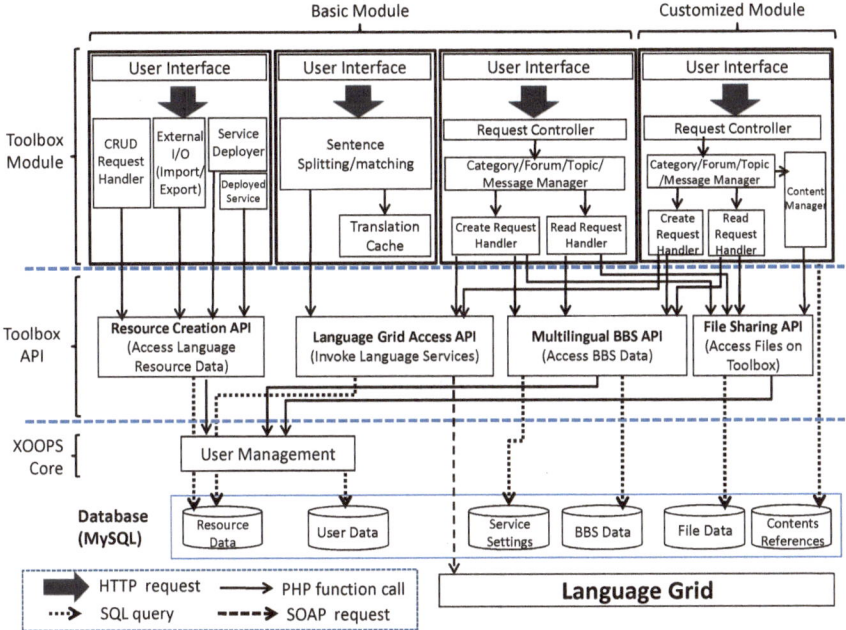

Fig. 3.9 Components of Language Grid Toolbox.

3.4.2 Development Policy

Since development resources are limited in the open source community, it is important to prevent development of incompatible derivations of modules. Therefore specifications of core components are discussed on the multilingual BBS and decisions are made by core members. Though anyone can modify the source code of Toolbox, the open source community allows only approved developers to commit the modified source code to the project repository. The repository therefore contains no derived versions of Toolbox API and XOOPS Core.

On the other hand, Toolbox modules focus more on quick feedback and flexible development in order to satisfy requirements in the field of intercultural collaboration. Therefore anyone can extend existing Toolbox modules and commit the source code to the project repository. Being deployed on the community site built based on Toolbox, the extended modules can easily be tested by the community members.

3.5 History of Language Grid Tools

The Language Grid has been used for the development of some intercultural communication support tools. In this section, we introduce the two major tools: Langrid Tools and Language Grid Playground. We also introduce the TransBBS in the Intercultural Collaboration Experiment (ICE2002) that preceded the Language Grid Project (Nomura et al. 2003). Intercultural Collaboration Experiment 2002 (ICE2002) was an Asian university-based project in which 32 students from Kyoto University, Shanghai Jiaotong University (China), Seoul National University and Handong University (South Korea), and the University of Malaya (Malaysia) developed software over the Internet. Since ICE2002 pursued collaboration among heterogeneous groups across country borders, participants never saw each other and communicated in their native languages, supported by machine translation.

ICE2002 provided participants with multilingual communication tools called TransBBS and TransWEB. The tools incorporate translation services for Chinese, Japanese, Korean, Malay, and English. TransBBS, a multilingual bulletin board system, was utilized as a space for ongoing discussion. TransWEB enabled participants to browse software development documents in their native languages. Communications in ICE2002 were held exclusively on TransBBS and TransWEB. In 2003 and 2004, they worked on research issues found during ICE 2002, such as analysis of human mental model forward MT, design of intercultural collaboration environment.

As the Language Grid project was started in 2006, some new Tools which replace old ones using the language services on the Language Grid were developed. Langrid Tools is a series of tools using a machine translator on the Language Grid for intercultural collaboration (Inaba et al. 2007). It includes an interface for inputting multilingual text, multilingual chat, and a multilingual shared blackboard (Fig. 3.10). Each is designed for supporting a specific form of intercultural collaboration.

The Language Grid project also investigated ways to support the need for multilingual communication among the members of two non-profit organizations – Pangaea (Mori, 2007) and the Japan Education and Resource Network (JEARN) (Naya, 2007). Pangaea developed virtual playgrounds where children around the world can meet, communicate, and connect. Personnel in the Pangaea offices in Japan, South Korea, Kenya, and Austria must communicate using their native languages. To meet this need, the Language Grid project provided Langrid chat, a tool that utilizing multilingual translation developed on the Language Grid. When a user inputs a sentence in his/her native language, back-translation results, via the target language set by the user, are returned in real time. The user can then confirm if the translation is reasonable.

JEARN is the Japanese center of the iEARN educational network and promotes international collaboration projects. For example, at its Natural Disaster Youth Summit, students created disaster safety maps of the areas surrounding their schools. These maps then form a "Global Disaster Safety Map." Participating countries include Japan, Russia, Taiwan, Armenia, Iran, Trinidad and Tobago, and Senegal. Students exchange information and discuss matters related to map creation using a BBS discussion board. However, most participants have poor English skills and thus they hesitate to speak up. The Language Grid project proposed enabling them to input to the BBS in their native language using Language Grid.

Pangaea needed a collaboration tool on the Language Grid while JEARN wanted to use its original BBS, but extended to provide a multilingual input tool called Langrid Input, a multilingual input interface for existing collaboration tools, such as a BBS. Input texts are translated in real time into various languages and sent to existing tools. Users can multi-lingualize existing tools by attaching the Langrid Input to them, and can also use the Langrid Input to edit specialized dictionaries.

Fig. 3.10 Collaboration tools (Langrid Chat)

The tools, however, do not provide APIs of their functions. Thus it is impossible to customize the functions according to individual communities' requirements. This is the reason Language Grid Playground was developed by Kyoto University (Morimoto et al. 2009). Language Grid Playground is a Web application that allows users to access language services on the Language Grid and to try out various language resources and language services via a browser. Language Grid Playground aims to be a showcase that displays all the Language Grid services and how they work, not to support intercultural collaboration in a multilingual community. Service configuration on the Language Grid Playground is therefore too complex for only communication. Examples of real-world challenges, such as creation of new language services using language resource composition, or application of Language Grid technologies to real-world sites with language needs, are also introduced through this website. The source code is open, like Toolbox, and reusable components, called "building blocks," are provided.

3.6 Conclusion

Although the Language Grid offers a lot of language services, we need an application system exploiting the services to support users in a multilingual community. The Language Grid Toolbox is a communication tool for intercultural collaboration. Contributions of this work are as follows:

- Allows community members to improve translation quality by creating language resources for their own community
- Provides basic functions for intercultural collaboration to activities in a multilingual community
- APIs of basic functions make it easier for individual communities to build customized functions according to their needs

Various organizations have already begun using Toolbox and registered community-specific language resources such as dictionaries, parallel texts, and Q&As. A municipality and a university have also developed new tools specialized for their needs.

In the future, we will establish a cycle of feedback from numerous multilingual communities and development by volunteer programmers in the open source community.

Acknowledgments   This work was partially supported by Strategic Information and Communications R&D Promotion Programme of the Ministry of Internal Affairs and Communications.

References

Aiken M, Hwang C, Paolillo J, Lu L (1994) A group decision support system for the Asian Pacific rim. Journal of International Information Management 3(2):1-13

Inaba R, Murakami Y, Nadamoto A, Ishida T (2007) Multilingual communication support using the language grid. Ishida T, Fussell SR, Vossen PTJM (eds) Intercultural Collaboration. Lecture Notes in Computer Sciences 4968, Springer-Verlag:118-132

Mori Y (2007) Atoms of bonding: communication components bridging children worldwide. Ishida T, Fussell SR, Vossen PTJM (eds) Intercultural Collaboration I. Lecture Notes in Computer Science 4968, Springer-Verlag: 335-343

Morimoto S, Sakai S, Gotou M, Cho H, Ishida T, Murakami Y (2009) Building blocks: layered components approach for accumulating high-demand web services. IEEE/ACM/WIC International Conference on Web Intelligence (WI-09): 430-433

Naya Y (2007) How intercultural disaster reduction education change students: a case study of an evening course senior high school in hyogo, japan. Ishida T, Fussell SR, Vossen PTJM (eds) Intercultural Collaboration. Lecture Notes in Computer Science 4968, Springer-Verlag

Nomura S, Ishida I, Yasuoka M, Yamashita N, Funakoshi K (2003) Open source software development with your mother language: Intercultural collaboration experiment 2002. The International Conference on Human-Computer Interaction (HCI2003): 1163-1167

Sakai S, Gotou M, Morimoto S, Morita D, Tanaka M, Ishida T, Murakami Y (2009) Language grid playground: light weight building blocks for intercultural collaboration. International Workshop on Intercultural Collaboration (IWIC-09): 297-300

Yamashita N, Ishida T (2006 a) Effects of machine translation on collaborative work. The International Conference on Computer Supported Cooperative Work (CSCW-06): 515-523

Yamashita N, Ishida T (2006 b) Automatic prediction of misconceptions in multilingual computer-mediated communication. The International Conference on Intelligent User Interfaces (IUI-06): 62-69

Part II

Composing Language Services

Chapter 4
Horizontal Service Composition for Language Services

Ahlem Ben Hassine[1], Shigeo Matsubara[2], and Toru Ishida[2]

1 National School of Computer Science (ENSI), Tunis University, Tunisia, e-mail: ahlembh@gmail.com

2 Department of Social Informatics, Kyoto University, Yoshida-honmachi, Sakyo-ku, Kyoto 606-8501, Japan, e-mail: {matsubara, ishida}@i.kyoto-u.ac.jp

Abstract In the Language Grid, automatically composing Web services is a crucial task. This task involves vertical and horizontal composition. Vertical composition consists of defining an appropriate combination of simple processes to perform a composition task. Horizontal composition consists of determining the most appropriate Web service from among a set of functionally equivalent ones for each component process. The latter is important in language services. For the horizontal composition of Web services, we propose a generic formalization of any Web service composition problem based on a constraint optimization problem (COP) and then propose an incremental user-intervention-based protocol to find the optimal composite Web service according to some predefined criteria at run-time.

4.1 Introduction

The Language Grid provides users with functions to combine language resources (e.g., bilingual dictionaries) or language processing functions (e.g., machine translators) and to add their own language resources to create new language services for their own intercultural activities (Ishida 2006). That is, combining a variety of language services allows users to make better use of the large quantity of language resources that have accumulated on the Internet. It will enable a language service to be built that is optimal for the actual field of activity performed by the intercultural collaboration.

Consider a specialized translation service with back translations. This service can be achieved by using a composite service. Several atomic services, such as machine translations, morphological analyzers, and specialized dictionaries can be combined to create the specialized translation service. However, this composition task might be difficult to realize because so many services with the same or similar ability exist. To overcome this difficulty and properly support users, we have developed a constraint-based Web service composition technique.

Our technique is based on the technologies of Web services. The great success of Web services, due especially to their rich applications made possible by open common standards, has led to their wide proliferation and a tremendous variety of Web services are now available. However, this proliferation has rendered the discovery and use of the most appropriate Web service arduous. These tasks are increasingly complicated, especially if the target is a composite Web service that must satisfy a user's long-term complex goal. The automatic Web service composition task consists of finding an appropriate combination of existing Web services to achieve a global goal.

We focus on the fact that many available Web services can fulfill the same task and we refer to these Web services as functionally equivalent Web services. In the sequel of this chapter, as is generally done in the literature, we refer to each of the subtasks making up the main goal as an *abstract* Web service and to each Web service able to perform a subtask as a *concrete* Web service. Solving the Web service composition problem involves two types of composition:

- *Vertical* composition is aimed at finding the "best" combination of *abstract* Web services, i.e., abstract workflow, in terms of achieving the main goal while satisfying all existing interdependent restrictions.
- *Horizontal* composition is aimed at finding the "best" *concrete* Web service, from among a set of available functionally equivalent Web services, i.e., executable workflow, to perform each *abstract* Web service. The quality of the response to the user's query (the composition task) strongly depends on the selected *concrete* Web services. The choice of a *concrete* Web service is dictated by functional (i.e., related to the inputs) and/or non-functional attributes (i.e., related to the quality of service attributes).

The main benefits gained by differentiating these two composition processes are: *i*) the Web service composition problem is simplified with reduced computational complexity, *ii*) avoiding any *horizontal* composition redundancy that may appear while searching for the "best" *combination* of *abstract* Web services, and mainly *iii*) ensuring more flexibility for user intervention, i.e., the user is able to modify/adjust the *abstract* workflow when needed.

This chapter consists of two main parts. The first is a generic formalization of any Web service composition problem as a constraint optimization problem (COP) in which we try to express most of the Web service composition problem features in a simple and natural way. Our main purpose is to develop a common and robust means of expressing any Web service composition problem that ideally reflects realistic domains. The second contribution is a real-time interactive protocol to solve any Web service composition problem by overcoming most of the limitations encountered above. Although there are various techniques for solving COPs, none of these consider the user interaction issue. The constraint optimization problem formalism is especially promising for ideally describing any realistic Web service composition problem, because this problem is a combinatorial problem that can be represented by a set of variables connected by constraints. Two approaches are proposed in this chapter, a centralized approach and a distributed approach.

This chapter is organized as follows. In Section 4.2, we explain why horizontal composition is needed in the language services domain. In Section 4.3, we present the proposed formalization. In Section 4.4, we describe a real-world scenario. In Section 4.5, we describe the proposed algorithm. In Section 4.6, we discuss possibilities of an extension of the previous algorithm. In Section 4.7, we compare the proposed techniques to the existing techniques. In Section 4.8, we conclude the chapter.

4.2 Why Horizontal Composition?

The language services domain has different characteristics from other domains such as supply-chain management. In the language services domain, the number of services included in a composite service is at most six or seven. On the other hand, a lot of functionally equivalent services exist that can be used to realize a subtask. For example, more than one hundred parallel dictionaries are available. This suggests that the challenge is not how to find the "best" combination of the *abstract* Web services but how to find the "best" *concrete* Web service from among a set of available functionally equivalent Web services.

Fig. 4.1 shows an example of vertical composition and horizontal composition. In vertical composition, a task of tailored-translation is given. First, the task is decomposed into the two subtasks of looking-up-dictionary and tailored-machine-translation and then a sequence of services accomplishing each subtask is searched for. The result is the best combination of the abstract Web services such as morphological-analysis, technical-term-extraction, technical-term-bilingual-dictionary, term-replacement, and machine-translation. Here, note that each service is an abstract Web service, that is, it is not bound to any concrete service.

In horizontal composition, on the other hand, a workflow of abstract Web services is given and the goal is to find a best combination of concrete Web services. For example, an abstract service of morphological-analysis can be bound to a concrete Web service such as LX-Suite, POSTAGE/K, FreeLing, or HAM.

Solving the horizontal Web service composition problem is not easy. The method of selecting the best service for each subtask and combining them to form a composite service does not work well because it does not guarantee to satisfy the constraints such as the user's budget constraint. The task of combining Web services has attracted the interest of many researchers, (McIlraith and Son 2002), (Sirin et al. 2004), (Lin et al. 2005), and several approaches have been reported. Most of these deal only with vertical composition, where only a single concrete Web service is available for each abstract one. Thus, their techniques cannot be applied to horizontal Web service composition.

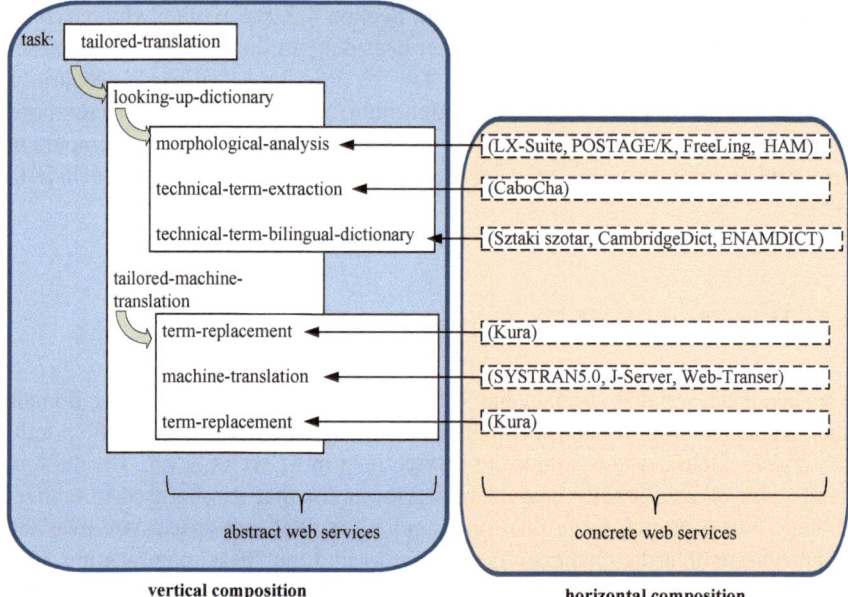

Fig. 4.1 Vertical composition and horizontal composition

To solve the problem of mixing and matching component Web services we have to consider various features. These features can be divided into two main groups:

- Features related to the user, including the user's constraints and preferences. For example, the user prefers J-Server over Google Translate as a machine translation service, while another user has the reverse preference.
- Features related to Web services; these can be divided into two subgroups, *internal* and *external* features. *Internal* features include quality of service (QoS) attributes, and *external* features include existing restrictions on the connection of Web services, (e.g., a hotel room should be reserved for the ISWC conference usually after booking the flight). *External* features are specified in the Web service ontology language, OWL-S (OWL Services Coalition 2003), through a set of control constructs such as *Sequence, Unordered, Choice*, etc.

As mentioned above, the tremendous number of functionally equivalent concrete Web services makes the search for an appropriate one, i.e., *horizontal* composition of concrete Web services, an NP-hard task (Canfora et al. 2005). This composition process also has the following characteristics.

- Information is often incomplete and uncertain.
- The environment is naturally distributed and dynamic.
- Many (non)-functional features, inter-related restrictions and especially user preferences may affect the quality of the response to a user's query.

Existing research efforts have tackled only some parts of the natural features of the Web service composition problem (Au et al. 2005), (Kuter et al. 2004), none have tried to deal with all of them. Moreover, some complex real-world problems require some level of abstract interactions with the user to refine the search for a valid composite Web service. Finally, very few studies have considered the validity of the information concerning a concrete Web service during the composition process and none have dealt with this question of validity during the execution process. We have learned from all these works and focused our research on the requirements of the Web service composition problem that are derived from the natural features of the problem, search-based user intervention and the information validity during the composition and execution processes. Our main goal is to provide a means by which an optimal composite executable workflow can be created for a given set of sub-tasks with their inter-relation restrictions, i.e., an abstract workflow.

4.3 Constraint-based Formalization of Horizontal Web Service Composition

The constraint satisfaction problem (CSP) framework is a key formalism for many combinatorial problems. The great success of this paradigm is due to its simplicity, its natural expressiveness of several real-world applications, and especially the efficiency of the existing underlying solvers. We therefore believe that the CSP formalism allows a better and more generic representation of any Web service composition problem. Hence, we formalize the Web service composition problem as a *constraint optimization problem* (COP) in which we have two kinds of constraints: *hard* and *soft* constraints.

A *static* CSP is a triplet (X, D, C) composed of a finite set X of n variables, each of which takes a value in an associated finite domain D and a set C of e constraints between these n variables (Montanari 1974). Solving a CSP consists of finding one or all complete assignments of values to variables that satisfy all the constraints. This formalism was extended to the COP to deal with applications where we need to optimize an objective function. A constraint optimization problem is a CSP that includes an objective function. The goal is to choose values for variables such that the given objective function is minimized or maximized.

We define a Web service composition problem as a COP by $(X, D, C, f(sl))$ where:

- $X=\{X_1,\ldots, X_n\}$ is the set of *abstract* Web services, each X_i being a complex variable represented by a pair $(X_i.in, X_i.out)$ where
  - $X_i.in = \{in_{i_1}, in_{i_2}, \ldots, in_{i_p}\}$ represents the set of p inputs of the *concrete* Web service, and
  - $X_i.out = \{out_{i_1}, out_{i_2}, \ldots, out_{i_q}\}$ represents the set of q outputs of the *concrete* Web service.

- $D=\{D_1, ..., D_n\}$ is the set of domains, each D_i representing possible *concrete* Web services that fulfill the task of the corresponding *abstract* Web service. $D_i=\{s_{ij}(s_{ij}.in, s_{ij}.out) \mid s_{ij}.in \subseteq X_i.in \text{ AND } X_i.out \subseteq s_{ij}.out\}$
- $C=C_S \cup C_H$
    - C_S represents the soft constraints related to the preferences of the user and to some Quality of Service attributes. For each soft constraint $C_{Si} \in C_S$ we assign the penalty $\rho_{C_{Si}} \in [0, 1]$. This penalty reflects the degree to which the soft constraint C_{Si} is not satisfied.
    - C_H represents the hard constraints related to the inter-*abstract* Web services relations, the OWL-S defined control constructs, and the preconditions of each *concrete* Web service. For each hard constraint, $C_{Hi} \in C_H$, we assign a weight $\perp$ (i.e. satisfaction is an imperative). It is noteworthy that C_H may also include some *hard* constraints specified by the user. These hard constraints can be *relaxed* upon request if no solution to the problem is found.
- For each *concrete* Web service we assign a weight to express the degree of user preference, $w_{s_{ij}} \in [0,1]$. Weights are automatically accorded to the values of variables in a dynamic way with respect to the goal.
- $f(sl)$ is the objective function to optimize, $f(sl)= \otimes_{s_{ij} \in sl}$ *(user's preferences, penalty over soft constraints, Quality of Service attributes, probability of information expiration)*, and sl is a solution of the problem defined by the instantiation of all the variables of the problem. In this work, we focus on optimizing both *i)* the user's preferences toward selected concrete Web services denoted by $\varphi(sl)$ and *ii)* the penalty over soft constraints denoted by $\psi(sl)$. The Quality of Service attributes and the probability of information expiration will be tackled in our future work.

Solving a Web service composition problem consists of finding a "good" assignment $sl^* \in Sol:=D_1 \times ... \times D_n$ of the variables in X such that all the hard constraints are satisfied while objective function $f(sl)$ is optimized according to Eq. 4.1.

$$f(sl^*) = arg\ max_{sl \in Sol} \otimes (\varphi(sl), \psi(sl)) \tag{4.1}$$

In this chapter, we maximize the summation of the user preferences for all *concrete* Web services involved in solution sl and minimize the summation of the penalties associated to all soft constraints according to Eq. 4.2.

$$f(sl^*) = arg\ max_{sl \in Sol} (\Sigma_{S_{ij} \in sl}\ w_{s_{ij}} - \Sigma_{C_{Si} \in C_S}\ \rho_{C_{Si}}) \tag{4.2}$$

Since the solution might be more than a sequence of *concrete* Web services, i.e., it may include concurrent *concrete* Web services, we use "," to indicate sequential execution and "‖" to indicate concurrent execution. This information is useful in the execution process. The obtained solution will have a structure such as

$sl=\{s_{1j}, \{s_{2j}\|s_{3k}\},s_{4h},...,s_{nm}\}$. This problem is considered to be a dynamic problem since the set of *abstract* Web services (the set of variables) is not fixed; i.e., an *abstract* Web service can be divided into other *abstract* Web services if no available *concrete* Web service can perform the required task. In addition, the set of values in the domain of each variable (the set of possible *concrete* Web services) is not fixed. *Concrete* Web services can be added to/removed from the system.

In the Web service composition problem, several control constructs connecting Web services can be used. The main ones, defined in the OWL-S description, can be divided into four groups and we describe our formalization of these four groups below.

- Ordered, which involves the SEQUENCE control construct, can be expressed by using a hard constraint. Each pair of *abstract* Web services linked by a sequence control construct are involved in the same $C_{Sequence}$ constraint.
- Concurrency involves the SPLIT, SPLIT+JOIN, and UNORDERED control constructs. The inherent aspect of the following proposed agent-based approach (Section 4.5) allows the formalization of this control construct in a natural way. Note that only "JOIN" will be associated with a C_{Join} constraint. SPLIT and UNORDERED will be modeled using an "empty" constraint, C_{empty}, that represents a universal constraint. This constraint will be used to propagate information about parallel execution to concerned variables in the following proposed protocol.
- Choice involves IF-THEN-ELSE and CHOICE control constructs. For each set of *abstract* Web services (two or more) related by the IF-THEN-ELSE or CHOICE control construct, the corresponding variables are merged into the same global variable (X_j for example), and their domains are combined and ranked according to the preference of the user. For example, given a set of m *abstract* Web services ($\{t_1,t_2,...,t_m\}$) related by the "CHOICE" control construct, we combine them into a global variable (X_k for example) and *rank* their domains. For their preconditions, we assign a sub-constraint to each condition $\{C_{cond_1}, C_{cond_2}, ..., C_{cond_m}\}$ and create a global constraint $C_{Choice} = \cup_i C_{cond_i}$. At any time we are sure that only one condition will be satisfied since $\cap_i C_{cond_i} = \varnothing$.
- LOOP, neither the CSP formalism nor any of its extensions can handle iterative processing. This will be considered in our future work.

4.4 Real-world Scenario

The main objective of the Language Grid project (Ishida 2006) is to enhance intercultural collaboration by increasing the accessibility and usability of existing language resources on the Web. Murakami et al. (Murakami et al. 2006) proposed an abstract workflow for a tailored translation, see Fig.4.2. In the following, we present our proposed formalization of this workflow.

- $X=\{X_1,X_2,X_3,X_4,X_5,X_6\}$, where each $X_i=(X_i.in,X_i.out)$ corresponds to one of the atomic services.
    - X_1 corresponds to the atomic service of morphological analysis; $X_1.in=\{originalSentence, sourceLang\}$; $X_1.out=\{morphemes\}$
    - X_2 corresponds to the atomic service of technical term extraction service; $X_2.in=\{morphemes\}$; $X_2.out=\{technicalTerms\}$
    - X_3 corresponds to the atomic service of technical term bilingual dictionary; $X_3.in=\{technicalTerms\}$; $X_3.out=\{technicalTermTranslated, technical-TermsIntermediateCode\}$
    - X_4 corresponds to the atomic service of term replacement service; $X_4.in=\{originalSentence, technicalTermTranslated, technicalTermsInter-mediateCode\}$; $X_4.out=\{intermediateCodeSentence\}$
    - X_5 corresponds to the atomic service of machine translation service; $X_5.in=\{intermediateCodeSentence\}$; $X_5.out=\{intermediateCodeSentenceTranslated\}$
    - X_6 corresponds to the atomic service of term replacement service; $X_6.in=\{intermediateCodeSentenceTranslated, technicalTermsIntermediate-Code, technicalTermsTranslated\}$; $X_6.out=\{originalSentenceTranslated\}$

- $D=\{D_1,D_2,D_3,D_4,D_5,D_6\}$, where

    - $D_1=\{$LX-Suite, POSTAGE/K, FreeLing, TreeTagger, Morpha, HAM$\}$
    - $D_2=\{$CaboCha$\}$
    - $D_3=\{$Sztaki szotar, CambridgeDict, ENAMDICT, UrdoWord, KamusJot$\}$
    - $D_4=\{$Kura$\}$
    - $D_5=\{$Kataku, SYSTRAN5.0, Reverso, Free Translation, J-Server, PeTra, Web-Transer$\}$
    - $D_6=\{$Kura$\}$

- $C=C_S \cup C_H$, where

    - C_H including
      $X_1.originalSentence \neq nil$;
      $X_2.morphemes = X_1.morphems$;
      $X_3.technicalTerms = X_2.technicalTerms$;
    - C_S including
      $Acc(X_5) \geq 0.7$ with $\rho_{C_{Si}}=0.6$, where the function of Acc returns the Web service result accuracy;
      $Cost(X_2) + Cost(X_4) \leq 1$ cent with $\rho_{C_{Si}}=0.3$, where the function of $Cost$ returns the Web service cost.

- The main objective is to find the best combination, sl, of the above *abstract* Web services and assign the most appropriate *concrete* Web services such that sl maximizes objective function $f(sl)$ defined in Section 4.3 Eq. 4.2. Note that, for simplicity, we assume pairwise independence between the values of the different domains. We will consider dependence issues in future work.

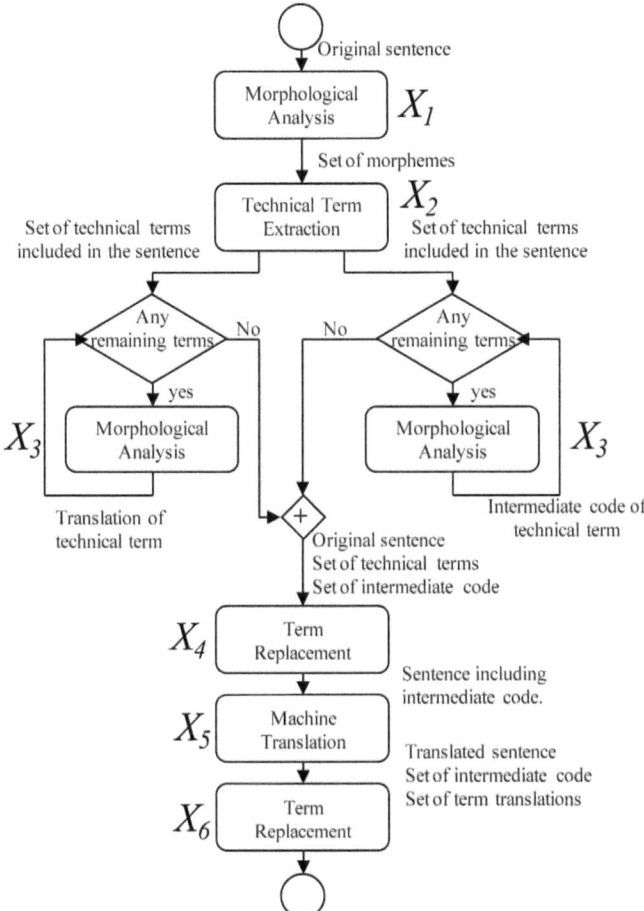

Fig. 4.2 The abstract workflow of the Language Resources composition problems.

4.5 Constraint Optimization Problem Interactive Algorithm for Solving the Web Service Composition Problem

The overall objective of our approach is to generate the *best* executable workflow (according to the aforementioned criteria) within a feasible time. Several constraint optimization problem algorithms can be applied to solve this problem, but none allows the intervention of the human user during the search process. In the following, we propose an algorithm (Algorithm 4.1) that allows human interaction with the system to enhance the solving process.

For each variable X_j we first determine a set of candidate *concrete* Web services, $Cand_{X_j}$, for its *abstract* Web service that satisfies all the hard constraints, C_{Hl} $\in C_H$ (Algorithm 4.1 line 4), and then we *rank* $Cand_{X_j}$ according to the objective function defined in Section 4.3. This ranked set is used to guide the selection of the next variable X_{j+1} in the search process. For X_{j+1} we start by applying the *join* operation to the received list $Cand_{X_j}$ and the current one $Cand_{X_{j+1}}$, i.e., join of $Cand_{X_j}$ and $Cand_{X_{j+1}}$ (Algorithm 4.1 line 12). The obtained sub-solutions are then *filtered* (Algorithm 4.1 line 12) according to the set of existing hard constraints. Finally, the resulting set of sub-solutions is ranked according to the objective function for optimization. If the set of candidates $Cand_{X_j}$ is large, to avoid explosion in the join operation, we select a fixed number of the most preferred *concrete* Web services for each variable, (i.e., a subset of candidates), and try to propagate these to the next variable. Whenever this subset does not lead to a complete solution, we backtrack and then seek a solution using the remaining candidates. The order of the values in the candidate set is established to avoid missing any solution. The obtained sets of sub-solutions are propagated to the next variable (Algorithm 4.1 line 16) and the same dynamic continues until all the *abstract* Web services are instantiated. If the set of candidate Web services becomes empty (i.e., none of the available Web services satisfies the hard constraints), or the set of sub-solutions resulting from the join and filter operations becomes empty and no more *backtracking* can be performed, the user is asked to relax some of his/her constraints (Algorithm 4.1 line 23). However, if the user's relaxed constraints involve the first instantiated variable in the search tree then the search process is reentered from scratch. It is noteworthy that three issues are possible in this algorithm, *i*) ask for user intervention whenever a local failure is detected, which may reduce the number of backtracks, *ii*) ask for user intervention only when a global failure is detected, no more backtracks can be performed, *iii*) store a trace of the explored search tree to be able to point directly to the variable involved in user relaxation and pursue the solving process and avoid some computational redundancy.

In addition, whenever we need any information concerning any *concrete* Web services, a request-message is sent to an information-providing Web service to get the necessary information along with both its validity duration and the maximum time required to execute the underlying Web service. The agent should maintain this time so that it can detect information expiration and perform the right decision (Algorithm 4.1 line 20). To deal with the main characteristic of this real-world problem, the dynamic environment, we maintain the validity of necessary information during the solving and execution processes, *totalTime*. *totalTime* should be less than the minimum validity time required for any Web service information. We use the following notations:

- $T_{plan}(sl)$: time needed to provide plan *sl*,
- $t_{exe}(s_i)$: time needed to execute one *concrete* Web service,
- $t_{val}(inf_j)$: estimated time before the expiration of solicited information *inf_j*.

Naturally, the validity of information is usually considered as uncertain. Hence, for each validity time a *probability of information alteration $p_{alt}(inf_i)$* can be associated with underlying information inf_i. We will consider this probability of information alteration in our future work. The maximal time required to provide a solution, T_{plan}, is defined by Eq. 4.3.

$$T_{plan}(sl) < \min_{\forall s_i \in sl} t_{val}(inf_j) - \Sigma_{s_j \in sl} t_{exe}(s_j) \qquad (4.3)$$

Algorithm 4.1 User-intervention-based algorithm for Web service composition.
WSCSolver(i, setSubSol, totalTime, checkedValues)
1: **if** $i > \|X\|$ **then**
2:     return *setSubSol*;
3: **end if**
4: $Cand_X[i] \leftarrow \{s_{ik} \in D_i \mid s_{ik}$ *satisfies all the $C_H\} \setminus$ checkedValues[i]*;
5: **if** *information required for any* $s_{ik} \in Cand_X[i]$ **then**
6:     Collect necessary information; Update t_{val}, t_{exe} and *totalTime*;
7: **end if**

8: *Rank $Cand_X[i]$ according to* $^W\!\!_{\mathcal{U}}$ *and* $^P\!c_{\mathcal{R}}$ *and while checking t_{val}, t_{exe} and to-talTime*;
9: *subSol* ← Ø;
10: **while** *subSol* = Ø **do**
11:     *subCand* ←subset of the *$Cand_X[i]$*; add(*checkedValues[i]*, *subCand*);
12:     *subSol* ←join *of setSubSol and subCand*; Filter and Rank *subSol* according to *f (subSol)*;
13: **end while**
14: **if** *subSol* ≠ Ø **then**
15:     add(*setSubSol*, *subSol*);
16:     return ***WSCSolver***(*i*+1, *setSubSol, totalTime, checkedValues*);
17: **else**
18:     **if** *i*>1 **then**
19:         reset to Ø all *checkedValues[j]* for *j*>*i*;
20:         Update *totalTime*; Update *setSubSol*;
21:         return ***WSCSolver***(*i*-1, *setSubSol, totalTime, checkedValues*);
22:     **else**
23:         *RelaxedConst* ←ask User to relax constraints involving X_k where *k*<*i*;
24:         Update(*C_H, C_S, RelaxedConst*);
25:         *i*←*j* such that $\forall X_k$ *involved in C_l and $C_l \in RelaxedConst$, X_j precedes X_k*;
26:         Update *setSubSol*;
27:         return ***WSCSolver***(*i*+1, *setSubSol, totalTime, checkedValues*);
28:     **end if**
29: **end if**

Each sub-solution based on expired information will be temporarily discarded but kept for use in case the agent cannot find any possible solution. This measurement is an efficient way to cope with Web services with effects characterized by information volatility because it allows for the forward estimation of the validity of information during both the composition process and the execution process.

4.6 Extended Algorithm

The main limitation of the previous algorithm is that it cannot be easily adapted to any alteration in the environment. Whenever a user decides to relax some of his/her constraints, and these constraints involve an already invoked variable, especially the first one in the search tree, the search for a solution must be recommenced from scratch. However, distributed approaches well support user intervention. In this solution, the same algorithm will be split among a set of homogeneous entities. Each entity will be responsible for one variable and the same algorithm will be performed in parallel by all entities. In case of conflict, i.e., no solution can be generated and no *backtrack* can be performed, the system will ask the user to relax some constraints. The concerned entity will update its view, generate new candidates and exchange them with the concerned entities. The process repeats until either a solution for the problem is generated or the lack of a solution is confirmed, even with all possible relaxations. Nevertheless, this distributed solution might be inefficient for some real-world scenarios that demand access to a specialized Web service. A specialized Web service maintains information about a set of Web services. Information on the involved Web services is considered private, which makes it difficult to gather and process at the same site the information needed on Web services. Hence, we believe that extending the above algorithm to a multi-agent system is more effective for realistic domains.

4.7 Discussion

In this chapter, we propose a generic formalization for a horizontal Web service composition problem based on a constraint optimization problem (COP) and then propose an incremental user-intervention-based protocol to find the optimal composite Web service according to some predefined criteria at run-time. We clarify our contributions by giving an overview of existing research.

Several solutions to the Web service composition problem have been reported including integer programming (IP)-based techniques (Aggarwal et al. 2004), (Zeng et al. 2004), non-classical planning-based techniques and logic-based techniques (McIlraith and Son 2002), (Narayanan and McIlraith 2002). Recently, some researchers have suggested applying existing artificial intelligence (AI) optimization techniques, such as genetic algorithms (GA), mainly to include some Quality of Service attributes in the search process. Regarding IP-based proposed solutions (Aggarwal et al. 2004), (Zeng et al. 2004), the authors assume linearity of the constraints and of the objective function. As for non-classical planning techniques, Sirin et al. proposed an HTN-planning based approach (Sirin et al. 2004) to solve this problem. Their efforts were directed toward encoding the OWL-S Web service description as a SHOP2 planning problem, so that SHOP2 can be used to automatically generate a composite Web service. As mentioned above, these studies implicitly assume that only a single concrete Web service is available for each abstract one. In addition, we believe that these planning techniques are difficult to scale up compared to constraint-based techniques.

McIlraith and Son (McIlraith and Son 2002) proposed an approach to building agent technology based on the notion of generic procedures and customizing user constraints. The authors claim that an augmented version of the logic programming language Golog provides a natural formalism for automatically composing services on the semantic Web. They suggested that this problem should not be considered as simple planning, but rather as the customization of reusable, high level generic procedures. These logic-based techniques also do not consider horizontal Web service composition and are difficult to scale up if a lot of functionally equivalent services exist.

Canfora et al. in (Canfora et al. 2005) proposed tackling the QoS-aware composition problem with Genetic Algorithms (GA). This approach tackles both vertical and horizontal compositions. However, to accomplish the Web service composition task, the Web service composition procedure may need to retrieve information from Web services while operating. Most studies have assumed that such information is static (McIlraith and Son 2002), (Sirin et al. 2004), (Canfora et al. 2005). The advantage of our proposal, especially the distributed algorithm for horizontal Web service composition problems, is that it complies with inherent characteristics of real-world problems such as the dynamism of the environment.

Other studies have assumed that an interactive process with the user can get all the necessary information as inputs. Nevertheless, the static information assumption is not always valid, and the information on various Web services may change, i.e., it may be "volatile information" (Au et al. 2005) either while the Web service composition procedure is operating or during execution of the composition process. Kuter et al. (Kuter et al. 2004) present an extension of earlier non-classical planning-based research efforts to better cope with *volatile* information. This arises when the information-providing Web services do not return the needed information immediately after it is requested (or not at all). In addition, Au et al. (Au et al. 2005) proposed two different approaches for translating static information into volatile information. They propose assigning a validity duration to each item of information received from information providing services. Our proposal also complies with the need to deal with such volatile and uncertain information during the composition and execution processes.

4.8 Conclusion

In the Language Grid, automatically composing Web services is a crucial task. The Web service composition problem is a challenging research issue because of the tremendous growth in the number of Web services available, the dynamic environment, and the fluidity of user needs. In this chapter, we have proposed a real-time interactive solution for the Web service composition problem. This problem involves vertical composition and horizontal composition, and we have focused on the latter. This work complements existing techniques dealing with vertical composition in that it exploits their abstract workflows to determine the *best* executable one according to predefined optimality criteria. We have developed a protocol that overcomes the published limitations of the existing work and complies with the inherent characteristics of real-world Web service composition problems such as the dynamism of the environment and the need to deal with volatile information during the composition and execution processes. Two main approaches were proposed in this chapter, the first is a user-intervention-based centralized approach and the second is a distributed version of the previous one that can easily handle any alteration in the environment.

Acknowledgments   This research was partially supported by National Institute of Information and Communications Technology (NICT) and a Grant-in-Aid for Scientific Research (A) (21240014, 2009-2011) from Japan Society for the Promotion of Science (JSPS).

References

Au T-C, Kuter U, Nau D (2005) Web service composition with volatile information. 4th International Semantic Web Conference (ISWC2005): 52-66

Aggarwal R, Verma K, Miller J, Milnor W (2004) Constraint driven web service composition in METEOR-S. 2004 IEEE International Conference on Services Computing (SCC2004): 23-30

Canfora G, Di Penta M, Esposito R, Villani ML (2005) An approach for QoS-aware service composition based on genetic algorithms. Genetic and Evolutionary Computation Conference (GECCO2005): 1069-1075

Kuter U, Sirin E, Parsia B, Nau D, Hendler J (2004) Information gathering during planning for web service composition. 3rd International Semantic Web Conference (ISWC2004): 335-349

Lin M, Xie J, Guo H, Wang, H (2005) Solving QoS-driven web service dynamic composition as fuzzy constraint satisfaction. IEEE International Conference on e-Technology, e-Commerce and e-Service (EEE2005): 9-14

McIlraith S, Son, TC (2002) Adapting Golog for composition of semantic web services. 8th International Conference on Knowledge Representation and Reasoning (KR2002): 482-493

Montanari U (1974) Networks of constraints: fundamental properties and applications to picture processing. Information Sciences 7: 95-132

Murakami Y, Ishida T, Nakaguchi T (2006) Infrastructure for language service composition. 2nd International Conference on Semantics, Knowledge, and Grid (SKG-06)

Narayanan S, McIlraith SA (2002) Simulation, verification and automated composition of web services. 11th International Conference on World Wide Web (WWW2002):77-88

OWL Services Coalition (2003) OWL-S: Semantic markup for Web services, OWL-S White Paper http://www.daml.org/services/owl-s/1.0/owl-s.pdf.

Sirin E, Parsia B, Wu D, Hendler J, Nau, D (2004) HTN planning for web service composition using SHOP2. Journal of Web Semantics 1(4): 377-396

Ishida, T (2006) Language Grid: an infrastructure for intercultural collaboration. IEEE/IPSJ Symposium on Applications and the Internet (SAINT-06): 96-100

Zeng L, Benatallah B, Ngu AHH, Dumas M, Kalagnanam J, Chang H (2004) QoS-aware middleware for web services composition. IEEE Transactions on Software Engineering 30(5): 311-327

Chapter 5
Service Supervision for Runtime Service Management

Masahiro Tanaka[1], Toru Ishida[2], and Yohei Murakami[1]

1 National Institute of Information and Communications Technology (NICT), 3-5 Hikaridai, Seika-Cho, Soraku-Gun, Kyoto, 619-0289, Japan, e-mail: {mtnk, yohei}@nict.go.jp

2 Department of Social Informatics, Kyoto University, Yoshida Honmachi, Sakyoku, Kyoto, 606-8501, Japan, email: ishida@i.kyoto-u.ac.jp

Abstract The Language Grid offers language services with a standardized interface and different non-functional properties. This allows us to create a specialized composite service for our own goals simply by selecting the appropriate services. The language services are, however, provided in various formats with their own policies. In an environment for service-collective intelligence, it is essential to have many service providers join by strongly ensuring that their policies are satisfied. In doing this, we therefore we have to solve the following problems. First, service composition relies on the products of various stakeholders that belong to different organizations, such as service products and composite service designers. This makes it difficult to modify existing services in line with given requirements. Next, selection of services may impose constraints on execution. We therefore often need to apply a certain amount of runtime adaptation toward a composite service in order to enforce given policies. To solve these problems, we proposed an architecture for runtime service management called Service Supervision. Service Supervision provides meta-level execution functions for composite services. These allow operators to modify behaviors of a composite service without changing its model. Service Supervision is also capable of effectively managing a comprehensive process of runtime service selection and adaptation in order to ensure the service providers' policies are satisfied. We implemented the Service Supervision prototype and showed that applying meta-level execution control barely decreases performance.

5.1 Introduction

With the maturing of service computing technologies, various programs and data have become available as Web services. Language services, including machine translators and dictionaries, are also available on the Language Grid. As described in the previous chapter, service interfaces are standardized according to the service

type. This allows us to realize various non-functional requirements by only selecting the appropriate service once a composite service is modeled based on the standardized interface of constituent services. For example, we can customize a composite service by combining a machine translator and a dictionary for a specific
domain by selecting an appropriate dictionary of technical terms.

Service providers often have a wide variety of policies, such as limitation of
transferred data and constraints on service combinations. To give service providers greater incentive to join a service composition platform, a composite service
that combines multiple services needs to be executed satisfying the policies of all
service providers concerned, while optimizing QoS.

From the early state of services computing research, many researchers have
tackled service composition that satisfies given requirements. Some proposed methods exist for selecting appropriate services from a set of functionally equivalent
services (Zeng et al. 2004) (Ben Hassine et al. 2006). Dynamic adaptation methods for composite services have been also proposed. These adopt aspect-oriented
programming (AOP) (Baresi et al. 2007) or a proxy between the composite service
execution engine and invoked services (Charfi and Mezini 2007).

However, many of the previous works suffer from limitations in a real, open
environment such as the Language Grid for the following reasons.

- Various stakeholders, such as service providers, composite service designers,
  and operators, typically belong to different organizations. Therefore modification of existing services for realizing required properties is unrealistic.
- Service selection and adaptation at runtime affect one another. This is why we
  need to consider a comprehensive process for them including steps of service
  selection and adaptation.

To solve the problems, we propose an architecture for runtime service management called Service Supervision, which consists of two parts: meta-level execution control and policy control. The former provides operators with a way to
change the behavior of composite services without changing the service model.
This allows operators to execute the services conforming to given policies even
when they do not have intellectual rights to modify the models. Policy control is
responsible for selecting/executing services using meta-level execution control. It
performs a comprehensive process of service selection, adaptation, and coordination. First, it tries to find a combination of services that satisfy policies of service
providers in a similar fashion to the previous work. But it adapts the services to
given policies by changing services' attributes if there is no service available to
satisfy those policies. The selection and adaptation are combined effectively based
on an extension of CSP.

The rest of this chapter is organized as follows. In Section 5.2, we describe the
design goal by showing a motivating scenario and our proposed architecture. Next
we explain execution control functions we implemented in Section 5.3, and then
describe the detail of the process of policy control using the control functions. In
Section 5.4, we show the experimental performance of the proposed framework.

After we introduce related work in Section 5.5, we conclude this chapter in Section 5.6.

5.2 Design Goal

In this section, we first describe a scenario of runtime management of a composite service. On a service-oriented collective intelligence platform like the Language Grid, we need to ensure service providers' policies are satisfied during execution of a composite service. Then we give an overview of the proposed architecture.

5.2.1 Scenario

A composite service for translation deployed on the Language Grid can serve as an example. The composite service combines a morphological analyzer, a machine translator, and dictionaries of technical terms. This service improves the translation quality of technical documents by translating technical terms in the given sentences using the dictionaries rather than the machine translator.

Fig. 5.1 shows the overview of the composite service. Squares containing circles represent service invocation activities. First, the given sentences are divided into morphemes by the morphological analyzer. Next, dictionaries find technical terms consisting of the morphemes and return their translation. Finally, the translator translates the entire sentences.

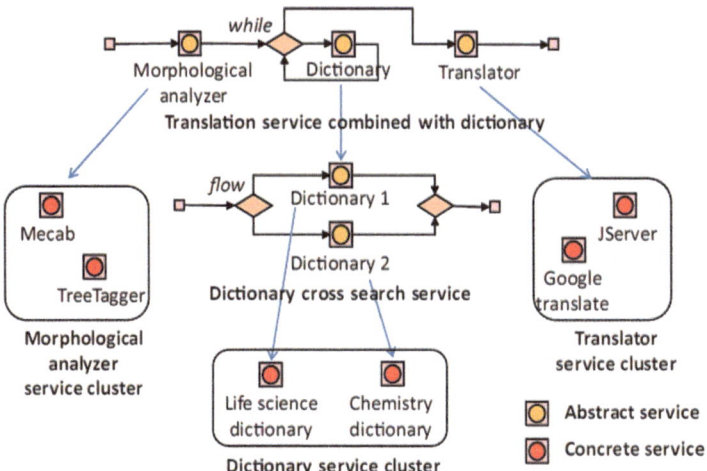

Fig. 5.1 A composite service for translation.

As shown in Fig. 5.1, we assume that a composite service is defined in a work-flow description language such as WS-BPEL. In a composite service, the constituent services define only the interfaces and are not bound to any endpoint. We refer to this as an *abstract service*. For example, on the Language Grid, an abstract service is defined for each service type, such as translators and dictionaries. Endpoints for the services are determined when the composite service is invoked. A service to which an endpoint is bound is called a *concrete service*.

On the Language Grid, all the information on concrete and composite services is managed by the Language Grid Service Manager. Currently, more than 90 concrete and 12 composite services are registered and various information on the services including license is managed on this manager.

A set of concrete services that is bound to an abstract service is called a *service cluster*. In Fig. 5.1, there are two concrete services in each service cluster. In our example, we bind one of these two to the morphological analyzer and the machine translator. For the dictionary, we first bind a composite service for cross-searching and then bind two concrete services to abstract services in the cross-search composite service. The Language Grid allows users to specify the hierarchical binding by describing the binding in the SOAP header of the request message.

We show the process of execution of this composite service below. First we select concrete services that satisfy the user's request and service providers' policies. In our example, we assume that the request is a Japanese-to-English translation and that the user specifies the life science and chemistry dictionaries for the two abstract dictionary services.

When receiving the request, the system selects concrete services for the rest of the abstract services. Suppose it first tries MeCab, which is a morphological analyzer for Japanese, and Google Translate, which provides translation from Japanese to English. The combination may have the following three problems.

The first problem is constraints on a combination of services. Assume the provider of the chemistry dictionary prohibits use of its service with Google Translate. In this case the system needs to select JServer, another machine translator that supports Japanese-English translation.

The second problem is constraints on execution of a constituent service. The JServer provider may limit the length of the input to 1,000 characters in order to reduce server load. In this case we need to introduce an adaptation process that divides long input into sentences before translation.

The third problem is constraints on execution of a composite service. Assume that both the life science and chemistry dictionaries are from the same provider and that the provider prohibits concurrent access to the two services in order to limit excess load from the user. In this case two dictionaries defined to execute in parallel should be controlled in order to perform sequential execution.

5.2.2 Architecture Overview

Here we propose an architecture to solve the problems described in the previous scenario. Fig. 5.2 gives an overview of this architecture.

The architecture in Fig. 5.2 consists of two parts: a meta-level execution controller and policy controller. The meta-level execution controller modifies behaviors of a running instance of a composite service by changing execution states, including values of variables and states of activities. It is also capable of controlling the interaction protocol to prevent execution failures by ensuring that behaviors of the composite service follow predetermined choreography. The policy controller first selects a combination of services that satisfy the service providers' policies. If no combination of available services to satisfy both the user's requirements and service provides' policies is found, it applies adaptation processes to change the properties of services.

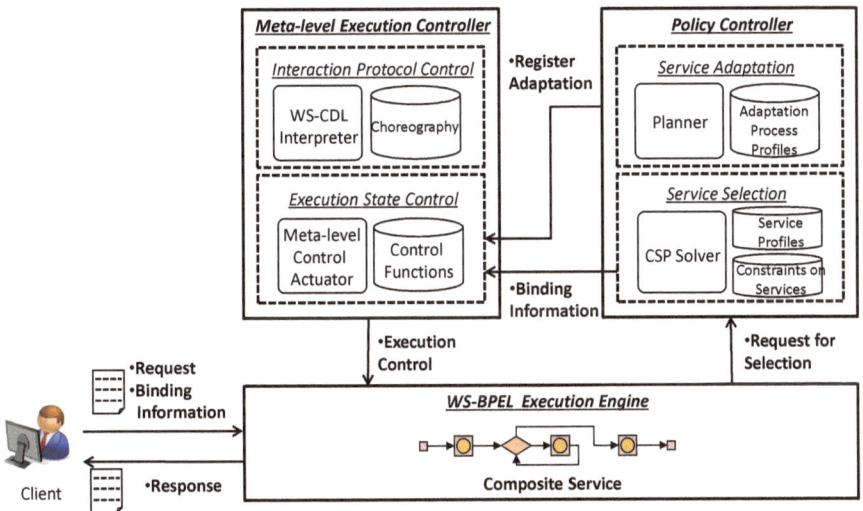

Fig. 5.2 An architecture for Service Supervision system.

5.3 Meta-level Execution Control

As a way to control behaviors of composite Web services, we adopt meta-level execution control. This is because runtime service management for satisfying service providers' policies requires much greater flexibility than proposed in previous work. Detailed comparison with previous work is shown in Section 5.6.

Table 5.1 shows a list of meta-level functions. The functions are provided via Web APIs. This is the reason we can define a composite Web service that controls the behavior of other composite Web services. To realize these APIs, we define states for an activity in a composite service. Ready indicates that the service is ready to be executed. Suspended indicates that the service is suspended after it becomes Ready. Running indicates that the service is being executed and Finished indicates that the execution of the service has finished. The composite service execution engine sets the state of activities as execution of a composite service proceeds.

Table 5.1 Meta-level control functions.

API	Effect
suspend	Suspend an activity whose state is *Ready*. The state of the suspended activity will be changed to *Suspended.*
resume	Resume an activity whose state is *Suspended.* The state of the suspended activity will be changed to *Running*.
terminate	Terminate the process of the composite service.
step	Execute the next activity in a composite Web service.
setBreakPoint	Set a breakpoint at an activity in a composite Web service and a callback Web service invoked when the execution stops at the breakpoint.
setExecutionPoint	Set the activity which is executed next.
getProcessState	Get the current state of all activities in a process of the composite service
setEndpoint	Set endpoints of an invocation in a composite Web service.
getVariable, setVariable	Get/Set variable defined in a composite Web service.

These APIs allow operators to change the order of service execution. This may violate policies of service providers when they define certain constraints of interaction protocols. Such constraints on the order of service execution can be issued as choreography by service providers. According to standards of Web service technologies, choreography is described as WS-CDL. Therefore we can check if an order of service execution satisfies the constraints using a WS-CDL interpreter. Fig. 5.3 shows the procedure for checking the order of service execution.

The algorithm in Fig. 5.3 first acquires states of all activities in the composite service. Next it puts activities whose states are Ready or Suspended into a queue. Then it checks that each activity can be accepted by the given choreography using the WS-CDL interpreter. If an activity is accepted, it is invoked. Otherwise, the state is changed to/continues as Suspended.

If all activities in the queue are in Suspended and there is no Running activity, execution of the composite service is terminated because no activity can be executed and the state will not be changed.

In our example, we can assume that concurrent access to the chemistry and life science dictionaries is prohibited. However, the composite service does not define the order of execution of the two services. Therefore the system monitors the state of execution and prohibits invocation of one of the dictionary services while another is running.

```
Function coordinateOrder()

 1:  choreography ← Protocol of service execution
 2:    based on model of composite service and
 3:    policies of service providers
 4:  currentState ← getProcessState()
 5:  queue ← getReadyActivity(currentState)
 6:        ⊔ getSuspendedActivity(currentState)
 7:  for each act in queue
 8:    if accept(choreography, currentState, act)
 9:      resume(act)
10:      return
11:    else
12:      suspend(act)
13:    end if
14:  end for
15:  if getRunningActivity(currentState) is empty
16:    terminateProcess()
17:  end if
```

Fig. 5.3 Adaptation process for division and merging of output.

5.4 Policy Control

The policy controller first tries to find a combination of concrete services that satisfies the constraints of service providers' policies. We formalize selection of services as a constraint satisfaction problem (CSP). Given the service profiles, a set of available concrete services, and policies of service providers, the selection of services are defined as follows.

A variable represents an abstract service in a composite service. If a composite service invokes other composite services, the set of variables contains variables of abstract services in all composite services. We provide an example of the definition for the translation composite service described in the previous section. As the composite services consists of a morphological analyzer, two dictionaries and a translator, variables x_{ma}, x_{dic1}, x_{dic2}, x_{trans} are defined. The variables have the corresponding domains as follows:

$$D_{ma} = \{x_{ma\_mecab}, x_{ma\_treetagger}\}$$
$$D_{dic1} = \{x_{dic\_life}, x_{dic\_chem}\}$$
$$D_{dic2} = \{x_{dic\_life}, x_{dic\_chem}\}$$
$$D_{trans} = \{x_{trans\_google}, x_{trans\_jserver}\}$$

We also show some of the attributes of concrete services below. The following definition represents that the MeCab morphological analyzer accepts only Japanese, and TreeTagger accepts English, German, French, Italian, and so on. For the

JServer translator, the supported language pairs and limitation of input sentences are defined.

$x_{ma\_mecab}.$ sourceLang = {Japanese}

$x_{ma\_treetagger}.$ sourceLang = {English, French, German, Italian, ...}

$x_{trans\_jserver}.$ langPair = {(Japanese to English)(English to Japanese), ...}

$x_{trans\_jserver}.$ maxInputLength = 1000

The constraints are shown below.

$C_1 = x_{trans}.$ maxInputLength $\geq$ length(Request. input)

$C_2 = $ exclusive$(x_{trans\_google}, x_{dic\_life})$

$C_3 = $ parallel_prohibited$(x_{dic\_life}, x_{dic\_chem})$

C_1 represents requirements based on the process of the composite service and shows that the limitation of input length of a translator must be longer than the input sentences. C_2 prohibits the combination of Google Translate and the life science dictionary. C_3 prohibits parallel execution of the chemistry dictionary and the life science dictionary.

In our example, we assume a request from a user, consisting of the following elements: sentences to be translated, the source language, and the target language.

input: Sentence to be translated(1500 characters in Japanese)

source language: Japanese

target language: English

The user can specify the concrete services bound to any abstract services in a composite service when invoking the composite service. For the abstract services for which the user does not specify concrete services bound to, the process in the Selection Layer selects concrete services. A user usually specifies concrete services when he/she knows how their attributes affect the result. Otherwise, the user delegates the selection to the system.

In our example, the user specifies the life science and chemistry dictionaries for two dictionaries in order to translate sentences in the area of biochemistry. On the other hand, the user does not specify concrete services for the morphological analyzer and the translator because he/she does not know which service can produce a better result.

The CSP that formalizes the above conditions has no solution. Therefore it is impossible to satisfy the user's requirements and service providers' policies using the available services. The combinations with the least number of violations are as follows. The former violates C_1 and C_3, and the latter violates C_2 and C_3.

$(x_{ma\_mecab}, x_{dic\_life}, x_{dic\_chem}, x_{trans\_jserver})$

$(x_{ma\_mecab}, x_{dic\_life}, x_{dic\_chem}, x_{trans\_google})$

The attributes of services that cause a violation are changed in the Adaptation Layer in order to resolve the violation. To determine which service should be adapted, we extended CSP based on the ideas of Open CSP (Faltings and Macho-Gonzalez 2005) and Partial CSP (Freuder and Wallace 1992).

In Open CSP, a new value for a domain is obtained when any combination of existing values cannot satisfy constraints. We show that the domain of a variable located in the deepest leaf of a search tree of a backtrack search definitely needs to be extended to resolve violations. Therefore we need to adapt a concrete service that corresponds to such a variable.

```
function: searchCombination(X, D, C)
Inputs:
  X: Variables ({X1, ..., Xn}),  D: Domains ({D1, ..., Dn}),
  C: Constraints

 1:  i←1, k←1, M←∞
 2:  while(i > 0)
 3:    if all values in Di are checked
 4:      reset xi,  i←i-1
 5:    else
 6:      xi←next value of Di
 7:      if ({x1, ..., xi}) satisfies C
 8:        k← max(k, i+1)
 9:      end if
10:      i←i+1
11:      if i > n
12:        if ViolationCount({x1, ..., xn}) = 0
13:          return {x1, ..., xn}
14:        end if
15:        if N > ViolationCount({x1, ..., xn})
16:          N ← ViolationCount({x1, ..., xn})
17:          currentSelection ←{x1, ..., xn}
18:        end if
19:        i←i+1
20:      end if
21:    end if
22:  end while
23:  xk'← findAdaptation(k, currentSelection)
24:  if xk' is failure
25:    return failure
26:  end if
27:  Dk ← Dk ∪ {xk'}
28:  Change order of variables (Move Xk
29:    to first as X1)
30:  return searchCombination(X, D, C);
```

Fig. 5.4 Algorithm for finding a combination of services.

Moreover, to determine which concrete service should be adapted, we also need to know the combination of services that gives the lowest violation count. Therefore we applied the Partial CSP concept, which finds a solution that gives the least violation when the problem is over-constrained.

Fig. 5.4 shows the algorithm that applies these ideas to the problem of finding a combination of services and determining a service to be adopted. The algorithm begins with a depth-first search (lines 1-22). The index of the deepest variable in the search tree is recorded as k. During the backtrack search, the lowest violation count and combination of services that gives the count are also respectively recorded as M and *currentSelection*.

It then extends the domain D_k giving k and *currentSelection* to the Adaptation Layer and again searches for a solution (lines 23-30).

If the Selection Layer cannot find a combination of services that satisfies all constraints, the Adaptation Layer adapts a service to constraints by changing attributes of services. This adapted service can be considered as a new service in the Selection Layer.

To find the appropriate adaptation processes, profiles of adaptation processes are stored in the Adaptation Layer. However, the implementation is in the AOP manager, which is an extension of the composite service execution engine. It is difficult for the standard framework to change the model of a composite service and deploy the new model if the adaptation processes applied are frequently changed, which is why the adaptation is realized by using AOP techniques.

Various adaptation methods for composite services using AOP have been proposed in previous works. One of the most flexible methods (Charfi and Mezini 2007) weaves a process described in WS-BPEL into the target composite service. We assume we adopt this method for our architecture and show implementation of the adaptation process in Fig. 5.5.

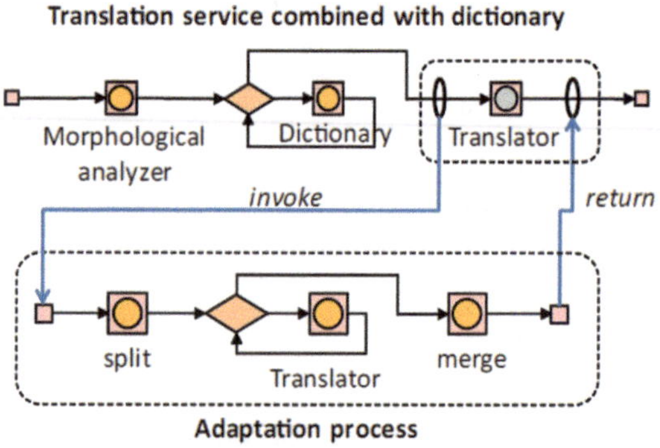

Fig. 5.5 Adaptation process for division and merging of output.

The adaptation process divides an input and merges the output before/after the target service is invoked. The invocation of the target service is located in the loop in the adaptation process. The invocation that is originally defined in a composite service is skipped.

Using the adaptation method described above, more than one adaptation process can be applied to one target service. We search for a sequence of adaptation processes by hill-climbing taking the count of violations as the evaluation value. The domain of translation services is extended as follows:

$$D_{trans} = \{x_{trans_{google}}, x_{trans_{jserver}}, a_{div_{merge}}(x_{trans_{jserver}})\}$$

We can obtain the following combination for which the violation count is reduced to one with the adapted service.

$$(x_{ma}, x_{dic1}, x_{dic2}, x_{trans}) =$$
$$(x_{ma\_mecab}, x_{dic\_life}, x_{dic\_chem}, a_{div\_merge}(x_{trans\_jserver}))$$

Some service providers have policies regarding execution, such as constraints on the order of service execution. Such constraints cannot be solved by adaptation of a service. Therefore we control the order of service execution in the Coordination Layer.

5.5 Experiment

In this section, we give examples of application of our method in order to discuss its applicability and performance. We take the document translation composite Web service, which splits and translates a document, as an example. In the composite service, translation services are invoked many times. We apply the following two controls to prevent possible failures.

- Assume the provider of the machine translation Web service limits the total number of invocations within a certain period. When the number of invocations exceeds the limit, change the endpoint of the machine translation Web service to select another such service. (Control 1)
- Assume the provider of the machine translation Web service limits the number of concurrent accesses. When the number of concurrent accesses exceeds the limit, change the endpoint to select another such service. When the number of concurrent accesses falls under the limit, change the endpoint back to that of the initial service. (Control 2)

First, we inspected the execution time of the document translation composite Web service for each control in order to demonstrate the practicality of our method. The input to the document translation composite Web service is a document consisting of five Japanese sentences to be translated into English. The limits placed on the total number of invocations and concurrent access number limits are both three.

Fig. 5.6 shows the results. In this experiment, we compared the execution time of the control based on our framework, Service Supervision, with the execution time of the equivalent control realized by modifying the document translation composite Web service. We executed multiple instances for each case. The time shown in the figure represents the average per instance of 10 trials.

The result shows that Service Supervision yields faster control than modifying the composite Web service in the case of one to three instances. This is because the invocation of the service-counting invocation of the translation service defined in the modified composite Web service takes longer than the access to information of another composite Web service via the meta-level control functions.

In the case of more instances, modifying the composite Web service yields faster control than Service Supervision. This is because there tends to be a relatively long queue of unprocessed interactions and it takes time to check whether they can be processed by the WS-CDL interpreter.

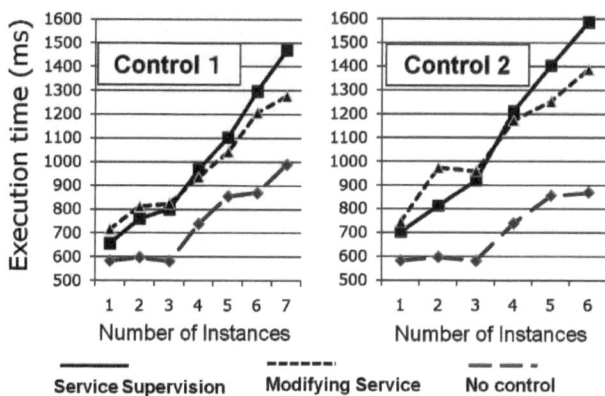

Fig. 5.6 Comparison of execution time.

The above result shows that the Service Supervision proposed in this work has a disadvantage in scalability of number of instances compared to the existing framework. However, the reduced performance is not serious when the number of active instances is small.

Next we compared the control complexity of supervision composite Web services to that of modified composite Web services in order to assess the cost of applying Service Supervision. We used the number of activities (atomic process steps in a composite Web service including service invocation, copying variables, and interactions with other composite Web services) and containers of control constructs, and maximum depth of nested structures as metrics. To choose the metrics, we consulted a previous work on business processes that addressed such metrics (Gruhn and Laue 2006).

Table 5.2 shows the complexity comparison results. For the supervision composite Web services, the sum of the numbers of activities and containers in such services and the document translation composite Web service to be controlled are in brackets because they are used together.

Table 5.2 Complexity of composite Web services.

	# of activities	# of containers	max depth of nest
Service Supervision (Control 1)	8 (17)	5 (7)	4
Modifying service (Control 1)	12	5	4
Service Supervision (Control 2)	10 (19)	6 (8)	5
Modifying service (Control 2)	15	7	5

When using Service Supervision, the sum of the number of activities and containers exceeds that of the document translation composite Web service modified to realize the same controls. One reason for this is that the supervision composite Web services have activities for interacting with the client and the composite Web service to be controlled. Another reason is that some of the processes that require a control construct are separated into the supervision composite service and composite Web service to be controlled. However, the difference is not significant because the difference in numbers of activities and containers does not increase in line with the complexity of the supervision composite Web service and composite Web services.

5.6 Related Work

In the architecture proposed in this work, service selection, adaptation, and coordination are performed during execution of a composite service. Many previous works have proposed methods for such service selection. For example, the method proposed in (Zeng et al. 2004) focuses on finding the combination of services that gives the best QoS. The method proposed in (Ben Hasinne et al. 2006) selects services considering service interfaces in addition to the QoS.

These works assume that a vast amount of services are stored in a service cluster. In reality, however, the number of services with equivalent functions is limited. This is why the previous works often cannot find a combination of services. Moreover, to handle the policies of service providers we need not only to find a static combination of services but also a dynamic adaptation and meta-level control of composite services.

There have also been some previous works in the area of dynamic adaptation. Most of these works can be classified into three types: weaving a new process based on aspect-oriented programming (AOP), using a proxy to monitor/change messages exchanged between a composite service and invoked services, and transforming the model of a composite service based on definition of additional processes.

AO4BPEL (Charfi and Mezini 2007) is a framework for realizing the AOP of composite services. It allows a user to define a pointcut in a WS-BPEL process and weave in a process described in WS-BPEL as advice. This can add processes for adaptation without changing the model of a composite service.

For service-oriented collective intelligence, however, various policies of service providers must be satisfied. This requires a comprehensive process of service selection, adaptation, and coordination. AOP is suitable for adaptation as described in the previous section, but is not flexible enough for coordination tasks such as controlling the order of service execution.

The work proposed in (Baresi et al. 2007) adopts a framework using a proxy. It checks if messages exchanged among composite services and constituent services satisfy the given conditions when the composite service execution engine invokes the constituent services. If any of these conditions is not satisfied, it performs some recovering processes, retries invocation, or changes the service to an alternative. But this focuses on adaptation of a single service and does not deal with the policies of all service providers concerned.

The methods that transform the model of composite services, such as (Mosincat and Binder 2008) do not need to modify the composite service execution engine. This is suitable for adding exception-handling processes, but the composite service needs to be deployed if the adaptation process changes.

(Moser et al. 2008) addressed the fact that BPEL lacks functionality for dynamic adaptation and monitoring. They proposed a method for dynamic service selection and managing QoS information by intercepting SOAP messages.

Meta-level control functions for Web services are proposed in (Tanaka et al. 2009). This work provides more flexible controls than the other works described above, but the flexibility often places too much load on platform operators. The architecture proposed in this work partially adopted the work focusing on satisfying constraints on execution.

Adaptive Workflow (van der Aalst et al. 1999) focuses on workflows that are mainly executed by humans. It aims to adapt to unexpected exceptions and changes in the environment. Some previous works adopt case-based reasoning, rule-based systems, and planning to realize adaptation (Weber et al. 2004; Casati et al. 2000).

5.7 Conclusion

On the Language Grid, many services with a different QoS and policies are available for each service type. Therefore we need to select those appropriate for optimizing the QoS while satisfying policies given by service providers. In this chapter, we proposed an architecture that performs a comprehensive process for service selection, adaptation, and coordination. The architecture is designed to satisfy policies of service providers while allowing users to select services according to their requirements.

The contributions of this chapter are as follows:

- We showed a framework using meta-level control functions in order to control behaviors of composite services without changing the models.
- We proposed an effective process of service selection and adaptation that relies on an extension of the constraint-satisfaction problem.

To realize service-oriented collective intelligence, various policies of service providers must be satisfied. This is the first work to focus on runtime service management in order to satisfy such policies based on the above features.

Acknowledgments   This work was supported by Kyoto University Global COE Program: Informatics Education and Research Center for Knowledge-Circulating Society, Strategic Information and Communications R&D Promotion Programme from Ministry of Internal Affairs and Communications and a Grant-in-Aid for Scientific Research (A) (21240014, 2009-2011) from Japan Society for the Promotion of Science (JSPS).

References

Baresi L, Guinea S, Plebani P (2007) Policies and aspects for the supervision of BPEL processes. 19th International Conference on Advanced Information Systems Engineering (CaiSE07): 340-354

Ben Hassine A, Matsubara S, Ishida T (2006) A constraint-based approach to horizontal web service composition. 5th International Semantic Web Conference (ISWC 2006): 130-143

Casati F, Ilnicki S, Jin LJ, Krishnamoorthy V (2000) Adaptive and dynamic service composition in eFlow. 12th International Conference on Advanced Information Systems Engineering (CaiSE00): 13-31

Charfi A, Mezini M (2007) AO4BPEL: an aspect-oriented extension to BPEL. World Wide Web 10(3): 309-344

Faltings B, Macho-Gonzalez S (2005) Open constraint programming. Artificial Intelligence 161(1-2): 181-208

Freuder EC, Wallace RJ (1992) Partial constraint satisfaction. Artificial Intelligence 58(1-3): 21-70

Gruhn V, Laue R (2006) Complexity metrics for business process models. 9th International Conference on Business Information Systems: 1-12

Ishida T (2006) Language Grid: an infrastructure for intercultural collaboration. 2006 IEEE/IPSJ Symposium on Applications and the Internet (SAINT-06):96-100

Moser O, Rosenberg F, Dustdar S (2008) Non-intrusive monitoring and service adaptation for ws-bpel. 17th International World Wide Web Conference (WWW 2008): 815-824

Mosincat A, Binder W (2008) Transparent runtime adaptability for BPEL processes. 6th International Conference on Service Oriented Computing (ICSOC 08): 241-255

Tanaka M, Ishida T, Murakami Y, Morimoto S (2009) Service supervision: coordinating web services in open environment. 2009 IEEE International Conference on Web Services (ICWS-09): 238-245

van der Aalst WMP, Basten T, Verbeek HMW, Verkoulen PAC, Voorhoeve M (1999) Adaptive workflow on the interplay between flexibility and support. The first International Conference on Enterprise Information Systems: 353-360

Weber B, Wild W, Breu R (2004) CBRFlow: enabling adaptive workflow management through conversational case based reasoning. 7th European Conference on Advances in Case-Based Reasoning (ECCBR04), Lecture Notes in Artificial Intelligence 3155, Springer: 434–448

Zeng L, Benatallah B, Ngu AHH, Dumas M, Kalagnanam J, Chang H (2004) QoS-aware middleware for web services composition. IEEE Transactions on Software Engineering 30(5): 311-327

Chapter 6
Language Service Ontology

Yoshihiko Hayashi[1], Thierry Declerck[2], Nicoletta Calzolari[3], Monica Monachini[3], Claudia Soria[3], and Paul Buitelaar[4]

1 OSAKA University, Toyonaka 5600043, Japan, e-mail: hayashi@lang.osaka-u.ac.jp

2 DFKI GmbH, D-66123 Saarbrücken, Germany, e-mail: declerck@dfki.de

3 ILC-CNR, 56124 Pisa, Italy, e-mail:{nicoletta.calzolari, monica.monachini, claudia.soria}@ilc.cnr.it

4 DERI, National University of Ireland, Galway, Ireland, e-mail: paul.buitelaar@deri.org

Abstract The Language Grid is a distinctive language service infrastructure in the sense that it accommodates a wide variety of user needs, ranging from technical novices to experts; language resource consumers to language resource providers. As these language services are various in type and each of them can be idiosyncratic in many aspects, the service infrastructure has to address the issue of interoperability. A key to solve this issue is not only to build the services around standardized resources and interfaces, but also to establish a knowledge structure that copes effectively with a range of language services. Given this knowledge structure, referred to as a service ontology, each language service can be systematically classified and its usage specified by a corresponding API. This not only enables the utilization of existing language resources but facilitates the dissemination of newly created language resources as services.

6.1 Introduction

The Language Grid (Ishida 2006), as thoroughly demonstrated in this book, can be distinguished from other language resources and technologies infrastructures[1] in the sense that it accommodates a wide variety of users: some users may be techni-

---

[1] CLARIN (http://www.clarin.eu/) is one of the representative initiatives in enabling eHumanities; more recently however, the META-NET (http://www.meta-net.eu/) initiative has been launched and will complement CLARIN in setting up a global infrastructure for language technologies and resources in more general contexts.

cally novice and only interested in consuming useful language services; while others might want to disseminate their own resources presumably to get evaluations through practical use. Therefore the Language Grid has to maintain a potentially large number of language services with varying functionalities.

The issue of *interoperability* (Calzolari 2008) arises here: as the underlying language resources are independently developed, they essentially exhibit idiosyncrasies in many aspects. A promising solution to solve this issue is to *servicize* a language resource while aiming at its standardization (Hayashi et al. 2008; Hayashi 2010). More specifically: standardized interfaces are necessary to wrap language processing tools/systems; standardized data formats are required for representing linguistic objects and language data resources. In addition and importantly, each language service has to be functionally classified and its usage should be specified by a corresponding Application Programming Interface (API).

To accomplish this, one needs to establish a shared knowledge structure that can descriptively cope with the variety of language services. Such a knowledge structure, referred to as a *language service ontology*, provides a comprehensive and formalized vocabulary that describes the language services and their associated linguistic elements.

This chapter presents the actual state of the developed language service ontology. Although it has been designed within the context of the Language Grid, it can nevertheless have a broader application. Those more general considerations are presented in Sections 6.2 and 6.3, while Section 6.4 reviews the current set of language services in the Language Grid. Further issues toward a comprehensive and practical ontology-driven language service infrastructure are discussed in Section 6.5, and the conclusions follow in Section 6.6.

6.2 Conceptual Framework of the Language Service Ontology

6.2.1 Necessity of an Ontological Foundation

Interoperability must be the most crucial issue, if we are to combine rather independently developed language processing tools and/or language resources to fulfill the requirements arising from an application, a fact which has led to a situation where data formats, annotation schemes, access methods and other features are all idiosyncratic. This obviously represents a burden for any user who wants to choose from existing resources and combine them appropriately.

To address this issue, a language service infrastructure should provide its resources as standardized services: standardized APIs are necessary for natural language processing (NLP) tools/systems; standardized data semantics as well as data format are required for language data resources. In addition and importantly, these services should be properly described by being based on comprehensive and shared knowledge which covers all possible elements of a range of language services. We refer to such a knowledge structure as a *language service ontology*, providing formalized and shared vocabulary for the language service descriptions. We have been developing this language service ontology in Web Ontology Language (OWL).

6.2.2 Triangular View of a Language Service

A goal of the Language Grid is to servicize every type of language resources in the Web-based language service infrastructure. Such a servicized resource is provided to the users through a computational process that accesses language data resources and/or operates upon linguistic objects. For example, a lexicon access service may extract and provide a part of the target lexicon, given a specific user query. Here, a computational process behind the service is invoked and returns the relevant part of the lexicon (linguistic object) by accessing the designated resource (language data resource). We refer to such a computational process as a language process. On the other hand, a syntactic parsing service may produce a syntactic annotation (linguistic object) on top of a given sequence of tokens with part-of-speech (POS) tags (linguistic object) by using a statistical language model (language data resource). This process-oriented view of a language service can be illustrated by a triangular structure as shown in Fig. 6.1, where three fundamental classes and the intrinsic relationships among them are depicted.

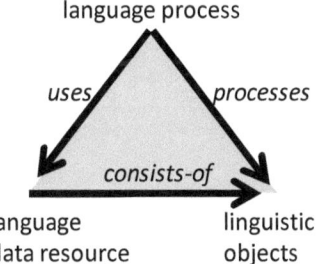

Fig. 6.1 Triangular view of a language service

This triangular diagram indicates that: (1) a language process operates upon linguistic objects by (2) using data resources, and that (3) a data resource consists of linguistic objects. Therefore, a language data resource can be created by organizing a set of linguistic objects each processed by language processes.

It should be noted here that the linguistic object class includes a range of linguistic annotations as well as linguistic expressions, which are the source of annotations; these types of abstract objects comprise the data to/from NLP tools/systems, as well as the content of language data resources. This triangular view of a language service establishes the conceptual framework of the language service ontology as developed below.

6.2.3 Top-level of the Language Service Ontology

Fig. 6.2[2] illustrates the top-level of the language service ontology; the upper half of the diagram realizes the triangle view of a language service depicted in Fig. 6.1. The lower half of the diagram additionally introduces some important classes. Each box in the diagram denotes a top-level class in the whole ontology; some of these classes further induce corresponding sub-ontologies.

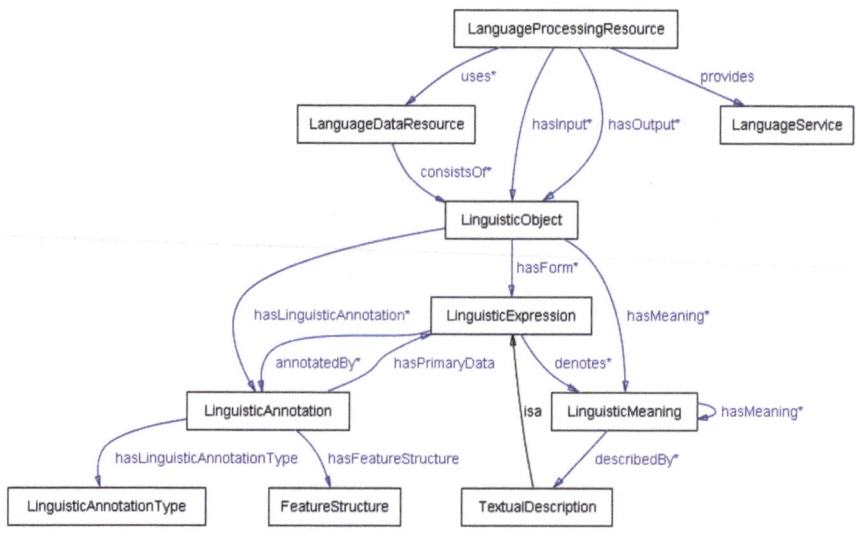

Fig. 6.2 Top-level of the language service ontology

Among these top-level classes, **LanguageService** is functionally the top-most one. As discussed in the previous subsection, a language service is provided by an instance of the **LanguageProcessingResource** class. Note that a language data resource does not provide a language service by itself; as it is a static resource, it is always activated through an access mechanism, which is an instance of a language processing resource subclass.

A language processing resource takes **LinguisticObject** as the input/output, and may use **LanguageDataResource**. **LanguageDataResource** consists of

---

[2] Figures like this in this chapter were automatically produced by the OntoViz plugin of the Protégé ontology editing tool.

instances of LinguisticObject, which might have been brought about by the results of LanguageProcessingResource.

LinguisticObject, according to Saussure tradition, can have linguistic forms
(LinguisticExpression) and meanings (LinguisticMeaning), where the former
denotes the latter. Additionally, a linguistic meaning can be described by Textu-
alDescription. Note here that an instance of the linguistic meaning class functions
as a place holder for representing a semantic equivalent relation among linguistic
objects. On the other hand, a LinguisticObject instance can be annotated by instances of LinguisticAnnotation, which should have actual annotation content
represented with FeatureStructure.

In further detailing some of the important sub-ontologies, we believe it is crucial to incorporate relevant international standards to address the issue of interoperability. In this sense, we have been looking at the frameworks for linguistic annotation and lexicon modeling discussed in ISO. The ISO frameworks for
linguistic annotation are incorporated into our ontology not only for specifying the
input/output data type of NLP tools, but also for defining the content type of corpora; while the framework for lexicon modeling is introduced to develop a taxonomy of lexicon classes, which obviously forms a part of the language data resource taxonomy.

6.3 Elementary Sub-Ontologies

This section develops sub-ontologies for three important classes: (1) linguistic annotation, (2) lexicon, a subclass of the language data resource class, and (3) language processing resource. A special emphasis is placed on the incorporation of
relevant international standards into the ontological configuration.

6.3.1 An Ontology for Linguistic Annotations

As already depicted in Fig. 6.2, a linguistic object could be multiply annotated,
and annotation content should be realized by an instance of the LinguisticAnnotation class. This is of crucial importance, because any framework for linguistic annotation has to be able to accommodate multiply layered annotations, given the
possibility that a target linguistic expression may be annotated by more than one
analyzer, each of which possibly does its job on a different linguistic level.

In addition, the ontological configuration for linguistic annotations should incorporate relevant international standards to address the interoperability issue.
Standardized linguistic annotations frameworks have been actively developed and
disseminated by the ISO TC37/SC4 committee. Among them, the most general
umbrella framework is given by the Linguistic Annotation Framework (LAF) (Ide

and Romary 2006), from which other specific frameworks have been derived. However, as none of these frameworks has been defined under an ontological perspective, we decided to ontologize and incorporate them into our language service ontology by just giving OWL specifications to the relevant parts of a framework.

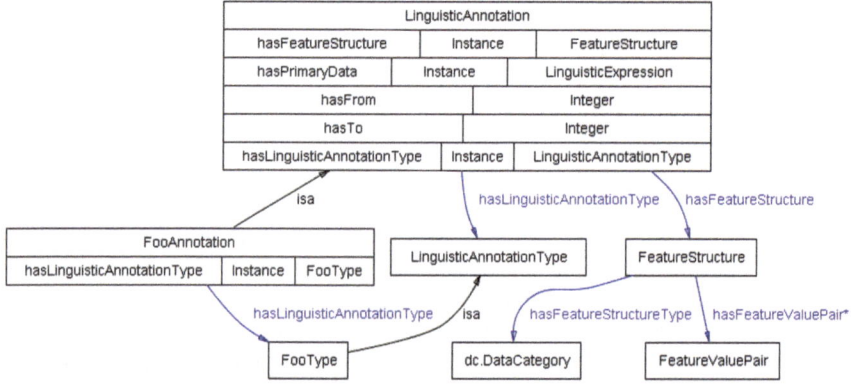

Fig. 6.3 Ontological configuration of linguistic annotations

Fig. 6.3 illustrates a high-level configuration of the sub-ontology for linguistic annotations, which corresponds to the LAF framework as follows.

- A linguistic annotation has primary data (an instance of LinguisticExpression) to which the annotation is attached.
- A linguistic annotation has a start and an end position to designate the span of the annotation in primary data. This allows implementation of the so-called *stand-off annotation* strategy, and hence enables multiple annotations on the same data region.
- The annotation content is realized by a FeatureStructure, which has a feature structure type and an arbitrary number of feature-value pairs.
- All feature types of a feature structure and the name and/or the value of a feature are selected from a pre-defined inventory of linguistic attributes (dc.DataCategory) defined outside of the language service ontology. Data Category Registry (DCR) (Broeder et al. 2010), also developed in ISO, may serve as the standardized inventory.

With the ontology described so far, any linguistic object in the proposed language service ontology can be typed according to the type of linguistic annotation it has. For example in Fig. 6.3, FooAnnotation, an imaginary subclass of LinguisticAnnotation, is defined to have a FooType linguistic annotation. This type information may be effectively utilized in dynamic composition of a composite language service, in which checking of the input/output constraints for the elemental atomic services is mandatory.

6.3.2 An Ontology for Lexicons

The class for language data resource (LanguageDataResource) is currently organized into subclasses for corpus (Corpus) and lexicon (Lexicon). The corpus class is further organized into subclasses according to the type of the corpus resource, which possibly includes the language of the resource. More specifically, a corpus subtype should be defined by the annotation types of the linguistic objects. Thus we have an interrelation between the corpus sub-ontology and the linguistic annotation sub-ontology.

Similarly but not identically, the lexicon class is organized into subclasses according to the type of lexical resource. More specifically, a lexicon subtype is defined by the type of lexical entry in the lexicon. Again we have an opportunity to incorporate relevant international standards into our language service ontology.

The international standard most relevant in this regard is Lexical Markup Framework (LMF) (Francopoulo et al. 2009), which has already been approved as the ISO standard ISO 24613:2008. The ultimate goal of LMF is to create a modular structure that will facilitate true content interoperability across all aspects of electronic lexical resources. The modular structure of LMF consists of a core package and a number of extensions for modeling a range of machine readable dictionaries (MRDs) and NLP lexicons.

Fig. 6.4 illustrates the ontological configuration of the LMF core model, and its incorporation into the language service ontology. Notice that there is a kind of dual structure: Imf.Lexicon is a subclass of LanguageDataResource, while *has_Imf.LexicalEntry* property is a subproperty of the *consistsOf* property; Imf.LexicalEntry is a subclass of LinguisticObject, while *has_Imf.Sense* is a subproperty of *hasMeaning*, etc.

The LMF extensions are presented by extending the LMF core package, giving us an opportunity to ontologize them by subclassifying the relevant top classes defined in the core package. Fig. 6.5 shows the taxonomy of the lexicon class, stating that each of the lexicon subclasses is defined in terms of the type of the lexical entries it has. A lexical entry type is also defined with the ontologized LMF. For example, BilingualDictionary, a subclass of MRD, is defined by restricting the domain of the *has_Imf.LexicalEntry* property to BilingualLexicalEntry, which in turn is a descendant subclass of the Imf.LexicalEntry.

In order to incorporate a new type of lexicon, we have to first introduce a new class for the lexical entry type, and then appropriately place it somewhere in the lexical entry class hierarchy, and finally define the corresponding lexicon class some appropriate place in the lexicon taxonomy.

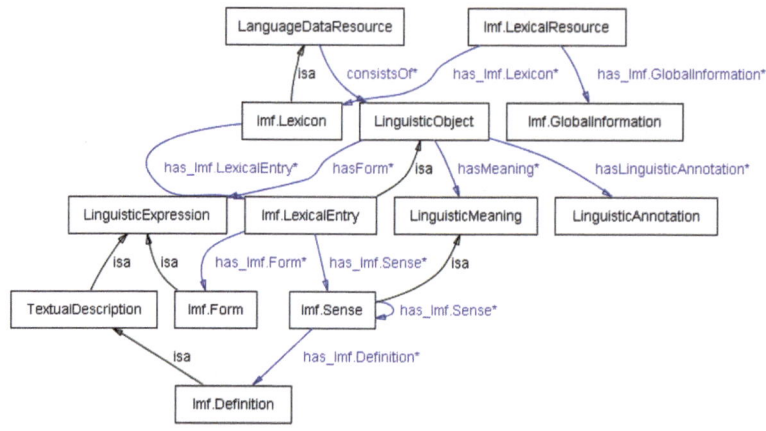

Fig. 6.4 Ontological configuration of the LMF core package

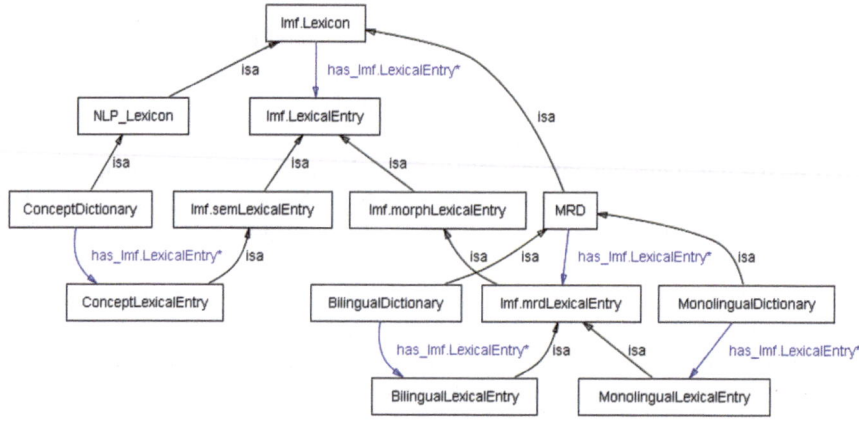

Fig. 6.5 Definition of the lexicon taxonomy

6.3.3 An Ontology for Language Processing Resources

Any NLP tools/system or language resource access mechanism is classified as a kind of language processing resource (Hayashi 2007). These resources are further sub-classed according to their functionalities. The top level of the language processing resource class currently consists of the following four subclasses.

- **AbstractReader, AbstractWriter**: These classes are introduced to define computational processes that convert to and from nontextual representation (e.g. speech) and textual representation (character strings).

- **LR_Accessor**: This class is introduced to define language resource access functionalities. It is first partitioned into **CorpusAccessor** and **DictionaryAccessor**, depending on the type of language data resource it accesses. Both classes are further subclassed according to the subtypes of the target language data resources.

- **LinguisticProcessor**: This class is introduced to define NLP tools/systems. Currently, the linguistic processor class is first partitioned into **LinguisticTransformer** and **LinguisticAnalyzer**. The transformer class is introduced to classify **Paraphraser** and **Translator**; both produce another linguistic expression from the given expression, while preserving the original meaning. The only difference between these classes is the sameness of the input/output languages; a translator produces an output expression in a language that is different from the language of the input expression. The resulting linguistic expression can be considered as a kind of annotation to the given expression.

Among these subclasses, **LR_Accessor** and **LinguisticAnalyzer** are of particular interest, because an instance of these classes may be wrapped as an atomic service and used as an element in a composite language service. These resources are further classified according to their functionalities; the functionality is largely characterized by the types of associated objects. More specifically, the types of language resources used and/or the types of input/output language objects induce the taxonomy of language processing resources.

Fig. 6.6 illustrates this principle: two processing resource subclasses **ConceptDictionaryAccessor** and **NLPAnalyzer1** are introduced for the sake of explanation. The former is a subclass of **LR_Accessor** being characterized by the target language data resource, that is **ConceptDictionary**; while the latter is distinguished from other processing resources by the input/output linguistic object types, that is **FooObject/BarObject**. Note that either of these linguistic object types is induced based on the type of the linguistic annotation (**FooAnnotation/BarAnnotation**) it has.

The input/output linguistic object types of a language processing resource play a crucial role in composing a composite language service, where two or more language processing resources form a so-called NLP pipeline or more complicated workflow. Suppose we are to get the syntactic annotation for an input sentence by using a particular syntactic parser that consumes an already POS-tagged word sequence. To make this happen, we need to feed the output of a POS-tagger to the syntactic parser. In this cascading scenario, the input data type of the syntactic parser has to be compatible with the output data type of the POS-tagger, requiring a *type-checking* operation at the composing stage, which can be accomplished by a kind of reasoning process that refers to the ontological knowledge.

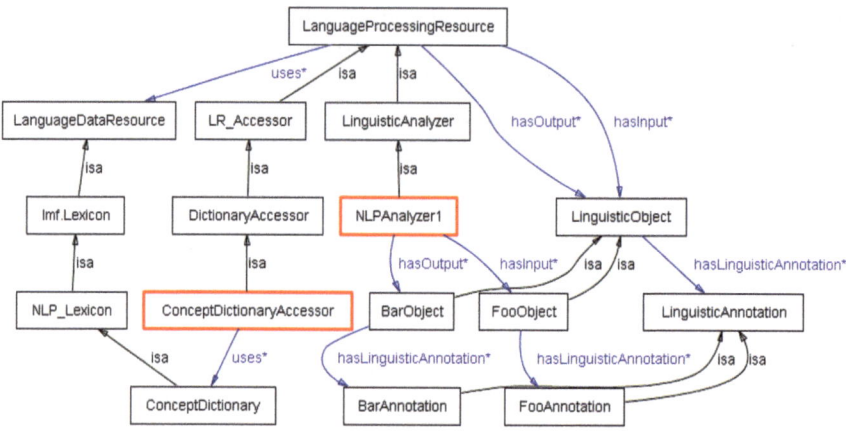

Fig. 6.6 Part of the language processing resource sub-ontology

6.4 Toward Ontology-grounded Language Web Services

6.4.1 Language Services in the Language Grid

The Language Grid is a Web-based multilingual language service infrastructure whose primary goal is to provide an environment for supporting a range of activities associated with intercultural collaboration. The envisaged majority of the users are non-expert in language technologies/language resources. The Language Grid, as of August 2010, accommodates more than 90 Web services, which are classified into one of the around 20 service types. A user can utilize the provided language services through appropriately defined APIs.

Fig. 6.7 shows a screenshot from the Language Grid Web site[3], where a user can search for a language service based on the service type and/or supported languages. The classification of the provided language services into one of the Language Grid service types does not yet completely reflect the language service ontology. It however substantially observes the ontological principles discussed so far. Table 6.1 lists major Language Grid service types and relates them to classes in the language service ontology. For example, the Language Gird service types, MORPHOLOGICAL ANALYSIS and DEPENDENCY PARSER, are classified as subclasses of LinguisticAnalyzer, while TRANSLATION is classified as a subclass of Translator.

---

[3] http://langrid.org/operation/service_manager/language-services

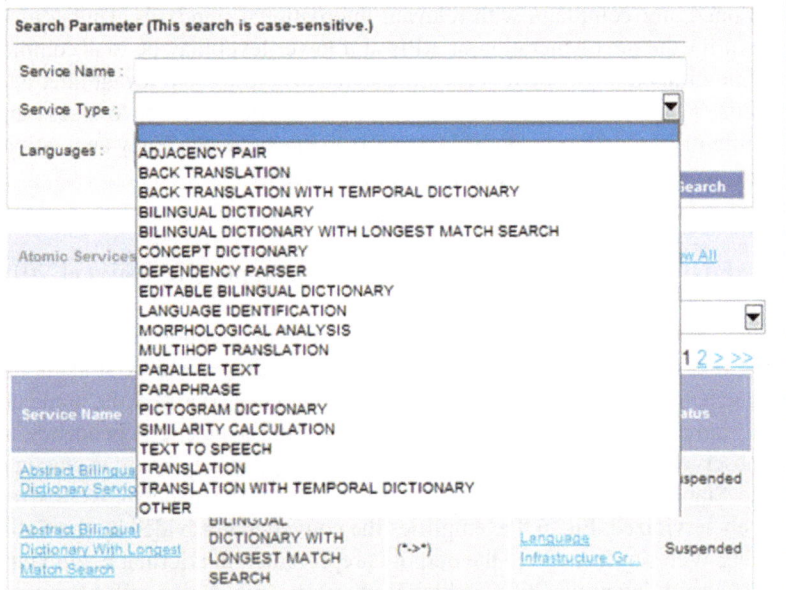

Fig. 6.7 Language Services in the Language Grid

Table 6.1 Major Language Grid service types

Language Grid service type	Class in the language service ontology	Input data type	Output (Annotation) type
TRANSLATION	**Translator**	sentence string (in language X)	sentence string (in language Y)
PARAPHRASE	**Paraphraser**	sentence string (in language X)	sentence string (in language Y)
CONCEPT DICTIONARY	**DictionaryAccessor**	query string	lexical entry
MULTILINGUAL DICTIONARY		query string	lexical entry
PARALLEL CORPUS	**CorpusAccessor**	query string	corpus entry
MORPHOLOGICAL ANALYSIS	**LinguisticAnalyzer**	sentence string	morphological annotation
DEPENDENCY PARSER		sentence string	dependency annotation

6.4.2 Trials of LR-standard-based Language Service

The Language Grid service APIs are designed so that non-expert users are able to use the services without great difficulty. The APIs however are not linguistically fine-grained, nor compliant with relevant international standards. Thus a possible direction for the next generation or APIs at a lower level may be to accommodate more fine-grained linguistic objects represented according to relevant international standards. Two trial Web services have been developed in order to assess the applicability of international standards: LAF in syntactic dependency annotation and LMF in representing WordNet-like semantic lexicons.

(a) LAF/GrAF-grounded dependency parser wrapper (Hayashi et al. 2010)

Syntactic dependency structures attract a great deal of attention as a representation of natural language utterances, presumably because they are more suitable for the subsequent semantic processing than phrase structures. To assess the applicability of LAF-based standardized schema for representing syntactic dependency structures observed in multiple languages, two actual dependency-based syntactic parsers, the Stanford parser for English[4] and CaboCha for Japanese[5], were wrapped and Web-servicized. Fig. 6.8 exemplifies the conversion provided by the CaboCha wrapping Web service; where the output is represented in a format compliant with GrAF (Ide and Suderman 2007), which is an XML serialization of LAF.

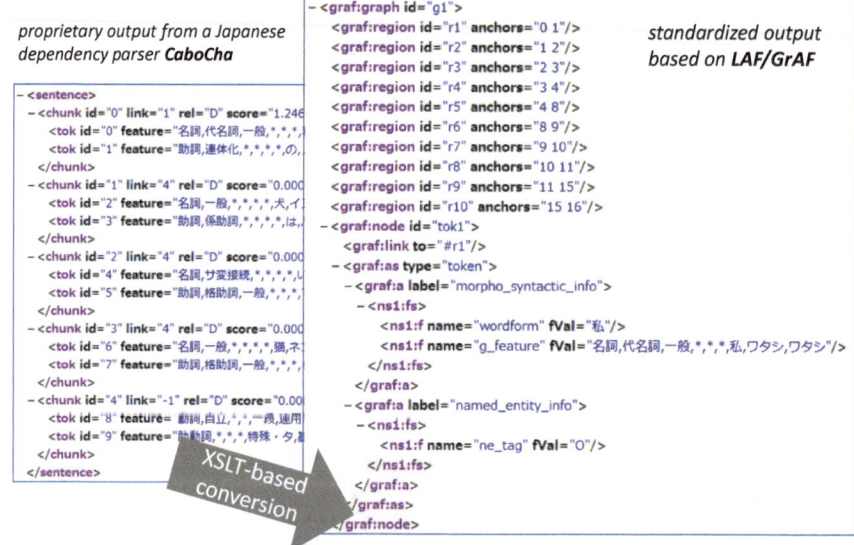

Fig. 6.8 Example of dependency structure conversion

---

[4] http://nlp.stanford.edu/software/lex-parser.shtml
[5] http://sourceforge.net/projects/cabocha/

The central component of the wrapper is an XSLT stylesheet that defines conversions from parser-proprietary formats to a GrAF-based standardized format. To develop this conversion process, GrAF's general graph schema has been subtyped to properly yet minimally define both the English and Japanese dependency structures. Two types of basic dependency unit were devised in the subtyping: one is word/token and the other is chunk/phrase. The latter is quite useful in representing chunk-based Japanese dependency structures. Note that this subtyping of GrAF is completely in line with the SynAF standard (Declerck 2008) which can be considered as "specialized LAF" for representing a variety of syntactic annotations.

(b) LMF-based semantic lexicon access (Savas et al. 2010)

The central idea behind the design of this service is: given a query, the primary functionality of lexicon access is to present a partial lexicon by extracting the relevant part of the target lexicon. Based on this idea, we implemented the system as a *RESTful* Web service whose input (query) is specified by the access URI and whose output is represented by a standardized XML data format.

In this service, LMF plays the central role: the access URI pattern basically reflects the lexicon structure as defined by LMF; the access results are rendered based on Wordnet-LMF (Soria et al. 2009) XML schema, which is a version of XML-serialization of LMF. The Web service currently provides access to Princeton WordNet 3.0, NICT Japanese WordNet (Bond et al. 2008), and additionally EDR Electronic Dictionary (Yokoi 1995) for technical assessment; all of these lexicons can be classified as a WordNet-like semantic lexicon.

```xml
<LexicalResource>
  <GlobalInformation label="/scope_web/wn-ja/word/form/銀行/"/>
  - <Lexicon languageCoding="ISO 639-3" label="Japanese Wordnet 3.0" language="jpn" owner="NICT" version="0.9">
    - <LexicalEntry id="w211859">
      <Lemma writtenForm="銀行" partOfSpeech="n"/>
      <Sense index="1" id="w211859_02787772-n" synset="jpn-09-02787772-n"/>
      <Sense index="2" id="w211859_13368318-n" synset="jpn-09-13368318-n"/>
      <Sense index="3" id="w211859_08420278-n" synset="jpn-09-08420278-n"/>
    </LexicalEntry>
  </Lexicon>
</LexicalResource>
```

Fig. 6.9 Result of the query: /wn-ja/word/form/銀行

Fig. 6.9 shows the access results using Japanese WordNet with the access URI /wn-ja/word/form/銀行, showing that the term "銀行" ("financial bank" in English) has three senses. Notice here that, according to the partial lexicon concept, the top element in the resulting XML document is <LexicalResource> whose immediate daughters are <GlobalInformation> (decorated with the access URI) and <Lexicon>.

(Savas et al. 2010) also proposed possible revisions to the current Wordnet-LMF schema that are required to accommodate innately bilingual/multilingual semantic lexicons like EDR, where the definition of a concept may be given in both Japanese and English. The proposal therefore relaxes the monolingual constraint posed by the current LMF specification.

6.5 Discussion

Toward a comprehensive and practical ontology-driven language service infrastructure, two issues should be further addressed: (1) the service ontology has to be well-detailed to accommodate all the elements associated with the current and potential language services; (2) a linkage mechanism that associates the ontological structure with concrete technical specifications has to be devised.

6.5.1 Detailing the Language Service Ontology

The language service ontology must be considerably expanded and detailed in order for it to be used as an effective vocabulary for describing a variety of language services. To accomplish this, we first need to recognize the current and potential elements of language services. As demonstrated in Section 5.1, an actual language service infrastructure such as the Language Grid provides us with a concrete list of such elements, we however have to go beyond to further enrich the list. In this sense, we should collaborate with similar efforts such as (Villegas et al. 2010), and reach a general consensus on a high-level structure of the language service ontology and the set of service APIs grounded on it as well.

6.5.2 Linking the Ontology to Technical Specifications

The current standard for giving a concrete technical specification to a Web service type is to assign a Web Service Description Language (WSDL) document. Although the WSDL document of a Web service gives the *syntactic description*, it does not deliver any *semantics* about the service. For example, the input/output data types defined in a WSDL document do not give us any ideas about which abstract linguistic object type is associated with which concrete data type. Therefore, to ensure the interoperability of a service and its service description, a syntactic definition (WSDL document) has to be augmented and interrelated with the background ontological knowledge.

Among the several possible solutions to this issue, we see adoption of the W3C recommendation Semantic Annotations for WSDL (SAWSDL) as the most feasible. With the sawsdl:modelReference construct provided by SAWSDL, we can semantically annotate a WSDL document by making references to the classes in the language service ontology. For example, Fig. 6.10 shows fragments of the semantically annotated WSDL document for the SimpleBilingualDictionary service type, where the input is a SimpleBilingualLexiconAccessQuery, which is a dedicated subclass of the LinguisticExpression.

```
...
<wsdl:operation name="searchSimpleBilingualDictionary"
      sawsdl:modelReference=
      "http://langrid.nict.go.jp/lso/lso#SimpleBilingualDictionaryAccessor">
   <wsdl:input message="sbd:searchSimpleBilingualDictionaryRequest"/>
   <wsdl:output message="sbd:searchSimpleBilingualDictionaryResponse"/>
</wsdl:operation>
...
<xsd:element name="searchSimpleBilingualDictionaryRequest"
      type="sbd:SearchQuery">
</xsd:element>
...
<xsd:complexType name="SearchQuery"
      sawsdl:modelReference=
      "http://langrid.nict.go.jp/lso/lso#SimpleBilingualLexiconAccessQuery">
      <xsd:sequence>
        <xsd:element name="SurfaceForm" type="xsd:string">
        </xsd:element>
        <xsd:element name="LanguageName" type="xsd:language"> </xsd:element>
        <xsd:element name="TargetLanguage" type="xsd:language"> </xsd:element>
      </xsd:sequence>
</xsd:complexType>
...
```

Fig. 6.10 Example of semantically annotated WSDL document

6.6 Conclusion

The language service ontology discussed in this chapter is one of the fundamental technologies in realizing the Language Grid, which is a trailblazing language service infrastructure. The language service ontology serves as a foundation on which various types of language services can be functionally classified and their usages specified via corresponding APIs. This knowledge structure may also play a role in disseminating newly created language *resources as services*.

However, as the language service ontology, in its current form, is still conceptual and might thus be partial and incomplete, it should be further expanded and detailed by also looking at other infrastructural efforts. This kind of activity naturally calls for world-wide collaboration as discussed in (Calzolari and Soria 2010);

it clearly states that "acting as community" is necessary to realize an open and distributed language infrastructure, while avoiding dispersed or conflicting efforts.

Acknowledgments   The presented work was partly supported by Strategic Information and Communications R&D Promotion Programme (SCOPE) of the Ministry of Internal Affairs and Communications of Japan. The first author of this chapter also thanks Chiharu Narawa and Bora Savas for their efforts associated with the SCOPE project. The second author, Thierry Declerck, was partly supported by Monnet (Multilingual ONtologies for NETworked knowledge), a FP7 R&D project co-funded by the European Commission with Grant No. 248458.

References

Bond F, Isahara H, Kanzaki K, Uchimoto K (2008) Boot-strapping a wordnet using multiple existing wordnets. LREC2008

Broeder D, Kemps-Snijders et al (2010) A data category registry and component-based metadata framework. LREC2010: 43-47

Calzolari N (2008) Approaches towards a 'lexical web': the Role of Interoperability. ICGL2008: 34-42

Calzolari N, Soria C (2010) Preparing the field for an open and distributed resource infrastructure: the role of the FLaReNet network. LREC2010

Declerck T (2008) A framework for standardized syntactic annotation. LREC2008

Francopoulo G, Bel N, et al (2009) Multilingual resources for NLP in the lexical markup framework (NMF). Language Resources and Evaluation 43(1): 57-70

Hayashi Y (2007) A linguistic service ontology for language infrastructures. ACL2007 (demo and poster sessions): 145-148

Hayashi Y, Declerck T, Buitelaar P, Monachini M (2008) Ontologies for a global language infrastructure. ICGL2008: 105-112

Hayashi Y (2010) Toward a standardized set of language service Web APIs. 2nd European Language Resources and Technologies Forum

Hayashi Y, Declerck T, Narawa C (2010) LAF/GrAF-grounded representation of dependency structures. LREC2010

Ide N, Romary L (2006) Representing linguistic corpora and their annotations. LREC2006

Ide N, Suderman K (2007) GrAF: a graph-based format for linguistic annotations. Linguistic Annotation Workshop: 1-8

Ishida T (2006) Language Grid: an infrastructure for intercultural collaboration. SAINT-06: 96-100, keynote address

Savas B, Hayashi Y, Monachini M, Soria C, Calzolari N (2010) An LMF-based web service for accessing WordNet-type semantic lexicons. LREC2010

Soria C, Monachini M, Vossen P (2009) WordNet-LMF: fleshing out a standardized format for wordnet interoperability. IWIC2009: 139-146

Villegas M, Bel N, Bel S, Rodriguez V (2010) A case study on interoperability for language resources and applications. LREC2010

Yokoi T (1995) The EDR electronic dictionary. Communications of the ACM 38(11): 42-44

Part III

Language Grid for Using Language Resources

Chapter 7
Cascading Translation Services

Rie Tanaka[1], Yohei Murakami[2], and Toru Ishida[3]

1 C&C Innovation Research Laboratories, NEC Corporation, Nara, 630-0101, Japan, e-mail: r-tanaka@ak.jp.nec.com

2 National Institute of Information and Communications Technology (NICT), Kyoto, 619-0289, Japan, e-mail: yohei@nict.go.jp

3 Department of Social Informatics, Kyoto University, Kyoto 606-8501, Japan, e-mail: ishida@i.kyoto-u.ac.jp

Abstract The Language Grid offers a broad array of language services such as dictionaries and translation, and cascading them enables people in different parts of the world to communicate with one another in their mother tongue. However, when cascading several translation services, words' meanings often drift due to the inconsistency, asymmetry and intransitivity of word selection. In this section, we propose context-based coordination to maintain the consistency of word meanings. For this, we put forth a method to automatically generate multilingual equivalent terms based on the use of bilingual dictionaries. We generated trilingual equivalent noun terms and implemented a Japanese-to-German-and-back translation, cascading four translation services. The evaluation results showed that the generated terms can cover over 58% of all nouns. Translation quality was improved by 41% for all sentences, and the quality rating for all sentences increased by an average of 0.47 points on a five-point scale.

7.1 Introduction

The number of online translation tools and dictionaries has increased rapidly and the Language Grid provides assorted language services in the form of Web services. This development permits easy access to translation services and encourages intercultural communication and collaboration among people with different first languages. However, it is practically impossible to cover all combinations of n languages due to the extremely high cost of developing (n^2-n) direct translation services. Cascading several translation services is a practical solution for these conditions. For instance, translation between French and the Japanese regional

Kansai dialect is possible by cascading translation services between French and Japanese, and between the standard Japanese dialect and Kansai dialect. Moreover, since a hub language for developing language resources is English, cascading translation services between English and non-English languages via English can realize communication between the non-English languages. However, cascaded services often result in drifting for meanings of words due to inconsistent word selection, which makes it difficult for communication to move forward. Establishing common ground among users in machine translation-mediated communication is known to be difficult (Yamashita et al. 2009); and one of the causes of this difficulty is inconsistent word selection (Yamashita and Ishida 2006).

For realizing consistent translation, this study uses the service computing framework and proposes the context-based coordination method of translation services. The difficulty in keeping consistent meanings between translation services can be said to be the same as the difficulty in maintaining the context of results between general Web services. We therefore regard the internal translation processes of services as black boxes and realize coordination between them instead of proposing a new machine translation technology. We propose the propagation of context across cascaded services by regarding the context as a set of multilingual equivalent terms. Research in the area of bilingual dictionaries has proposed methods to match meanings of words of different languages by combining multiple dictionaries. We refer to these methods and propose a method to automatically generate equivalent multilingual terms based on available bilingual dictionaries. We use a multiagent architecture as one means of implementation, wherein the coordinator agent gathers and propagates the context from/to translation agents in the same way as an intermediate agent (Decker et al. 1997).

We implemented a coordinated Japanese-to-German-and-back translation service by cascading four translation services in this architecture, and obtained results indicating substantial improvement in the translation quality. This implies that high-quality translations can be extracted from existing translation services and bilingual dictionaries without modifying their internal coding systems, and context-based Web service composition techniques contribute to service quality, which is a frequently considered issue for component technologies.

7.2 Related Work

In the area of natural language processing, certain approaches have been proposed to solve or improve cascaded translation. In phrase-based statistical machine translation (SMT), methods with no direct corpora between the source and target languages have been proposed (Utiyama and Isahara 2007, Wu and Wang 2007). In this approach, the phrase-table required for SMT between the source and target languages is generated by combining phrase tables between the source and pivot languages and the pivot and target languages. The phrase and lexical translation probabilities in the new table are estimated from original corpora, enabling more accurate selection of translated phrases. The other approach for word selection problems has proposed the linguistic annotation method (Kanayama and Watanabe 2003). This method embeds lexical and syntactical information for a source sentence into the intermediated sentence. However, the above approaches cannot immediately be put into practice because it is not easy to prepare the enormous and reliable corpora required to merge phrase tables, or to apply the linguistic approach to all translation services. Moreover, in the above method, when intermediated words have ambiguities the translated words in the target language do not always have the same meanings as the original words. We propose a method of coordinating cascaded translations with context outside each translation system, without changing it or preparing additional language processing systems.

In the area of services computing and Web service composition, the framework which we use, the *WS-Coordination* (Web Services Coordination)[1] specifications enable propagation of the service ID or port number as "CoordinationContext" to solve the semantic problems of service composition. It is also used to automatically match input and output data types (Ben Hassine et al. 2006). A method of meta-level control for composite Web services in an open environment, known as Service Supervision, has been proposed for designers who are not authorized to modify each component Web service (Tanaka et al. 2009). In terms of improving the performance of composite Web services with diverse interfaces and various clients, a context-aware approach called a situated Web service (SiWS) has been proposed (Matsumura et al. 2006). We also adopt this approach to coordinate word selection with context from outside the Web services. Another method proposed combining language resources and middleware architecture to integrate deep and shallow natural language processing components (Bramantoro et al. 2008). This approach uses both language resources and language processing components as Web services: our context-based coordination approach can contribute to the improvement of combined services in such areas.

7.3 Overview of Context-Based Approach

7.3.1 Issues in Composite Translation Services

We conducted several experiments using the Language Grid and classified word selection errors into three categories (Tanaka et al. 2009): inconsistency, asymmetry and intransitivity. *Inconsistency* is when translations of the same source word vary among different sentences. *Asymmetry* is when the back-translated word is different from the source word. The impact of these errors on communication has

---

[1] http://www-106.ibm.com/developerworks/library/ws-coor

already been analyzed (Yamashita and Ishida 2006). Quantitative results with interview data show that lexical entrainment (Brennan and Clark 1996) is disrupted by asymmetries since they interfere with echoing. *Intransitivity* is when the word sense drifts across the cascaded machine translators.

Case 1
Source sentence (English): Please add that picture in this <u>paper</u>.
→Translation (Japanese): *Douzo, sono shashin wo kono <u>ronbun</u> no naka ni tsuika shinasai.*
                                  (Please add that picture in this <u>thesis</u>.)
Case 2
Source sentence (English): Please send me this <u>paper</u>.
→Translation (Japanese): *Douzo, kono <u>kami</u> wo watashi ni okuri nasai.*
                                  (Please send me this <u>paper</u>.)

(a) Inconsistency in word selection

• Japanese user (Japanese): *Kinou watashitachi ha <u>pa-ti-</u> wo shita.*
                                  (We had a <u>party</u> yesterday.)
→Translation (English): There was a <u>party</u> yesterday.
• English user (English): How was the <u>party</u>?
  →Translation (Japanese): *<u>Tou</u> ha doudeshita ka?* (How was the <u>political party</u>?)

(b) Asymmetry in word selection

Source sentence (Japanese): *Kanojo no <u>ketten</u> ha ookina mondai da.*
                                  (Her <u>shortcoming</u> is a big problem.)
→Translation (English): Her <u>fault</u> is a big problem.
→Translation (German): *Ihre <u>Schuld</u> ist ein großes Problem.*
                                  (Her <u>responsibility</u> is a big problem.)

(c) Intransitivity in word selection

Source sentence (Japanese): *Kyo no yushoku no tame ni <u>tako</u> wo katte kite kudasai.*
                                  (Please get some <u>octopus</u> for today's dinner.)
→Translation (English): Please get <u>octopus</u> for today's dinner.
→Translation (German): *Besorge <u>Tintenfisch</u> für das Abendessen von heute bitte.*
                                  (Please get <u>cephalopods</u> for today's dinner.)
→Translation (English): Please procure <u>squid</u> for the dinner of today.
→Translation (Japanese): *Douzo, kyo no dina no tame ni <u>ika</u> wo nyushu shinasai.*
                                  (Please procure <u>squid</u> for today's dinner.)

(d) An example including both asymmetry and intransitivity in word selection
Fig. 7.1 Issues in composite translation services

Fig. 7.1 presents examples of problems encountered by cascaded translation services. All original Japanese and German sentences in this chapter are italicized and their English translations are provided in parentheses. (a) is an example of inconsistency, wherein the English word "paper" is translated into the Japanese *ron-bun* (thesis) in Case 1, while the same word is translated into *kami* (paper) in Case 2. Asymmetry is presented in (b). In the first step of the machine translation-mediated communication, the Japanese word *pa-ti* (party), which means a social gathering, is translated into English correctly. Yet when an English user echoes the word "party," it is translated into the Japanese word *tou* (political party). Intransitivity is presented in (c). The Japanese word *ketten* (shortcoming), which means a weakness of character, is translated into English word "fault" which can have the same meaning, but mistranslated to the German *Schuld* (responsibility). This is because the intermediate English "fault" has several meanings, and the English-German translator has no knowledge of the context for the preceding Japanese-English translation. An example including both asymmetry and intransitivity is presented in (d). This is an example of a Japanese-German back-translation generated by combining Japanese-English, English-German, German-English, and English-Japanese translation services. Back translation is frequently used to examine the quality of translation. First, the Japanese source word *tako* (octopus) is translated correctly to the English "octopus." Second, in the English-German translation, the translated German *Tintenfisch* (cephalopod)—meaning a mollusk with tentacles, such as an octopus or squid—is selected. Though this word selection is not necessarily incorrect, it results in inappropriate selection of the English word "squid" by extracting the meaning of squid in the next step of the cascaded translation. Therefore, the back-translated Japanese word *ika* (squid) is different from the source word *tako* (octopus). All problems depicted in Fig. 7.1 result from inconsistency in word selection.

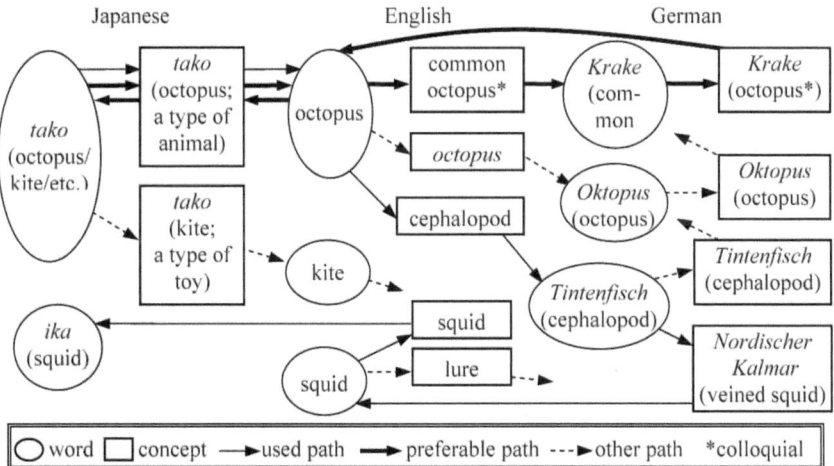

Fig. 7.2 Conceptual picture illustrating the translation of the word "octopus"

7.3.2 *Word Selection in Composite Translation Services*

Fig. 7.2 is the conceptual picture illustrating the word selection of the example shown in Fig. 7.1(d). The words are presented in circles, and concepts in squares. The picture is obtained using bilingual dictionaries. For instance, the Japanese-

English dictionary describes the Japanese word *tako* (octopus/kite/etc.) as a type of animal as well as a type of toy, and the English "octopus" is translated as the type of animal. The solid arrows indicate the translation path in each translation.

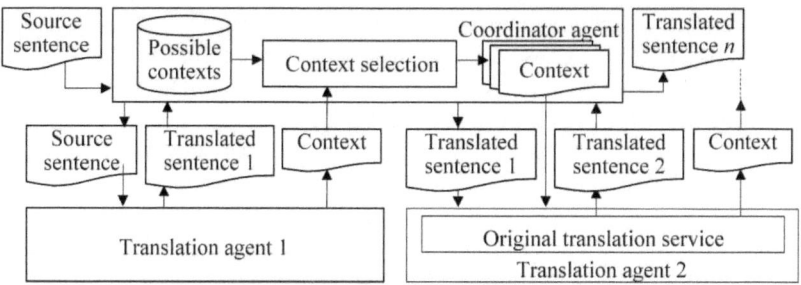

Fig. 7.3 Multiagent architecture for context-based approach

Though the translated words are directly combined with source words within actual translation services, it is supposed that such selections of words and concepts are performed conceptually. In Fig. 7.1(d), in the English-German and German-English translations, the concept of "cephalopod" was selected for the English "octopus"; the German *Tintenfisch* (cephalopod) was selected for the concept; and the concept of *Nordischer Kalmar* (veined squid), which is a type of squid, was selected for the German word. As a result, the meaning of the translated words was changed from octopus to squid. In contrast, in the path indicated by bold arrows, the meaning was kept consistent. In order to realize such consistent selection, a mechanism that considers the correspondence across all languages, not just between two languages, is required.

7.3.3 Context-Based Pivot Translation Service with Multiagent Architecture

We propose a multiagent architecture for a context-based pivot translation service, as shown in Fig. 7.3. The coordinator agent, which plays the role of controlling the entire translation, gathers and propagates context from/to the translation agents in addition to requesting that they translate the sentence. It possesses all possible contexts internally, selects all contexts that suit the context reported by the translation agent, and transfers them to the next translation agent. Translation agents possess in-built functionality for the original translation service; they perform translations by taking into account the context provided by the coordinator agent, update the context, and transfer the result to the coordinator agent. They have knowledge of the languages and make language-specific processes or decisions. Context can be represented in several ways, such as a set of characteristic words in a document or surrounding text. Since context in one language can be translated to other languages with multilingual equivalent terms, we represent context by sets of equivalent terms, not sets of terms in one language. In our architecture, we consider a set of terms in the source sentence as context in the source language and use equivalent terms as propagated context.

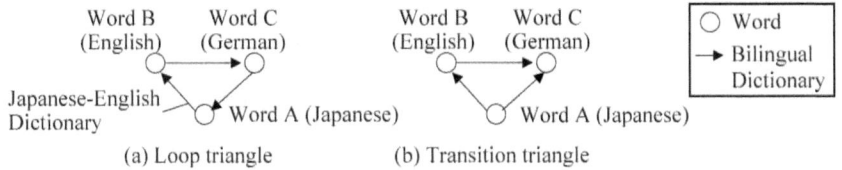

(a) Loop triangle   (b) Transition triangle

Fig.7.4 Two types of shapes of triangles

7.4 Generating Multilingual Equivalent Terms

The set of equivalent terms can be generated by analyzing generic bilingual dictionaries. For instance, multilingual equivalent terms can also be developed manually, as in the case of EuroWordNet (Vossen 1998). However, since it is costly and difficult to manually develop multilingual dictionaries that include all words in all languages, we need an automated method. One previous work on this subject proposed a method to match concepts for different languages using bilingual dictionaries (Tokunaga and Tanaka 1990). In this method, correspondences between concepts are obtained by representing a dictionary by a graph. In the graph, words and their concepts are shown as vertices and mapping relations between words and concepts are shown as direct edges. If the graph contains a cyclic route through two words and two concepts, the concepts included in the route are considered the same.

We extended this idea to generate a set of trilingual equivalent terms (hereinafter a *triple*). We represent mappings of words belonging to different languages in the form of a graph; words are shown as vertexes, and mappings in bilingual dictionaries as directed edges. If the graph contains a triangle, three words are considered equivalent terms. Fig. 7.4 shows the two types of triangles: *loop* and *transition*. The loop triangle starts from a source language, refers to dictionaries three times and returns to the source language. The transition triangle refers to dictionaries to locate transitive and direct routes between the source and target languages. It is easy to generate a triple from such triangles. We call these loop-type triples.

Example 1 – Loop triangle representing "sky"

Fig. 7.5 shows an example of a loop triangle, starting with the Japanese word *sora* (sky/heaven/midair). Words such as "sky" are extracted by looking them up in a Japanese-English dictionary. The German word *Himmel* (sky/heaven) is obtained by looking up the word "sky" in an English-German dictionary. Since the source Japanese word is extracted from a German-Japanese dictionary, {*sora* (sky/heaven/midair), sky, *Himmel* (sky/heaven)} is considered a triple. Continuing this process yields further triples.

In related research on dictionary formulation, a method to construct a bilingual dictionary using a third language as an intermediate is proposed (Tanaka and Umemura 1994). This study takes the example of generating a Japanese-French dictionary by connecting Japanese-English and English-French dictionaries. It addresses the problem that a French word meaning something different from the original Japanese word is obtained due to ambiguity in the intermediate English word. This problem is solved through inverse consultation with French-English and English-Japanese dictionaries. We focus on obtaining more reliable equivalent terms when dictionaries exist between each pair of languages and differ from the above research in terms of our assumptions and objectives. To realize coordination even when sufficient dictionaries are not available, methods such as inverse consultation are required in order to obtain equivalent terms.

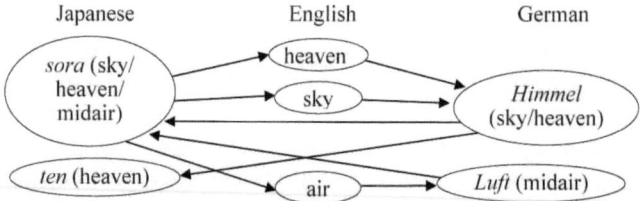

Fig. 7.5 Loop triangle representing the sense of "sky"

This method for three languages can easily be extended to four or more languages by combining triples generated in each subset of the three languages. It is noteworthy that a triangle does not always imply equivalent terms. In the case where word A has word sense C_1 and C_2, word B has C_2 and C_3, and word C has C_3 and C_1, no shared sense exists between the three words. Assume that each word in a triple has n senses with uniform distribution, the probability of sharing the same sense is 0.83 for $n = 2$ and 0.91 for $n = 3$. This probability approaches 1 as n increases. In practice, the term frequencies of n senses are unequal, and the actual probability is higher than the calculated one. Thus we can obtain reliable equivalent terms by combining triples if the number of languages increases.

7.5 Context-based Coordination Algorithms

Algorithms of the multiagent architecture for the context-based coordination are shown in Fig. 7.6 and Fig. 7.7. These algorithms are simple implementations of our multiagent model. Let machine translator MT_i input source sentence s_i and output translated sentence t_i. Let the translation agent MTA_i receive source sentence s_i, generate and modify t_i, and output s_{i+1}, which is a source sentence of

MTA_{i+1}. Let the coordinator agent CA repeat the coordination process from MTA_1 to MTA_n and receive s_{n+1} as the final result in the target language. Multilingual equivalent terms in n languages are grouped into n-tuples. The context T_i is a set of n-tuples and the i-th word in each n-tuple in T_i is included in s_i. In an n-tuple $(w_1, ..., w_n)$, the words $w_2, ..., w_n$ have the same meaning as w_1, i.e., the same meaning as original sentence s_1, and their use assures the correct translation.

Algorithm 1: COORDINATOR-AGENT CA

```
 1: s_i /* Source sentence */
 2: o_i /* A word in sentence s_i */
 3: MTA /* An ordered list of translation agents (MTA = {MTA_1, MTA_2, ..., MTA_n}) */
 4: MTA_i = {(s_i, s_{i+1})} /* A translation agent; a set of pairs of sentence s_i and s_{i+1} */
 5: T_i /* A set of n-tuples (w_1, w_2, ..., w_n), where w_k is included in s_k (k≤i);
           All n-tuples are n-lingual equivalent terms */
 6: Q_k /* A set of pairs (o_i, m_{i+1}), where o_i∈s_i and m_{i+1} is the modified translated word for o_i */
 7: when received (ask, s_1) from user do
 8:     T_1←{(w_1, w_2, ..., w_n)| w_1∈s_1};
 9:     for each MTA_i in MTA do
10:         send (request, (s_i, T_i)) to MTA_i;
11:         when received (response, (s_{i+1}, Q_i)) do;
12:             T_{i+1}←SELECT-POSSIBLE-N-TUPLES (T_i, Q_i);
13:         end do;
14:     end loop;
15:     send (reply, s_{n+1}) to user;
16: end do;
```

Algorithm 2: SELECT-POSSIBLE-N-TUPLES (T_i, Q_i) return T_{i+1}

```
 1: T_{i+1}←Φ;
 2: for each pair (o_i, m_{i+1}) in Q_i do
 3:     T_{i+1}←T_{i+1}∪{(w_1, w_2, ..., w_n)|( w_1, w_2, ..., w_n)∈T_i, w_i=o_i and w_{i+1}=m_{i+1}};
 4: end loop;
 5: return T_{i+1};
```

Fig. 7.6 Algorithms of the coordinator agent CA

First, CA prepares the initial context T_1 from s_1 received from the user and starts translation. After MTA_i returns the translated sentence s_{i+1} and Q_i — representing word pairs of the source word in s_i and translated word in s_{i+1}—CA generates a new context T_{i+1} for the $i+1$-th translation by narrowing down T_i such that the $i+1$-th word in each n-tuple appears in s_{i+1} by the SELECT-POSSIBLE-N-TUPLES procedure. T_{i+1} may contain ambiguity in word selection for the $i+2$-th word, as more than two n-tuples containing the same j-th word ($1 \leq j \leq i+1$) can exist with different $i+2$-th words. If there are several candidates for the $i+2$-th word, the $i+1$-th translation agent MTA_{i+1} determines the most appropriate one. The choice is noted to CA by Q_{i+1}, and CA reflects it in the next translation.

MTA_i generates a translated sentence t_i using MT_i to create P_i—a set of word pairs of source word o_i and translated word c_{i+1}—using the GET-WORD-PAIRS-USED-BY-MT procedure. One way to implement this function is to divide s_i and t_i into morphemes and map between them using bilingual dictionaries. Then, MTA_i

modifies words in P_i based on the context T_i using the procedure CREATE-WORD-PAIRS-TO-BE-USED and Q_i. Since T_i preserves the words used in the preceding i translations, the translated words excluded from T_i may have different meanings. Such words are replaced by words included in T_i, selected from among a few candidates if T_i contains ambiguity. Finally, t_i is modified by the procedure MODIFY-TRANSLATED-SENTENCE, wherein the words are replaced using P_i and Q_i. The word selection process can be improved through several methods; for instance, by referring to term frequency or priority of words in the case the translation agent possesses this information. If the full document or conversation logs are available, this information can be utilized by CA to create an initial context T_1.

Algorithm 3: SERVICE-AGENT MTAi

1: t_i /* Translated sentence */
2: $MT_j=\{(s_i, t_i)\}$ /* A translation service; a set of pairs of s_i and t_i */
3: c_{i+1} /* A word in sentence t_i */
4: P_i /* A set of pairs (o_i, c_{i+1}), where $o_i \in s_i$ and $c_{i+1} \in t_i$ */
5: **when** received (request, (s_i, T_i)) **from** CA **do**
6:     $t_i \leftarrow MT_j(s_i)$;
7:     $P_i \leftarrow$ GET-WORD-PAIRS-USED-BY-MT (s_i, t_i);
8:     $Q_i \leftarrow$ CREATE-WORD-PAIRS-TO-BE-USED (P_i, T_i);
9:     **if** $Q_i \neq P_i$ **then**
10:       $s_{i+1} \leftarrow$ MODIFY-TRANSLATED-SENTENCE (t_i, P_i, Q_i);
11:     **else** $s_{i+1} \leftarrow t_i$;
12:     **end if** ;
13:     send (response, (s_{i+1}, Q_i)) to CA;
14: **end do**;

Algorithm 4: CREATE-WORD-PAIRS-TO-BE-USED (P_i, T_i) **return** Qi

1: $Q_i \leftarrow \Phi$;
2: **for each** pair (o_i, c_{i+1}) **in** P_i **do**
3:     **for each** n-tuple $(w_1, w_2, ..., w_n)$ **in** T_i **do**
4:       **if** $o_i \in (w_1, w_2, ..., w_n)$ and $c_{i+1} \in (w_1, w_2, ..., w_n)$ **then**
5:         $Q_i \leftarrow Q_i \cup \{(o_i, c_{i+1})\}$;
6:       **end if**;
7:     **end loop**;
8:     **if** $(o_i, c_{i+1}) \notin Q_i$ **then**
9:       $m_{i+1} \leftarrow i+1$th word in n-tuple selected from $\{(w_1, w_2, ..., w_n)|o_i \in (w_1, w_2, ..., w_n)\}$;
10:       $Q_i \leftarrow Q_i \cup \{(o_i, m_{i+1})\}$;
11:     **end if**;
12: **end loop**;
13: **return** Q_i;

Fig. 7.7 Algorithms of the translation agent MTA

Example 2 – Context-based translation of sentence shown in Fig. 7.1(d)

Here we explain the translation process for the sentence shown in Fig. 7.1(d). In this example, the replacement of target words is limited to nouns. Fig. 7.8 shows the process of the English-German translation agent MTA_2 after the Japanese-English translation agent MTA_1 completes its translation process. In the first step, the coordinator agent CA receives the Japanese source sentence $s_1 =$ "*kyo no yushoku no tame ni tako wo katte kite kudasai* (Please get some octopus for today's dinner)." sets all possible *n*-tuples including the words in s_1 and transfers s_1 and T_1 to MTA_1. MTA_1 then translates s_1 into the English sentence $t_1 =$ "Please get octopus for today's dinner." using the Japanese-English translation service MT_1. MTA_1 obtains pairs P_1 of words in s_1 and t_1: $P_1 = \{\{$*tako* (octopus), octopus$\}$, $\{$*yu-shoku* (dinner), dinner$\}\}$. MTA_1 then examines the translated words. For example, if T_1 contains triples including both *tako* and "octopus," MTA_1 realizes that they share the same meaning. If that is not the case, the triples may remain incomplete, and MTA_1 has to abandon efforts to maintain context. If the triples are complete, then triples including both *tako* and "octopus," as well as those including both *yu-shoku* and "dinner," should be contained in T_1. Therefore, translated words are not modified: $Q_1 = P_1$ and $s_2 = t_1$. MTA_1 then sends s_2 and Q_1 to CA and CA generates the new context T_2. For example, both triples of T_1 including both *tako* and "octopus" are to be included in T_2, as shown in Fig. 7.8.

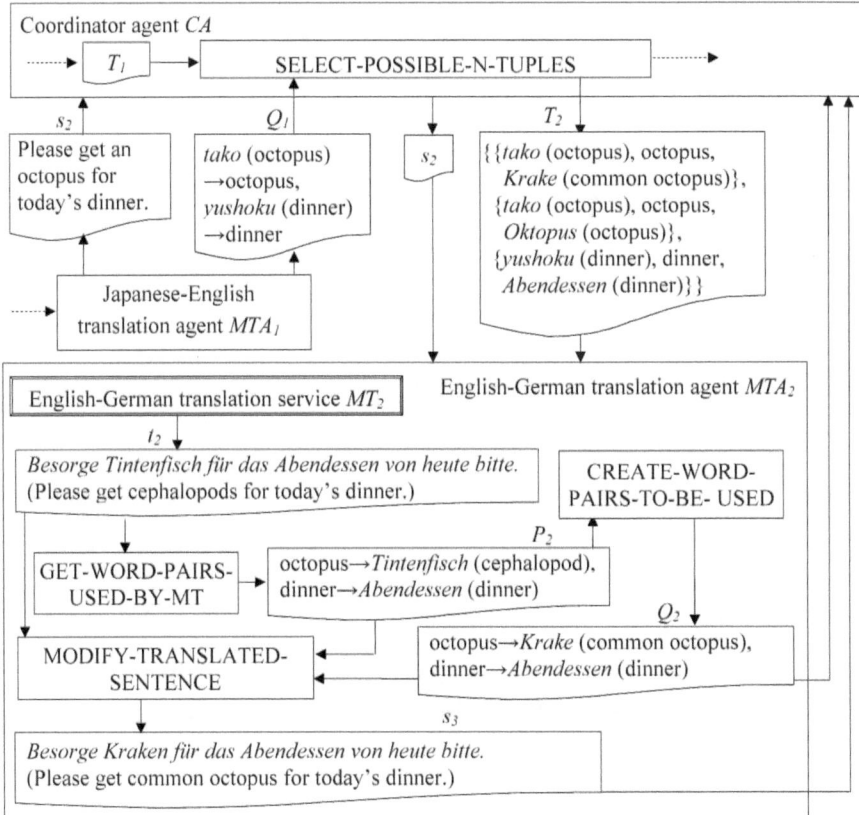

Fig. 7.8 Example of Coordinated Translation Services

In the second step, s_2 and T_2 are sent to the second English-German translation agent MTA_2. MTA_2 translates s_2 to the German sentence $t_2 =$ "*Besorge Tintenfisch*

für das Abendessen von heute bitte (Please get cephalopods for today's dinner)."
Pairs P_2 are then obtained: $P_2 = \{\{$octopus, *Tintenfisch* (cephalopod)$\}$, $\{$dinner, *Abendessen* (dinner)$\}\}$. It appears that the word *Tintenfisch* has semantically drifted, as there is no triple in T_2 that includes both "octopus" and *Tintenfisch*. Thus it is replaced by a word that is included in a triple in T_2, which also includes "octopus." If the first triple in Fig. 7.7 is selected, Q_2 would be $\{\{$octopus, *Krake* (common octopus)$\}$, $\{$dinner, *Abendessen* (dinner)$\}\}$. MTA_2 modifies t_2 to s_3: $s_3 =$ "*Besorge Kraken für das Abendessen von heute bitte* (Please get common octopus for today's dinner)." s_3 is finally returned to the user.

Table 7.1 Bilingual dictionaries used to obtain triples

Dictionary	Number of headwords
Genius Japanese-English dictionary	31,944 (noun)
Concise Japanese-German dictionary	38,487(all words)
Oxford English-German dictionary	31,180 (noun)
Crown German-Japanese dictionary	34,255 (noun)

7.6 Evaluation

We generated triples of Japanese, English and German, and implemented the co-ordinated pivot translation with context. For simplicity, we limited the part-of-speech to nouns. We analyzed the Japanese-German back-translation to check the effectiveness of our method on the problem of asymmetry in word selection, and analyzed the Japanese-German multi-hop translation to check the effectiveness on the problem of intransitivity in word selection.

7.6.1 Evaluation of Method of Generating Multilingual Equivalent Terms

We constructed Japanese-English-German triples limiting their parts-of-speech to nouns. Table 7.1 lists the dictionaries used and the number of triples obtained from them. We constructed triples from the triangle shown in Fig. 7.4 (a) and (b). We obtained 15,627 loop-type triples and 13,757 transition-type triples, with a total of 21,914 triples without overlaps.

We first analyzed the effectiveness of the 21,914 triples in covering arbitrary Japanese documents. We used the term frequency of nouns in a Web corpus storing 470 million sentences that totaled five billion Japanese words (Kawahara and Kurohashi 2006). The triples appeared to cover 58% of all nouns in the corpus and 40% of all part-of-speech words. If the triples are used in descending order of term frequency, 6,000 triples can cover 50% of nouns and 38% of all part-of-speech words. This implies that a relatively small number of triples can cover the majority of frequently used nouns. Second, we analyzed how much the generated triples can cover the actual translation. We prepared the Japanese sentences, translated them into English and obtained the pairs of Japanese source words and English translated words. The pairs were obtained by using morphological analysis and a Japanese-English dictionary. Source Japanese sentences were selected from the Machine Translation Test Set provided by the NTT Natural Language Research Group (Ikehara et al. 1994). Then, we randomly selected 100 sample sentences and checked whether each pair can be covered by a triple, namely, whether any triple, which includes Japanese, English and German words, includes both the source word and translated word. We resultantly obtained 175 pairs of source and translated noun words from 85 sentences, and triples could cover 105 pairs in 65 sentences. Though proper cover percentage depends on the machine translation, morphological analysis and dictionary, it appears that the generated triples can be applied to the actual translation at a high rate.

Source sentence (Japanese; A): *Torakku ga michi wo fusaide ita.*
                              (A truck was blocking the road.)
B: *Torakku ha houhou wo samatageta.* (A truck was blocking the method.)
C: *Torakku ha michi wo samatageta.* (A truck was blocking the road.)

(a) Example of an improvement from 4 (Most) to 5 (All)

Source sentence (Japanese; A): *Shachou ha roudousha wo tsukau.*
                              (The boss employs laborers.)
B: *Daitouryou ha roudousha wo tsukau.* (The president employs laborers.)
C: *Shachou ha roudousha wo tsukau.* (The boss employs laborers.)

(b) Example of an improvement from 3 (Much) to 5 (All)
Fig. 7.9 Examples of changes of translation scores

7.6.2 *Evaluation of Coordinated Pivot Translation*

We then conducted a preliminary evaluation of the quality of Japanese-German back-translation using the cascade of Japanese-English, English-German, German-English and English-Japanese translations. We compared the source Japanese sentence (A), back-translated Japanese sentence generated without coordination (B), and that generated with coordination (C). For accuracy, we took subjective evaluation by three native Japanese speakers. The subjects were asked to evaluate the translation quality on a five-point scale representing how much of the original meaning of sentence A was conveyed through sentences B and C (5-All, 4-Most, 3-Much, 2-Little, 1-None). We used the same source sentences as in section 7.6.1. In the 3,718 sample sentences provided, there were 458 sentences in which modification of the translated words occurred in the translation process, and we randomly selected 100 sentences from the 458. The results of Welch's test show a difference in quality between B and C with a confidence level greater than 98%.

On average, the translation quality improved for 41% of all sentences and the score increased by an average of 0.47 points using context-based coordination. The quality improved in the case of 34% of the sentences previously assigned a rating of 4 when translated without coordination. Similarly, sentences with ratings of 3, 2 and 1 showed improvements for 32%, 49%, and 60% of sentences, respectively, with the context-based approach. Words in back-translated Japanese sentence B, which had different meanings from the source words, numbered 143 in 100 sentences, with 89 words modified. An example of modification is shown in Fig. 7.9. In this example, without coordination (B), the Japanese words *michi* (road) and *shachou* (boss) were mistranslated to *houhou* (method) and *daitouryou* (president). The first error occurs because the intermediate English word "way" has several meanings.

7.7 Conclusion

This study proposes a method for context-based coordination to overcome mistranslation in several cascaded translation services, which occurs because of inconsistent word selection. Our approach seeks to propagate context across combined translation services. Treating context as a set of multilingual equivalent terms, we propose obtaining all possible terms based on triangle forms formed by the relationships between words and translated words extracted from bilingual dictionaries. Our triangle method can easily be extended to four or more languages, and it is efficient in obtaining a sufficient amount of terms. We proposed a multiagent architecture as one way to implement coordination with propagated context, wherein the coordinator agent gathers and propagates context from/to translation agents. The evaluation results show that the generated equivalent noun terms cover 58% of nouns and 40% of all parts-of-speech appearing in arbitrary sentences, and translation quality improved in 41% of the total 100 sentences used, with the quality rating increasing an average of 0.47 points on a five-point scale.

By considering the translation services as black boxes, a substantial improvement in translation quality was realized. The advantage of our approach is that we can improve the translation quality with no corpora, training of translation services with training sentences or changing the inner systems. We only use the available language resources and add some components outside existing translation services. Our method enables easy realization of a range of translations between various languages by cascading language services on the Language Grid. This improvement is also significant in the intercultural collaboration domain (Ishida et al. 2007). A context-based coordination approach will play an important role in quality improvement of the component service that comprises the composite service, which is a frequently considered issue for component technologies.

Acknowledgments   This collaborative research was conducted between NICT and Kyoto University during author Rie Tanaka's master's degree studies at Kyoto University. It was supported by the Kyoto University Global COE Program: Informatics Education and Research Center for Knowledge-Circulating Society, Strategic Information and Communications R&D Promotion Program from Ministry of Internal Affairs and Communications, and a Grant-in-Aid for Scientific Research (A) (21240014, 2009-2011) from the Japan Society for the Promotion of Science (JSPS).

References

Ben Hassine A, Matsubara S, Ishida T (2006) A constraint-based approach to horizontal web service composition. ISWC-06: 130-143

Bramantoro A, Tanaka M, Murakami Y, Schäfer U, Ishida T (2008) A hybrid integrated architecture for language service composition. ICWS-08: 345-352

Brennan SE, Clark HH (1996) Conceptual pacts and lexical choice in conversation. Journal of Experimental Psychology: Learning, Memory, and Cognition 22(6): 1482-1493

Decker K, Sycara K, Williamson M (1997) Middle-agents for the internet. IJCAI-97: 578–583

Ikehara S, Shirai S, Ogura K (1994) Criteria for evaluating the linguistic quality of Japanese to English machine translations. Journal of Japanese Society for Artificial Intelligence 9(5): 569-579 (in Japanese)

Ishida T(2006) Language grid: an infrastructure for intercultural collaboration. SAINT-06: 96-100

Ishida T, Fussell SR, Vossen P (Eds) (2007) Intercultural collaboration. Lecture Notes in Computer Science 4568, Springer-Verlag

Kawahara D, Kurohashi S (2006) Case frame compilation from the web using high-performance computing. LREC-06

Kanayama H, Watanabe H (2003) Multilingual translation via annotated hub language. MT-Summit IX: 202-207

Matsumura I, Ishida T, Murakami Y, Fujishiro Y (2006) Situated web service: context-aware approach to high speed web service communication. ICWS-06: 673-680

Tanaka K, Umemura K (1994) Construction of a bilingual dictionary intermediated by a third language. COLING 94: 297-303

Tanaka M, Ishida T, Murakami Y, Morimoto S (2009) Service supervision: coordinating web services in open environment. ICWS-09: 238-245

Tanaka R, Ishida T, Murakami Y (2009) Towards coordination of multiple machine translation services. JSAI 2008 Conference and Workshops, Revised Selected Papers, Lecture Notes in Artificial Intelligence 5447, Springer-Verlag: 73-86

Tanaka R, Murakami Y, Ishida T (2009) Context-based approach for pivot translation services. IJCAI-09: 1555-1561

Tokunaga T, Tanaka H(1990) The automatic extraction of conceptual items from bilingual dictionaries. PRICAI-90: 304-309

Utiyama M, Isahara H (2007) A comparison of pivot methods for phrase-based statistical machine translation. HLT-NAACL: 484-491

Vossen P (Ed) (1998) EurowordNet: a multilingual database with lexical semantic networks. Dordrecht, Netherlands: Kluwer. http://www.hum.uva.nl/ ewn/.

Wu H, Wang H (2007) Pivot language approach for phrase-based statistical machine translation. ACL'07: 856-863

Yamashita N, Inaba R, Kuzuoka H, Ishida T (2009) Difficulties in establishing common ground in multiparty groups using machine translation. CHI09: 679-688

Yamashita N, Ishida T (2006) Effects of machine translation on collaborative work. CSCW-06: 515-523

Chapter 8
Sharing Multilingual Resources to Support Hospital Receptions

Mai Miyabe[1], Takashi Yoshino[2], and Aguri Shigeno[3]

1 Graduate School of Systems Engineering, Wakayama University, 930 Sakaedani, Wakayama, Japan, email: miyabe@yoslab.net

2 Faculty of Systems Engineering, Wakayama University, 930 Sakaedani, Wakayama, Japan, email: yoshino@sys.wakayama-u.ac.jp

3 NPO Center for Multicultural Society Kyoto, 143 Manjuji-cho Shimogyo-ku, Kyoto, Japan, email: aguri@tabunka-kyoto.org

Abstract In the medical field, there exists a serious problem with regard to communications between hospital staff and foreign patients. According to statistics, many countries worldwide have a low rate of literacy. Illiterate people engaging in multilingual communication face problems. Therefore, this situation requires the provision of support in various ways. Currently, medical translators accompany patients to medical care facilities, and the number of requests for medical translators has been increasing. However, medical translators cannot provide support at all times. Therefore, the medical field has high expectations from information technology. However, a useful system has yet to be developed and introduced in the medical field for practical use. In this chapter, we propose a multilingual communication support system called "M^3." M^3 uses parallel texts and voice data to achieve high accuracy in communication between people speaking different languages. The Language Grid provides various parallel texts provided by a multilingual parallel text sharing system and parallel text providers. The proposed system can obtain and share parallel texts using Web services via the Language Grid.

8.1 Introduction

Opportunities for multilingual communication in Japan have increased due to the increase in the number of foreigners in Japan. When people communicate in their nonnative language, the differences in languages prevent mutual understanding among communicating individuals (Aiken 2002, Tung and Quaddus 2002). These differences in languages have to be overcome in order for multilingual communication to occur. In this study, we focus on the support for multilingual communication in the medical field. Currently, medical translators accompany patients to medical care facilities, and the requests for medical translators to accompany patients are increasing. However, medical translators cannot provide support in cases in which round-the-clock support is required or in case of emergencies. Thus, a system that supports accurate multilingual communication is required. In the medical field in particular, accurate translations are very important. Medical care directly impacts both human life and health. To overcome the language barrier in communication, machine translation is used for communication that uses native language (Yoshino et al. 2008, Inaba 2007). Despite recent advances in machine translation technology, it is still very difficult to obtain highly accurate translations. Inaccurate translation adversely affects communication, and an incorrect machine translation can cause serious problems. Thus, in the medical field, it is difficult to apply a support system that uses machine translation. We need to consider a system that uses accurate translations.

In Japan, there are foreigners who are illiterate in Japanese and natives who are illiterate in their native language. According to statistics, many countries worldwide have a low rate of literacy. In some countries, illiterate people account for more than 70% of the adult population. The actual illiterate population can be estimated to be larger because most countries estimate their illiterate population to be lower than it really is. If an illiterate person and his/her conversational partner speak the same language, the conversational partner can provide support to the illiterate person through a verbal explanation. However, if they speak different languages, it is difficult for the conversational partner to provide information on texts to the illiterate person through a verbal explanation. Therefore, illiterate people engaging in multilingual communication face problems. We need to develop a method to provide support to illiterate people engaging in multilingual face-to-face communication.

In this chapter, we propose a parallel text based support system for multilingual communication at hospital reception desks. This system provides reliable communication using correct translations. The Language Grid (Ishida 2006) provides various parallel texts that are provided from a multilingual parallel text sharing system and parallel text providers. The proposed system can obtain and share parallel texts using Web services via the Language Grid.

8.2 Related Work

Our research is related to two aspects: support for multilingual communication using parallel texts and support for illiterate people using voice data.

Parallel texts are lines of text in one language paired with translations of the text in other languages. In other words, parallel texts are accurate translations prepared in advance that are meant to improve the efficiency and accuracy of medical treatment (Wang et al. 2002). Face-to-face communication systems using parallel texts are now in use. One of these is a support system using speech-to-speech translation for foreign travelers (Ikeda et al. 2002). Another topic of research is a tool that supports communication between speakers of different languages and uses parallel texts for speech recognition (Imoto et al. 2006). In these systems, the user inputs speech, and the system outputs a translated sentence, but the system cannot output sentences that have not been previously registered. Speech translation systems using phrase translation for communication in the medical field have also been proposed (Rayner et al. 2003, Chung et al. 2005). Even these systems, however, provide insufficient support for the medical field. We need a common system that can register, share, and use parallel texts among several hospitals. In our research, we develop a system that shares parallel texts on the Internet.

In order to provide support to illiterate people, it is necessary to read out the text data verbally. Some studies have employed speech synthesis as a text-to-speech technology (ElAarag and Schindler 2006). Recently, the quality of speech synthesis has improved. Moreover, text-to-speech technology has been applied for providing support to visually impaired people (Sporka et al. 2005, Chirathivat et al. 2007). An interface that provided support to illiterate people has been discussed (Leporini et al. 2003). However, an interface that supports illiterate people has not been adequately discussed. Both visually impaired people and illiterate people require support through voice data. However, illiterate people require a different type of support from that required by visually impaired people because the former can look at a display and texts. It is necessary to develop an interface that provides support to illiterate people. In our research, for illiterate people, we propose an interface that provides support using voice data.

8.3 Development of a Multilingual Medical Reception Support System

8.3.1 System Design Concept

Our design concepts of the multilingual medical reception support system are as follows:

(1) Retrieval and registration of parallel text using a Web service

Groups and communities working together can easily create a huge body of parallel texts. Conversation support systems use Web services to reserve and share parallel texts by retrieving and registering them. A Web service is defined by the W3C as a software system designed to support interoperable machine-to-machine interaction over a network. Web services can cooperate with one another and are scalable. They can also use parallel texts easily.

(2) User-friendly interface

Hospital reception staff and patients use these systems differently. Hospital staff use the system regularly. Patients, however, use the system less frequently, meaning they are less expert. Therefore, the system provides two types of system interface: a simple one for patients and a multifunctional one for hospital staff. The use of a touch screen instead of a keyboard makes the system easier to use.

(3) Support for illiterate people

In this study, we develop a method that provides support to illiterate people when they use the system that is operated using the touch screen. Although illiterate people cannot understand the meaning of the texts that are shown on the display, they can operate the system by viewing the display. Therefore, illiterate people can use the system if they can understand the meaning of the texts. We provide support to illiterate people by implementing the text-to-speech function. In the system operated by the touch screen, the following problems have to be solved for the realization of the text-to-speech function.

- Text-to-speech for all texts shown on the display

  We should enable the reading out of all texts shown on the display, in order to provide support to illiterate people. Although illiterate people cannot understand the meaning of the texts that are shown on the display, they can operate the system by viewing the display. Therefore, we need to enable a readout of only that text that an illiterate person cannot understand and not all the texts.

- Screen area

  In the system operated by the touch screen, the sizes of the interfaces operated by users need to be sufficient for the users to touch. The screen area of the system is limited compared with that of a mouse-driven system. Therefore, we require a method in which there is no dependence on the screen area.

We consider that these problems may be solved by the following solutions.

- Text-to-speech conversion by suitable selections by users

  If users touch the text shown on a display, only the touched text is read out verbally.

- Operation of text-to-speech function separate from operation of the touch screen

  The text-to-speech function is not usually used in the system. Therefore, we separate the operation of this function from that of the main functions. The function is physically implemented to be operated separately from the touch screen.

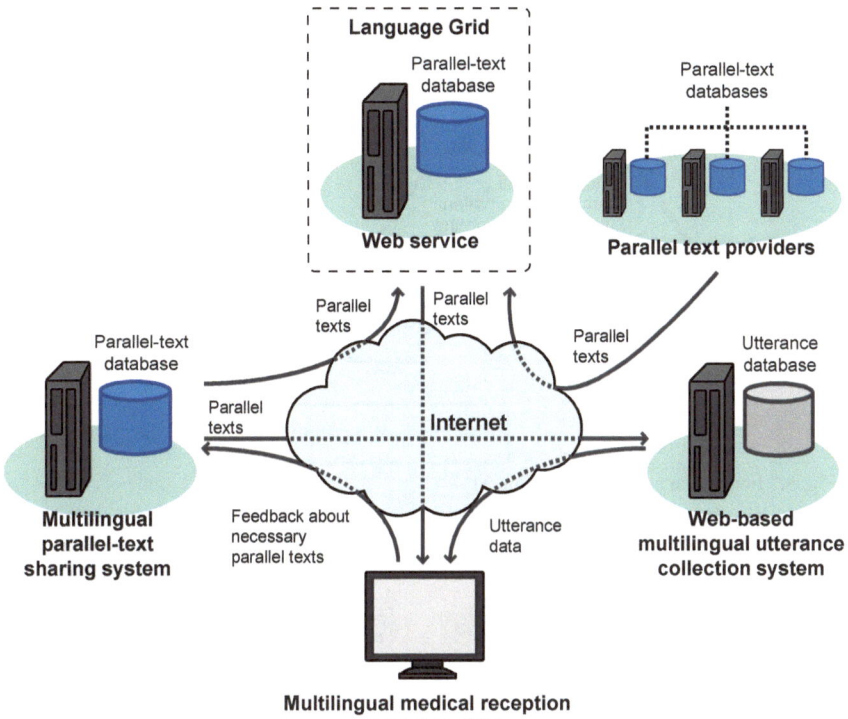

Fig. 8.1 System configuration

8.3.2 *System Configuration*

We have developed a support system for multilingual medical reception termed M^3. M^3 supports face-to-face communication and the procedure followed at hospital receptions.

Fig. 8.1 shows the configuration of the proposed system. Various parallel texts are provided on the Internet by parallel text providers, a multilingual parallel-text sharing system (Yoshino et al. 2009a) that collects and shares parallel texts, etc. The Language Grid provides various parallel texts through a multilingual parallel text sharing system and parallel text providers. The proposed system can obtain and share parallel texts using Web services via the Language Grid. When the proposed system's users find the required parallel texts are unavailable, they can feed back requests for parallel texts to the multilingual parallel-text sharing system. On the basis of the feedback data, the lack of parallel texts can be corrected, and the proposed system can share parallel texts as required in the medical field.

We use two types of Web services: an example service and a parallel text service. The example service provides Japanese questions that are used by hospital staff. The parallel text service provides parallel texts of Japanese questions and candidate responses to the questions. These services are divided because they are

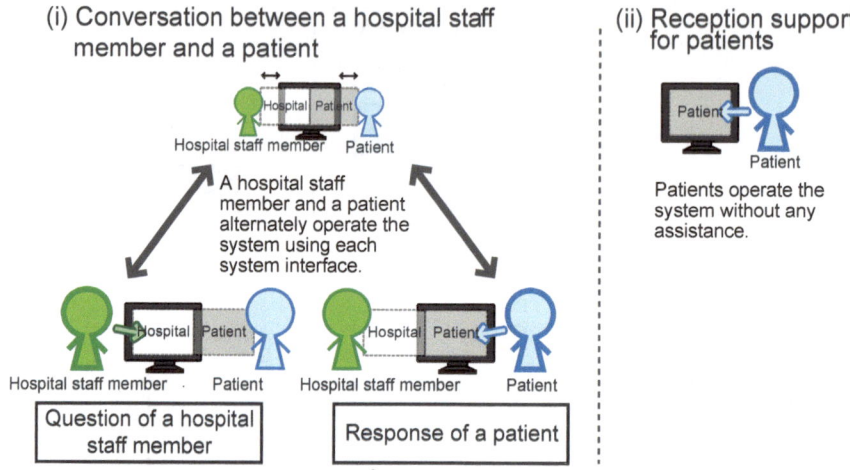

Fig. 8.2 Image of a conversation using M^3

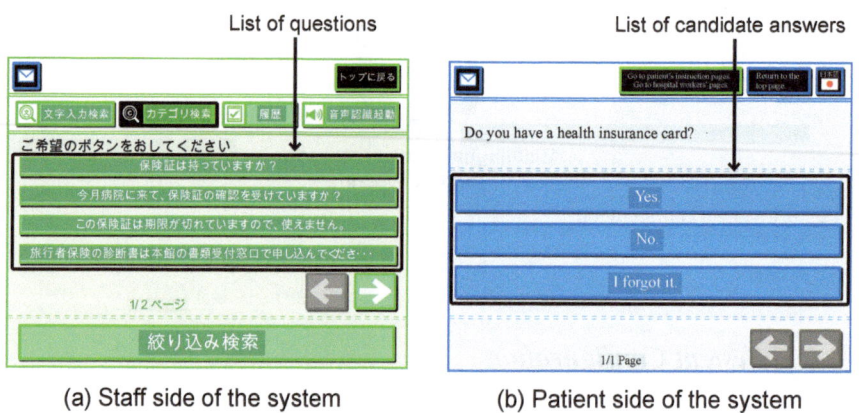

(a) Staff side of the system   (b) Patient side of the system

Fig. 8.3 Screenshot of conversation function

easy to combine with a parallel text collecting system. By using these services, we can obtain and share the necessary parallel texts among hospitals.

8.3.3 Conversation Function

Users operate M^3 using a touch screen. Fig. 8.2 shows the image of a conversation using M^3. When a hospital staff member and a patient communicate, they alternately operate the system each using a different system interface. When a patient receives support for following the required procedure at the hospital reception, he/she operates the system without receiving any further assistance.

Fig. 8.3 (a) is a screenshot of the staff side of the system. The users of the system are Japanese. Hospital staff communicates with patients using this system. A hospital staff member questions a patient and he/she responds. When the hospital staff member selects a category of questions, the system retrieves parallel texts for a given hospital reception scenario from the Web service. The parallel texts obtained are shown as a list of questions on the screen. When a user selects and sends a parallel text from the list of questions, the selected question and the candidate answers are displayed translated into the patient's language on the patient side of the system.

Fig. 8.3 (b) shows a screenshot of the patient side of the system. The users of this version of the system speak English. The parallel text that is sent by the staff side of the system is labeled as the question and the candidate answers are as shown in the list of candidate answers. When a user selects and sends a response, the selected response is translated into Japanese and is displayed on the staff side of the system.

8.3.4 Text-to-speech Function

In the medical field, accurate translations are required. Thus, the medical field also requires voice data of appropriate nuance.

In this study, we use the real utterance data via a Web-based multilingual utterance collection system (Yoshino et al. 2009b). The Web-based multilingual utterance collection system collects and provides real utterance data. The real utterance data are registered by a person speaking in his/her native language. Therefore, the data express the appropriate nuance.

However, we cannot provide the support by voice data if the Web-based multilingual utterance collection system does not have utterance data. Thus, we use the system in combination with voice synthesis. We use AITalk and AITalk International, developed by AI, Inc., as the voice synthesis system.

The procedure of the text-to-speech function is as follows:

(1) A user selects a text and then requests to play the voice data of the text.
(2) The function performs a query on the Web-based multilingual utterance collection system.
(3) If the system has real utterance data of the selected text, the function downloads and plays the data.
(4) If the system does not have utterance data, the function plays the voice data using voice synthesis.

Our system can provide data that are more appropriate by using the real utterance data preferentially.

We develop two modes of the system: the normal operation mode and the text-to-speech mode. Fig. 8.4 shows a screenshot of the text-to-speech mode. Users can

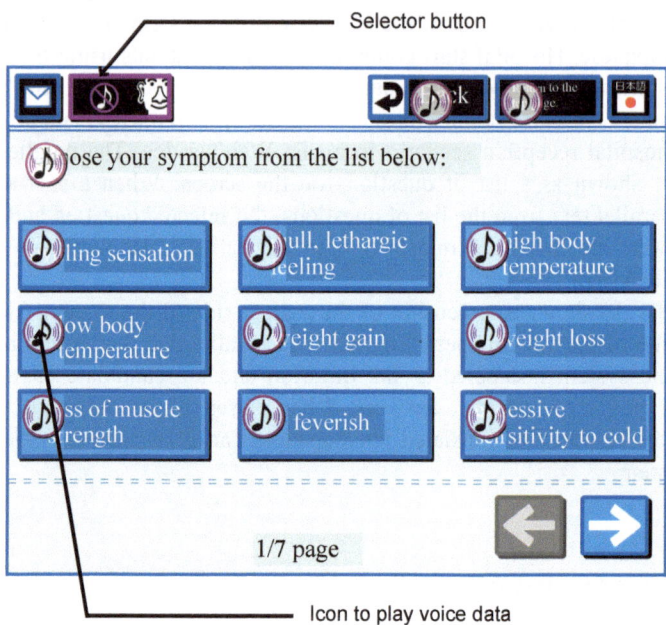

Fig. 8.4 Screenshot of the text-to-speech mode

switch between these two modes in order to perform a normal operation or a text-to-speech operation when they press the selector button. The text-to-speech mode is superimposed on the normal operation mode. When users press the icon to play voice data, the texts selected by them are read out verbally.

8.3.5 Other Functions

M^3 provides the following other functions:
  (1) Questionnaire function
      Fig. 8.5 (a) shows a screenshot of the questionnaire function. In this function, the candidate symptoms are shown in the list of symptoms when the patient clicks on the region exhibiting a symptom in the chart of the human body. When a patient selects a symptom, the selected region and the symptom are translated into Japanese.
  (2) Q&A function
      Fig. 8.5 (b) shows a screenshot of the Q&A function. This function provides FAQs for a hospital.
  (3) Assistance with reception procedures function

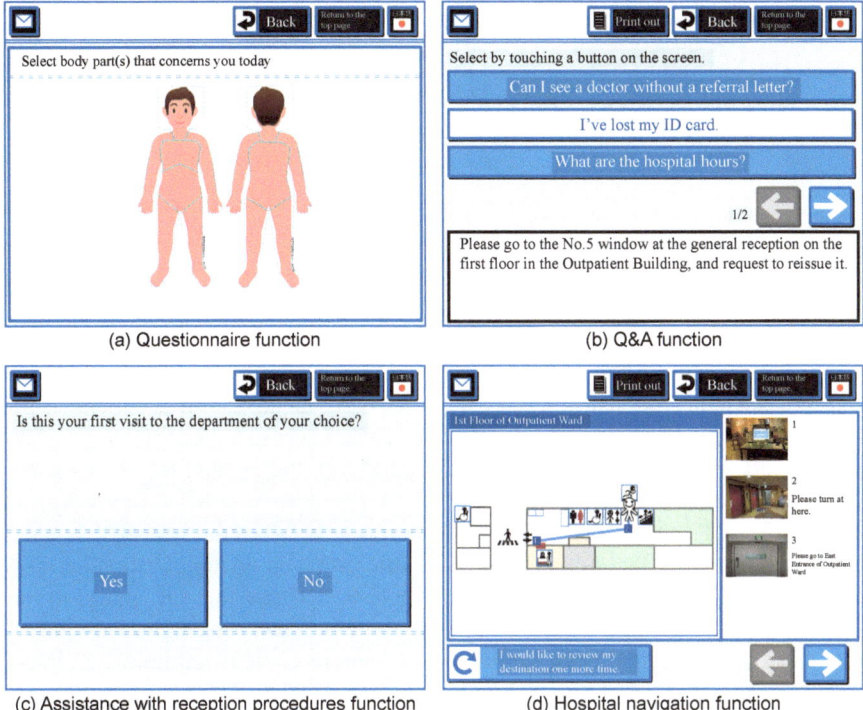

(a) Questionnaire function   (b) Q&A function

(c) Assistance with reception procedures function   (d) Hospital navigation function

Fig. 8.5 Screenshots of other functions

Fig. 8.5 (c) shows a screenshot of the assistance with reception procedures function. In this function, a patient can go through a series of Q&A on "assistance with reception procedures."

(4) Hospital navigation function

Fig. 8.5 (d) shows a screenshot of the hospital navigation function. In this function, when a patient selects the destination, the system displays the route map.

8.3.6 *Use of the System at Hospitals*

We have installed our system in the Kyoto City Hospital, Kyoto University Hospital, and Rakuwakai Otowa Hospital in Japan. Fig. 8.6 is a photograph of the system at the Kyoto University Hospital. These systems are currently in operation.

8.4 Experiments and Analysis

8.4.1 Experiment 1: Comparing the Proposed and Conventional Systems

We carried out a conversation experiment to examine the effect on communication of using different interfaces. The subjects were ten students from Wakayama University. They were trained on the use of the system before conducting the experiment.

In the experiment, we assigned the subjects the roles of hospital staff and patients. We carried out the experiments using the conventional and proposed systems. In the conventional system, a hospital staff member and a patient use a printed list of parallel texts for conversation. The subject searches for the specified parallel text from the printed list and then points out the parallel text to his interlocutor.

In Tables 8.1 and 8.2, there were few differences between the systems.

We found that different interfaces have little effect on communication because of the values of questions (1) and (2) in Table 8.3. These are with regard to the following: "Interfaces do not have to be the same because perspectives are different" and "Different interfaces are intuitive." Therefore, we determined that interfaces based on standpoint are useful when the users' standpoints are different.

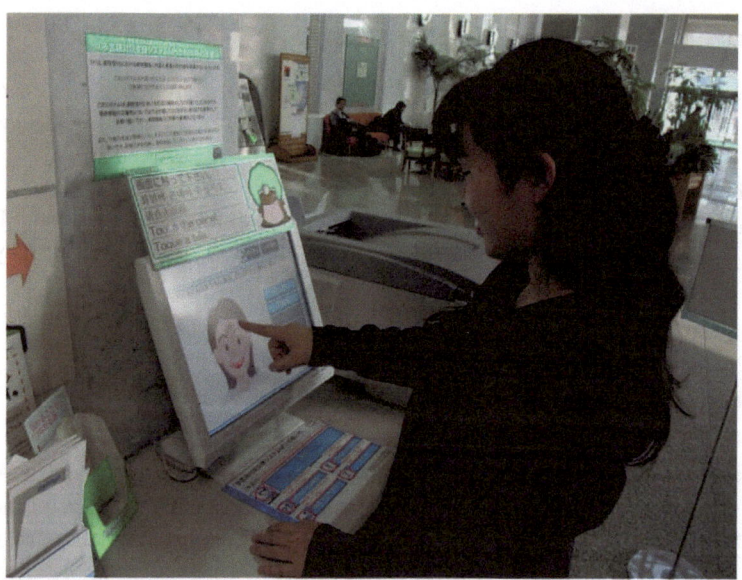

Fig. 8.6 Photograph of the system at the Kyoto University Hospital

Table. 8.1 Results of the questionnaire on the staff side of the system in experiment 1

Questions		Average
(1)	I could find the specified parallel text more easily than I could use the conventional system.	4.0
(2)	Using this system, for a given patient response time, I did not experience more stress than with the conventional system.	3.6
(3)	I could converse more smoothly by using the proposed system than by using the conventional system.	4.3

Table. 8.2 Results of the questionnaire on the patient side of the system in experiment 1

Questions		Average
(1)	I could respond to questions more easily by using the proposed system than by using the conventional system.	4.2
(2)	Using this system, for a given staff response time, I did not experience more stress than with the conventional system.	3.3
(3)	I could converse more smoothly by using the proposed system than by using the conventional system.	4.0

We did not allow the subjects to converse in Japanese. We allowed only gestures or nods based on the assumption that neither the hospital staff nor the patient could converse with each other in the same language.

Tables 8.1, 8.2, and 8.3 are the results of the questionnaire in which a five-point Likert scale was used for the evaluation—1: strongly disagree, 2: disagree, 3: neutral, 4: agree, and 5: strongly agree.

8.4.2 Experiment 2: Evaluation of the Text-to-speech Function

We performed an experiment using the text-to-speech function in order to evaluate its efficiency and determine the problems encountered in the method. The subjects of the experiment were ten students from Wakayama University.

In the experiment, the subjects played the voice data of more than three sentences using the Q&A function of M^3. After the experiment, we asked the subjects to fill out a questionnaire on the text-to-speech function.

Table 8.4 shows the results of the questionnaire. We used a five-point Likert scale for the evaluation—1: strongly disagree, 2: disagree, 3: neutral, 4: agree, and 5: strongly agree.

From the results of question (1) shown in Table 8.4, we found that the subjects were able to switch between modes with ease. From the results of question (2) shown in Table 8.4, we found that the subjects were able to play the voice data easily. In the free description of the questionnaire, subjects replied as follows: "It was easy to understand how to play the voice data because icons to play voice data were shown."

Table. 8.3 Results of the questionnaire on both systems in experiment 1

Questions		Average
(1)	I felt that the displays were inconsistent.	2.1
(2)	I think that the difference in displays influenced the communications.	1.8
(3)	I used a touch screen.	3.9
(4)	I could operate the touch panel easily.	4.0

Table. 8.4 Results of the questionnaire in experiment 2

Questions		Average
(1)	I could switch between each mode easily.	4.1
(2)	I could play the voice data easily.	3.9
(3)	I think it was easy to understand how to play the voice data.	3.7

8.5 Conclusion

The medical field has high expectations from information technology, and it requires a system that supports accurate multilingual communication. We have developed a multilingual medical reception support system called M^3, which uses accurate translation tools called parallel texts to facilitate reliable communication through conversations between hospital staff and patients. Various parallel texts are provided on the Internet by parallel text providers, a multilingual parallel text sharing system that collects and shares parallel texts, etc. The Language Grid provides various parallel texts through a multilingual parallel text sharing system and parallel text providers. The proposed system can obtain and share parallel texts using Web services via the Language Grid. When the proposed system's users find the required parallel texts unavailable, they can feed back requests for the necessary parallel texts to the multilingual parallel text sharing system. On the basis of the feedback data, the lack of parallel texts can be corrected, and the proposed system can share parallel texts as required in the medical field.

However, it is difficult for the system that uses parallel texts to provide support to illiterate people because it provides text-based support. Therefore, we developed a method to provide support to illiterate people engaging in multilingual face-to-face communication.

We performed an experiment to examine the effect of the proposed system and method. The results of the experiment are as follows.

(1)   The proposed system effectively uses parallel texts to support multilingual communication. The results of the experiment on multilingual conversa-

tion show that correct multilingual communication is possible using parallel texts.

(2) An interface based on users' perspectives can improve communication. A comparison of our system and the conventional system showed that the interface was easy to use.

(3) The subjects were able to use the text-to-speech function easily.

Acknowledgments This work was partially supported by the Strategic Information and Communications R&D Promotion Programme (SCOPE) of the Ministry of Internal Affairs and Communications of Japan.

References

Aiken M (2002) Multilingual communication in electronic meetings. ACM SIGGROUP, Bulletin 23(1): 18-19

Chirathivat J, Nakdej J, Punyabukkana P, Suchato A (2007) Internet explorer smart toolbar for the blind. The 1st International Convention on Rehabilitation Engineering & Assistive Technology: in conjunction with 1st Tan Tock Seng Hospital Neurorehabilitation Meeting: 195-200

Chung JW, Kern R, Lieberman H (2005) Topic spotting common sense translation assistant. CHI '05 extended abstracts on Human factors in computing systems: 1280-1283

ElAarag H, Schindler L (2006) A speech recognition and synthesis tool. The 44th Annual Southeast Regional Conference: 45-49

Ikeda T, Ando S, Satoh K, Okumura A, Watanabe T (2002) Automatic interpretation system integrating free-style sentence translation and parallel text based translation. The Workshop on Speech-to-Speech Translation: Algorithms and Systems, vol.7: 85-92

Imoto K, Sasajima M, Shimomori T, Yamanaka N, Makoto Y, Yasyyuki M (2006) A multi modal supporting tool for multi lingual communication by inducing partner's reply. The 11th International Conference on Intelligent User Interfaces (IUI '06): 330-332

Inaba R (2007) Usability of multilingual communication tools. Lecture Notes in Computer Science 4560, Springer: 91-97

Ishida T (2006) Language grid: an infrastructure for intercultural collaboration. 2006 IEEE/IPSJ Symposium on Applications and the Internet (SAINT-06): 96-100

Leporini B, Andronico P, Buzzi M (2003) Designing search engine user interfaces for the visually impaired. ACM SIGCAPH Computers and the Physically Handicapped 76: 17-18

Rayner M, Bouillon P, von Dalsem V, Isahara H, Kanzaki K, Hockey BA (2003) A limited-domain English to Japanese medical speech translator built using REGULUS 2. The 41st Annual Meeting on Association for Computational Linguistics, vol.2 (ACL '03): 137-140

Sporka AJ, Němec V, Slavík P (2005) Tangible newspaper for the visually impaired users. CHI'05 extended abstracts on Human factors in computing systems: 1809-1812

Tung LL, Quaddus MA (2002) Cultural differences explaining the differences in results in GSS: implications for the next decade. Decision Support Systems 33(2): 177-199

Wang B, Cheng X, Bai S (2002) Example-based phrase translation in Chinese-English CLIR. The 25th Annual International ACM SIGIR Conference on Research and Development in Information Retrieval: 435-436

Yoshino T, Fujii K, Shigenobu T (2008) Availability of web information for intercultural communication. 10th Pacific Rim International Conference on Artificial Intelligence (PRICAI 2008): 923-932

Yoshino T, Fukushima T, Miyabe M, Shigeno A (2009a) A web-based multilingual parallel corpus collection system for the medical field. The 2009 ACM International Workshop on Intercultural Collaboration (IWIC'09): 321-324

Yoshino T, Fukushima T, Nisimura R (2009b) A web-based multilingual utterance collection system for the medical field. 5th International Conference on Web Information Systems and Technologies (WEBIST 2009): 370-375

Chapter 9
Exploring Cultural Differences in Pictogram Interpretations

Heeryon Cho[1] and Toru Ishida[2]

1 Department of Interaction Science, Sungkyunkwan University, Seoul 110-745, Korea, e-mail: heeryon@skku.edu, heeryon@gmail.com

2 Department of Social Informatics, Kyoto University, Yoshida-Honmachi, Kyoto 606-8501, Japan, e-mail: ishida@i.kyoto-u.ac.jp

Abstract Pictogram communication is successful when participants at both ends of the communication channel share a common pictogram interpretation. Not all pictograms carry a universal interpretation, however; the issue of ambiguous pictogram interpretation must be addressed to assist pictogram communication. To unveil the ambiguity possible in pictogram interpretation, we conduct a human subject experiment to identify culture-specific criteria employed by humans by detecting cultural differences in pictogram interpretations. Based on the findings, we propose a *categorical semantic relevance measure* which calculates how relevant a pictogram is to a given interpretation in terms of a given pictogram category. The proposed measure is applied to categorized pictogram interpretations to enhance pictogram retrieval performance. The WordNet, the ChaSen, and the EDR Electronic Dictionary registered to the Language Grid are utilized to merge synonymous pictogram interpretations and to categorize pictogram interpretations into super-concept categories. We show how the Language Grid can assist the cross-cultural research process.

9.1 Introduction

In recent years, advances in information communication technology have enabled people to easily create, publish, and share various images such as photographs, movies, and illustrations on the World Wide Web. Meanwhile, tag-based image management applications such as Flickr and YouTube have come into wide use, allowing users to add tags, a prevalent form of metadata, which are later incorporated into the image search process, to enhance image retrieval (Marlow et al. 2006). Among the various images shared by people, we focus on *pictograms* or pictorial symbols that carry semantic interpretations. An example of well-known pictograms are road signs, but in this paper, we look at a special kind of pictogram used in computer-mediated intercultural communication, in particular, those used in a children's email system (Takasaki 2007).

Pictograms have clear pictorial similarities with some object (Marcus 2003), and a person who can recognize the object depicted in the pictogram can interpret the meaning associated with the object. Pictorial symbols, however, are not universally interpretable. For instance, the cow is a source of nourishment to westerners who drink milk and eat its meat, but it is an object of veneration to many people in India; hence, a picture of a cow could be interpreted quite differently by Protestants and Hindus (Kolers 1969). The pictograms we handle also exhibit such ambiguity in interpretation; they are designed by Japanese college art students who are non-experts in pictogram design, and no strict design process was applied to ensure a universal interpretation. Therefore, using these pictograms in communication may lead to misunderstanding between the communicating parties.

Given such ambiguous pictograms, our goal is (1) to analyze the ambiguities in pictogram interpretation and (2) to propose a way to assist pictogram selection so that communicating parties can achieve better pictogram communication. Our research is motivated by the overarching goal of enabling children from different cultures to communicate with each by using just pictograms; this is not the case when natural language is involved since at least one child (who is monolingual as is often the case) would have to communicate using a second language. We use various language resources such as thesauri, morphological analyzers, and concept dictionaries registered to the Language Grid to process cross-cultural pictogram interpretations.

To achieve our first goal, we conduct a human subject experiment to identify cultural differences in pictogram interpretations. We employ thirty pictograms containing U.S. and Japanese pictogram interpretations as stimuli, and use questionnaires and interviews to ask U.S. and Japanese subjects to identify cultural differences in pictogram interpretations. Synonymous English pictogram interpretations are merged using the WordNet (Fellbaum 1998), an English thesaurus, and variants in Japanese notations are integrated using the ChaSen (Matsumoto et al. 1997), a Japanese morphological analyzer; both language resources are registered with the Language Grid. As a result of the human subject experiment, five criteria for detecting cultural difference in cross-cultural pictogram interpretations are identified.

To achieve our second goal, we propose a *categorical semantic relevance measure*, which calculates how relevant a pictogram is to a given interpretation, using categorized pictogram interpretations. Our approach first categorizes the pictogram interpretations into five pictogram categories and then calculates the *semantic relevance* of a word query (or an interpretation) and a set of pictogram interpretations given to a pictogram to rank relevant pictograms. Five first-level classifications in the EDR Electronic Dictionary (Yokoi 1995) registered to the Language Grid are taken as the five pictogram categories. We show that the categorized approach performs better than the uncategorized approach in pictogram retrieval tasks.

To summarize, we (1) identify five human cultural difference criteria in cross-cultural pictogram interpretations and (2) propose a *categorical semantic relevance measure* which can be incorporated into pictogram retrieval to assist pictogram selection. In the following section, the experimental setup and the results of the human cultural difference detection experiment are described. Section 9.3 outlines the semantic relevance measure, the pictogram categorization process, and the performance evaluation of the proposed measure. Section 9.4 further discusses the evaluation result, and Section 9.5 lists related works. Finally, Section 9.6 concludes this paper.

9.2 Human Cultural Difference Detection Criteria

Detecting cultural differences requires an understanding of culture. More than a hundred definitions of culture exist (Kroeber and Kluckhohn 1952), but Geertz (1973) defines culture as "a historically transmitted pattern of meanings embodied in symbols." If culture can be viewed as 'a pattern of meanings,' it may also be viewed as 'a pattern of interpretation' or 'a pattern of semantics'; therefore, we view the detecting of cultural differences as detecting 'semantic' differences.

Existing computational methods for calculating semantic differences (or dissimilarities) in two documents make use of, for example, the vector space model (Manning and Schütze 1999) and hierarchical semantic nets (Rada et al. 1989). Applying such semantic dissimilarity calculations to the detection of cultural differences in pictogram interpretations could be easily envisaged, but whether existing computational methods are sufficient to detect cultural differences needs to be carefully studied. For this reason, we conduct a human subject experiment to understand how humans detect cultural differences in pictogram interpretations.

9.2.1 Experimental Setup for Human Subject Experiment

A pictogram web survey was conducted in the U.S. and Japan to collect cross-cultural pictogram interpretations with possible cultural differences. The two countries were selected for their cultural distinctness (Hall 1976, Hofstede and Hofstede 2005). A total of 120 pictograms were surveyed for U.S.-Japan pictogram interpretations, and 30 out of 120 cross-cultural pictogram interpretations were selected as stimuli for the human cultural difference detection experiment. Cho et al. (2009) gives a detailed description of the stimuli selection process.

Table 9.1 shows an example of the U.S.-Japan pictogram interpretations collected from the web survey. As shown in the table, a pictogram can have various interpretations such as talking and laughing, which describe some kind of action, or friends and happy group, which describe some kind of people. We see that 20% of the U.S. respondents interpret the pictogram as "talking, conversation" whereas 42% of the Japanese respondents interpret it as "to lie, liar, lie." A positive/negative perceptional difference in the U.S.-Japanese respondents is evident in the pictogram interpretations.

Table 9.1 Example of U.S.-Japan pictogram interpretations

U.S. Interpretation			Japanese Interpretation	
talking, conversation	20%		to lie, liar, lie	42%
friends	19%		double-dealing	20%
party	17%		deceive	12%
joking	11%		scheme	8%
gossip	9%		dual personality	6%
laughing	9%		boast, big talk	6%
happy group	8%		backbiting	6%
happy	7%		-	-

Six human subjects participated in a two-part cultural difference detection experiment which consisted of (1) answering a questionnaire and (2) responding to a post-questionnaire interview. Three subjects were U.S. nationality English teachers living in Japan with fair understanding of Japanese; the remaining three subjects were Japanese graduate students with graduate-school level English knowledge. All six subjects were paid for their participation.

During the questionnaire-answering part of the experiment, the subjects were instructed to first mark the two countries' interpretations for similar interpretations, and then select one of the four Venn diagrams which depicted the relationship between the two countries' pictogram interpretations. The relationships were (1) a disjoint relation, (2) an intersecting relation, (3) a subset relation where U.S. interpretations subsume Japanese interpretations, and (4) a subset relation where Japanese interpretations subsume U.S. interpretations.

Based on the two countries' pictogram interpretations and their percentages, similar interpretations, and the relationship between the two countries' interpretations, each human subject assessed the level of cultural difference in 30 U.S.-Japan pictogram interpretations. A seven-point Likert scale ("Strong cultural difference exists = 7" to "Absolutely no cultural difference = 1") was used to determine the degree of cultural difference in pictogram interpretations.

After the questionnaire was answered, each subject was interviewed for one hour for their reasons behind the cultural difference assessment; they were asked to elucidate why they thought certain pictograms had cultural differences while others didn't.

Table 9.2 lists the top three interpretations for each of the 30 U.S.-Japan pictogram interpretations used in the human subject experiment. The bold-lettered pictograms (12 out of 30 pictograms: P01, P02, P10, P11, P12, P13, P14, P15, P16, P21, P28, and P30) were judged by the human subjects as having cultural differences in pictogram interpretations.

Table 9.2 Top 3 U.S.-Japan pictogram interpretations and percentages (continues)

U.S.	%	Japan	%
P01 (AVG: 6.83, RANK: 2)			
exercise	46	okay	44
stretch	14	circle	21
jump rope	11	correct answer	14
P02 (AVG: 6.17, RANK: 5)			
mad	44	no-no	59
angry	39	penalty	19
no	6	no	5
P03 (AVG: 4.00, RANK: 18)			
woman	37	woman	78
man	21	mom	9
mom	17	adult female	8
P04 (AVG: 4.00, RANK: 19)			
man	46	man	74
dad	17	adult man	12
woman	12	dad	10
P05 (AVG: 4.00, RANK: 20)			
up	30	there	36
there	30	that	31
point	13	over there	14
P06 (AVG: 3.50, RANK: 24)			
down	34	here	41
here	28	this	30
near	12	near	8
P07 (AVG: 4.17, RANK: 17)			
late	31	future	36
time	24	time passes	17
10 minutes	10	after 10 minutes	16
P08 (AVG: 4.67, RANK: 14)			
on time	31	now	46
time	22	time	19
now	10	time now	9
P09 (AVG: 4.67, RANK 15)			
early	34	past	42
10 minutes ago	13	10 minutes ago	21
before	11	time turned back	20
P10 (AVG: 5.50, RANK: 10)			
scared	29	cold	64
worried	17	scared	27
cold	16	shiver	7
P11 (AVG: 6.00, RANK: 7)			
sly	26	sneer	22
sneaky	25	*hehehe* (laugh)	20
smile	13	doubt	20
P12 (AVG: 6.33, RANK: 3)			
mischievous	20	cool	59
happy	16	handsome	22
smart	14	boast	12

U.S.	%	Japan	%
P13 (AVG: 5.83, RANK: 8)			
happy	43	cute	76
pretty	21	beautiful woman	11
nice	10	dazzle	5
P14 (AVG: 6.00, RANK: 6)			
happy	24	cute	47
cute	21	beautiful woman	24
in love	13	dazzle	7
P15 (AVG: 5.67, RANK: 9)			
whistling	43	nonchalant	38
no	13	humph	19
blow	8	pout	14
P16 (AVG: 5.17, RANK 11)			
thinking	24	I, me	61
face	16	cheek	13
me	14	face	9
P17 (AVG: 3.67, RANK: 23)			
cake	29	cake shop	93
pie	22	cake	7
bakery	18		
P18 (AVG: 3.83, RANK: 21)			
food	43	supermarket	87
grocery store	31	grocery store	7
food groups	8	food	4
P19 (AVG: 3.50, RANK: 25)			
sour	53	sour	48
full	14	delicious	36
happy	12	full stomach	6
P20 (AVG: 3.67, RANK: 22)			
confused	73	think	48
thinking	8	question	17
question	7	why?	13
P21 (AVG: 7.00, RANK: 1)			
talking	20	lie	42
friends	19	double-dealing	20
party	17	deceive	12
P22 (AVG: 4.67, RANK: 13)			
talking	33	speak	23
praying	21	announcement	17
thinking	16	thank you	15
P23 (AVG: 4.50, RANK: 16)			
winner	49	athletic event	45
win	23	first place	28
event	10	victory	13
P24 (AVG: 2.33, RANK: 30)			
chewing	42	delicious	67
happy	14	eat	10
yummy	13	fun	9

Table 9.2 Top 3 U.S.-Japan pictogram interpretations and percentages

U.S.	%	Japan	%		U.S.	%	Japan	%
P25 (AVG: 3.17, RANK: 28)					P28 (AVG: 6.17, RANK: 4)			
happy	31	delicious	24		**Eiffel Tower**	**48**	**Tokyo Tower**	**47**
chewing	18	eat	21		**Paris**	**24**	**tower**	**35**
yummy	17	so-so	16		**tower**	**17**	**Eiffel Tower**	**8**
P26 (AVG: 2.83, RANK: 29)					P29 (AVG: 3.33, RANK: 27)			
TV	18	information	35		carnival	31	amusement park	69
media	15	media	22		amusement park	20	amusement	19
radio	15	radio	15		games	15	entertainment	6
P27 (AVG: 3.50, RANK: 26)					P30 (AVG: 5.00, RANK: 12)			
hobbies	19	hobby	87		**world**	**45**	**world**	**26**
fishing	16	play	5		**Paris**	**24**	**earth**	**24**
activities	15	fishing	3		**travel**	**17**	**electric wave**	**10**

9.2.2 Result of the Questionnaire

Table 9.3 shows the top 12 average cultural difference assessment values given by the six human subjects: columns US1, US2, and US3 indicate the cultural difference assessment values given by the U.S. subjects; columns JP1, JP2, and JP3 indicate the assessment values given by the Japanese subjects. The numerical value "7" indicates "Strong cultural difference exists" and "1" indicates "Absolutely no cultural difference." The values are sorted in descending order of the average assessment value so that the pictograms having a greater cultural difference lie at the top.

Table 9.3 Cultural difference assessments of the top 12 culturally different interpretations

PICTOGRAM	US1	US2	US3	JP1	JP2	JP3	AVG	SD
P21	7	7	7	7	7	7	7.00	0.00
P01	7	7	7	7	7	6	6.83	0.37
P12	6	7	7	6	5	7	6.33	0.75
P28	6	6	6	6	6	7	6.17	0.37
P02	6	6	7	6	7	5	6.17	0.69
P14	6	6	6	6	5	7	6.00	0.58
P11	6	7	3	6	7	7	6.00	1.41
P13	6	7	7	5	3	7	5.83	1.46
P15	5	7	7	5	4	6	5.67	1.11
P10	5	7	7	6	2	6	5.50	1.71
P16	5	6	5	6	3	6	5.17	1.07
P30	5	5	5	5	4	6	5.00	0.58

Note: US1-US3 indicate the U.S. subjects; JP1-JP3 indicate the Japanese subjects; 7 = Strong cultural difference exists, 6 = Cultural difference exists, 5 = Cultural difference exists somewhat, 4 = Undecided, 3 = Rather no cultural difference, 2 = No cultural difference, and 1 = Absolutely no cultural difference.

We interpreted average cultural difference assessment values of 5.0 or greater (AVG ≥ 5.0) to mean some kind of cultural difference exists; this is because the numerical value "5" corresponds to "Cultural difference exists somewhat" in the seven-point Likert scale. A total of 6 pictograms (P21, P01, P12, P28, P02, and P14) were unanimously assessed by the six subjects to have some kind of cultural difference. P21 had the highest average cultural difference value of 7.0.

Fig. 9.1 Thirty pictograms used as stimuli in the questionnaire

The images of the 30 pictograms used as stimuli in the questionnaire are shown in Fig. 9.1. The pictograms surrounded by bold solid lines were judged by the human subjects to have cultural differences in U.S.-Japan pictogram interpretations.

9.2.3 Result of the Post-Questionnaire Interview

Face-to-face interviews were conducted with the six subjects to elucidate the reasons behind their cultural difference assessments. The human subjects considered the following aspects of the U.S.-Japan pictogram interpretations when assessing cultural differences:

- Similar/dissimilar interpretations in the two countries
- Percentage or ranking of the interpretations
- Conformity/variance of semantics within one country's interpretations
- Presence of proper nouns (e.g., country names)
- Positive/negative connotation in the interpretations

With regard to the top 12 pictograms with cultural differences (Table 9.3), the subjects assessed them to have cultural differences for the following reasons:

- Few similar interpretations exist between the two countries. (All pictograms except P28)
- Quite a few similar interpretations exist, but the percentages of those interpretations are different between the two countries. (P01, P02, P10, P11, P12, P13, P14, P15, and P16)
- Conformity of semantics is observed in one country's interpretations while variance is observed in the other's interpretations. (P10, P12, and P14)
- Proper nouns such as the name of a country or a city exist in the interpretations. (P28 and P30)
- Negative connotation in the interpretations is observed in one country while positive connotation is observed in the other. (P11, P12, P15, and P21)

9.3 Assisting Pictogram Selection Using Semantic Relevance

The criteria the human subjects employed in assessing the cultural differences in pictogram interpretations include not only the semantic similarity/dissimilarity of the two countries' interpretations, but also the percentage of the similar interpretations. This suggests that we need to consider both the semantic similarity and the percentage of the pictogram interpretations when devising a way to assist pictogram selection. Note that the diversity of the interpretation is observed both *across the two countries* and *within one country*. For example, the U.S. interpretations in Table 9.1 include actions (talking, joking, laughing), state of mind (happy), person(s) (friends, happy group), and event (party). To tackle the semantic ambiguity in pictogram interpretation, we simplify our problem by focusing on the pictogram interpretation of one country (U.S.) from here on.

9.3.1 Semantic Relevance Measure

We assume that pictograms each have a list of interpretation words and ratios as per Table 9.1. Each unique interpretation word has a ratio or a probability, and it indicates how much support people give to that interpretation. For example, in the case of Table 9.1, it can be said that more people support talking (20%) as the interpretation of the given pictogram than laughing (9%). The higher the probability is of a specific interpretation word in a pictogram, the more that pictogram is accepted by people as having that interpretation. We define a *semantic relevance measure* of a pictogram to be a measure of relevancy between a word query and a set of interpretation words in a pictogram.

Let w_1, w_2, ... , w_n be the interpretation words of pictogram e. Let the probability of each interpretation word in a pictogram be $P(w_1|e)$, ... , $P(w_n|e)$. For example, the probability of the interpretation word talking for the Table 9.1 pictogram can be calculated as $P(talking|Pictogram_{Table9.1}) = 0.2$. Thus the simplest expression that assesses the relevancy of a pictogram e in relation to a word query w_i can be defined as follows:

$$P(w_i|e) \tag{9.1}$$

This probability, however, does not take into account the similarity of interpretation words. For instance, when "talking" is given as the query, pictograms having similar interpretation words like speaking or communicating, but not talking, fail to be measured as relevant since only the probability is considered. To resolve this issue, we need to define some kind of similarity, or *similarity*(w_i, w_j), between interpretation words. Using the similarity, we can define the *semantic relevance measure* or $SR(w_i, e)$ as follows:

$$SR(w_i, e) = \sum_j P(w_j|e) similarity(w_i, w_j) \tag{9.2}$$

There are several similarity measures. We draw upon the definition of similarity given by Lin (1998) which states that the similarity between A and B is measured by the ratio between the information needed to state the commonality of A and B and the information needed to fully describe what A and B are. Here, we calculate the similarity of w_i and w_j by counting how many pictograms contain certain interpretation words. When there is a pictogram set E_i having an interpretation word w_i, the similarity between interpretation words w_i and w_j can be defined as follows:

$$similarity(w_i, w_j) = |E_i \cap E_j| / |E_i \cup E_j| \tag{9.3}$$

$|E_i \cap E_j|$ is the number of pictograms having both w_i and w_j as interpretation words. $|E_i \cup E_j|$ is the number of pictograms having either w_i or w_j as an interpretation word. Based on Equation (9.2) and Equation (9.3), the *semantic relevance* or the measure of relevancy to return pictogram e when word w_i is given as a query can be calculated as follows:

$$SR(w_i, e) = \sum_j P(w_j|e) |E_i \cap E_j| / |E_i \cup E_j| \tag{9.4}$$

The calculated semantic relevance values fall between one and zero, which denotes that either a pictogram is completely relevant to the interpretation (or a word query) or completely irrelevant. Using the semantic relevance values, pictograms can be ranked from very relevant (value close to 1.0) to not at all relevant (value close to 0). As the value nears zero, pictograms become less relevant; hence, a cut-off point is needed to discard the less relevant pictograms. Setting an ideal cut-off point that satisfies all word query and pictogram interpretations is difficult, since all words contained in the pictogram, regardless of how much or little each interpretation word is related to the query, influence the semantic relevance calculation. One way to restrict the diversity of pictogram interpretations is to select a set of interpretation words more related to the query, and use those selected words in the semantic relevance calculation to reduce the effect of less-related interpretation words. With this idea, we propose a semantic relevance calculation on *categorized* interpretations; we perform a priori categorization of the interpretation words.

9.3.2 Categorizing the Pictogram Interpretations

To categorize the diverse pictogram interpretations containing both similar and dissimilar words, we classified them into related perspectives by utilizing the Headconcept Dictionary and Concept Classification Dictionary in the Concept Dictionary of the EDR Electronic Dictionary (Yokoi 1995) which is registered with the Language Grid. The SUMO ontology (Niles and Pease 2001) was another candidate for categorizing pictogram interpretations, but we chose EDR for three reasons: (1) we needed to handle both Japanese and English pictogram interpretations, and EDR provided both the English and Japanese headconcepts; (2) the first level classes located directly below the SUMO ontology's Entity Class were Abstract Class and Physical Class, but these classes were more abstract than the first level classifications defined in EDR; (3) EDR was specifically developed for natural language processing, so it was more appropriate to our research purpose which involved pictogram communication.

To categorize the pictogram interpretations, we defined *five pictogram categories* by appropriating the five first level classifications in the Concept Dictionary of the EDR. The five first level classifications were:

(1) human or subject whose behavior (actions) resembles that of a human
(2) {matter} an affair
(3) event/occurrence
(4) location/locale/place
(5) time

We designated the five pictogram categories as (1) AGENT, (2) MATTER, (3) EVENT, (4) LOCATION, and (5) TIME; each mapped to the aforementioned first level classifications, respectively. Using the five pictogram categories, each pictogram interpretation word was categorized into appropriate pictogram categories through the following steps: first, concept identifier(s) of the interpretation word was obtained by matching the interpretation word string to the English headconcept string in the Headconcept Dictionary; then, the first level classification(s) of the concept identifier was obtained by climbing up the super-sub relations defined in the Concept Classification Dictionary. Cho et al. (2008) gives more details on the a priori categorization of pictogram interpretation words.

Applying the semantic relevance calculation to categorized interpretations will return five *categorical semantic relevance values* for each pictogram. We take the highest categorical value and compare it with the cut-off point to determine whether the pictogram is relevant or not. Once the relevant pictograms are selected, the selected pictograms are then sorted according to the semantic relevance value of the query's major category. For example, if the query is "park," then the relevant pictograms are first selected using the highest categorical semantic relevance value of each pictogram, and once the relevant pictograms are selected, the pictograms are ranked according to the categorical semantic relevance value of the query's major category, which in this case is the LOCATION category. The resulting list of pictograms is a ranked list of pictograms starting with the most relevant pictogram at the top.

9.3.3 Pictogram Retrieval Performance Evaluation

The performance of three pictogram retrieval approaches, (1) a string match approach, (2) a not-categorized semantic relevance approach, and (3) a categorized semantic relevance approach were evaluated. The baseline approach for comparison was a simple string match of the query word to the pictogram interpretation words with probabilities greater than the cut-off point. This is the same as selecting pictograms with $P(w_j|e) > cut\text{-}off\ point$ where w_j equals the query.

Five human judges constructed a relevant pictogram set which consisted of 188 pictogram interpretation words and a ranked list of relevant pictograms for each word. The judges were all undergraduate students and they were paid for their tasks. The relevant pictogram set was constructed through the following steps: first, a questionnaire containing 188 pictogram interpretation words with candidate pictograms, each listing all interpretation words, was given to the five human judges, and for each interpretation word, the human judges were asked to (1) judge whether each candidate pictogram could be interpreted as the given word (i.e., judged either as relevant or not relevant), and (2) if judged as relevant, write down the ranking among the relevant pictograms; then the judges' assessment data were averaged and variances were calculated to select and rank relevant pictograms for each interpretation word. If three or more judges decided that the pictogram was relevant, the pictogram was selected as relevant. Otherwise, the pictogram was discarded. Average rankings among the selected pictograms were calculated based on the rankings given by the human judges; if average rankings were the same among two or more pictograms, variances were calculated to give higher ranking to the pictogram with lower variance. As a result, a ranked relevant pictogram set for 188 words was created and used in the evaluation.

Table 9.4 Mean precision and recall of the three pictogram retrieval approaches

Cut-Off	Precision			Recall		
	SR-CAT	SR-NOCAT	STR-MATCH	SR-CAT	SR-NOCAT	STR-MATCH
0.10	0.25810	0.34883	0.98056	1.00000	0.99867	0.22615
0.15	0.36467	0.46397	0.99275	0.99823	0.97442	0.17766
0.20	0.46512	0.57565	1.00000	0.98980	0.94174	0.14752
0.25	0.57928	0.67917	1.00000	0.95713	0.86184	0.08901
0.30	0.66786	0.73870	1.00000	0.93784	0.72376	0.07704
0.35	0.70442	0.79100	1.00000	0.86527	0.59734	0.06640
0.40	0.74880	0.84497	1.00000	0.82768	0.47810	0.05044
0.45	0.76979	0.87760	1.00000	0.72214	0.35887	0.03183
0.50	0.81036	0.89655	1.00000	0.60657	0.20222	0.02739

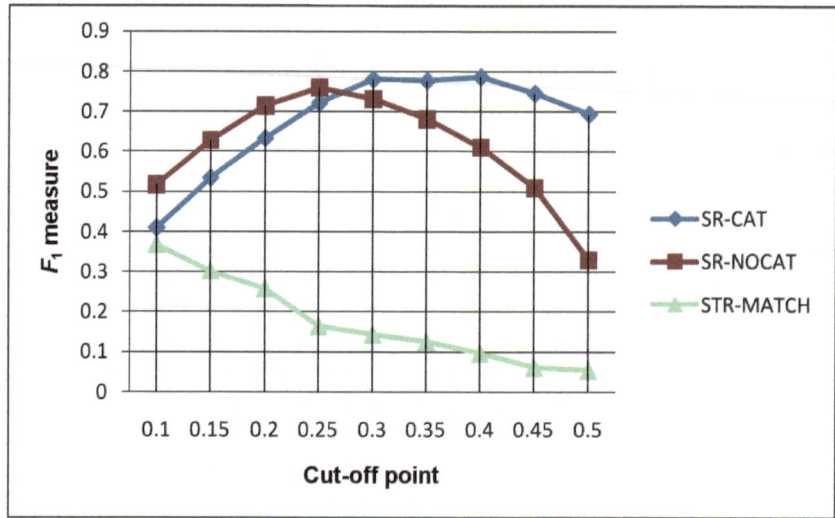

Fig. 9.2 F_1-measure comparison of the three pictogram retrieval approaches

The mean precision, mean recall, and F_1-measure (van Rijsbergen 1979) of 188 retrieval tasks using the three pictogram retrieval approaches were calculated using nine different cut-off points from 0.1 to 0.5 with 0.05 intervals. Table 9.4 shows the mean precision and recall values of the three approaches at different cut-off points. Fig. 9.2 shows the F_1-measure values: the SR-CAT indicates the categorized semantic relevance approach; the SR-NOCAT indicates the not-categorized semantic relevance approach; the STR-MATCH indicates the baseline string match approach. Note that the mean precision values were calculated using the valid tasks that returned at least one result. For example, in the case of 0.5 for cut-off point, only 9 retrieval tasks returned at least one pictogram for the STR-MATCH approach; hence, the mean precision of the STR-MATCH approach was calculated using only those 9 tasks. We see that the retrieval performance is improved by applying semantic relevance and word categorization (SR-NOCAT, SR-CAT).

9.4 Discussion

We see in Fig. 9.2 that a broader cut-off range, roughly 0.25 to 0.5, is obtained by the categorized approach for F_1-measure values greater than 0.7 (SR-CAT); in contrast, the not-categorized approach has a steeper curve with a narrower cut-off range roughly between 0.2 and 0.33 (SR-NOCAT). The categorized approach returns a wider range of stable F_1-measure values because the interpretation words are grouped into related perspectives prior to the calculation of the semantic relevance value. This enables targeted semantic relevance calculation on the words that are more related to each other. Consequently, the recall is improved without damaging precision. Table 9.4 confirms this; the recall range of SR-CAT is tighter with the values between approximately 0.6 and 1.0 whereas SR-NOCAT is broader with the recall values between approximately 0.2 and 1.0. Meanwhile, the precision values fall between approximately 0.25 and 0.8 for SR-CAT and 0.35 and 0.9 for SR-NOCAT.

Our method can be applied to various image management applications such as clipart search systems or online photo-sharing systems as long as the images are labelled with *descriptive* tags, and those tags have some form of numeric value that expresses how much support the tag receives from the users. With regard to the gathering of the pictogram interpretations, the wide spread usage of tag-based applications enables us to gather human interpretations in the form of tags. Moreover, if user profile and IP address information can be utilized, we can realistically obtain cross-cultural interpretation data (or metadata).

9.5 Related Work

Existing pictogram communication systems such as Minspeak (Baker 1982) and IconText (Beardon 1995) use a fixed set of icons and system-defined sentence generation procedures to create pictogram messages. By contrast, the pictogram email system (Takasaki 2007) we looked at in this paper uses an open set of pictograms where new pictograms are continually added to an existing set of pictograms; the system provides a two-dimensional canvas interface where a user can freely place one or more pictograms onto the canvas to create pictogram messages. Hence, no system-defined pictogram sentence generation procedure is imposed on the user. While the pictogram sentence creation strategy of the existing systems (Baker 1982, Beardon 1995) utilizes a fixed set of pictograms and predefined sentence generation procedures to generate clearly defined pictogram sentences, our system (Takasaki 2007) uses an unfixed set of pictograms as candidates for conveying intended meaning, so the selection of the most relevant pictogram follows the sentence creation strategy. Therefore, we focused on the pictogram selection stage, and proposed a way of using the categorized semantic relevance measure to assist the process of pictogram selection.

Related research on tags (which could be viewed as a kind of interpretation given by the user) unifies browsing by tags and visual features for intuitive exploration of image databases (Aurnhammer et al. 2006) or helps users browse large-scale annotations in a semantic, hierarchical, and efficient way (Li et al. 2007). Aurnhammer et al. (2006) augments navigation within an image database by combining image tags with visual features of the images while Li et al. (2007) utilizes tags and URLs to browse similar documents or browse documents in a top-down manner; in both cases, the aim is to improve users' browsing experience through tags. By contrast, we use only the tags (or the interpretation word) and the ratio (or the probability) of the tags to assist users with the selection of more relevant pictograms.

9.6 Conclusion

With the goal of assisting intercultural pictogram communication, we looked at the special kind of pictograms used in a children's email system. To tackle the ambiguity inherent in pictogram interpretations, we conducted a human subject experiment to understand how humans detect cultural differences in pictogram interpretations. We utilized the WordNet (an English thesaurus) and the ChaSen (a Japanese morphological analyzer), which are registered with the Language Grid, to process the English and Japanese pictogram interpretations. Through a two-part study consisting of answering a questionnaire and responding to a post-questionnaire interview, we identified five criteria for the detection of cultural differences. Of these criteria, the human subjects mainly emphasized the similarity/dissimilarity and the agreement percentage of the pictogram interpretations.

Based on the findings of our human experiment, we devised a method that selects and ranks relevant pictograms which are more likely to be interpreted as intended; we proposed the *categorical semantic relevance measure*, which calculates how relevant a pictogram is to a given interpretation in terms of a pictogram category. The five first-level classifications in the EDR Electronic Dictionary registered with the Language Grid were taken as the five pictogram categories to categorize the multifarious pictogram interpretations. The proposed measure defines the relevance probability and the similarity measurement of the categorized pictogram interpretations. We evaluated our measure through multiple pictogram retrieval tasks, and confirmed that the proposed measure improves pictogram retrieval performance.

During our cross-cultural research process, we were able to facilitate the processing of the English and Japanese pictogram interpretations by utilizing the thesauri, morphological analyzers, and concept dictionaries registered with the Language Grid. We believe that many cross-cultural studies that require multilingual word-processing can likewise benefit from the various language resources registered to the Language Grid.

Acknowledgments   We thank the following people for their valuable contributions to this research: Yumiko Mori, Toshiyuki Takasaki, Takekazu Hanada (all at the NPO Pangaea), Dr. Naomi Yamashita (NTT Communication Science Laboratories), Prof. Satoshi Oyama (Hokkaido University), Prof. Tomoko Koda (Osaka Institute of Technology), and Dr. Rieko Inaba (Kyoto University). This research was done while the first author was a member of the Ishida & Matsubara Laboratory at Kyoto University, and was supported by the Japanese Government (Monbukagakusho) Scholarship program funded by the Ministry of Education, Culture, Sports, Science and Technology (MEXT) of Japan.

References

Aurnhammer M, Hanappe P, Steels L (2006) Augmenting navigation for collaborative tagging with emergent semantics. 5th International Semantic Web Conference, Lecture Notes in Computer Science 4273, Springer: 58–71

Baker BR (1982) Minspeak, a semantic compaction system that makes self-expression easier for communicatively disabled individuals. Byte 7(9): 186–202

Beardon C (1995) Discourse structures in iconic communication. Artificial Intelligence Review 9(2-3): 189-203

Cho H., Ishida T, Oyama S, Inaba R., Takasaki T (2008) Assisting pictogram selection with categorized semantics. IEICE Transactions on Information and Systems E91-D (11): 2638-2646

Cho H, Ishida T, Yamashita N, Koda T, Takasaki T (2009) Human detection of cultural differences in pictogram interpretations. 2009 Int'l Workshop on Intercultural Collaboration: 165–174

Fellbaum C (1998) Wordnet: an electronic lexical database. MIT Press, Cambridge

Geertz C (1973) The interpretation of cultures. Basic Books, New York,

Hall E (1976) Beyond culture. Doubleday & Company, New York

Hofstede G, Hofstede GJ (2005) Cultures and organizations: software of the mind. McGraw-Hill, New York

Kolers P (1969) Some formal characteristics of pictograms. American Scientist 57(3): 348-363

Kroeber AL, Kluckhohn C (1952) Culture: a critical review of concepts and definitions. Harvard University Peabody Museum of American Archaeology and Ethnology Papers 47: 181

Li R, Bao S, Fei B, Su Z, Yu Y (2007) Towards effective browsing of large scale social annotations. 16th Internationl World Wide Web Conference: 943-952

Lin D (1998) An information-theoretic definition of similarity. 15th International Conference on Machine Learning: 296-304

Manning CD, Schütze H (1999) Foundations of statistical natural language processing. MIT Press, Cambridge

Marcus A (2003) Icons, symbols, and signs: visible languages to facilitate communication. Interactions 10(3): 37–43

Marlow C, Naaman M, Boyd D, Davis M (2006) HT06, tagging paper, taxonomy, Flickr, academic article, to read. 17th Conference on Hypertext and Hypermedia: 31-40

Matsumoto Y, Kitauchi A, Yamashita T, Hirano Y, Imaichi O, Imamura T (1997) Japanese morphological analysis system ChaSen manual. NAIST Technical Report, NAIST-IS-TR97007.

Niles I, Pease A (2001) Towards a standard upper ontology. 2nd International Conference on Formal Ontology in Information Systems: 2-9

Rada R, Mili H, Bicknell E, Blettner M (1989) Development and application of a metric on semantic nets. IEEE Transactions on System, Man and Cybernetics 19(1): 17–30

Takasaki T (2007) Design and development of a pictogram communication system for children around the world. 2007 International Workshop on Intercultural Collaboration, Lecture Notes in Computer Science 4568, Springer: 193–206

van Rijsbergen C (1979) Information retrieval. Butterworths, London

Yokoi T The EDR electronic dictionary. Communication of the ACM 38(11): 42–44

Part IV

Language Grid for Communication

Chapter 10
Intercultural Community Development for Kids around the World

Toshiyuki Takasaki[1, 2], Yumiko Mori[2], and Alvin W. Yeo[3]

1 Department of Social Informatics, Kyoto University, Yoshida-Honmachi, Sakyo-ku, Kyoto, Japan, email: toshi@ai.soc.kyoto-u.ac.jp

2 NPO Pangaea, Cocon Karasuma Building 4F 620, Kyoto, Japan, email: {toshi, yumi}@pangaean.org

3 Faculty of Computer Science and Information Technology, Universiti Malaysia Sarawak, Sarawak, Malaysia, email: alvin@fit.unimas.my

Abstract Communication methods and tools are key factors in developing online intercultural communities, especially when community members use their own mother tongue. This chapter introduces a case of an online intercultural community for international youths in NPO Pangaea. Youths and volunteer staff are from different countries and communication in this community is not English-based. Pictograms are used for youth communication and machine translations are used for staff communication. This chapter reports the participatory design and development processes of a pictogram communication system for youths and multilingual community site for staffs. Community-based communication tools such as Pangaea Staff Community Site receive benefits from the Language Grid technology in its aspect of a collective intelligence, because the Language Grid enables community users such as Pangaea volunteers to improve machine translation quality, for example, by adding a Pangaea community dictionary.

10.1 Introduction

Information communication technologies play important roles in social enterprises such as Non Governmental Organizations. Especially when their domains involve international activities with people around the world, the use of Internet communication tools is essential to develop intercultural communities. This chapter introduces one case in which Pangaea, an R&D NPO to facilitate intercultural exchange among youths, designed and developed online communication tools for youths worldwide as well as their international volunteer staff. The language barrier was one of the biggest issues in developing this intercultural community.

There were many monolingual youths and the volunteer staff spoke several different languages. As the Pangaea mission is to respect diversity in cultures, it needed to provide communication tools without forcing users to use one language such as English. In such circumstances, the goal of youth communication was defined not as delivering precise information but rather realizing heart-to-heart communication for fostering bonds among the participants. The solution was to design and develop a pictogram communication system.

The goal of staff communication, on the other hand, was defined as exchanging useful information for creating and maintaining better youth programs and realizing effective administration for the international volunteer staff. The communication solution was to apply machine translation tools. Pangaea Community Site was developed on top of the Language Grid technology. Any community-based communication tool can receive maximum benefit from the Language Grid technology due to its collective intelligence, because the Language Grid enables community users to improve the quality of machine translation, for example, by combining its own dictionary created by community users such as volunteer staff.

Pangaea is a non-profit research and development initiative with the goal of creating a 'Universal Playground', an intercultural community for youths. It creates an ICT environment where youths, aged between nine and sixteen, can develop a personal and emotional 'bond' with each other around the world. Geographical and language barriers as well as differences in social background are major factors that limit the opportunities for youths to experience these 'bonds.' Pangaea offers an online environment and tools through which youths can spontaneously enjoy getting to know each other, share their experiences, and collaborate despite being physically and linguistically separated. Using the Internet as a catalyst and connector, Pangaea provides a range of opportunities for youths to 'bond' through Peace Engineering.

It also creates and implements playful and collaborative activity menus called Pangaea Activities at Pangaea's various local locations such as schools and youth centres. As of August 2010, Pangaea Activities were active at four locations in Japan, two locations in Malaysia (Kuching, Sarawak and Bario, Sarawak), and one location each in Kenya, Austria, and Korea. Both simultaneous and non-simultaneous activities are available at these locations. "Meeting", "Communicating", and "Connecting", Pangaea aims to develop contents and tools to make these tasks enjoyable to the young participants as discussed in (Mori 2007). PangaeaNet has been developed as a non-simultaneous activity platform of a social network system (SNS). It is an online Universal Playground where youths can communicate with each other and can share their work.

This chapter introduces two communication methods: pictogram communication for youths and machine translation communication for staffs. The first part of the chapter shows how the pictogram communication software for international youths was designed and used. The last part describes the use of an online communication system of machine translation that was developed for the staff community.

10.2 Communication Analysis in Youth Community

A common language was needed to realize communication among the intercultural Pangaea youth participants since most do not understand English. Any dependence on English would imply the existence of superior and inferior languages. In Pangaea, pictograms were designed and pictogram communication software was developed. This chapter shows how the pictograms were designed and how youths used them to develop their intercultural community.

Prior to the choice of a communication method among youths, the following issues were taken into consideration as discussed in (Takasaki and Mori 2007):

(1) The communication method should realize heart-to-heart communication.

(2) The communication method should respect cultural diversity and self-identity.

(3) The communication method should be useful without the need to learn new languages.

(4) The communication method should be effectively supported by the Internet.

Possible global communication methods were considered to identify which ones meet all the above points. There were three candidates: artificial text-based languages, machine translation, and visual languages.

First, Esperanto is probably the most well known artificial text-based language. Though Esperanto is useful, it requires learning the language from scratch and this is not practical for youth communication. So, artificial languages were not selected.

Second, machine translation systems were surveyed. Though it enables the exchange of messages without learning any new language, there are many unsupported languages such as Khmer in Cambodia. Japanese to English machine translation services were tested on youths' texts such as transcripts from chat sessions and email. The quality of translation was not adequate at that time.

Third, visual languages were evaluated. Marcus (2003) stated that the main communication systems that use pictograms can be placed into three categories: Universal signs, Signs for the handicapped, and Smilies. Road signs, direction boards at airports, and the symbols of each sport played in the Olympic game are universal signs. The second category of pictograms includes Augmentative Alternative Communication (AAC) such as Blissymbolics of (Bliss 1965) and (Olaszi et al. 2004), PIC of (Maharaj 1980), and Elephant memory of (Ingen-Housz 1999.) For example, Blissymbolics are relatively abstract with syntax. AAC supports people with severe communication disabilities to be more socially active. The third category includes pictograms that decorate text messages as shown in (Rivera et al. 1996) such as emoticons and pictograms in cell phones. Some teenagers use cell phones to send email messages that consist entirely of pictograms with rich emotional content.

By reviewing these communication methods, it was concluded that a pictogram system would be the most practical and realistic solution for this youth communication case. Although a pictogram system is not so good for conveying precise information, it can be useful to facilitate heart-to-heart communication and well satisfies the conditions above.

The selection of pictograms started with Ogden's vocabulary list in (Ogden 1932), which consists of approximately 850 words. However, some words were obsolete. Also, experiments on pictogram message composition were conducted. The subjects were youths between 9 and 15 years old in Japan, Korea, and Kenya. They were asked to compose pictogram messages by drawing pictures by hand. Their messages were observed and taken into account when selecting the pictograms. Approximately 550 words were listed and designed by design volunteers. Through pictogram online surveys as described in (Takasaki 2006) and pictogram research surveys such as (Koda and Ishida 2006), approximately 450 pictograms were designed for the Communicator (Fig 10.1.) These pictograms are researched from cultural aspects in (Cho et al. 2007).

Fig. 10.1 A screenshot of Communicator, pictogram communication software for youths

10.3 Use of Pictograms in Youth Community

In Pangaea Activities, youth participants in each location compose pictogram messages. At the time of data collection, there were approximately 450 pictograms. Youth participants were from three cities in Japan (Tokyo, Kyoto and Mie), Seoul, Korea, Vienna, Austria, and Nairobi, Kenya. The 152 youths were all between 9 and 15 years old. Pictograms are listed in tabbed folders in the top half of the screen as shown in Fig 10.1. System operation was not controlled, and use of the Communicator was not forced. In order to analyze pictogram communication among these participants, 1,311 messages were selected that consisted of more than four pictograms out of the 2,228 sent messages. Participants were asked what their messages meant after composing them. It was revealed that there are mainly three communication patterns in pictogram messages: syntactic description, artistic drawing, and storytelling.

10.3.1 Syntactic Description

Pictograms were utilized to replace text words and phrases in the Syntactic Description pattern. In this survey, Syntactic Descriptions were found in all four countries, in all locations.

One of the significant characteristics is that all messages ran from left to right like text sentences by following verbal syntax (Fig. 10.2). The pictograms were equally spaced (roughly) and most messages start in the upper left corner. "I" or "You" pictograms were used. Each message consisted of one of more sentences and each sentence began on a new line.

Fig. 10.2 An example of Syntactic Description pictogram message. "I like Reading and Computer. I want to fly to your country Austria and meet you."

Fig. 10.3 Repeating pictogram to show stronger or bigger. Top: "I love Cat, and Dog and Bird, Animals!" Bottom: "I was shocked by your house!!!!"

In some cases, emotion levels such as 'like' or 'love' were expressed by repeated use of the 'heart' pictogram as shown in Fig. 10.3 top, while multiple "exclamation marks" were used for emphasis as shown in Fig. 10.3 bottom. And some messages contained mathematical description as shown in Fig.10.4.

Fig. 10.4 Strengthening meaning by using numbers. I wish to give you an invitation card, I like you 100 times.

10.3.2 Artistic Drawing

Pictogram messages, which are drawn as if they are one picture, follow the Artistic Drawing pattern. Participants used Communicator's pictogram composing field as a drawing canvas to make the Artistic Drawing messages. Participants first visualized the message in their mind. They composed the message by positioning the pictograms vertically and horizontally. Pictogram separation also has meaning. By connecting or combining pictograms, size, weight, length, or width can be expressed. Artistic Drawing messages were used most frequently by participants at the same activity location, in another words, they knew each other on a face-to-face basis. Comic style expressions were observed in some of these messages (Fig.10.5.) This influence was especially strong among the Japanese and Korean participants whereas they were rare in Austria and Kenya.

Fig. 10.5 Use of Comic style expression in Artistic Drawing. "I think about visiting your home and having apple snack." *Receiver has uploaded her apple house to PangaeaNet.

10.3.3 Story Telling

Some participants made pictogram messages in story style and so these are categorized as Story Telling messages. Pictograms are located in chronological order. Arrows (→) were used between pictograms in some Story Telling messages. Pictograms were frequently positioned from left to right, then down, and right to left as shown in the message of a Kenyan boy in Fig.10.6.

Fig. 10.6 An example of Story Telling message. "Hello, flowers for you, I am bit shy, but fine to visit me. I play catch ball with my friend and got hit by a ball, and cried. Bit stupid of me."

10.3.4 Statistics

64.7% of 1,311 sent messages with more than four pictograms per message were Syntactic Description pattern whereas 20.7% were Artistic Drawing pattern and 14.6% followed Story Telling pattern. Participants were free to send pictogram messages or not to send to anyone listed on PangaeaNet.

50.1% of messages were sent to participants who were in the same location. 22.6% were sent to participants who lived in the same country but in different locations. 26.7% were sent to foreign countries. 55.0% of messages sent within the same location (Type A), 72.0% to the same language group (Type B), and 76.9 % of messages sent overseas (Type C) belong to Syntactic Description pattern.

Table 10.1 The number of messages in each message pattern: receiver's location, communication patterns. 'A' represents message sent within the same location. 'B' messages were intended for the same country, but different location and children have never met. 'C' are messages sent to foreign countries or intercultural setting. Messages counted here are only those with more than four pictograms per message.

	Num. of Subjects	Syntactical			Artistic			Story Telling			
		A	B	C	A	B	C	A	B	C	
Me	33	69	59	54	67	18	7	43	25	7	
Shibuya	24	64	61	69	68	13	8	11	10	7	
Kyoto	17	101	74	55	20	4	3	15	7	6	
Suginami	19	109	18	21	38	2	4	28	3	10	
Seoul	42	14	0	53	3	0	6	1	1	11	
Vienna	13	8	1	11	2	0	0	3	0	3	
Kenya	5	0	0	7	0	0	8	0	0	1	
Total	153	365	213	270	198	37	36	101	46	45	1311
Ratio		0.430	0.251	0.318	0.731	0.137	0.133	0.526	0.240	0.234	

The ratio of Syntactic Description in Type C appears quite high. Most of those messages used more than eight pictograms per message. 17.4% of Type C had over 8 pictograms per message, while Type A is the lowest at 13.4%, Type B is

14.2%. Participants seemed to have the intention to communicate with the inter-cultural group using more pictograms, because they may have thought that the dif-ference in culture or language required more explanation than delivering messages to children in the same location.

10.4 Communication Analysis of Staff Community

10.4.1 International Volunteer-Based Staff Community

As is the case with international NGOs, Pangaea owes a lot to its adult staff, espe-cially to international volunteers. Staff consist of core staff and volunteer staff. Basically, core staff get paid while volunteer staff do not. Five core staff work in Pangaea; they are a content creator, technical engineer, designer, and administra-tive workers. Approximately 340 volunteers support Pangaea; 160 people are in Japan, the remainder are outside Japan. These volunteers are facilitators, technical facilitators, back-office volunteers, and technical development volunteers. Facili-tators and technical facilitators participate in Pangaea Activity of youths. Facilita-tors support preparation of Pangaea Activity and participate to help youth partici-pants. Technical facilitators prepare digital tools such as computers and digital cameras, participate in the activities to help youth participants use these tools, and upload artwork of youths to servers. There are approximately three to eight facili-tators and one to three technical facilitators. Back-office volunteers help with of-fice tasks such as documentation, accounting service, and translation. Technical development volunteers support system development such as computer software and web applications. Volunteers vary in age, nationality, language, and back-ground.

Pangaea has its Headquarters in Japan and has its activity locations in Japan, Korea, Malaysia, Austria and Kenya. Activity locations are in primary or sec-ondly schools, universities, youth centres, and commercial places. For example, there are two activity locations in Malaysia, one in UNIMAS, a national univer-sity, and one in SMK Bario, a school in a very rural area. One of the unique as-pects of Pangaea activity locations is that both developed countries and develop-ing countries participate in the activity. Some locations are equipped with a high speed Internet infrastructure and high-spec computers whereas others have satel-lite Internet connections and second-hand computers. As described in (Parikh 2009), trials of ICT projects have been conducted in rural areas.

For example, the Bario location of Pangaea is located in a very remote rural vil-lage on the island of Borneo. It is a village of 1,000 people near the Malaysia-Indonesia border between Sarawak, Malaysia and Kalimantan, Indonesia. (Mohamad et al. 2010) describes that most of the facilities own their power supply equipment such as generators or solar panels. Most houses and lodges are not equipped with hot water for showering. Though cell phones can be used in Bario since October 2009, Internet connection is limited to special facilities such as tele-centers. The connection is the satellite Internet system called VSAT. As it is a re-mote and challenging ICT field, Bario gave rise to the statement that "if you can successfully implement a project in Bario, you can do so anywhere" in (Yeo et al. 2007).

10.4.2 Designing Pangaea Community Site for Staff Powered By Language Grid Technology

One of the most important roles of Pangaea core staff is to keep track of Pangaea Activities in each location. Accordingly, facilitators and technical facilitators were asked to write a report when they participated in a Pangaea Activity. If prob-lems occurred, core staff had to make some decisions or give instructions to local staff. But there is a language issue. Pangaea does not set English skill as a prereq-uisite. For example, there are many staff who do not speak English in Austria, Korea and Japan and it is usually difficult to allocate human interpreters or trans-lators due to the tight budget of the NGO.

There were requests from the volunteer staff that they would like to communi-cate online with other staff, but they faced the language issue again. Youths com-municate and make friends with international participants by using pictograms as shown earlier, but the staff had no access to the system. Furthermore, the reason for online staff communication was different from that of the youths. Staff said that they would like to share information about their facilitation methods and ex-change questions and information about Pangaea Activity. Thus, pictogram or non-verbal communication was not appropriate and verbal communication was necessary.

Pangaea core staff started to think about creating an online community site, a BBS-style (Bulletin Board System) communication platform for all staff. They named it Pangaea Community Site. In order to resolve the language issue, they tried some machine translation services that were accessible from the Web. Unfor-tunately, they found that many machine translation results were not good enough. They wanted to have some way of enhancing the quality of machine translation and started to look around for such technologies or methodologies. Pangaea core staff knew of the Language Grid technology created by NICT (National Institute of Information Communication Technology) in Japan. Their focal point was ma-chine translation combined with community dictionaries. By creating a commu-nity-specific dictionary Pangaea could be assured of creating a machine translation service with much higher quality than general machine translators. Because Pan-gaea is a community-based activity, the Pangaea community dictionary could be collaboratively created by the international volunteer staff. So, Pangaea core staff decided to introduce the Language Grid technology in its community site system as shown in Fig 10.7(a.) The back translation function is convenient for checking machine translation results and contributes to higher quality machine translation.

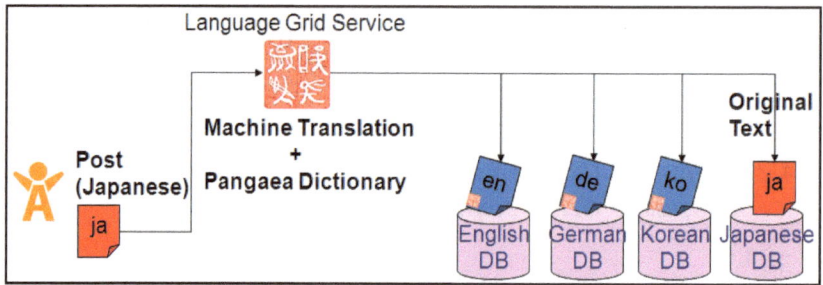

(a)   Message posting flow of machine translation combined with community dictionary.

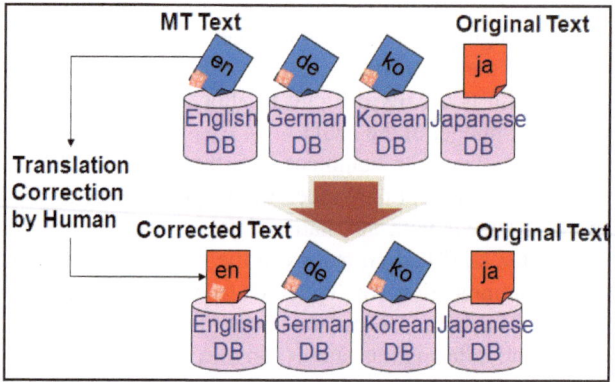

(b) Flow of a human modification of machine translation results.

Fig. 10.7 System design of Pangaea Community Site.

In addition, a human correction function was proposed. It allows users to modify the machine translation result of each message on the BBS. Because users are core staff and volunteer staff and share common ground in Pangaea context, it is expected to be easier for users to modify machine translation results as shown in Fig 10.7 (b.)

The use case of Pangaea Community Site is as follows:

[Step 1] A user logs in at the top page with his/her user name and password and enters a thread list page.

[Step 2] A user selects a thread. Each thread has a three-level hierarchical structure such as {Pangaea Activity Report}>{Bario}>{Facilitator Report}.

[Step 3] A message list with user name and message title in the thread are shown. A user selects a message that he/she would like to read.

[Step 4] The message and reply message(s) if any are shown.

[Step 5-1: Post a message] When a user clicks on the "Post" button, a message form is shown. The user fills in the form with a title and message text and clicks

"Translate" button to check the back translation result in all languages. The user can modify his/her original title and message and check the back translation again. When a user finishes the back translation check, the user clicks on the "Post" button to post the message.

[Step 5-2: Modification] If the message language is not the original message language, there is a "Modify translation" button on a screen. When a user clicks on the "Modify translation" button, an editable message form that is filled with a machine translation result text is shown. The user edits the text and clicks the "Post" button when done.

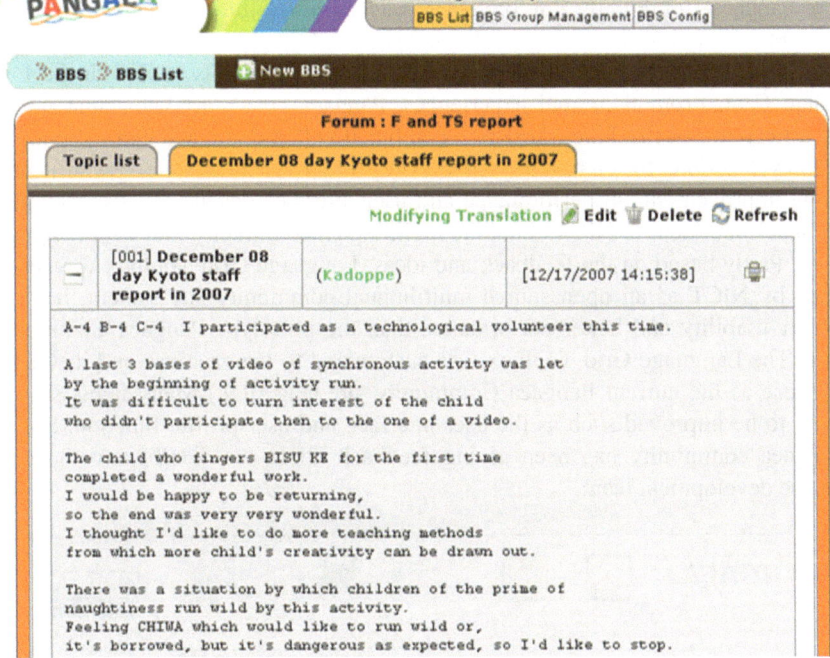

Fig. 10.8 Screenshot of a prototype of Pangaea Community Site

10.5 Use of Machine Translation for Staff Community

10.5.1 Prototyping Pangaea Community Site

The first version of Pangaea Community Site was prototyped in 2007 by Pangaea core staff and technical development volunteers (Fig 10.8.) It was implemented as a Web application by customizing Rubricks, an open-source CMS (Contents Management System) framework. It was deployed on an open-base solution consisting of a Linux server, Apache web-server, MySQL database and Ruby interpreter. The

Pangaea Community Site prototype was introduced to Pangaea staff in December 2007. It remains in actual operation and is often used by international users. Volunteer staff post activity reports every time they participate in a Pangaea Activity. It dramatically improves communication especially between core staff and volunteer staff such that core staff can keep track of activities of volunteer staff.

10.5.2 Transferring the idea to Language Grid Toolbox

The Pangaea Community Site prototype was shown to the Language Grid development team in NICT at some small conferences. At that time, the NICT team was thinking to create a general purpose multilingual community tool with the Language Grid. From their real experiences, Pangaea core staff knew that human modification and machine translation combined with a domain-specific dictionary are key functions for community sites. Also, they noticed that the system needed some improvements in performance and user interface design. So, Pangaea gave feedback and ideas to NICT about the multilingual community tool with Language Grid. Partly based on the feedback and ideas, Language Grid Toolbox was developed by NICT as an open source multilingual community site system. It offers higher usability and better performance than the prototype Pangaea Community Site. The Language Grid Toolbox was customized to Pangaea use and it was put into use as the current Pangaea Community site (Fig.10.9.) Many items still remain to be improved such as the user interface and user profile function. So, the Pangaea community has been giving feedback about the Toolbox to the open source development team.

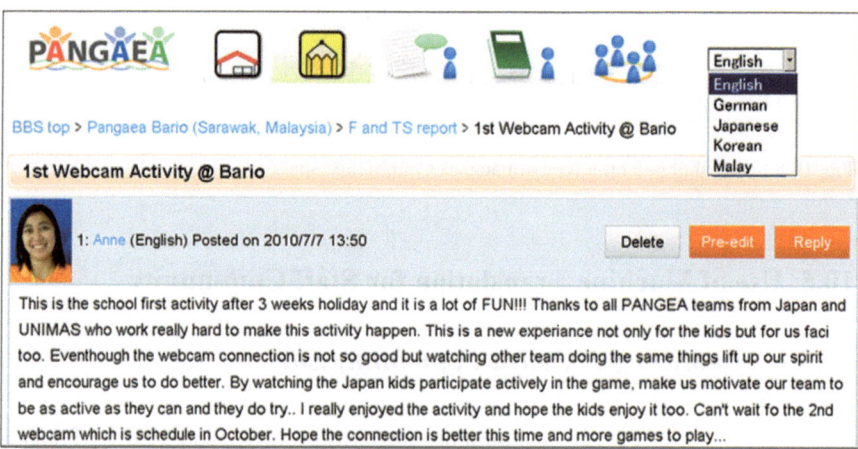

Fig. 10.9 A screenshot of the Toolbox version of Pangaea Community Site

The current Pangaea Community site has a total of 262 user accounts; 111 Japanese staff, 42 Korean staff, 3 Austrian staff, and 106 Malaysian staff. The number of posted messages was 1457; 212 English messages, 993 Japanese messages, 242 Korean messages, and 10 Malay messages. The number of all human-corrected messages was 236. Table 10.2 shows statistics for the corrected messages. For example, 15 machine-translated messages that were originally posted in English and translated into Japanese by machine translation were corrected by community members. In the process of human correction, users frequently found some words that triggered mistranslation. Those words were registered into the Pangaea community dictionary by them or Pangaea core staff to prevent subsequent mistranslation. There are currently 1,665 entries in the current Pangaea community dictionary.

Table 10.2 Statistics of human-corrected machine translations.

Original message Language	Corrected Language of translated messages	The number of Human Corrections of machine translations
English	German	3
English	Japanese	15
English	Korean	3
English	Malay	3
Japanese	German	28
Japanese	English	39
Japanese	Korean	29
Japanese	Malay	28
Korean	German	15
Korean	English	19
Korean	Japanese	39
Korean	Malay	15

10.6 Conclusion

This chapter showed how the intercultural community for international youths has been developed by discussing the case of Pangaea.

First, pictogram-based communication among international youths was explained. Because heart-to-heart and 'equal' communication were prioritized over the forced use of English, pictograms were incorporated into the communication method adopted by the Pangaea intercultural youth community. Pictogram design proceeded iteratively with feedback from actual youth users. Users' messages revealed that pictogram messages can be categorized into three patterns: syntactic description, artistic drawing, and storytelling.

Second, the participatory design process of the multilingual Pangaea Community Site for staff was described. Machine translation was introduced for staff communication, but initial results were rather poor in quality. Because Pangaea is supported by many international volunteers, the system makes maximum use of collective intelligence and it asks human users to enhance translation performance. The know-how of the system was transferred to the Language Grid Toolbox system being developed by NICT.

In this manner, a community-based communication tool could receive maximum benefit from the collective intelligence provided by the Language Grid technology, because the Language Grid enables community users to improve quality of machine translation, for example, by adding domain-specific dictionaries created by community users such as volunteer staff.

Acknowledgments   The authors would like to thank Prof. Toru Ishida of Kyoto University and members of NICT Language Grid project for advice and support. The authors would also like to acknowledge the cooperation of the youth and staff community of NPO Pangaea. The development of Pictogram Communication software was partially supported by the Exploratory Software Project of Information Technology Promotion Agency Japan. The development of the first version of the Community Site system was partially supported by the Asian Neighbours Network Program of The Toyota Foundation. This research was also supported by the Global COE Program on Informatics Education and Research Center for Knowledge-Circulating Society.

References

Bliss CK (1965) Semantography (blissymbolics). Sydney Semantography Publications

Cho H, Ishida T, Yamashita N, et al (2007) Culturally-situated pictogram retrieval. In: Ishida T, Fussell SR, Vossen PTJM (ed): Intercultural Collaboration I. Lecture Notes in Computer Science 4568, Springer-Verlag Berlin: 221-235

Ingen-Housz T (1999) The elephant's memory: in search of a pictorial language. Learning Technology Review(Spring and Summer): 2-25

Koda T, Ishida T (2006) Cross-cultural comparison of interpretation of avatars' facial expressions. 2006 IEEE/IPSJ Symposium on Applications and the Internet (SAINT-06): 130-136

Maharaj S (1980) Pictogram ideogram communication. Saskatoon, SK. The Pictogram Centre, Saskatchewan Association of Rehabilitation Centres

Marcus A (2003) Icons, symbols, and signs: visible languages to facilitate communication. Interactions 10 (3), ACM Press: 37-43

Mohamad R, Yeo AW, Abdul Aziz N, et al (2010) Borneo children in an international digital playground: intercultural issues and idiosyncrasies. The 3rd International Conference on Intercultural Collaboration (ICIC 2010): 103-110

Mori Y (2007) Atoms of bonding: communication components bridging children worldwide. Intercultural Collaboration, Lecture Notes in Computer Science 4568, Springer-Verlag Berlin: 335-343

Ogden CK (1932) Basic English, a general introduction with rules and grammar. Paul Trebor & Co.

Olaszi P, Koutny I, Kálmán SL (2004) From bliss symbols to grammatically correct voice output: a communication tool for people with disabilities. International Journal of Speech Technology 5(1): 49-56

Parikh TS (2009) Engineering rural development, Communications of the ACM 52(1): 54-63

Rivera K, Cooke NJ, Bauhs J (1996) The effects of emotional icons on remote communication. CHI Conference Companion: 99-100

Takasaki T (2006) Pictnet: semantic infrastructure for pictogram communication. The Third International WordNet Conference (GWC-06): 279-284

Takasaki T, Mori Y (2007) Design and development of a pictogram communication system for children around the world. Intercultural Collaboration, Lecture Notes in Computer Science 4568, Springer-Verlag Berlin: 193-206

Yeo AW, Johari A, Suhaila S, et al (2007) ICTs in the rural communities: engaging remote communities towards a knowledge-based society. International Library Conference: Sarawak 2007, Kuching, Sarawak, Malaysia

Chapter 11
Language-Barrier-Free Room for Second Life

Takashi Yoshino[1] and Katsuya Ikenobu[2]

1 Faculty of Systems Engineering, Wakayama University, 930 Sakaedani, Wakayama, Japan, email: yoshino@sys.wakayama-u.ac.jp

2 Graduate School of Systems Engineering, Wakayama University, 930 Sakaedani, Wakayama, Japan, email: s105003@sys.wakayama-u.ac.jp

Abstract A three-dimensional (3D) online virtual space, such as Second Life, becoming a familiar communication medium is a possibility because of the widespread use of the Internet. Some people view Second Life as the successor of the Internet. However, as in the real world, in the virtual world also language differences pose significant barriers to intercultural communications. We can consider a virtual space to be the simulated environment of a real space. We consider the Language Grid to be the multilingual language environment of the future that can include a variety of language resources. We have developed communication support systems that facilitate multilingual chat in Second Life, called language-barrier-free rooms. The objective of this study is to develop a communication support system in virtual space that is identical to a system in real space. We will use the findings of the experiment to enhance the communication support systems in real space. From the results of the experiments and those of the trial experiments of the communication systems, we obtained the following result. In virtual space where communication similar to that in the real world can be simulated, we observed that human adjustment of the machine translations is necessary.

11.1 Introduction

Some people view Second Life and other so-called metaverses, which are virtual worlds in three-dimensional space (3D), as the successors of the Internet. These virtual worlds are not games, and they are receiving considerable attention as people have started perceiving them as being potentially far more profound than any other online pastimes. Second Life can be a prospective platform for a completely new 3D network that could offer more socializing opportunities and communication channels than the real world.

Most of the current computer technologies can be easily used in virtual space. Therefore, the use of complex combinations of technologies is also possible in virtual space. We can consider a virtual space to be the simulated environment of a real space. The number of user accounts on Second Life has increased to more than 13 million. Approximately 43% of these users are English-speakers[1], and English is used even in chats with non-English speakers. However, there are many users who cannot speak English fluently, and therefore, language becomes a communication barrier in the virtual world as it is in the real world.

Several studies have proposed methods that support communication in a virtual space (Isbister et al. 2000). These studies aim to enable communication through verbal conversations between persons speaking a common language. Thus far, no research has been carried out on communication support systems for facilitating multilingual chatting in a virtual space. The Internet and technologies supported by high-performance computers have enabled communication in the virtual world for the first time.

Currently, most of the communication between remote environments is carried out using a PC and keyboard by machine translation. In the future, the development of speech translation technology will enable communication between people who cannot speak in a common language in a real space. However, this technology has unresolved problems.

The following two steps were carried out in this study:

(1) We performed simulation of a virtual environment to facilitate communication between people who cannot speak in a common language in a real space. The results of the simulation were used to enhance communication support systems in real space.

(2) We compared the results obtained for communication through machine translations in real space with those obtained for the communication system developed by us for a three-dimensional virtual environment.

The ultimate aim of communication support for facilitating multilingual communication is to support communication between people who cannot speak in a common language in a real-life activity. We studied human behavior by using a three-dimensional visualization space that was the simulation of a real space in a complex environment. We have developed conversation-component-visualization systems powered by the Language Grid. The Language Grid provides certain types of multilingual resources that are easy to use and also facilitates multilingual processing. We consider the Language Grid to be the multilingual language environment of the future that would include a variety of language resources. The purpose of this study is to develop a system that imitates a real space in a virtual space, and we obtain our findings from the comparison of this and a real space.

In the study described in this chapter, we have developed communication support systems in Second Life, called language-barrier-free rooms. First of all, we have developed two types of multilingual communication environments: fixed-type and portable-type environments. We proposed the use of the back-translation

[1]Second Life Virtual Economy Key Metrics (BETA).

technique for achieving reliable communication between people who cannot speak in a common language in a virtual space, and we evaluated the basic performance of the communication support system. In addition, we constructed a multilingual lecture room in which the back translation technique is employed. Moreover, we simulated and developed a dictionary registration system in which words used in conversations were registered, and we compared our dictionary writing system with conventional Web-based systems. Finally, we compared the multilingual communication environment in a virtual space with that in a real space.

11.2 Related Work

Sugawara et al. researched communications in a three-dimensional virtual space (Sugawara et al. 1994). They developed a three-dimensional virtual space, called InterSpace, for their research. In InterSpace, there is an agent who mediates communications in a virtual space. This agent has achieved asynchronous communications in a virtual space. Then, an open experiment was carried out on the Internet using InterSpace. The effect of the development of communities and the use of the communications media was studied in this experiment.

Matsuda et al. developed a virtual society, called PAW, and carried out an open experiment (Matsuda 2002). From the result of the open experiment, they presented the user's profile, the effect of an event, the feature of communities, and the communication tools for using all these together.

Nakanishi et al. studied the impact of a three-dimensional virtual space communication environment (Nakanishi et al. 1999). From a comparison of this environment with a face-to-face environment, they found that the environment of the three dimensional virtual space contributes to an increase in the switch frequency of the speaker.

Human agent interaction via machine translation needs to be investigated in the future (Pallay et al. 2009).

Our research differs from the abovementioned researches; we discuss the possibility of communication among speakers who cannot speak in a common language by using machine translation in a virtual space.

11.3 Multilingual Chat Support System

We have developed a multilingual chat support system by using an object[2] that is built in an event-driven-type script in a three-dimensional virtual space. Portable and fixed translation systems are intended as multilingual chat communications

---

[2] An "object" is a form combined by "prim," which is the basic object in Second Life.

support. In the following subsections, we discuss the support form in the three-dimensional virtual space and then describe the portable and fixed translation systems.

11.3.1 Support Form of Multilingual Chat Support System

Table 11.1 shows the advantages and the disadvantages of a fixed and a portable communication support system in a virtual space.

Table 11.1 Advantages and disadvantages of a fixed and a portable communication support system in a virtual space

	Advantages	Disadvantages
Fixed	- It is easy to manage and update software because the software is in an object. - The language of the other person is shown clearly by the bench. - It is easy for users to operate the avatar because a user can use translation only while sitting on the bench. - The translation bench can be shown clearly using a translation function.	- The translation chat can be carried out only in that particular area. - One translation object can be translated only in one pair of languages.
Portable	- A user can use the translation function everywhere. - One HUD can support multiple language pairs.	- A user needs to update the translation system by himself/herself because the translation function is in the object. - The language of the other person is not shown clearly. A user needs to ask his/her language in advance. - A user has to operate the HUD for translation. - Because the user is not aware that the other person is using a machine translation function, there could be a lot of confusion.

In the case of the fixed system, the translation object was set up in a certain pre-decided place. When a user (avatar) went to this place, he/she could use the translation chat system. It was necessary to prepare a separate translation object for each translation language for such a system[3]. The advantage of this system was that the other party's language was specified by the place where it sat.

The operation "Sit an avatar" is an easy operation that is often used in Second Life. The fixed machine translation function was displayed in the three dimensional virtual space. Therefore, other users could recognize that the other party is

---

[3] This limitation was a problem in Second Life.

using the machine translation system. In the case of the portable system, the translation object was displayed on the user's screen as a head-up display (HUD[4]). This feature of the portable system did not place limitations on where the user could use the translation functions, so communications that used translation chat could be carried out everywhere. It was necessary to select the translation language for a portable system on HUD; further, it was necessary to know the other party's language beforehand[5]. When a portable system was used, sentences in two or more languages were suddenly displayed while chatting because the machine translation function was not displayed in the three-dimensional virtual space. This could confuse the other party.

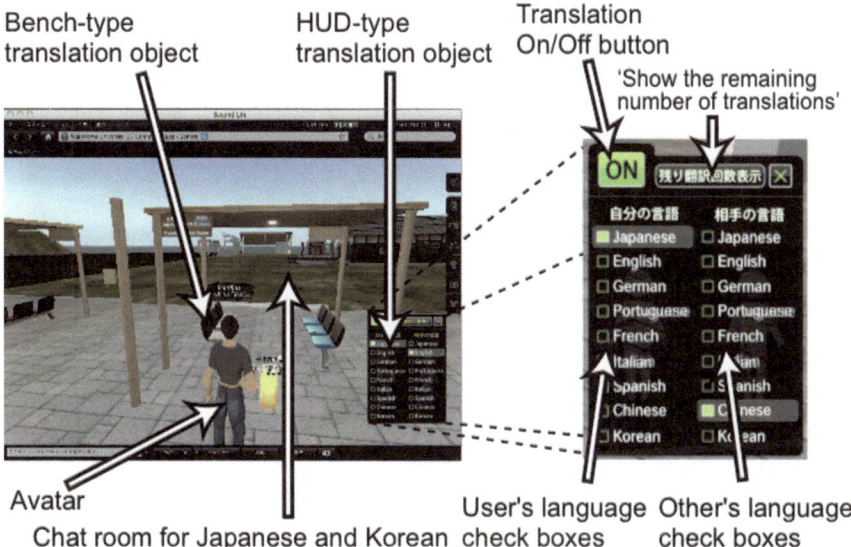

Fig. 11.1 Screenshot of a multilingual chat support system

11.3.2 Structure of Multilingual Chat Support System

The multilingual chat support system that we have developed is shown in Fig. 11.1.

(1)   Fixed translation system (Bench-type translation object)

---

[4] A head-up display (HUD) is a transparent display that presents information without requiring the user to look away from his/her usual viewpoint.

[5] When this system was developed, neither the user's national origin nor information on the user's language was offered in Second Life. However, now, a user's language can be known.

"Chat room for Japanese and Chinese" in Fig. 11.1 is a fixed translation object. We set up Japanese–English, Japanese–Chinese, and Japanese–Korean chat rooms. The procedure for using the translation chat room was as follows:

a. A user clicked the bench-type translation object in the translation chat room, and then the avatar of the user sat on the bench.

b. The chat sentence was translated automatically during the chat. The appearance of the chat communication in the chat room is shown in Fig. 11.2. Each user sat on the bench on the native language side. The input chat sentences were machine translated and displayed as a chat sentence.

Bench-type translation object for Japanese   **Bench-type translation object for Chinese**

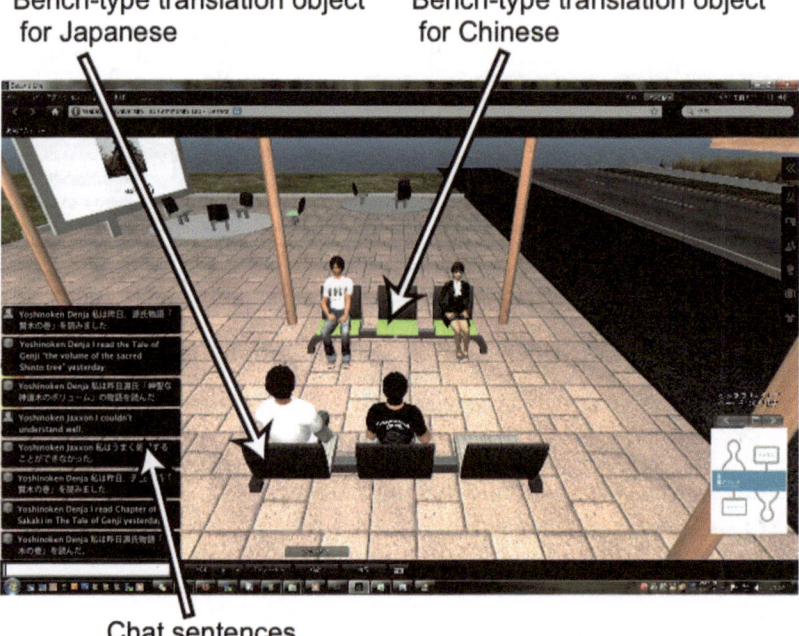

Chat sentences

Fig. 11.2 Screenshot of a chat communication in the translation chat room

(2)   Portable translation system (HUD-type translation object)

The expanding HUD-type translation object in Fig. 11.1 is a portable translation object, which can translate between Japanese, English, Chinese, and Korean by switching the language tab. The procedure for using the HUD-type translation object was as follows:

a. The user installed the HUD-type translation object in his/her avatar.

b. The user clicked the language selection tab according to the partner's language and his/her own language.

c. The chat sentence was translated automatically during the chat.

11.3.3 Back Translation

Back translation is the process of translating a sentence that has already been translated into another language back to the original language. Back translation enables users to check the accuracy of a message using their own native language.

A sample conversation is shown in Fig. 11.3. The translation sentence was displayed only on the input user's side and not on the other party's side. When the input sentence had a mistake, the sentence could not be machine-translated correctly. When an unknown word or complex syntax was used even when the input sentence was correct, the translation would most likely be incorrect. In previous studies, the user confirmed the back-translation result before he/she presented it to the other party's side (Yoshino et al. 2008). When the user judges that there is a problem in the back-translation result, he/she can correct the input sentence (Miyabe et al. 2009) (Miyabe and Yoshino 2009).

A chat in a virtual space communication demands real-time translation. Therefore, the user can correct the sentence if he/she finds that the translation result is not correct.

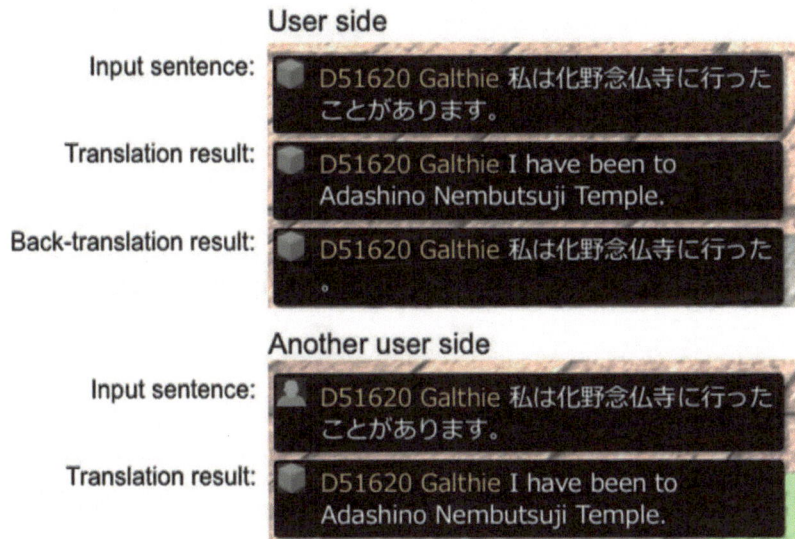

Fig. 11.3 Example of multilingual chat communication

11.3.4 System Configuration

Fig. 11.4 shows the system configuration of the multilingual chat support system. The input sentence that the translation object (Bench-type translation object in the translation chat room and the HUD-type object) received from the Second Life server passed through the relay server (Fig. 11.4 (B)).

The relay server authenticated the user, limited the translation frequency, and recorded the user log. Then, the input sentence was sent to the translation server (Fig. 11.4 (D)) through the Language Grid (Ishida 2006) server (Fig. 11.4 (C)).

The relay server sent the translated sentence to the Second Life server (Fig. 11.4 (B)). Finally, the translation object displayed the translated sentence in Second Life. The back translation was carried out using a similar procedure.

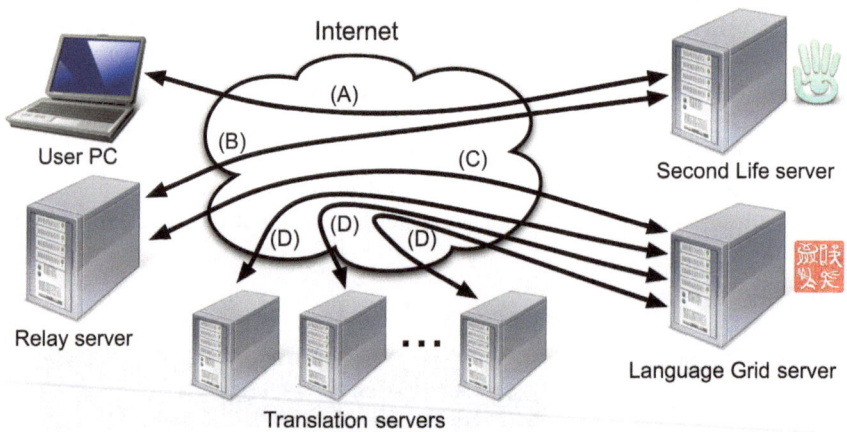

Fig. 11.4 System configuration of the multilingual chat support system.

11.4 Experiment of Multilingual Chat Support System

We conducted two kinds of multilingual chat experiments. The procedure and the result of the experiments are shown.

11.4.1 Portable Multilingual Chat Communication System

We carried out an experiment using the portable multilingual chat communication system. In the experiment, five Japanese university students chatted with some unspecified general users in Second Life.

The purpose of the experiment was to investigate the problems that occurred during the use of the portable multilingual chat communication system in Second Life. The procedure of the experiment was as follows:

(1) A subject installed the portable translation system (HUD-type translation object) in his/her avatar.

(2) The subject went to an island (called SIM in Second Life) where the other avatar existed.

(3) The subject had a conversation among the general users on Second Life and chatted to them.

The duration of each experiment was approximately 20 to 30 minutes.

In the experiment, the translation system was not able to translate sentences in many cases. Many Second Life users used clipped forms for chat. Some users incorrectly used capital and small letters while spelling out a word. Moreover, even if the chat with a general user on Second Life was translated, it was not possible to follow the conversation because the translation could not keep up with the speed of the conversation. Subjects were ignored by almost everyone on Second Life.

Table 11.2 shows the questionnaire result of the experiment using the portable translation system. We obtained good results with respect to the necessity and ease-of-use of the system from the questionnaire (Table 11.2 (2), (5), and (7)). However, the results with respect to the actual use of the system in Second Life were poor (Table 11.2 (1), (3), and (4)). We found that the sentences of the other party and those of the subject were often translated incorrectly. The main reasons given by the subjects, for not being able to carry out a good chat conversation, (Table 11.2 (3)) were as follows:

Table 11.2 Advantages and disadvantages of a fixed and a portable communication support system in a virtual space

Questionnaire items	Average	Standard deviation
(1) The translation result of my chat sentence was correct.	2.2	0.16
(2) I think that the back translation is necessary.	4.6	0.24
(3) I understood the meaning of the foreigner's (the other party of the chat) sentence from the translation.	2.8	0.56
(4) I am satisfied with the accuracy of the translation.	2.0	0.40
(5) I understood the usage of the translation function at once.	4.0	0.40
(6) A problem occurred in the translation system while chatting.	2.2	1.36
(7) I think that the machine translation in the chat is useful.	3.6	1.04

We used a five-point Likert scale for the evaluation, with 1 = Strongly disagree, 2 = Disagree, 3 = Neutral, 4 = Agree, and 5 = Strongly agree.

- I hardly understood the content of the chat. However, I think that the translation depends on the content of the sentence.
- I think a peculiar word was often used in the chat ('You' is shown 'u'). I did not know what was said at all because the contents of the chat were too unusual.
- Because the translation results were not too correct, I could not understand the conversation well.

We found that the chat in Second Life was similar to the chats on the Internet. The users did not care much about grammar and spelling. When the subjects used the portable translation system, the other party did not answer with consideration for such a special situation.

11.4.2 Fixed Multilingual Chat Communication System Result and Discussion

Experimental Procedure

We carried out the experiment using the fixed multilingual chat communication system with the purpose of investigating the problems that could occur during its use in Second Life.

In the conversation experiment, we verified the following items:

- Can you carry out a serious conversation using this system?
- Does the meaning of the other party's sentence change because of the machine translation?
- How can we verify that the machine translation function is effective?

From the result of the experiment using the portable system, it was concluded that most of the conversation was not established. We thought that this was because of the following two reasons:

- The other party did not understand the purpose of the conversation.
- The conversation was not meant for machine translation.

Therefore, we gave the subject a purpose "Question your partner by using machine translation." The subjects were seven Second Life users whose native language was English. We recruited the experimental subjects from the official Web page of Second Life. The participating subjects were offered a reward of 10L\$~ 30L\$ in Second Life currency.

The procedure of the experiment was as follows:

(1)   We guided the subject to the translation chat room.
(2)   We told the subject that this was an experiment to verify the effectiveness of machine translation.
(3)   We asked the subject to ask a Japanese interlocutor 10 different questions.
(4)   The Japanese interlocutor requested rephrasing of questions that could not be understood from the translation result.
(5)   When the translation of the rephrased sentence also did not make much sense, the Japanese interlocutor asked the subject to change the question.

The Japanese interlocutor was one of the authors. In the experiment, the subjects did not use back translation. They could only see their input sentences and the translated sentences. We screen-captured the entire experiment and recorded all the sentences that were exchanged during the chat.

Result and Discussion

Table 11.3 shows the Japanese interlocutor's understanding of the subjects' questions. The Japanese interlocutor judged whether a translated question was understandable. The subjects were asked to rephrase questions that the Japanese interlocutor did not understand. From Table 11.3, it can be concluded that the translation result for many of the questions was understandable.

Table 11.3 Judgment result of the Japanese interlocutor's understanding of the subjects' question.

Subjects	Question of subject			
	Apprehensible	Inapprehensible	Average number of characters	Average number of words
A	7	3	74.8	14.6
B	10	0	39.5	7.6
C	10	0	31.9	6.2
D	8	2	53.1	10.0
E	9	1	57.9	10.7
F	9	1	46.7	9.9
G	10	0	66.2	13.1
Average	9.0	1.0	52.9	10.3

Some of the problems that hindered accurate translation, and hence the overall chat communication, were as follows:

(1) The subjects hardly used clipped forms in the chat. We had explained to the subjects that the experiment was about verifying the effectiveness of machine translation in advance. However, we did not explain the features of machine translation and the problems caused by the use of clipped forms.

(2) The subjects often made spelling mistakes. Therefore, the machine translation failed. A couple of examples are shown below.

Input sentence: Who are your <u>favorate</u> singers/music groups?

Translation result: favorate 歌手/音楽グループは誰であるか？

(The Japanese translation means 'Who is singer/music group?' but 'favorate' cannot be translated because the spelling of "favorate" is incorrect.)
Input sentence: It is a very well <u>desgined</u> welcome area.

Translation result: それは非常によく desgined された喜ばしいエリアである。

(The Japanese translation means 'It is a very joyous area' but 'desgined' cannot be translated because the spelling of "desgined" is incorrect.)

(3) When the Japanese interlocutor said that he did not understand the translated sentence, the subjects rephrased the sentence. The subject followed the following rephrasing method:

• The subject numbered each sentence.
• The subject supplemented the meaning by using parentheses.

Some of the examples are as follows:

First input sentence: I am making up questions, it is ok. Next question: This skirt comes in Copy/No Mod/No Trans, can you make the skirt in Copy/Mod/No Trans? I am small, so I have to edit the skirt.

Second input sentence: (1) I am making up questions, it is ok. (2) This skirt comes in Copy/No Mod/No Trans, can you make the skirt in Copy/Mod/No Trans? I am small, so I have to edit the skirt.

(After the subject placed (1) and (2) at the beginning of the sentence, he asked the Japanese interlocutor to specify which sentence was poorly translated.)

(4)   The subjects divided a long sentence.

First input sentence: When I am speaking (typing) to a Japanese person, what symbol should I use to make each idea/statement easier to seperate?

Second input sentence: The English tend to put many subjects in their statements. Is there a symbol that would make it easier for you to understand the change of thought?

(5)   When a subject noticed a mistake in the input, he/she would input only the corrected form of the incorrect word in the next line.

First input sentence: can you tell mehow many cans of beer would be left in a carton of 24 cans, if I drank eight cans of beer?

Second input sentence: me how*

(In the first input sentence, he input "me how" as "mehow")

11.5 Application for Multilingual Communication

We have developed some support systems for facilitating multilingual communication in Second Life. We present three systems: a multilingual classroom, a bilingual dictionary making system, and conversation-component-visualization systems for Second Life and for the real world. These systems show how the real world can be imitated in the virtual world.

11.5.1 Multilingual Classroom

We have developed a multilingual classroom in Second Life. This is an application for multilingual communication through online chat. In the virtual environment, the lecturer can lecture the students in Japanese, and the attending students can converse in Chinese, Korean, and English. We show that they can communicate with one another in a multilingual classroom via machine translation.

Fig. 11.5 shows a snapshot of the multilingual classroom. There are translation chairs for a lecturer and students, and the slides used in the lecture are projected on a wall in the classroom. When an avatar sits on the chair, the chat messages can be translated from the student's language to the lectures' language. The data format of the slide is standard image format. These slides can be directly prepared using Microsoft PowerPoint. In the chat area shown in Fig. 11.5 (enlarged view), the messages (A) and (C) are the input sentences of the users, and the messages (B), (D), (E), and (F) are the translated sentences.

We received the following feedback from the teacher in charge of the foreign students' class. Some teachers were concerned about the accuracy and effectiveness of the machine translation because a considerable number of technical terms were used in the lecture. This problem can be solved by using the Language Grid because the Language Grid includes many advanced language resources obtained from all over the world, which are permitted to be shared. To realize such a multilingual lecture room, a technical dictionary has to be developed.

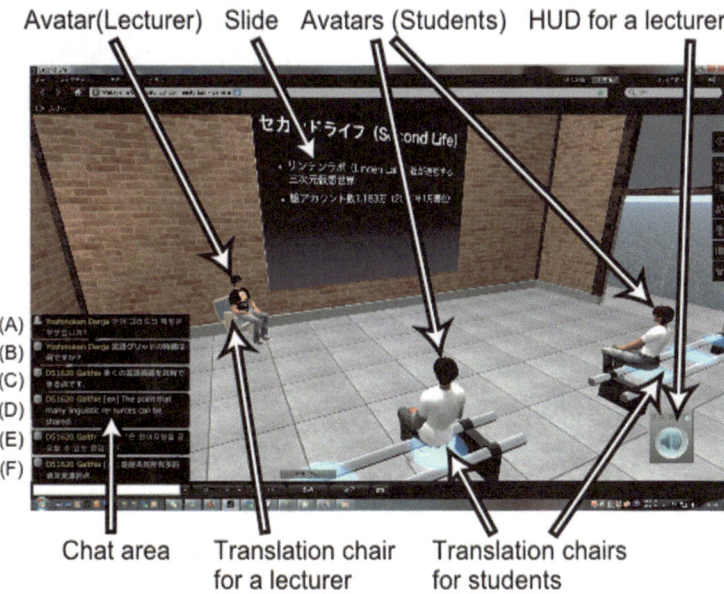

Fig. 11.5 Screenshot of a multilingual classroom

11.5.2 Bilingual Dictionary Registration System

We have developed a bilingual dictionary registration system on Second Life. Fig. 11.6 shows the screenshot of the objects in Second Life that facilitate dictionary registration. When an avatar touches an object, the user can register a pair of terms in the dictionary.

We compared the registration system on Second Life with the problem of requiring a PC to access the Internet in the real world. We received the following feedback from the users about the two systems:

- *The registration system on Second Life is easy to use because it is tailor-made for Second Life. I felt that accessing the Web page for the registration was troublesome.*
- *I found that the input procedure on Second Life is not understood easily.*

Thus, the opinions of users are divided. The registration of words in a dictionary in the virtual world was performed via online chat. We think that the dictionary registration system developed by us was not suitable for a virtual world that imitates the real world well. This problem is similar to the problem of requiring a PC to access the Internet in the real world. We found that it is difficult to facilitate machine translation in the real world.

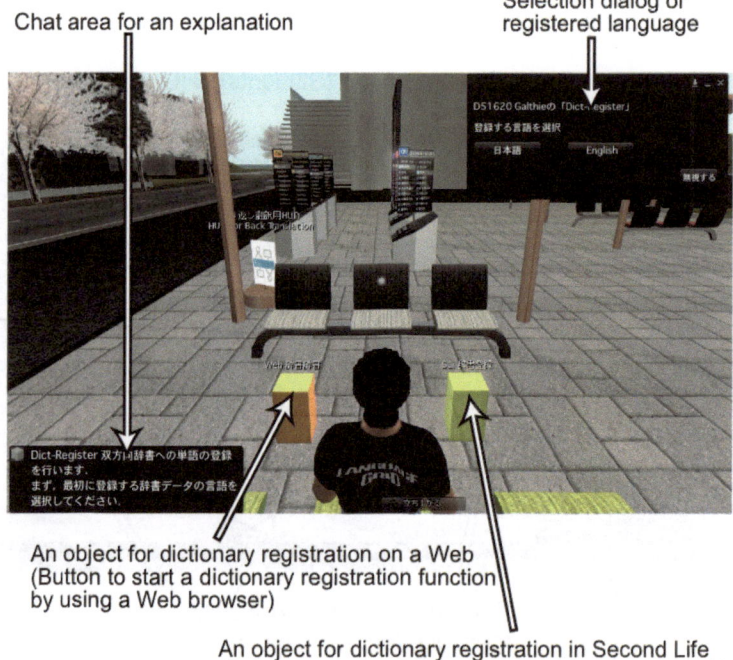

Fig. 11.6 Screenshot of objects in Second Life for dictionary registration

11.5.3 Conversation- Components-Visualization Systems for Second Life and for Real World

It is necessary to understand the language of the person with whom we are conversing. It is difficult to have a conversation with someone who speaks in a different language. Therefore, we have developed conversation–component-visualization systems that provide an opportunity to persons who do not know a common language to converse with each other in 3D online virtual space Second Life and in Augmented Reality (AR). We compared the multilingual communication environment in virtual space with that in a real space. We used the AR technology and head mounted display (HMD) for presenting the information obtained from conversations in the real world.

The left panel of Fig. 11.7 shows screenshots of a conversation-component-visualization system in Second Life. We use a bench-type translation object for the system. When an avatar sits on a translation chair, his/her chat messages can be translated using the Language Grid and can be visualized on a conversation visualizing board.

The right panel of Fig. 11.7 shows a photograph of a conversation–component-visualization system that uses AR. When a user sits on a chair that has a visual marker for AR, his/her chat messages can be translated using the Language Grid and visualized on a conversation visualizing board for AR.

From the results of the comparison experiments using Second Life and AR, we found that voice modulation and the body language of each interlocutor can help the other interlocutors in understanding the conversation more clearly. We found that the system using AR is more effective than that in Second Life in facilitating multilingual conversations.

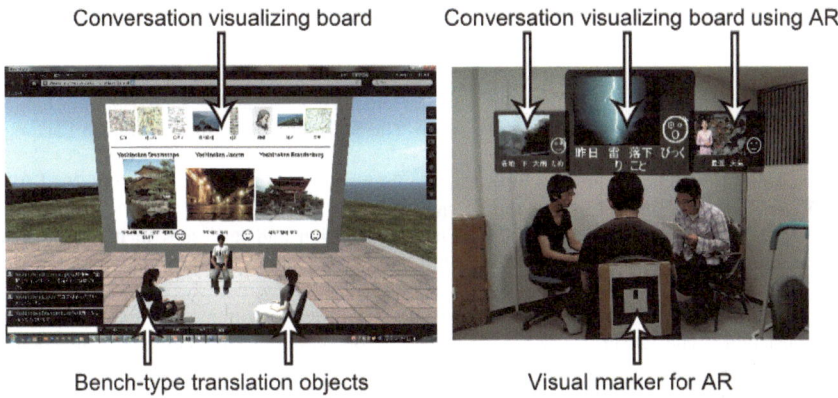

Fig. 11.7 Screenshot of a conversation-component-visualization system in Second Life (left). Photograph of a conversation-component-visualization system using Augmented Reality in the real world (right)

11.6 Conclusion

We have developed multilingual communication support systems, called language-barrier-free rooms, powered by the Language Grid. The purpose of this study is to develop a system that imitates a real space in a virtual space, and we report our findings in experiments comparing use of the system with similar experiments in real space.

The following two results were obtained in this study:

(1) In a virtual space, we observed that when machine translation is used, human adjustment is also necessary to compensate for the limitations of the machine translation. The observed adjustments in behavior were made use of in real-space systems that facilitate communication through machine translations.

(2) We developed communications environments for facilitating communication between people who cannot speak in a common language; these environments in virtual space are identical to those in real space. We performed an operation to access information that is available on the Internet, for example, through the Web and databases, in a virtual space. In the virtual world, the operational procedure tended to be more complex. In a real space, since it was not possible for the operation to access information without using a PC, it is assumed that such problems are encountered in real space.

Currently, the multilingual chat communication support system in Second Life has been opened to the public as a trial.

Acknowledgments This work was partially supported by a Grant-in-Aid for Scientific Research (B), No. 19300036, 2007-2009 and No. 22300044, 2010-2012.

References

Isbister K, Nakanishi H, Ishida T, Nass C (2000) Helper agent: designing an assistant for human-human interaction in a virtual meeting space. The SIGCHI Conference on Human Factors in Computing Systems: 57-64

Ishida T (2006) Language Grid: an infrastructure for intercultural collaboration. 2006 IEEE/IPSJ Symposium on Applications and the Internet: 96-100

Matsuda K, Miyake T, Kawai H (2002) Culture formation and its issues in personal agent-oriented virtual society: "paw^2". The 4th International Conference on Collaborative Virtual Environments: 17-24

Miyabe M, Yoshino T, Shigenobu T (2009) Effects of undertaking translation repair using back translation. The 2009 ACM International Workshop on Intercultural Collaboration (IWIC'09): 33-40

Miyabe M, Yoshino T (2009) Accuracy evaluation of sentences translated to intermediate language in back translation. 3rd International Universal Communication Symposium (IUCS 2009): 30-35

Nakanishi H, Yoshida C, Nishimura T, Ishida T (1999) Freewalk: a 3D virtual space for casual meetings, IEEE Multimedia 6(2): 20-28

Pallay C, Rehm M, Kurdyukova E (2009) Getting acquainted in Second Life: human agent interactions in virtual environments. The International Conference on Advances in Computer Entertainment Technology (ACE 2009): 36-43

Sugawara S, SuzukiG , Nagashima Y, Matsuura M, Tanigawa H, Moriuchi M (1994) Interspace: networked virtual world for visual communication, IEICE Transactions on Information and Systems E77-D(12): 1344-1349

Yoshino T, Fujii K, Shigenobu T (2008) Availability of web information for intercultural communication. 10th Pacific Rim International Conference on Artificial Intelligence (PRICAI 2008): 923-932

Chapter 12
Conversational Grounding in Machine Translation Mediated Communication

Naomi Yamashita[1] and Toru Ishida[2]

1 NTT Communication Science Laboratories, 2-4 Hikaridai Seika-cho Soraku-gun Kyoto Japan, e-mail: naomiy@acm.org

2 Department of Social Informatics, Kyoto University, Yoshida-Honmachi, Sakyo-ku, Kyoto Japan, e-mail: ishida@i.kyoto-u.ac.jp

Abstract When people communicate in their native languages using machine translation, they face various problems in constructing common ground. This study, based on the Language Grid framework, investigates the difficulties of constructing common ground when pairs and triads communicate using machine translation. We compare referential communication of pairs and triads under two conditions: in their shared second language (English) and in their native languages using machine translation. Consequently, to support natural referring behaviour in machine translation mediated communication between pairs, our study suggests the importance of resolving the asymmetries and inconsistencies caused by machine translations. Furthermore, to successfully build common ground among triads, it is important for addressees to be able to monitor what is going on between a speaker and other addressees. The findings serve as a basis for designing future machine translation embedded communication systems. The proposed design implications, in particular, are fed back to the Language Grid development process and incorporated into the recent Language Grid Toolbox.

12.1 Introduction

An increasing number of multilingual organizations and Internet communities are proposing machine translation for communication support. In spite of the growing demands for machine translation to facilitate multilingual communication, little is known about the features of machine translation mediated communication. It has been reported that low quality translations complicate mutual understanding. For example, Ogden et al. have identified translation errors as the main source of inaccuracies that complicate mutual understanding (Ogden et al. 2003). Climent found that typographical errors are also a big source of translation errors that hinder mutual understanding (Climent et al. 2003). Despite these findings, we still lack an understanding of how machine translation affects communication; the previous studies have exclusively put focus on translation qualities, not taking into account how people actually ground each others' utterances during conversation. There-fore, the studies presented in this chapter consider how people ground each others' utterances in machine translation mediated communication. The underlying ques-tions of this chapter are: how do people build on each others' utterances when they do not share the same language? Is translation quality (namely accuracy and flu-ency) all that matters for conducting efficient communication? What else (i.e. new technology or support) can we do besides improving translation quality? Answer-ing such questions will help provide a foundation for designing future machine translation for communication use.

In this chapter, based on two case studies (Yamashita and Ishida 2006; Yama-shita et al. 2009), we tackle the questions stated above; we uncover some of the factors that complicate conversational grounding when multiparty groups (pairs and triads) communicate via machine translation. In particular, we highlight the issues of how machine translations hinder the exploitation of our everyday social skills (such as lexical entrainment, echoing in ratification process), and lead the communicators to ineffective communication.

The studies presented in this chapter are closely interrelated with the Language Grid, which provides language support to various multilingual communities. First, by looking closely into those communities, which actually use machine translation for their activities, we were able to identify problems inherent in machine transla-tion mediated communication. Particularly, the second study was inspired by an interview with an NPO that has been receiving substantial support from the Lan-guage Grid to manage its overseas offices. Second, in our controlled experiment, we were able to use the same communication tool used in the actual community to study the difficulties identified in the interview. The Language Grid was an ideal platform to examine machine translation mediated communication, with the choices of top quality machine translations and stability. Lastly, the findings in our study served as a basis for subsequent studies on machine translation mediated communication (e.g., Chapter 14). The design implications were also fed back to the development process of the Language Grid Project. Since the design implica-tions proposed in the studies have proven to improve multilingual communication, they have been incorporated into the current Language Grid Toolbox (see Chapter 7).

In the remainder of this chapter, we first introduce the theoretical foundation guiding our work. Next, we present two studies that tested the difficulties of con-versational grounding in machine translation mediated communication. The first study focused on machine translation mediated communication between pairs and the latter focused on triads. We conclude with a discussion of the practical impli-cations of our findings and some issues raised by our studies.

12.2 Grounding and Referential Communication

Interpersonal communication is considerably more efficient when people share a greater amount of common ground– mutual knowledge, beliefs, assumptions, goals, etc. (Clark 1996; Clark and Marshall 1981; Clark and Wilkes-Gibbs 1986). According to Clark, reference is a collaborative process: speakers and addressees work together to establish common ground (Clark and Marshall 1981; Clark and Wilkes-Gibbs 1986). One way they do so is by adopting the same perspective on a referent. Once speakers and their partners have enough evidence to believe that they are talking about the same thing, mapping is grounded between the referent and the perspective (Brennan and Clark 1996). Conversational grounding (Clark 1996), then, refers to a process by which "common ground is updated in an orderly way, by each participant trying to establish that the others have understood their utterances well enough for the current purpose." During the grounding process, people typically become aware of what others do and do not know (Clark and Haviland 1977), and such information helps them formulate appropriate utterances, which leads to effective communication (Clark and Haviland 1977; Grice 1975).

Many social psychological communication studies have employed what has come to be called a "referential communication task." This task allows us to examine the adequacy of communication. Referential communication tasks are not the only way to objectively assess the adequacy of communication, but they have been extensively used (Clark and Marshall 1981; Fussell and Krauss 1992; Krauss and Glucksberg 1969). The most notable research applying this task, for example the studies conducted by Clark (Clark and Wilkes-Gibbs 1986), studied how participants arrange an identical set of figures into matching orders. In each trial, one partner (the Director) is given a set of figures in a predetermined order. The other partner (the Matcher) is given the same figures in a random order. The Director must explain to the Matcher how to arrange the figures in the predetermined order. Typically, this matching task is repeated for several trials, each using the same figures but in different orders. The process of agreeing on a perspective on a referent is known as *lexical entrainment* (Brennan and Clark 1996; Garrod and Anderson 1987). Studies using referential communication tasks have shown that once a pair of communicators has entrained on a particular referring expression for a referent, they tend to abbreviate this expression in subsequent trials.

12.3 Case Study 1: Machine Translation Mediated Communication between Pairs

Since conversational grounding is of such importance to effective communication, communication tools must be designed in such a way that they facilitate conversational grounding, or at least do not hinder the nature of conversational grounding. However, machine translation seems to hinder some of the characteristics inherent in conversational grounding, leading the communicators to ineffective communi-cation.

The first case study aims to uncover the problems inherent in machine transla-tion mediated communication between pairs (Yamashita and Ishida 2006). We highlight the interactional aspect of machine translation mediated communication (i.e. how pairs construct common ground in machine translation mediated com-munication), leaving out the translation quality aspect. The questions of particular interest in this study are: how do speakers and addressees establish common ground when using machine translation? How do they make a reference and iden-tify it without sharing identical referring expressions? Can an addressee smoothly identify a referent after the speaker's referring expressions have been shortened?

12.3.1 Experimental Design

In this study, eight pairs from three different language communities–China, Korea, and Japan–worked on referential tasks in their shared second language (English) and in their native languages using a machine translation embedded chat system. In the experiment, pairs sat in different rooms. Each pair was presented with the same ten Tangram figures arranged in different sequences and instructed to match the arrangements of figures using a multilingual chat system (Fig. 12.1). After matching their arrangements, their figures were placed in two new random orders, and the procedure was repeated. They carried out the task twice in English and twice in their native languages using machine translation. The details of the ex-periment procedure are provided below:

Step (1): Participants engaged in a short-term free discussion on how to sup-port intercultural collaboration using Annochat to become familiar with it. Before matching the figures, participants were told that: a) each person has the same ten figures in different orders; b) their task was to match the arrangements of the fig-ures; and c) they could use any strategy to accomplish the task.

Step (2): Each pair worked on four matching tasks:

Step (2-1), 1st trial in English: Each participant accessed a URL individually arranged immediately before the experiment and got a figure set. Participants matched their arrangements in English.

Step (2-2), 2nd trial in English: As in Step (2-1), each participant got a figure set in which the same figures were arranged in different orders.

Step (2-3), 1st trial in native languages: Each participant got a new figure set whose figures differed from those in Step (2-1) and (2-2). Participants matched ar-rangements in their native languages using machine translation.

Step (2-4), 2nd trial in native language: Participants' figures were placed in two new random orders, and then the procedure was repeated.

The two figure sets (used in English and in native languages) were counterbal-anced for order. The experimental design was incomplete in that language condi-tion was not counterbalanced for order.

Step (3): Following the four matching tasks, participants were interviewed about ease of creating utterances, ease of understanding utterances, how efficiently they conducted the matching tasks, how difficult the matching task was, the usefulness of machine translation, and their English proficiency.

12.3.2 Apparatus: AnnoChat

For the experiment, a multilingual chat system, "AnnoChat" (Fig. 12.1), was prepared that automatically translates each message into the other languages. The machine-translation software embedded in AnnoChat is a commercially available product that is rated as one of the very best translation programs on the market, in terms of translation quality. The chat interface allows users to select their browsing and typing languages from Chinese, English, Korean, and Japanese. For example, a Japanese participant who has selected Japanese for his browsing and typing language will be able to read and write in Japanese. Similarly, when a pair selects English as their browsing and typing language, they can both read and write in English.

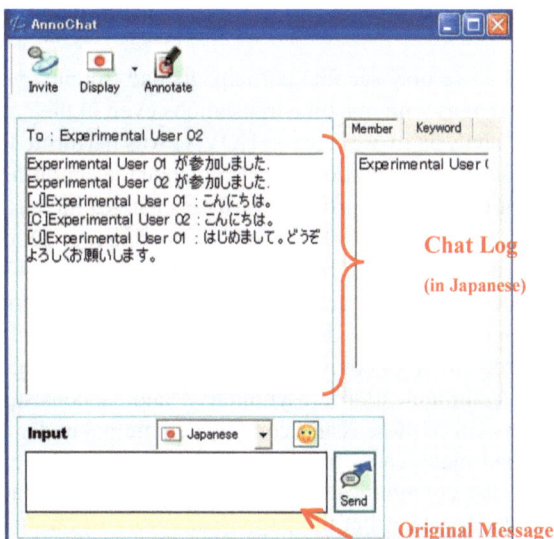

Fig. 12.1 AnnoChat interface (for Japanese participants)

12.3.3 Results: Referential Communication between Pairs

The most efficient way to identify a referent consists of two steps called a "basic exchange": (a) the presentation of a referring expression and (b) its acceptance

(Clark and Wilkes-Gibbs 1986). The rate of basic exchanges typically increases in later trials because they can be based on prior mutually accepted descriptions (Clark and Wilkes-Gibbs 1986). To see whether efficiency differs between conversations in English and those in machine translation mediated communication, we compared the average proportion of basic exchanges in each media condition for each trial.

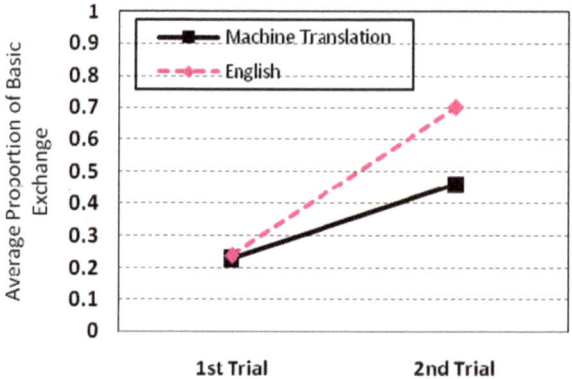

Fig. 12.2 Average proportion of basic exchanges in the first and second trials of each condition.

From Fig. 12.2, we may see that participants had trouble identifying the referents in basic exchanges with machine translations even in their second trials. A repeated measures analysis of variance (ANOVA) was performed on the proportion of basic exchanges, using condition order and language conditions as repeated factors. It turned out that the proportion of basic exchanges increased significantly in second trials ($F[1,7]=68.60$, $p<.001$). There was no main effect of language condition. We found a slight language by trial interaction ($F[1,7]=4.47$, $p=.07$).

To better understand how machine translation made referential communication inefficient, we analyzed the log data of our experiment more closely. As a result, we found two problems that complicated mutual understanding in machine translation mediated communication: "asymmetry" and "inconsistency". Below, we will explain how each of these issues complicated mutual understanding.

First, we found many cases in which communication broke down in machine translation mediated communication due to the asymmetric nature of translation (Fig. 12.3). To understand what the participants were trying to communicate, we translated both the Chinese and Japanese messages into English. Also to share the automatically translated messages, we further translated the Japanese and Chinese translated messages into English, referring to the automatically translated results of the Chinese and Japanese. The original message is underlined and the translated output from machine translation is italicized.

Japanese Screen (translated in English)	Chinese Screen	Chinese Screen (translated in English)
J: 1 is a dancing lady. C: *It jumped.* J: 3 is a person with his head down.	J: 1是跳的女性 C: 是跳的 J: 朝向了下的人是3	J: *1 is a dancing lady.* C: *Ok, a dancing one.* J: *A person looking down is 3.*

Fig. 12.3 Asymmetric issues in machine translation mediated communication

In the above excerpt, the Japanese participant is explaining his first figure, and the Chinese participant shows that she understands the message. From the interview we learned that in her response, she carefully responded, deliberately echoing the same word the Japanese participant had used, to emphasize that she understood the message. However, since the Chinese to Japanese translation translated "dance" into "jump," the Japanese participant got confused. He breaks off matching his first figure and starts explaining his third figure. The Japanese participant mentioned in the interview that he could not understand what his partner meant, so he decided to proceed with another figure that looked easier to match. In sum, it appears that echoing as a ratification behavior was disrupted by the asymmetric nature of machine translations.

Second, regarding the inconsistency issues, we found that participants had problems abbreviating referring expressions over trials when using machine translations. When two people in conversation refer repeatedly to the same object, the referring expressions are typically simplified and shortened (Krauss and Glucksberg 1969), and the expressions converge on the same or similar referring expressions (Brennan 1996; Brennan and Clark 1996). There are two main strategies for shortening referring expressions: simplification, and less often, narrowing (Clark and Wilkes-Gibbs 1986). With simplification, certain details, usually adjectives, are omitted while retaining the referent's overall image, as in "a guy running with shiny gold-rimmed glasses" to "a guy running with gold-rimmed glasses." With narrowing, the focus of a perspective is narrowed to just one part of a figure. The perspective typically moves to a peripheral but distinctive part, as in "a guy running with shiny gold-rimmed glasses" to "gold-rimmed glasses."

To see how participants abbreviated referring expressions in their second trials, we classified each of a speaker's referring expressions on the second trial in each condition into one of four categories: identical, narrowed, simplified, and different (Table 12.1).

Table 12.1 Abbreviation of referring expressions in the 2nd trial

	Identical	*Narrowed*	*Simplified*	*Different*
English	33%	6%	50%	11%
Machine Translation	58%	22%	14%	6%

As shown in Table 12.1, participants using machine translation rarely short-ened referring expressions in a simplified manner (F[1,7]=25.53, p=.001). Instead, they often identified a figure by using *exactly* the same referring expressions as on the first trial (e.g., Fig. 12.4) or by using a distinctive narrowed term from the re-ferring expression in the first trial (e.g., Fig. 12.4) (F[1,7]=138.03, p<.001).

To see why the speakers did not shorten their lengthy referring expressions in their second trial, we examined the conversations in our experiment in further de-tail. As shown in Fig. 12.4, we found many cases in which machine translation translated messages quite differently in the first and second trials, even when the referring expressions overlapped considerably.

Japanese Screen (translated in English) <First Trial>	Chinese Screen (translated in English) <First Trial>
J: My second figure looks like an animal. J: It has four feet and a tail. C: That's my the 9th.	J: My second figure is like an animal. J: It has four feet and a tail. C: That's my 9th.
<Second Trial>	<Second Trial>
J: My second figure is an animal with a tail and four feet. C: What kind of meaning and rice boy? J: My second figure looks like an animal. J: It has four feet and a tail. C: Oh, I understand, and am the 8th.	J: My role of a young handsome beau is a boy with a tail and 4 feet. C: What do you mean? A handsome boy? J: My second figure is like an animal. J: It has four feet and a tail. C: I got it. It's my 8th figure.

Fig. 12.4 Inconsistency issues in machine translation mediated communication.

In the excerpt above, a Chinese participant and a Japanese participant matched one of the Tangrams in two sentences: "looks like an animal" and "it has four feet and a tail." In their second trial, the Japanese speaker tried to explain the same figure in one sentence: "an animal with a tail and four feet." In ordinary conversa-tion, the addressee would obviously recognize the meaning of the sentence (i.e., recognize the original in the new version). However, machine translation gener-ates something quite different ("My role of a young handsome beau is a boy with a tail and 4 feet.") based on very small changes. As a result, the reference becomes uninterpretable, and the Japanese speaker reuses exactly the same explanation he gave in the first trial. In the post-experimental interview, the Japanese participant said, "I got afraid of rephrasing an expression. I thought it was a reliable way to use the same referential expression as in the first trial." In sum, participants using machine translation tend, in their second trial, to use the same referring expressions as they did in the first trial or to select distinctive terms from the first trial to safely identify figures without misunderstandings.

12.4 Case Study 2: Machine Translation Mediated Communication among Triads

To mitigate the problems found in the first case study, a novel solution called *back translation* (Shigenobu 2007) has been proposed. Back translation provides speakers with the awareness of how their utterances are translated into other languages by retranslating the translated utterances back into the speaker's language. Studies have demonstrated that the technique improves translation quality in machine translation mediated communication (Shigenobu 2007). Despite this breakthrough, some problems remain unresolved in multiparty machine-translation-mediated communication. Even with the use of back translation, an addressee in a three-way machine-translation-mediated communication cannot monitor how the speaker's utterance is translated to the other addressee. For example, speaker A's message is translated into B's and C's languages simultaneously and back translations from both languages are shown to A. However, B (C) cannot monitor the translation between A and C (B). Furthermore, the two addressees (B and C) cannot be aware whether they share the same information (i.e.. A's utterance). Finally, addressee B (C) cannot be aware what addressee C (B) did and did not understand of A's utterance.

Such difficulties seem to cause a significant problem when grounding conversation via machine translation. Indeed, an interview with an NPO which has been using a machine-translation-embedded chat system for two years revealed that they were facing particular difficulties when conducting multiparty group meetings. All of the interviewees mentioned that it was virtually impossible to conduct a group meeting when the total number of languages within the group was larger than two. Inspired by such interviews, the second case study aims to clarify the reasons why machine translation mediated conversation is so difficult when the number of group members is larger than two (Yamashita et al. 2009). We build on the first case study by expanding the experiment on referential communication from pairs to triads. Specifically, we compose triads whose members come from three different language communities—China, Korea, and Japan—and compare their referential communication under two conditions: in their shared second language (English) and in their native languages using machine translation.

12.4.1 Design

In this study, thirteen triads (total of thirty-nine participants) from different language communities—China, Korea, and Japan—participated in the experiment.

Nine triads participated in a referential communication task using their native languages through machine translation; four triads participated in the same referential communication task using a common language (English, which is not their native language). The experimental design was a between-subjects design for comparing referential communications carried out using a method similar to the above two-language case. The experiment's procedure was as follows:

Step(1): On arrival, participants were taken to a room and asked to complete experimental consent forms. Next, participants were taken to a room partitioned into three compartments with a computer in each, and asked to sit in front of one of the computers. Participants were then given explanations of how to use Langrid Chat and an overview of the experiment. Participants were told that a) each person has the same set of figures in different orders; b) there are three roles: one Director and two Matchers; c) the Director must explain each figure one by one until both Matchers arrange their figures in the Director's order; d) the matching task is repeated six times using the same figures but in different orders, and each time the role of Director is rotated.

Step(2): As a pre-study, the participants engaged in a short-term referential communication task using three Tangram figures (different from those used in the next step). The pre-study was conducted to let participants familiarize themselves with Langrid Chat.

Step(3): Triads were presented with eight Tangram figures arranged in different sequences, and they were instructed to match the arrangements of figures using Langrid Chat.

12.4.2 Apparatus: Langrid Chat

For the experiment, we used a machine-translation-embedded chat system called "Langrid Chat" (Ishida 2006) (Fig. 12.5). The machine-translation software embedded in Langrid Chat is a commercially available product that is rated as one of the very best translation programs on the market, in terms of translation quality. Langrid Chat is also equipped with a back translation function: when a user types a sentence into the typing area, the system automatically translates the sentence into other languages, retranslates them back into the original language, and shows them to the user (Fig. 12.5 (right)). Back translation is provided in real time so that users can edit their messages before sending them to others.

The chat interface allows each user to select his/her browsing and typing language from Chinese, English, Korean, and Japanese. For example, a Japanese participant who selects Japanese for his browsing and typing language can read and write in Japanese. Similarly, when a triad selects English as their browsing and typing language, they can both read and write in English.

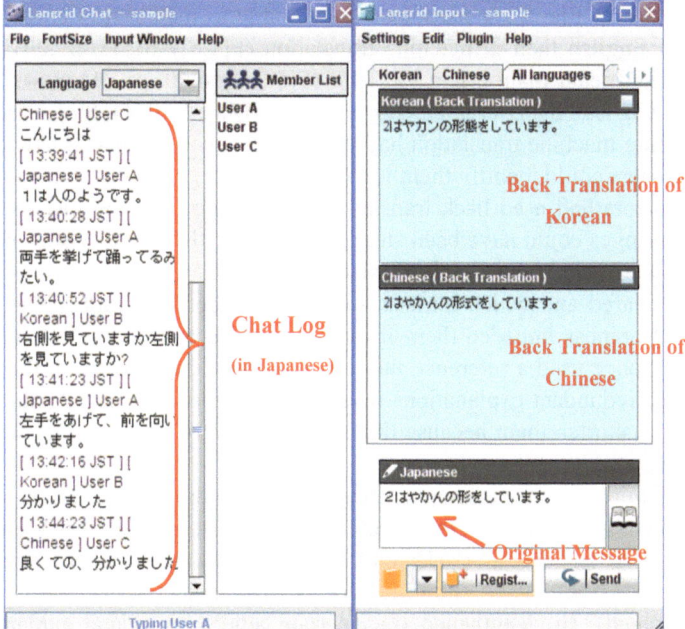

Fig. 12.5 Langrid Chat interface (for Japanese participants)

12.4.3 Results: Referential Communication among Triads

Similar to the first case study, we started with examining how much Directors improved in making appropriate references over trials; we calculated for each trial the rate of participants matching the figures through basic exchanges (i.e., the most efficient way to match a figure: a Director proposing a reference and two Matchers accepting the reference immediately). Then, we performed a repeated measure ANOVA on those rates.

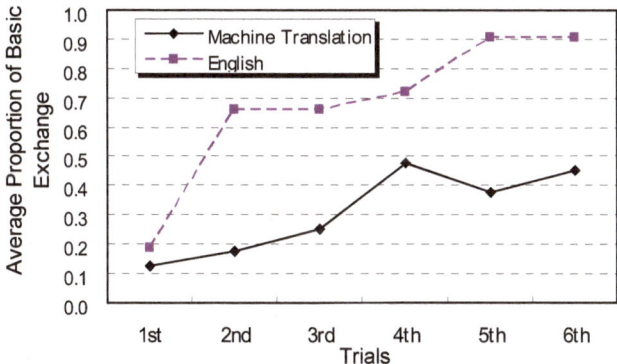

Fig. 12.6 Average proportion of basic exchanges among triads.

As shown in Fig. 12.6, participants were able to match the figures more efficiently in English than in machine translation ($F[1,8]$)=61.43, $p<.001$). We also found a significant main effect for Trial ($F[5, 40]$=6.40, $p<.01$) as well as a significant Language by Trial interaction ($F[5,40]$=12.0, $p<.001$). It appeared that Directors using machine translation had difficulty improving their references so that both Matchers could identify them immediately.

If Directors had used back translation more rigorously, the increasing rate of basic exchanges could have been steeper. However, the problem does not lie only in the disinclination to use back translation. Directors were not aware which terms could be shared and which terms could not be shared with all of the members. Such unawareness impeded them from constructing appropriate references; even when they once used a reference that could be shared among all of the members, they added redundant explanations when some problems occurred, and they were reluctant to shorten them because they were not aware which references could be shared among all members.

To examine whether participants can abbreviate this expression on subsequent trials, we compared the lengths of referring expressions of the same Director between the first and second cycles and classified for each referent whether the referring expression was (i) shortened (i.e., certain adjectives or/and explanations are eliminated), (ii) lengthened (i.e., certain adjectives or/and explanations are added), or (iii) other (identical or totally differentiated). For each participant, we calculated the rates of shortened and lengthened referring expressions.

Although the difference was not significant, participants shortened their referring expressions slightly more when using English (Avg: 45%) than machine translation (Avg: 31%) ($F[1,8]$=3.98, $p=.08$). As a more interesting finding, participants lengthened their referring expressions significantly more when using machine translation (Avg: 19%) than English (Avg: 6%) ($F[1,8]$=5.21, $p<.05$). It seems that participants had trouble finding referring expressions that could be shared with all three members. Even in a case where a Director's reference was smoothly accepted by the Matchers in the first cycle, the Director sometimes lengthened his or her referent in the second cycle because the reference could not be used between the two Matchers (when one of the Matchers became the Director). The excerpt below captures this tendency (figure 12.7).

As shown in Fig. 12.7, it appears that the Directors could not determine which terms to omit and which to keep (from 4th to 6th trial). We infer that Directors are reluctant to abbreviate their referring expressions once a new adjective and/or explanation is added during their mutual acceptance process, since they do not know which terms are translated correctly among all language pairs or why a new explanation has been added. To minimize their collaborative effort, it seems that they adopt a strategy of listing several references so that some parts of the list will be correctly translated in the translations of any language pair. We speculate that such difficulties in sharing the same reference will increase as the number of languages increases in multiparty machine translation mediated communication.

Japanese Screen (translated in English) <First Trial> **Director**	Korean Screen (translated in English) <First Trial>	Chinese Screen (translated in English) <First Trial>
J: Number 2 is a horse.	J: Number 2 is a horse.	J: Number 2 is a horse.
<Second Trial>	<Second Trial> **Director**	<Second Trial>
K: Number 4 is	K: Number 4 is a person standing upside down.	K: 4 times
(snip)		
J: Mr. B. Which number is the animal?	J: Mr. B. Which number is the animal?	J: Mr. B. Which number is the animal?
K: Animal?	K: Animal?	K: Animal?
(snip)		
J: Which number is the creature with a square tail?	J: Which number is the creature by which a tail is a square?	J: A tail, what number is a square creature?
C: An animal will be 8 days.	C: An animal is 8 days.	C: Animal is number 8.
K: I wouldn't know what to say, but something like an animal is 4 times most.	K: I don't know what you are saying but the most animal like thing is number 4.	K: Something like whatever animal says, is it wasteful, an unclear one is 4 times most.
<Third Trial>	<Third Trial>	<Third Trial> **Director**
C: It seems to be an animal.	C: It seems to be an animal.	C: It looks like an animal.
C: Horse.	C: Horse.	C: Horse.
<Fourth Trial> **Director**	<Fourth Trial>	<Fourth Trial>
J: Horse. Animal.	J : Horse. Animal.	J : Horse. Animal.
J: Tail is square.	J: A tail is square.	J: A tail is square.
<Fifth Trial>	<Fifth Trial> **Director**	<Fifth Trial>
K : It's an animal.	K: It's an animal.	K : It's an animal.
K: Its seems to be a word which raised its foreleg.	K: It's a shape of a horse raising its front legs.	K: A word is the design which entered a foreleg.
<Sixth Trial>	<Sixth Trial>	<Sixth Trial> **Director**
C: Animal, it seems to be a horse.	C: Animal, it seems to be a horse.	C: Animal, seems to be a horse.
C: There is a square on the right side.	C: There is a square on the right side.	C: There is a square on the right side.

Fig. 12.7 Difficulties in abbreviating referring expressions among triads.

12.5 Discussion

The results provide insight into the effects of machine translation on referential communication. From our first case study, we found that (1) due to the asymmetries in machine translations, echoing, which is an important way part of the ratification process in lexical entrainment (Brennan and Clark 1996), is disrupted; (2) Since machine translations do not translate the same terms consistently throughout the conversation, the process of shortening referring expressions is also disrupted. Subsequently, from our second case study, we found the following difficulties in constructing common ground in multiparty machine translation mediated communication: (1) due to the discrepancy between translation from A to B and that from A to C, participants cannot share the same conversational content with others (2) since machine translations do not allow the participants to monitor how each utterance is translated into the other languages, participants cannot be aware of what information they share and do not share with others.

Our findings from the two studies suggest four recommendations for the design of future machine-translation-embedded communication systems to support natural referring behavior.

- Machine translations of each pair of languages should coordinate and resolve asymmetries.

- Machine translations should take into account contextual information (particularly terms used in the recent past) and resolve inconsistency issues.

- Machine translations should provide addressees with an awareness of how a speaker's utterance is translated to other addressees using different languages (e.g., whether it is translated correctly or which part of the utterance is mistranslated) in order to alleviate the problems caused by discrepancy between translation from A to B and that from A to C.
- Machine translations should provide speakers with an awareness of how their utterances are translated between addressees (i.e., whether the terms they are using can also be used between addressees).

It is worth noting that the first design implication has proven to be effective and has been incorporated into the Language Grid (Chapter 7).

We should note, however, that the results may vary according to the experimental setting (such as tasks and communication medium used). For example, participants in our experiment often used exactly the same referring expressions throughout the process to ensure consistent translation. Identifying a figure using the same expression might be useful in cases where the participants continuously work together and frequently refer to the same referents, as in our experiment. Although people have remarkably good memories for the expressions they entrain on (Krauss and Glucksberg 1969), we speculate that it would be difficult for participants to remember lengthy expressions exactly when working intermittently.

12.6 Conclusion

Earlier studies of machine translation have focused almost exclusively on translating written (unidirectional) documents. Many natural language processing researchers have become experts on developing high quality translation algorithms of certain language pairs in one direction. Thus, most research in machine translation has not taken into account interaction (dual-directional) factors. Also, machine translations have commonly been evaluated by the adequacy and fluency of translated single sentences. Our study raises concerns about the mismatch between such history of machine translation and the nature of communication. Many of the issues raised in this study are caused by the fact that machine translation systems consist of an aggregation of unidirectional translation systems. These issues cannot be resolved by simply improving the translation quality of single sentences. We believe that there is a need to consider a new definition of translation quality that improves machine translation mediated communication.

Acknowledgments   This research is partially supported by International Communications Foundation and the Kyoto University Global COE Program: Informatics Education and Research Center for Knowledge-Circulating Society. We would like to express our sincere gratitude to Susan Fussell for providing significant help in improving the studies. We would also like to thank Hideaki Kuzuoka for his assistance and insightful comments. We also thank Rieko Inaba and Takashi Yoshino for their assistance in running the experiments.

References

Brennan SE (1996) Lexical entrainment in spontaneous dialogue. International Symposium on Spoken Dialogue: 41-44

Brennan SE, Clark HH (1996) Conceptual pacts and lexical choice in conversation. Journal of Experimental Psychology: Learning, Memory, and Cognition 22(6): 1482-1493.

Clark HH (1996) Using language. Cambridge, UK, Cambridge University Press

Clark HH, Haviland SE (1977) Comprehension and the given-new contract. In Freedle RO (Ed.), Discourse Production and Comprehension, Ablex, Norwood: 1-40

Clark HH, Marshall CR (1981) Definite reference and mutual knowledge. In Joshi AK, Webber BL, Sag I (Eds.) Elements of discourse understanding, Cambridge Univeristy Press, Cambridge: 10-63

Clark HH, Wilkes-Gibbs D (1986) Referring as a collaborative process. Cognition 22: 1-39

Climent S, More J, Oliver A, Salvatierra M, Sanchez I, Taule M, Vallmanya L (20003) Bilingual newsgroups in Catalonia: a challenge for machine translation. Journal of Computer Mediated Communication 9(1)

Fussell SR, Krauss RM (1992) Coordination of knowledge in communication: effects of speakers' assumptions about what others know. Journal of Personality and Social Psych 62(3): 378-391

Garrod S, Anderson A (1987) Saying what you mean in dialogue: a study in conceptual and semantic co-ordination. Cognition 27: 41-48

Grice HP (1975) Logic and conversation. In Cole P, Morgan JL (Eds.) Syntax and Semantics 3: Speech Acts, Seminar Press, New York: 113-127.

Ishida T (2006) Language Grid: an infrastructure for intercultural collaboration. 2006 IEEE/IPSJ
    Symposium on Applications and the Internet (SAINT-06): 96-100
Krauss RM, Glucksberg S (1969) The development of communication: competence as a function
    of age. Child Development 40(1): 255-266
Krauss RM, Fussell SR (1990) Mutual knowledge and communicative effectiveness. In Galla-
    gher J, Kraut RE, Egido C (Eds.) Intellectual Teamwork: Social and Technological Founda-
    tions of Cooperative Work, Erlbaum, Hillsdale: 111-146
Ogden B, Warner J, Jin W, Sorge J (2003) Information sharing across languages using MITRE's
    trim instant messaging
Shigenobu T (2007) evaluation and usability of back translation for intercultural communication.
    International Conference on Human-Computer Interaction (HCII-07) 10: 259-265
Takano Y, Noda A (1993) A temporary decline of thinking ability during foreign language proc-
    essing. Journal of Cross-Cultural Psychology 24: 445-462
Yamashita N, Inaba R, Kuzuoka H, Ishida T (2009) Difficulties in establishing common ground
    in multiparty groups using machine translation. CHI09: 679-688
Yamashita N, Ishida T (2006) Effects of machine translation on collaborative work. CSCW2006:
    515-524

Part V

Language Grid for Translation

Chapter 13
Humans in the Loop of Localization Processes

Donghui Lin

National Institute of Information and Communications Technology (NICT), 3-5 Hikaridai, Seika-Cho, Soraku-Gun, Kyoto, 619-0289, Japan, e-mail: lindh@nict.go.jp

Abstract The Language Grid is a service-oriented infrastructure for language services. In the Language Grid, machine translation services play important roles in supporting multilingual activities for communities. Although the effectiveness of using machine translation services for multilingual communication has been shown in previous reports, the gap between human translators and machine translators remains huge especially in the domain of localization processes that require high translation quality. In this chapter, we aim at improving localization processes by introducing humans into the loop to utilize machine translation services. We try to compare several different types of localization processes (i.e., absolute machine translation processes, absolute human translation processes and processes by human and machine translation services) in the dimensions of translation quality and translation cost. The experiment results show that monolinguals can help improve the translation quality of machine translators with the aid of community dictionary services, and that collaboration of human and machine translation services make it possible to reduce the cost compared with absolute human translations.

13.1 Introduction

In recent years, more and more machine translation services have become available on the Internet that are provided by companies and research institutes. People use these machine translation services to browse information in different languages and communicate with other people who speak different languages. However, the gap between human and machine translation services remains huge. On the one hand, machine translators always have limitations in translation quality and therefore are seldom used for translating documents which require a high quality translation. On the other hand, human translators are not always available in the real world and the cost of translations of highly-trained bilingual individuals is always high. Although most of the previous studies show the possibility of combining human and machine translators for supporting multilingual communication, there is little consideration of how to apply such approaches for supporting professional translation that requires high business qualities in the real world, e.g., localization processes.

The Language Grid is developed to share many available language resources that are distributed on the Internet with different interfaces, including machine translation services, dictionary services and so on. Community users can combine existing language services, and create new language services for their own purposes as well. For example, machine translation services and community dictionary services can be composed to improve translation quality in the Language Grid. Moreover, the Language Grid is also designed to enable humans to be in the loop of processes. Therefore, the Language Grid offers the possibilities for improving traditional localization processes. Based on various language services provided on the Language Grid, we aim at improving localization processes by composing human and machine translation services. When introducing humans into the loop of localization processes, we consider both monolinguals and bilinguals. Monolinguals are considered in the localization processes because they are always more available and cost less than bilinguals. In more detail, monolinguals are introduced to modify the translation results produced by the machine translation services, while bilinguals are introduced to check the modification results and also translate the contents that cannot be modified by the monolinguals.

To evaluate the effectiveness of introducing humans into the machine translation processes, we conduct experiments to compare the translation qualities and costs using several different localization processes, including absolute machine translation processes, absolute human translation processes and translation processes by human and machine translators. By introducing humans in the loop of localization processes based on the Language Grid, we expect that (1) monolinguals could help improve the translation qualities of machine translation services with the aid of community dictionary services, and (2) collaboration of humans and machine translators could reduce translation cost compared with absolute human translations.

The remainder of the chapter is organized as follows: we first explain how the Language Grid can help to improve localization processes in Sect. 13.2. In Sect. 13.3, localization processes composing human and machine translation services are proposed. Section 13.4 shows a case study of translation processes with experiments. The analysis and discussion of the experiments is shown in Sect. 13.5. In Sect. 13.6, we introduce some related work. Section 13.7 is the conclusion of this research.

13.2 Language Grid for Localization Processes

The Language Grid collects language resources (e.g., machine translation services, dictionary services, parallel text services, morphological analysis services and so on), which are wrapped as atomic Web services by standard interfaces. Moreover, a series of composite services with advanced functions have also been developed based on the atomic services. Fig. 13.1 shows a composite machine translation service which was developed with a WS-BPEL specification (Alves et al. 2007) in the Language Grid, which combines several atomic services including morphological analysis service, a multilingual dictionary service, a machine translation service, and so on. By combining dictionary services and other services, the translation quality can be improved compared with the atomic machine translation service (Inaba et al. 2007) (Ishida 2010).

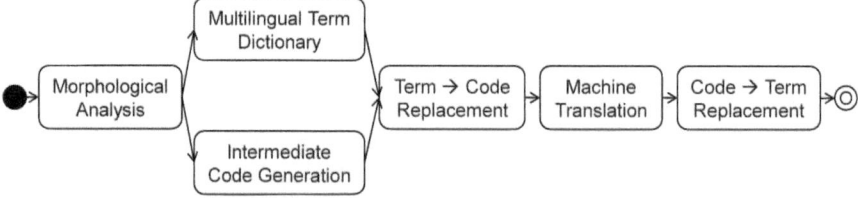

Fig. 13.1 Composite machine translation service on the Language Grid

The Language Grid promises to improve traditional localization processes based on the following features.

Variety of language services. Since users have different requirements for translation quality, it is necessary to provide different services/composite processes with different quality for the same function. In the Language Grid, language services are categorized into several classes. For each service class, multiple services/composite processes are provided for different requirements. For example, the translation service class includes atomic machine translation service (e.g., Google Translator, J-Server, Parsit, Toshiba, Translution, Web-Transer, YakushiteNet and so on), two-hop machine translation service, composite machine translation service combined with bilingual dictionary, and so on.

Customization of language services. The Language Grid enables community users to deploy their own language services following the standard interfaces. Therefore, users can flexibly choose atomic translation services or composite translation services (e.g., any combination of atomic translation services and global dictionaries or user dictionaries for composite machine translation service combined with dictionaries) on the Language Grid for their own requirements. Moreover, it is also possible to combine humans with the composite translation services on the Language Grid..

13.3 Composing Humans and Machine Translation Services

In the area of machine translation, translation results were evaluated based on two dimensions in previous reports, i.e., adequacy and fluency (White et al. 1994).

Adequacy refers to the degree to which the translation communicates information present in the original, while fluency refers to the degree to which the translation is well-formed according to the grammar of the target language. In this research, we also use these dimensions to evaluate the translation results.

Although many types of translation services/processes are provided in the Language Grid, automatic machine translation services can never have perfect fluency and adequacy on average even when they are combined with dictionaries or other services for quality improvement. For example, the composite service in Fig. 13.1 might be able to deal with the requirement for online chatting among people in different countries, while it is difficult to use such a service to write business documents or translate product manuals. Therefore, we consider combining machine translation services and human activities in cases of localization processes. As for humans in the loop of localization processes, monolinguals and bilinguals can be considered. When there is an existing machine translation service (either atomic service or composite service as described in Sect. 13.2), the human activities may be combined with the machine translation service in different ways to improve the whole process:

(1) Introduce a monolingual revision activity for preprocessing the source sentences for machine translation, e.g., changing long sentences into short ones or changing the sequence of words to one which may be handled by machine translation services more easily;

(2) Introduce a monolingual revision activity for post-processing the output translation results by improving the fluency of the machine translation results;

(3) Introduce a bilingual revision activity for post-processing the revision results products by the monolinguals.

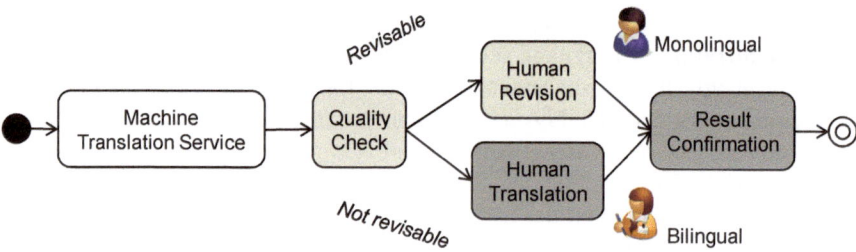

Fig. 13.2 Introducing humans into the loop of localization processes

In this research, we mainly consider localization processes where human roles are induced to process the translation results. In more detail, we focus on the process as shown in Fig. 13.2. The proposed process combines machine translator, monolinguals and bilinguals, where *Machine Translation Service* indicates the atomic machine translation service or composite machine translation service provided by the Language Grid. Monolinguals are introduced to revise the translation results of the machine translators, while bilinguals are introduced to check the revision results and also to translate the contents that cannot be revised by the monolingual revisers. The process can be realized by describing the human activities using BPEL4People (Kloppmann et al. 2005) to extend the existing machine translation services on the Language Grid.

13.4 Experiment Settings

The localization processes are effective if translation quality keeps high while translation cost keeps low. Therefore, both translation quality and translation cost must be considered when evaluating localization processes. First, the translation quality is expected to be kept high compared with the absolute human processes since we still have human roles in the proposed processes. Second, the translation cost is expected to be kept low since we include machine translation services and monolingual human roles in the proposed processes that might be less expensive than bilingual human roles.

We have the following hypotheses for the experiments: (1) composing monolinguals and community dictionary services improves the translation quality of machine translators, and (2) collaboration of human and machine translators reduces the cost compared with the absolute bilingual translation.

13.4.1 Translation Processes

In this research, we use the two dimensions (fluency and adequacy) that we have introduced in Sect. 13.3 to evaluate the quality of translations using the method in the DARPA TIDES Project at University of Pennsylvania, with a five-level score for each dimension. For example, when evaluating the Chinese translation result, the evaluation criteria of fluency is 5: Flawless Chinese, 4: Good Chinese, 3: Nonnative Chinese, 4: Unfluent Chinese, 5: Incomprehensible, and the evaluation criteria of adequacy is 5: All, 4: Most, 3: Much, 4: Little, 5: None.

We use the following processes in this experiment. *MT* is an atomic machine translation service. *MT+Dic* is a composite translation service with dictionary as shown in Fig. 13.1. *MT+Mono* and *MT+Dic+Mono* are collaborative translation processes by monolinguals and machine translation services (omitting the bilingual activities in Fig. 13.2). *MT+Mono+Bi* and *MT+Dic+Mono+Bi* are collaborative translation processes shown in Fig. 13.2. Machine translation services are atomic translation services in *MT+Mono* and *MT+Mono+Bi*, and composite translation services combined with a dictionary in *MT+Dic+Mono* and *MT+Dic+Mono+Bi*. *Bi* is an absolute human process. *Bi+TM* is an absolute human process with the aid of tools like translation memory which can automatically complete 15% of the translation tasks. The descriptions of the above processes are given in Table 13.1 in detail.

Table 13.1 Translation processes in the experiments

Process	Description
MT	An atomic Japanese-Chinese machine translation service.
MT+Dic	A composite Japanese-Chinese machine translation service combined with user dictionaries.
MT+Mono	An atomic Japanese-Chinese machine translation service combined with human tasks. The human tasks are conducted by a Chinese monolingual person to revise the understandable machine translation results.
MT+Dic+ Mono	A composite Japanese-Chinese machine translation service combined with user dictionaries and human tasks. The human tasks are conducted by a Chinese monolingual person to revise the understandable machine translation results.
MT+Mono+ Bi	An atomic Japanese-Chinese machine translation service combined with human tasks. The human tasks are conducted by a Chinese monolingual person to revise the understandable machine translation results and a Chinese-Japanese bilingual person to confirm the correctness of the revised results in *MT+Mono* as well as translating the unrevised parts in *MT+Mono*.
MT+Dic+ Mono+Bi	A composite Japanese-Chinese machine translation service combined with user dictionaries and human tasks. The human tasks are conducted by a Chinese monolingual person to revise the understandable machine translation results and a Chinese-Japanese bilingual person to confirm the correctness of the revised results in *MT+Dic+Mono* as well as translating the unrevised parts in *MT+Dic+Mono*.
Bi+TM	A human translation process conducted by a Japanese-Chinese bilingual person with translation memory software.
Bi	A human translation process conducted by a Japanese-Chinese bilingual person without any Web services or translation memory software.

For each process described in Table 13.1, we run 17 process instances to translate a Japanese sentence to a Chinese sentence. The Japanese sentences are randomly picked from a description manual for a digital camera from a Japanese company for localization, with average sentence length of 42 Japanese characters.

13.4.2 Machine Translation Services and Humans

Machine translation services used in the experiments include an atomic machine translation service and a composite machine translation service as shown in Fig. 13.1. Main language services used in our experiments are provided in the Language Grid by wrapping language resources including J-Server Japanese-Chinese machine translation service provided by Kodensha Co., Ltd, Mecab Japanese morphological analysis service provided by NTT Communication Science Laboratories, and a user Japanese-Chinese dictionary service for digital cameras which covers 18.75% of words in the Japanese sentences for execution.

Human tasks in the experiments are conducted by a Japanese-Chinese bilingual translator and a Chinese monolingual reviser with the cost of 30 units and 15 units per hour respectively.

13.5 Analysis

In our experiments, we analyze the translation quality and cost of different translation processes as described in Sect. 13.4.

13.5.1 Translation Quality

Table 13.2 presents the experimental results of fluency and adequacy of translation for *MT*, *MT+Dic*, *MT+Dic+Mono*. Besides, we also evaluate the translation quality for *MT+Mono* with the average fluency as 3.5 and adequacy as 3.3. Results of *MT+Mono+Bi*, *MT+Dic+Mono+Bi*, *Bi+TM* and *Bi* are not listed because fluency and adequacy are both 5 for each instance. The result shows that the machine translation quality in *MT* is limited and cannot meet the requirements for localization processes. However, it can be improved by using a composite translating service by combining dictionaries and other services. For *MT+Dic*}, adequacy of the translation result is not less than 3 in 88% of process instances (15 of 17). By combining machine translator and dictionaries, the translation quality can be further improved from *MT* to *MT+Dic* (fluency: 2.8 to 3.2, adequacy: 3.0 to 3.7). Composing monolingual human tasks with the composite translation service with dictionaries, the translation quality can be further improved from *MT+Dic* to *MT+Dic+Mono* (fluency: 3.2 to 4.5, adequacy: 3.7 to 4.4). There is also an interesting observation that the adequacy of translation result in *MT+Dic* (adequacy: 3.7) is even better than that of *MT+Mono* (adequacy: 3.3), which means that collaborative translation by human and machine translator also has limitations if the original translation quality is not good. The result reveals that community dictionary services are very important to improve machine translation quality. In one word, the results in Table 13.2 give evidence to support our first hypothesis that composing monolingual roles and dictionary services improves the translation quality of machine translators. We can also see that the improvement is very effective when the original translation quality (fluency and adequacy) of machine translation is around the level of 2 to 4.

Table 13.2 Experimental results of translation qualities in different processes.

Process	Fluency			Adequacy		
Instance	*MT*	*MT+Dic*	*MT+Dic+Mono*	*MT*	*MT+Dic*	*MT+Dic+Mono*
#1	5	5	5	5	5	5
#2	4	5	5	4	5	5
#3	2	3	5	2	4	4
#4	2	2	5	3	3	5
#5	1	1	1	1	2	2
#6	5	5	5	5	5	5
#7	1	2	5	2	3	5
#8	2	4	5	2	4	5
#9	1	1	1	2	2	2
#10	3	3	5	4	4	3
#11	3	3	5	4	4	5
#12	5	5	5	3	5	5
#13	3	3	5	3	4	5
#14	3	3	5	4	4	5
#15	4	4	5	3	3	5
#16	3	3	5	3	3	5
#17	1	3	5	1	3	4
Average	2.8	3.2	4.5	3.0	3.7	4.4

13.5.2 Translation Cost

Table 13.3 presents the experimental results on translation cost and time duration for *MT+Mono+Bi, MT+Dic+Mono+Bi, Bi+TM* and *Bi*, which have equal translation qualities with fluency and adequacy both 5 and can be used as localization processes. The results show that collaborative translation processes by human and machine translator (*MT+Mono+Bi* and *MT+Dic+Mono+Bi*) can reduce the translation cost compared with the human translation process (*Bi* and *Bi+TM*) by up to 35%. However, the time duration of the four processes do not significantly differ from each other since we simply add the execution duration of the machine translator and human tasks for all 17 process instances when computing the execution duration in collaborative translation processes (*MT+Mono+Bi* and

MT+Dic+Mono+Bi). However, if we consider the parallel execution of process instances and human tasks, the execution duration is expected to be reduced in collaborative translation processes (*MT+Mono+Bi* and *MT+Dic+Mono+Bi*). In summary, the results in Table 13.3 give evidence to support our second hypothesis that collaboration of human and machine translators may reduce the cost compared with the absolute bilingual human translation.

Table 13.3 Comparison of translation cost and duration for different translation processes

Process	Human	Time	Cost
Bi	Bilingual (1)	40min	20.00
Bi+TM	Bilingual (1)	35min	17.50
MT+Mono+Bi	Bilingual (1) Monolingual (1)	39min	16.50
MT+Dic+Mono+Bi	Bilingual (1) Monolingual (1)	36min	13.00

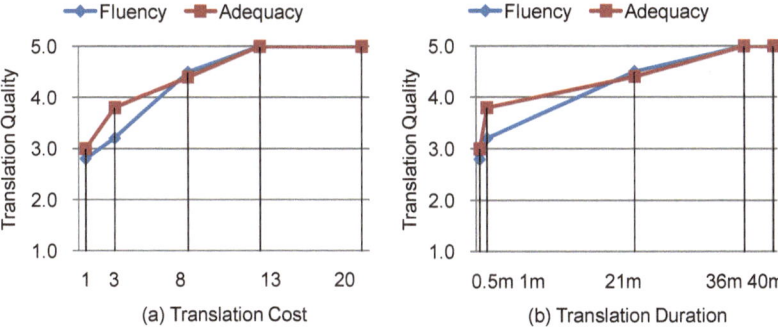

Fig. 13.3 Translation cost and duration (Processes from left to right in each chart: *MT, MT+Dic, MT+Dic+Mono, MT+Dic+Mono+Bi, Bi*)

Fig. 13.3 shows the relationship between translation quality and translation cost/duration for five different processes: *MT, MT+Dic, MT+Dic+Mono, MT+Dic+Mono+Bi* and *Bi*. The result shows that both execution cost and execution duration increase from *MT, MT+Dic, MT+Dic+Mono, MT+Dic+Mono+Bi* to *Bi*, which means that more cost and duration are required to get higher translation quality. For *MT* and *MT+Dic* that consist of automatic services only, the cost and duration are much less compared with processes composed of both human and services. However, the acquired translation quality is also very limited. For *MT+Dic+Mono+Bi* and *Bi* with the requirements of perfect translation quality, the cost and duration are many times more than those of *MT* and *MT+Dic*. *MT+Dic+Mono+Bi* which is composed of both human and Web services saves 20% execution cost compared to *Bi* which is a completely human process. The experiment result also shows that execution duration of *MT+Dic+Mono+Bi* and *Bi* do not significantly differ from each other since we simply add the execution duration of the services and human tasks for all 17 process instances when computing the execution duration of *MT+Dic+Mono+Bi*. However, if we consider the parallel execution of process instances and human tasks, the execution duration can be reduced significantly in *MT+Dic+Mono+Bi*. The translation quality of *MT+Dic+Mono* is not perfect compared to *MT+Dic+Mono+Bi* and *Bi*, but at a relatively high level compared to *MT* and *MT+Dic*. The execution cost and execution duration of *MT+Dic+Mono* are more than *MT* and *MT+Dic*, but much less than *MT+Dic+Mono+Bi* and *Bi* (save about 50%).

13.5.3 Discussion

Since the experimental results are based on an experiment of very small scale, we cannot simply conclude that the hypotheses in Sect. 13.4 are true for all cases. Actually, when inducing human activities to keep high translation quality, the translation cost is affected in different ways by the varying execution rate of human activities and machine translation services in the proposed localization processes. In cases where human activities are induced but not efficiently executed, the translation cost of a composite process comprising both machine translation services and human activities is even higher than an absolute human process. In the experiments we conduct, the monolingual human task *human revision* is executed in 88% of process instances in *MT+Dic+Mono* and *MT+Dic+Mono+Bi*. To analyze how the execution rate of *human revision* would affect the translation cost of the proposed process, we conduct further simulations. To keep the translation quality at fluency=5.0 and adequacy=5.0, we use *MT+Dic+Mono+Bi* as the simulation process. We conduct the simulation by varying the execution rate (rr) of the monolingual human task *human revision* with other settings the same as we have described in Sect. 13.4.2. For example, rr=25% means that the execution probability of *human revision* in *MT+Dic+Mono+Bi* is 25%. We simulate several cases (rr=100%, 75%, 50%, 25%, 0%) for all the 17 process instances. The simulation result is shown in Table 13.4. From the result, we can see that with the increase of rr, translation cost and translation duration both decrease. The case of rr=100% can save 38.5% of translation cost and 15.6% of translation duration compared to the case of rr=0%, where monolingual human activity is intended to be induced to revise the translation result but actually nothing can be revised and all the translations are done again by the bilingual human translator. The simulation also has the result that the execution cost and execution duration of the case rr<55% in *MT+Dic+Mono+Bi* are even more than those in *Bi* because of the wasted execution of composite machine translation services and monolingual human tasks. The simulation is conducted with IBM's Websphere Business Modeler Advanced V6.2.

To cover translation quality and translation cost, composition of human activities and machine translation services can be regarded as a promising approach. However, it is necessary to consider how to design mechanisms to reduce translation cost while keeping the translation quality. Although the experimental results in this chapter might not be significant from a statistical perspective, many lessons can be obtained from an empirical perspective as a fundamental trial of composing human and machine translation services for improving localization processes. We have also observed several important issues concerning controlling human tasks that should be considered in the future. First, although this chapter mainly focuses on the translation quality and translation cost of localization processes composed of both human and machine translation services, the design of interaction mechanisms among human and translation services, and between human activities in a localization process is actually an important issue to be considered. If the interactions are not effective, translation cost might be increased because of the additional interaction cost. Second, in composite processes it is necessary to unify human activities and Web services in order to control human assignment, quality control of human tasks, dynamic human service selection and so on. Third, dynamic management of human task execution is also important for reducing the cost of human tasks.

Table 13.4 Simulation results of translation cost and time for different translation revision rate

Items	Revision rate of translation result in MT+Dic+Mono+Bi				
	rr = 100%	rr = 75%	rr = 50%	rr = 25%	rr = 0%
Cost	14.75	17.50	19.25	22.25	24.00
Time	38min	39min	41min	43min	45min

13.6 Related Work

Web service composition has been an important issue for the past several years in the service-oriented computing area. Recently, QoS-aware service composition has become the focus in this area (Zeng et al. 2004) (Aggarwal et al. 2004) (Menascé 2002) (Cardoso et al. 2004). The work of Zeng et al. (Zeng et al. 2004) is among the earliest on QoS-aware service composition. The authors propose a multidimensional QoS model for Web service composition including dimensions of execution price, execution duration, reputation, successful execution rate and availability. In this research, we also use QoS dimensions like execution cost and execution duration for analysis. However, we also consider the application-specific QoS (fluency and adequacy of translation) and focus more on it.

Human activities have been considered in workflow management from the perspective of linking organization elements and business process (Zhao et al. 2008) and from the perspective of organization management (Zur Muehlen 2004).

BPEL4People has been used to specify human tasks in previous work (Russell and Aalst 2008) (Zhao et al. 2008) (Mendling et al. 2008). However, our research is the first to use human tasks for improving application-specific QoS and conduct experiments in the language domain in the real world to analyze the composition of human activities and machine translation services.

In the area of intercultural collaboration, machine translators have been applied in multilingual communication in previous research. From the point of view of communication analysis, effects and difficulties of using machine translation in collaborative work have been discussed (Yamashita and Ishida 2006) (Yamashita et al. 2009). Moreover, it has been reported that combining community dictionaries and machine translators can improve mutual understanding in multilingual communications (Inaba et al. 2007). Further, effectiveness of collaborative translation by machine translators and monolingual human has been shown in some work (Hu 2009) (Morita and Ishida 2009). However, the effects of applying machine translation services in localization processes with the aid of human activities are rarely observed in this area, which is the focus of this research.

13.7 Conclusion

The Language Grid provides the possibility of combining human and machine translators to improve localization processes in the real world. The main contribution of this chapter is to propose an approach to composing human activities and machine translation services for localization processes considering both translation quality and translation cost. First, we propose the approach of improving localization processes by composing human and machine translation services based on the Language Grid, a language service platform that we have developed. Then, we show how to conduct localization processes on the Language Grid. Further, we conduct experiments to compare translation qualities and costs using several translation processes, including absolute machine translation processes, absolute human translation processes and translation processes involving both human and machine translators. The experimental results show that (1) composing monolingual roles and dictionary services improves the translation quality of machine translators, and (2) collaboration of human and machine translators is possible to reduce the cost compared with absolute bilingual human translation. The proposed approach is expected to be applied in localizing community contents within local communities.

Acknowledgments   The author would like to thank Mr. Yoshiaki Murakami at Navix Co., Ltd., Japan for his collaborative work and valuable advice. This work was partially supported by Strategic Information and Communications R&D Promotion Programme from Ministry of Internal Affairs and Communications, Japan.

References

Aggarwal R, Verma K, Miller J, Milnor W (2004) Constraint driven web service composition in METEOR-S. 2004 IEEE International Conference on Services Computing (SCC 2004):23–30

Alves A, Arkin A, Askary S, Barreto C, Bloch B, Curbera F, Ford M, Goland Y, Guızar A, Kartha N, et al (2007) Web services business process execution language version 2.0. OASIS Standard 11

Cardoso J, Sheth AP, Miller JA, Arnold J, Kochut K (2004) Quality of service for workflows and web service processes. Journal of Web Semantics 1(3):281–308

Hu C. (2009) Collaborative translation by monolingual users. 27th international conference extended abstracts on Human factors in computing systems: 3105–3108

Inaba R, Murakami Y, Nadamoto A, Ishida T (2007) Multilingual communication support using the Language Grid. Intercultural Collaboration. Lecture Notes in Computer Science 4568, Springer, Berlin: 118-132

Ishida T (2006) Language Grid: an infrastructure for intercultural collaboration. IEEE/IPSJ Symposium on Applications and the Internet (SAINT-06):96-100

Ishida T (2008) Service-oriented collective intelligence for intercultural collaboration. IEEE/WIC/ACM International Conference on Web Intelligence and Intelligent Agent Technology (WI-IAT '08) 1:4–8

Ishida T (2010) Intercultural collaboration using machine translation. IEEE Internet Computing, January/February 2010:26–38

Kloppmann M, Koenig D, Leymann F, Pfau G, Rickayzen A, von Riegen C, Schmidt P, Trickovic I (2005) WS-BPEL extension for people–BPEL4People. Joint white paper, IBM and SAP.

Menascé DA (2002) QoS issues in web services. IEEE Internet Computing 6(6):72–75

Mendling J, Ploesser K, Strembeck M (2008) Specifying separation of duty constraints in BPEL4People processes. 11th International Conference on Business Information Systems (Bis 2008):273-284

Morita D, Ishida T (2009) Collaborative translation by monolinguals with machine translators. 13th International Conference on Intelligent User Interfaces:361–365

Murakami Y, Ishida T (2008) A layered language service architecture for intercultural collaboration. 6th International Conference on Creating, Connecting and Collaborating through Computing (c5 2008):3–9

Russell N, Aalst WM. (2008) Work distribution and resource management in BPEL4People: capabilities and opportunities. 20th International Conference on Advanced Information Systems Engineering, Lecture Notes in Computer Science 5074, Springer, Berlin, Heidelberg:94-108

White J, O'Connell T, O'Mara F (1994) The ARPA MT evaluation methodologies: evolution, lessons, and future approaches. 1st Conference of the Association for Machine Translation in the Americas:193-205

Yamashita N Ishida T (2006) Effects of machine translation on collaborative work. 20th Conference on Computer Supported Cooperative Work:515-524

Yamashita N, Inaba R, Kuzuoka H, Ishida T (2009) Difficulties in establishing common ground in multiparty groups using machine translation. 27th International Conference on Human Factors in Computing Systems:679–688

Zeng L, Benatallah B, Ngu AHH, Dumas M, Kalagnanam J, Chang H (2004) QoS-aware middleware for web services composition. IEEE Transactions on Software Engineering, 30(5):311-327

Zhao X, Qiu Z, Cai C, Yang H (2008) A formal model of human workflow. 2008 IEEE International Conference on Web Services:195-202

Zur Muehlen M (2004) Organizational management in workflow applications–issues and perspectives. Information Technology and Management 5(3-4):271–291

References

Chapter 14
Collaborative Translation Protocols

Daisuke Morita[1]* and Toru Ishida[2]

1 NTT Information Sharing Platform Laboratories, 9-11 Midori-Cho 3-Chome Musashino-Shi, Tokyo, 180-8585 Japan, e-mail: morita.daisuke@lab.ntt.co.jp

2 Department of Social Informatics, Kyoto University, Yoshida-Honmachi, Sakyo-ku, Kyoto, 606-8501 Japan, e-mail: ishida@i.kyoto-u.ac.jp

Abstract In this chapter, we present a protocol for collaborative translation, where two non-bilingual people who use different languages collaborate to perform the task of translation using machine translation (MT) services. The key idea of this protocol is that one person, who handles the source language and knows the original sentence (source language side), evaluates the adequacy between the original sentence and the translation of the sentence made fluent by the other person, who handles the target language (target language side). In addition, by determining whether the meaning of the machine-translated sentence is understandable, it is ensured that the two non-bilingual people can do the above tasks without stopping the protocol. As a result, this protocol 1) improves MT quality; and 2) terminates successfully only when the translation result becomes adequate and fluent. An experiment shows that when the protocol terminates successfully, the quality of the translation is increased to about 83 percent for Japanese-English translation and 91 percent for Japanese-Chinese translation. We contributed to the Language Grid Project by proposing a new way to use MT services efficiently in real fields.

14.1 Introduction

Due to internationalization and the spread of the Internet, the number of multilingual groups where the native languages of the members differ is increasing. In the past, communication among such groups typically took place in one language, which was in many cases English. However, members who are required to communicate in a non-native language frequently find communication difficult (Takano and Noda 1993) (Aiken et al. 1994) (Kim and Bonk 2002), thus such collaboration tends to be ineffective (Aiken 2002) (Tung and Quaddus 2002).

---

* This research was conducted at Kyoto University when this author was affiliated to this university.

Machine translation (MT) is useful for realizing some level of multilingual communication, because participants can pick up the general meaning even if some words are badly translated (Nomura et al. 2003). However, most MT systems make many translation errors. More precisely, many of the machine-translated sentences are generally neither adequate nor fluent. In intercultural and multilingual collaboration based on MT, translation errors have caused mutual misconceptions (Ogden et al. 2003). Moreover, it is difficult to identify translation errors because of the asymmetric nature of MT (Yamashita and Ishida 2006).

An internationally active NPO tried to enhance information sharing among members by developing a multilingual BBS system using technologies of the Language Grid (Ishida 2006) as a platform of language resources. However, there were many cases where information sharing did not work because of the above nature of MT. The Language Grid Project needs to not only provide a platform of resources, but also to research how to use them efficiently.

In this chapter we present protocols of collaborative translation, where two non-bilingual people who use different languages collaborate to perform the task of translation with MT systems (Morita and Ishida 2009b). This protocol does not assume the presence of bilingual people, and has been designed to solve on-site problems. The collaborative translation protocol 1) improves MT quality; and 2) is fairly likely to terminate successfully with an adequate and fluent translation result.

This chapter is organized as follows. In Section 14.2, we show activities of a group working in the intercultural field as an example and clarify issues to be addressed by the research of how to use MTs efficiently in real intercultural fields. In Section 14.3, we describe the collaborative translation protocol in detail and reveal that problems described in the previous section are solved. Additionally, we evaluate the success rate and the reliability of the collaborative translation protocol in an experiment described in Section 14.4. Section 14.5 introduces some related work, and we conclude this chapter in Section 14.6.

14.2 Human-Assisted Machine Translation

14.2.1 Practice in the Field of Intercultural Collaboration

As an example of a group working with the technologies of the Language Grid, we introduce an internationally active NPO based in Japan. This NPO has participants in Japan, South Korea, Austria, and Kenya and has a variety of native languages such as Japanese, Korean, German and English. In order to foster information sharing and invigorate intergroup discussion, this group developed their own web BBS system using MTs. In this system, each person edits articles in his or her native language. The articles are translated via this system to the other three lan-

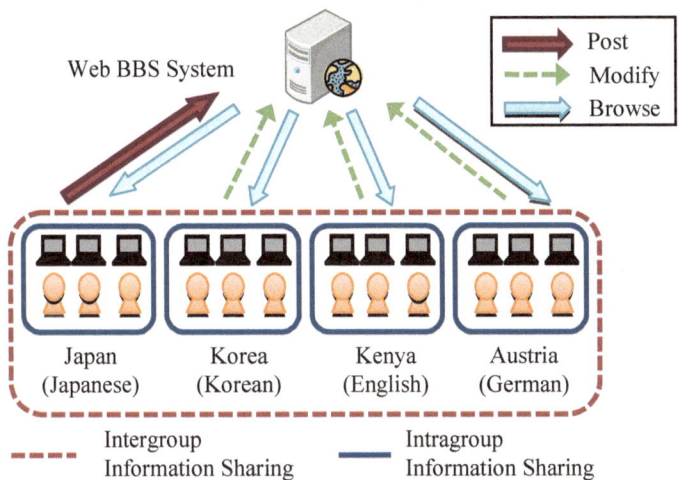

Web BBS System

Post
Modify
Browse

Japan   Korea   Kenya   Austria
(Japanese)   (Korean)   (English)   (German)

---- Intergroup
Information Sharing

—— Intragroup
Information Sharing

Fig. 14.1 Illustration of the web BBS system of the NPO group

guages. This enables other people to read the article in their own native language. However, the quality of MT is often imperfect. This can make it difficult to share information internationally. To overcome this problem, this system enables people to correct errors in machine-translated sentences manually. Human modification of machine-translated sentences allows us to improve the fluency by the correction of grammatical errors and the adequacy by using the shared background of the group (Callison-Burch 2005) (Maybury et al. 2005). An illustration of this web BBS system is shown in Fig. 14.1. In this figure, posting a Japanese article is taken as an example. Machine-translated sentences can be modified to be natural expressions, which makes intragroup information sharing easier.

14.2.2 Problems in Modifying Machine Translation Output

Human-assisted machine translation is a useful method for enhancing intercultural collaboration, but there are two main problems with implementing it. The problems are described below.

Example 1: Misinterpretation of the meaning of a machine-translated sentence

The Japanese sentence "He needed a week to cure a cold" was translated into English as "*He was necessary to correct a cold for 1 week.*" Since there were diction and grammar errors in this English sentence, this sentence was modified into a natural expression by the native English speaker. However, he or she modified this English sentence to "He should recover from a cold within 1 week." This modified English sentence differs in meaning from the original Japanese sentence.

A person modifying a machine-translated sentence can never understand the original meaning of the sentence. Therefore, he or she might misinterpret the meaning and create an erroneous sentence.

Example 2: Incomprehension of the meaning of a machine-translated sentence

The Japanese sentence "His belly is sticking out" was translated into English as "*A stomach has gone out to him.*" A native English speaker cannot understand the meaning of this machine-translated English sentence. Therefore, this sentence remained unmodified.

It is almost impossible to modify phrases of a machine-translated sentence that the reader cannot make sense of. Such phrases tend to remain unmodified. As a result, information about such phrases cannot be shared.

Problems of human-assisted machine translation are summarized as follows:

- It cannot be determined that a modified machine translation has the same meaning as the corresponding original sentence
- Phrases in the machine-translated sentence that a person cannot make sense of remain unmodified

14.3 Collaborative Translation

14.3.1 Definition

Participants in a collaborative translation task are two non-bilingual people: one person who handles the source language (source language side), and the other person who handles the target language (target language side). An MT system performs the task of translation. While the original document cannot be revised, the source language side can submit alternatives to the original sentences to the MT system to create reference material.

The source language side and the target language side play different roles. The target language side cannot determine whether a machine-translated sentence has the same meaning as the original sentence. However, he or she can determine whether the machine-translated sentence is fluent. Therefore, he or she can modify the non-fluent sentences to be more fluent. We assume that the sentences modified by monolingual people are always fluent. Like the target language side, the source language side cannot determine whether the machine-translated sentence has the same meaning as the original sentence. However, given the machine translation of a sentence modified by the target language side, the source language side can de-

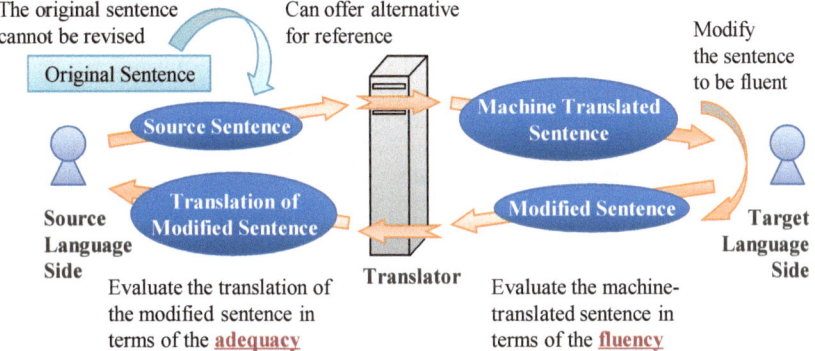

Fig. 14.2 The basic concept of collaborative translation

termine whether the back-translation of the modified sentence has the same meaning as the original sentence. He or she can thus determine whether a machine-translated sentence has the same meaning as the original sentence.

The above definitions are illustrated in Fig 14.2.

14.3.2 Protocol

In order to work together efficiently, it is essential to establish shared knowledge or common ground on the subjects (Clark and Brennan 1991) (Krauss and Weinheimer 1964). The process of establishing common ground consists of the presentation phase to present information to the addressees and the acceptance phase to confirm that addressees have received the information correctly (Clark and Brennan 1991). In collaborative translation, the presentation phase is the transmission of a machine-translated sentence to the target language side. The acceptance phase is all processes following the presentation phase. The protocols must be designed to ensure that the correctness of the translation result can be confirmed in the acceptance phase.

Fig. 14.3 shows the formal statement of the basic protocol, which is the minimal protocol to perform collaborative translation. This protocol is detailed below.

This protocol starts by sending the machine-translated sentence of the original sentence to the target language side (1. Transmission of Source Sentence). The target language reader cannot modify the machine-translated sentence if he or she cannot understand its meaning. Therefore, he or she determines that its meaning is understandable before modifying it. (2. Readability Determination of Translation).

Let s be a source sentence.

Let c, a, and f be boolean functions. For any sentence x, $c(x)$ indicates that the content of x is understandable, $a(x, s)$ indicates that x adequately captures the meaning of a source sentence s, and $f(x)$ indicates that x is fluent.

Let m and t be functions. For any sentence x, $m(x)$ indicates a human modification of x, and $t(x)$ indicates a machine translation of x. For instance, $m(t(s))$ indicates a human-modified version of a machine translation of the source.

Let p be the number of modifications made by the source language side, the maximum value permitted is P. Let q be the number of modifications made by the target language side, the maximum value permitted is Q.

1) [Source Language Side: Transmission of Source Sentence]
   Let $p := 0$
   Transmit s to the target language side
       Goto 2)
2) [Target Language Side: Readability Determination of Translation]
   Let $t(s)$ be a machine translation of s
   If not $c(t(s))$
       Request the source language side to modify s
       Goto 6)
   Else If $c(t(s))$
       Let $q := 0$
       Goto 3)
3) [Target Language Side: Modification of Translation]
   Let $q := q + 1$
   If $q \geq Q$
       Terminate protocol with label *Unsuccessful*
   Else If $q < Q$
       Let $m(t(s))$ be a human modification of $t(s)$ such that $f(m(t(s)))$
       Transmit $m(t(s))$ to the source language side
       Goto 4)
4) [Source Language Side: Readability Determination of Back-Translation]
   Let $t(m(t(s)))$ be a machine translation of $m(t(s))$
   If not $c(t(m(t(s))))$
       Request the target language side to modify $m(t(s))$
       Goto 3)
   Else If $c(t(m(t(s))))$
       Goto 5)
5) [Source Language Side: Adequacy Determination of Back-Translation]
   If $a(t(m(t(s))), s)$
       Terminate protocol with label *Successful*
   Else If not $a(t(m(t(s))), s)$
       Goto 6)
6) [Source Language Side: Modification of Source Sentence]
   Let $p := p + 1$
   If $p \geq P$
       Terminate protocol with label *Unsuccessful*
   Else If $p < P$
       Let s be a human modified source sentence
       Goto 2)

Fig. 14.3 The formal statement of the collaborative translation protocol

If it is not understandable, the source language side is required to paraphrase the original sentence and submit the new version to machine translation. Generally speaking, MTs tend to output different expressions even if the source sentence is only slightly changed. The target language side keeps requesting the source language side to paraphrase the original sentence until the meaning of the machine-translated sentence becomes understandable. Only after its meaning is understandable does the target language side make it fluent. (3. Modification of Translation). After the target language side finishes the modification, the source language side starts to evaluate the adequacy of the modified sentence. Using the same approach as the target language side, the source language side determines if the meaning of the back-translation is understandable. (4. Readability Determination of Back-Translation). If it is understandable, he or she determines if the translation of the modified sentence has the same meaning as the original sentence. (5. Adequacy Determination of Back-Translation). If the back-translation sentence has the same meaning, it is recognized that the modified machine translation not only is fluent, but also has the same meaning as the original sentence. Consequently, the protocol can terminate successfully. If the back-translation sentence does not have the same meaning, it can be seen that the interpretation of the machine-translated sentence by the target language side is likely to differ from the meaning of the original sentence. Therefore, the source language side paraphrases the original sentence again and presents the different expression of the machine-translated sentence to the target language side (6. Modification of Source Sentence).

In order to guarantee that the protocol always terminates, the maximum modification iterations of the source language and the target language, P and Q, are defined. When translation quality is not improved by repeated processings of the protocol, the improvement is not likely to be attained in this protocol, so the protocol should be aborted at a proper stage. Moreover, the number of paraphrases is not endless. A past intercultural collaboration study (Nomura et al. 2003) reported that eight modifications of the original sentence was the upper limit (set by a very enthusiastic participant). However, this is viewed as a rare case, so it is reasonable to set the iteration limit to four or five.

14.3.3 Prototype System

A prototype system for collaborative translation was designed to implement the protocol and evaluate its effectiveness (Morita and Ishida 2009a). This system was developed using AJAX technologies as a browser-based application. Web services of MTs provided by the Language Grid Project (Ishida 2006) were used as the MT modules. The prototype system divides a document into sentences, and processes each sentence independently. The user client GUI displays the status of each sentence, and guides the source language side and the target language side on what to do. More precisely, the states of progress, including modification, readability eval-

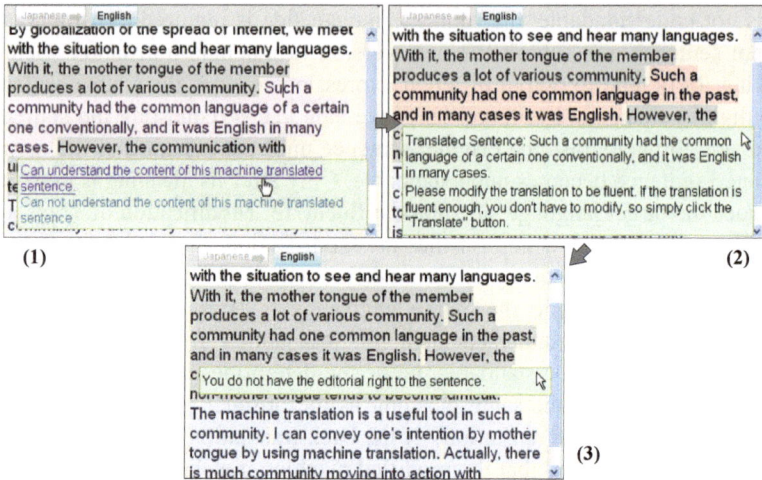

Fig. 14.4 The screen transitions in the target language side's turn in Japanese-English translation

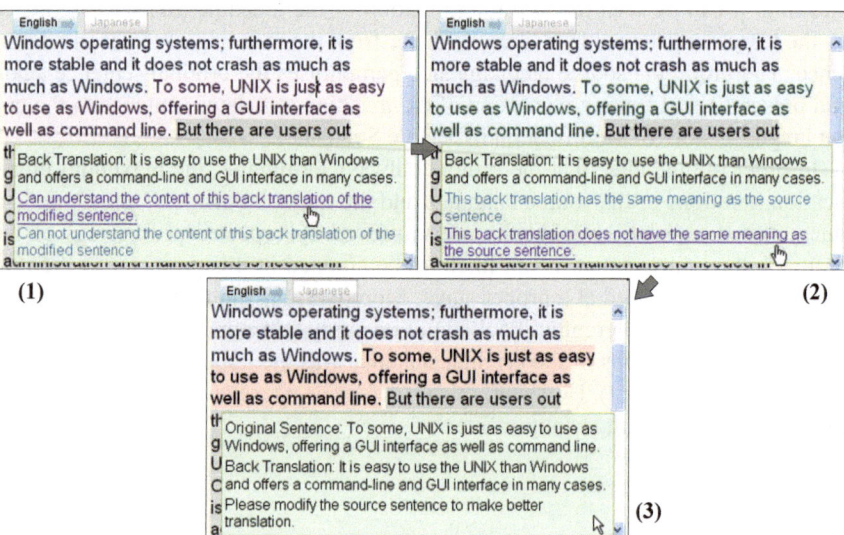

Fig. 14.5 The screen transitions in the source language side's turn in English-Japanese translation

uation, and adequacy evaluation are displayed by highlighting the respective sentences. When a sentence is selected, explanations of what to do or criteria for the evaluation of readability or accuracy are displayed in a pop-up box. Users perform collaborative translation by following the directions provided by the user client.

Fig. 14.4 shows the screen transition at the target language side's turn in Japanese-English translation. The user evaluates, (1), the readability of the machine-translated sentence and if it is human-readable, modifies, (2), it to make it fluent.

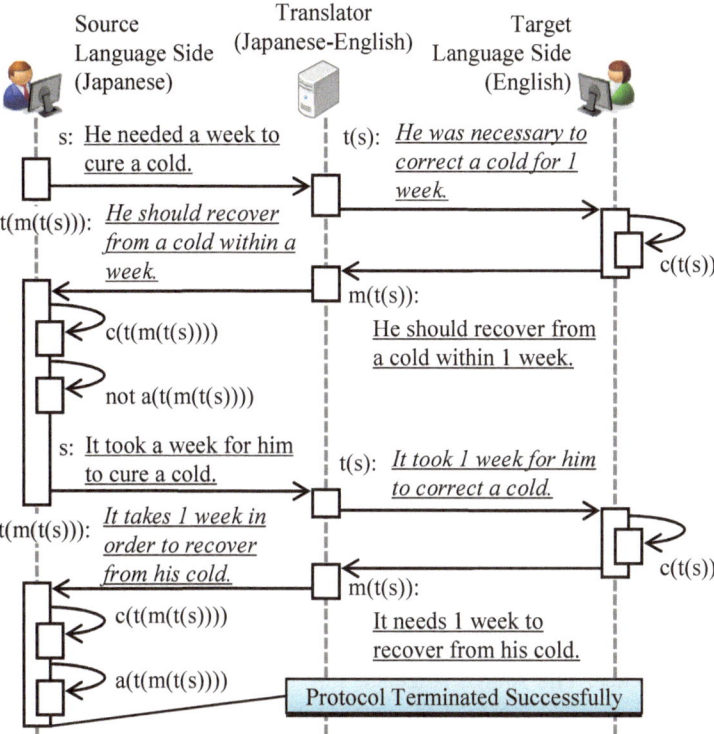

Fig. 14.6 The problem of Example 1 is solved by collaborative translation protocol (translators' outputs are shown in *italic*)

After that, (3), the target language side user cannot edit the sentence until the end of the source language side's turn. Fig 14.5 shows the screen transition in the source language side's turn in English-Japanese translation. The user evaluates, (1), the readability of the back-translation of the modified sentence and if it is human-readable determines, (2), whether it has the same meaning as the source sentence. If it does not, the user modifies, (3), the source sentence again.

14.3.4 Effectiveness

Fig. 14.6 shows how the collaborative translation protocol solves the problem of the target language side's misinterpretation (Example 1). In the first turn, the target language side wrongly corrected the machine-translated sentence due to his or her misinterpretation. However, the source language side saw that the back-translation of the modified sentence did not have the same meaning as the original sentence. This showed that the target language side may have misinterpreted the

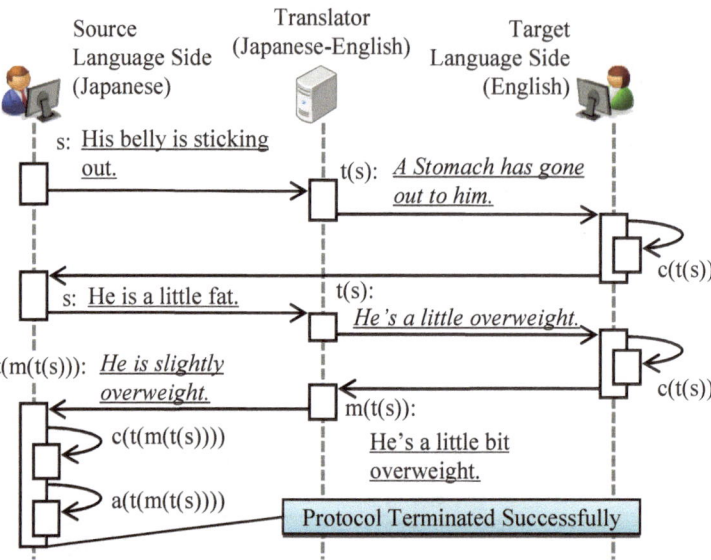

Fig. 14.7 The problem of Example 2 is solved by the collaborative translation protocol (translators' outputs are shown in *italic*)

translated sentence. The source language side modified the source sentence, and the target language side received the corresponding machine-translated sentence. In the second turn, the target language side corrected it with the understanding that the first correction was wrong. Finally, the source language side determined that the last back-translation had the same meaning as the original sentence. To sum up, it was recognized that the translated sentence had the same meaning as the original sentence. The target language side's misinterpretation can be detected and corrected by applying the protocol.

Fig. 14.7 shows how the protocol solves the problem of unreadable sentences (Example 2). In the first turn, the target language side could not understand the meaning of the machine-translated sentence. Therefore, the protocol requested the source language side to modify the source sentence. In the second turn, the target language side received the latest machine-translated sentence which used different wording. Its meaning was understandable, so the target language side modified it as necessary. The source language side determined that the back-translation had the same meaning as the original sentence. Therefore, it was recognized that the translated sentence had the same meaning as the original sentence. The protocol can continue even if the content of a machine-translated sentence is not understandable.

These examples show that the protocol can solve two common problems with human-assisted machine translation. However, MTs tend to cause errors, and there are human factors such as difficulties in consistent judgment and different criteria about the assessment of translation adequacy. Because of these factors, although the protocol terminates successfully, the translation result could have a different meaning from the source sentence. Therefore, we confirmed the protocol's effectiveness in an experiment (Section 14.4).

14.4 Evaluation

14.4.1 Setting

We evaluated the collaborative translation protocol in an experiment on the prototype system.

We used an MT test set provided by NTT Communication Science Laboratories. This set consists of 3,718 Japanese sentences with English translations. In this experiment, 100 randomly selected sentences were used as the test set. Japanese-English and Japanese-Chinese translations were conducted and three pairs of participants were made for each language pair to minimize human effects. The values P and Q, the maximum number of modifications, were set to three.

We also evaluated the effectiveness of a back-translation method, which is frequently used to improve the quality of machine-translated sentences in many real fields of intercultural collaboration. We aimed to show that the collaborative translation protocol is superior to this conventional method of improving MT quality. For the back-translation method, the maximum number of modifications of the source sentence was also set to three and if the subject could not determine that the back-translated sentence had the same meaning as the original sentence within the modification limit, we deemed that the back-translation method terminated unsuccessfully.

The results of collaborative translation, back-translation, and pure MT were scored by bilingual readers on a scale of 5 (All, Most, Much, Little, and None) in terms of translation adequacy. Translation adequacy means how well the translation matches the reference(s) in *meaning*, thus this is explicitly distinguished from translation fluency. Ratings were conducted by three people and the median was used as the final evaluation value. Since it is postulated that manually modified sentences are always fluent, the fluency of the translated sentences were not evaluated in this experiment.

14.4.2 Results

Success Rate. For Japanese-English translation, the rates of successful termination were 67 percent for back-translation, and 70 percent for collaborative translation. For Japanese-Chinese translation, the corresponding rates were 78 percent for

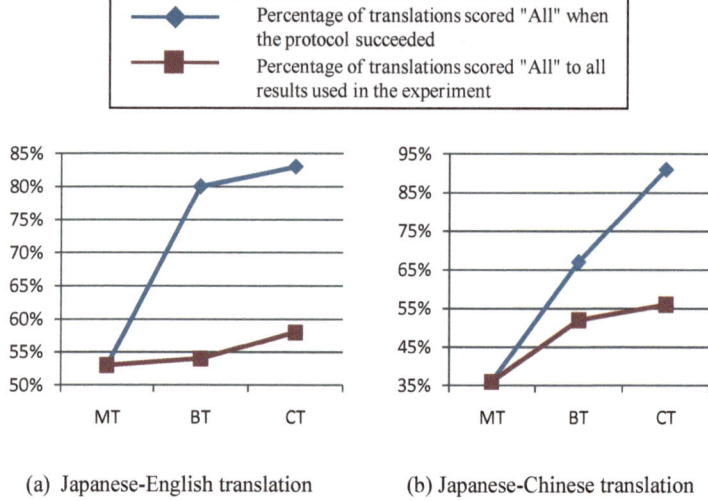

(a) Japanese-English translation   (b) Japanese-Chinese translation

Fig. 14.8 Results of collaborative translation (CT), back-translation (BT), and pure MT (MT)

back-translation, and 62 percent for collaborative translation. Correlation between success rates of collaborative translation and of back-translation were not observed, and those rates are in the same range.

Translation Adequacy. Fig. 14.8 shows a graph of evaluated values of adequacy for pure MT, back-translation and collaborative translation in Japanese-English translation and Japanese-Chinese translation. The blue line with diamond marks in each graph indicates the percentage of translations that scored "All" in terms of translation adequacy when the protocol terminated successfully and the red line with square marks indicates the percentage of translations that scored "All" over all results used in the experiment (that is, including sentences where the protocol terminated unsuccessfully). In terms of pure MT, these percentages are always the same. When the collaborative translation protocol terminated successfully, 83 percent of Japanese-English translation and 91 percent of Japanese-Chinese translation were scored "All". This result shows that the translation quality is likely to be high if the collaborative translation protocol terminates successfully. As mentioned above, there is a possibility that the adequacy of the translated sentences could be low even if the collaborative translation protocol terminates successfully, but the possibility is relatively low. Besides, when comparing the results of collaborative translation with the results of back-translation, collaborative translation is superior to back-translation in terms of translation adequacy in both Japanese-English and Japanese-Chinese translation.

Table 14.1 shows changes in the evaluated value of the adequacy of the collaborative translation from the value of pure MT in Japanese-English translation and Japanese-Chinese translation. Since this experiment was conducted with three participant pairs, 300 result sentences of collaborative translation were available. 5 percent of the Japanese-English collaborative translation and 1 percent of the Japanese-Chinese collaborative translation got a lower evaluated value in adequacy against the results of pure MT, but this shows that most of the results of collaborative translation are higher than or equal to corresponding results of MT in terms of translation quality. In other words, there is very little possibility that collaborative translation degrades the MT quality, it is more likely to improve the MT quality.

14.5 Related Work

Aiken et al. developed *Polyglot*, which is a multilingual group support system with 40 different languages based on *Google Translate*, and observed communication between an English speaker and different non-English speakers (Aiken et al. 2010). They reported that communication between English and some European languages (such as Dutch, Danish, Swedish, German, Norwegian, Estonian and Slovenian) has much less misunderstanding. However, this is mainly because Google Translate achieves better translation results between Germanic languages, which include English. Since MT between English and most other languages including Asian languages is rather poor, researchers have to deal with MT's weakness in multilingual communication.

Albrecht et al. developed *The Chinese Room*, which is a support tool of human correction of English sentences translated from non-English sentences by MTs (Albrecht et al. 2009). This system helps English speakers to modify the mistranslated parts of machine-translated English sentences by visually presenting additional linguistic information such as alignments, parts-of-speech, segmentations, glosses and other translation candidates. However, since it is not easy to obtain these language resources for all possible languages, this system lacks versatility.

Table 14.1 Changes of translation quality for each test sentence from pure MT to collaborative translation

(a) Japanese-English translation

		CT					
		5	4	3	2	1	F
	5	117	10	0	2	3	27
	4	21	5	0	0	0	22
MT	3	15	5	4	0	0	18
	2	11	1	2	0	0	16
	1	11	1	1	0	1	7

(b) Japanese-Chinese translation

		CT					
		5	4	3	2	1	F
	5	84	2	1	0	0	21
	4	30	6	0	0	0	18
MT	3	39	1	1	0	0	22
	2	16	2	1	2	0	51
	1	2	0	0	0	0	1

In addition, even if the main purpose is presenting linguistic information like alignment, not the content of the source sentence, effectiveness of presenting sentences that are described in unfamiliar languages should be investigated.

Approaches to much the same translation problems proposed by Hu et al. (Hu et al. 2010) (Hu 2009) are very similar to those proposed in this chapter. They made three assumptions: the translation channel is noisy, internal details of the translation channel remain hidden, and the participants have little or no skill with regard to the foreign language. These assumptions equally apply to our definition of collaborative translation (Section 14.3.1). The protocol of translation developed by Hu et al. is much simpler: the source language speaker sends the source text through the translation channel, whose output is edited by the target language speaker and sent back the back-translation, and the protocol consists of a few round-trips. On the basis of the protocol, Hu et al. tried to solve the problems by designing a rich user interface which allows the target language speaker to infer the intended meaning of the source sentence through negotiations with the source language speaker by exchanging external information such as relevant images, translated Web pages and multiple machine-translated results. We agree with their argument that information redundancy supports the target language speaker's inference to some extent. However, they did not adequately consider the cases where participants cannot make sense of the machine-translated sentences like Example 2 (Albrecht et al. also reported that participants could also elect to "pass" any part of a sentence if they found it too difficult to correct), and where translation results are not sufficiently improved by repetitive round-trips of translation processes. Therefore, it can be considered that developing the fundamental framework of the protocol with attention to its continuing and terminating features like the protocol we proposed in this chapter is a very helpful approach to the problems of collaborative translation.

14.6 Conclusion

Our main research contribution is a protocol that establishes and simplifies collaborative translation. It solves the problems common to multilingual translation-based applications. In addition, this protocol 1) improves MT quality; and 2) is fairly likely to terminate successfully with a translation result which is adequate and fluent. We clarified the value of the target language side making the machine-translated sentences fluent. The source language side evaluates the translation quality by determining whether the back-translation of the modified sentence has the same meaning as the original sentence. Only 53 percent of Japanese-English translation and 36 percent of Japanese-Chinese translation were perfect translations in pure MT. However, when the collaborative translation protocol terminated successfully, 83 percent of Japanese-English translation and 91 percent of Japanese-Chinese translation were perfect. These results revealed that collaborative translation is much more likely to result in good translations. Thus, we contributed to the Language Grid Project with an approach to solve the problem of how to use MTs efficiently in real fields of intercultural collaboration.

Acknowledgments   This work was supported by a Grant-in-Aid for Scientific Research (A) (21240014, 2009-2011) from Japan Society for the Promotion of Science (JSPS), Strategic Information and Communications R&D Promotion Programme from Ministry of Internal Affairs and Communications, and Kyoto University Global COE Program: Informatics Education and Research Center for Knowledge-Circulating Society.

References

Aiken M (2002) Multilingual communication in electronic meetings. ACM SIGGROUP Bulletin 23(1): 18–19

Aiken M, Hwang C, Paolillo J, Lu L (1994) A group decision support system for the Asian Pacific Rim. Journal of International Information Management 3(2): 1–13

Aiken M, Park M, Lindblom T (2010) Integrating machine translation with group support systems. International Journal of Business and Management 5(5): 25-35

Albrecht J, Hwa R, Marai GE (2009) The Chinese room: visualization and interaction to understand and correct ambiguous machine translation. In Computer Graphics Forum 28(3): 1047-1054

Callison-Burch C (2005) Linear B system description for the 2005 NIST MT evaluation exercise. NIST Machine Translation Evaluation Workshop

Clark HH, Brennan SE (1991) Grounding in communication. In Resnick LB, Levine RM, Teasley SD (eds) Perspectives on socially shared cognition, American Psychological Association, Washington DC

Hu C (2009) Collaborative translation by monolingual users. 2009 International Conference on Human Factors in Computing Systems: 3105-3108

Hu C, Bederson BB, Resnik P (2010) Translation by iterative collaboration between monolingual users. ACM SIGKDD Workshop on Human Computation: 54-55

Ishida, T (2006) Language Grid: an infrastructure for intercultural collaboration. 2006 IEEE/IPSJ Symposium on Applications and the Internet (SAINT 2006): 96–100

Kim KJ, Bonk CJ (2002) Cross-cultural comparisons of online collaboration. Journal of Computer Mediated Communication 8(1)

Krauss RM, Weinheimer S (1964) Changes in reference phases as a function of frequency of usage in social interaction. A preliminary study. Psychonomic Science 1: 113-114

Maybury M, Griffith J, Holland R, Damianos L, Hu Q, Fish R (2005) Virtually integrated visionary intelligence demonstration (VIVID). In MITRE technical papers

Morita D, Ishida T (2009a) Collaborative translation by monolinguals with machine translators. In International Conference on Intelligent User Interfaces (IUI 2009): 361-365

Morita D, Ishida T (2009b) Designing protocols for collaborative translation. In International Conference on Principles of Practice in Multi-Agent Systems (PRIMA 2009), Lecture Notes in Computer Science 5925, Springer, Berlin: 17-32

Nomura S, Ishida T, Yamashita N, Yasuoka M, Funakoshi K (2003) Open source software development with your mother language: intercultural collaboration experiment 2002. International Conference on Human-Computer Interaction (HCI 2003) 4: 1163–1167

Ogden B, Warner J, Jin W, Sorge J (2003) Information sharing across languages using MITRE's trim instant messaging

Takano Y, Noda A (1993) A temporary decline of thinking ability during foreign language processing. Journal of Cross-Cultural Psychology 24(4): 445–462

Tung LL, Quaddus MA (2002) Cultural differences explaining the differences in results in GSS: implications for the next decade. Decision Support Systems 33(2): 177–199

Yamashita N, Ishida T (2006) Effects of machine translation on collaborative work. International Conference on Computer Supported Cooperative Work (CSCW 2006): 515–524

Chapter 15
Multi-Language Discussion Platform for Wikipedia Translation

Ari Hautasaari[1], Toshiyuki Takasaki[1], Takao Nakaguchi[2], Jun Koyama[3], Yohei Murakami[4], and Toru Ishida[1]

1 Department of Social Informatics, Kyoto University, Kyoto, 606-8501, Japan, e-mail: {arihau, toshi} @ai.soc.i.kyoto-u.ac.jp, ishida@i.kyoto-u.ac.jp

2 NTT Advanced Technology Corporation, 12-1 Ekimae-Honmachi, Kawasaki-Ku, Kanagawa, 210-0007, Japan, e-mail: takao.nakaguchi@ntt-at.co.jp

3 EIP.Co.,Ltd., Uda Bldg. 2F 4-1-13 Shinmachi, Nishi-ku, Osaka-shi, Osaka, 550-0013, Japan, e-mail: koyama@eip.co.jp

4 National Institute of Information and Communications Technology, 3-5 Hikaridai, Seika-Cho, Soraku-Gun, Kyoto, 619-0289, Japan, e-mail: yohei@nict.go.jp

Abstract The multilingual Wikipedia is the largest existing collaboratively edited encyclopedia, where several translation communities are working towards translating Wikipedia articles. The different language communities are largely independent in terms of policy creation, behavior and community mechanisms. We conducted a case study on the Wikipedia community from a multilingual point of view to better understand community behavior. We also conducted a collaborative Wiki-to-Wiki translation experiment using machine translation tools provided by the Language Grid. Based on the findings of the two studies we designed and developed a multi-language discussion platform for Wikipedia translation communities. In this chapter, we discuss the results of the case study and a laboratory experiment and how the results are applied to facilitate the creation of multilingual collective intelligence in Wikipedia through a multi-language discussion platform.

15.1 Introduction

Wikipedia is a free, collaboratively edited online encyclopedia supported by the Wikimedia Foundation. Since its launch in 2001, the multilingual Wikipedia has grown rapidly, exceeding 16,000,000 articles in more than 270 languages. Currently, the English Wikipedia is the largest in terms of active contributors as well as the number of articles. However, since the main language of Internet users is gradually shifting away from English, there is an increasing need to enhance the quality of Wikipedia in other languages as well.

In the multilingual Wikipedia, users from different language backgrounds often have to rely on their second or third language in order to effectively communicate with other Wikipedia users. Moreover, in the different language Wikipedia, discussions are usually conducted in the respective language making it impossible for users with insufficient language ability to participate in the discussion. In order to improve the quality of the multilingual Wikipedia, it is necessary to bridge the language gap between different Wikipedia communities and provide technology to support large-scale article translation between different language Wikipedia.

In this chapter, we first discuss the results of a case study on the Wikipedia communities to analyze the requirements for multilingual discussion support in real Wikipedia communities. Secondly, we present the results of a Wiki-to-Wiki translation experiment, where the experiment participants used machine translation as a supporting tool. Based on the case study and the experiment results, we developed a multi-language discussion platform to support the Wikipedia translation communities with the Language Grid Extension. The Language Grid Extension enables Wikipedia users to select and combine machine translators and multilingual dictionaries registered in the Language Grid as an extension to the MediaWiki software. Wikipedia contributors are able to make use of the available machine translators and dictionary creation function to improve the quality of the multilingual Wikipedia through translation activities, and engage in multilingual machine translation mediated discussions in Wikipedia.

15.2 Wikipedia Translation Community

In this section, we discuss the volunteer-based Wikipedia translation community members and related communities, such as in *Wikimedia Commons*, from a multilingual viewpoint. Furthermore, we give examples of real multilingual discussions conducted in Wikipedia.

15.2.1 Guidelines

The Wikipedia communities have raised some policies on translation and discussion, and most of the policies are established through discussions among Wikipedia community members. In effect, the Wikipedia community also respects and facilitates the multilingual nature of knowledge in Wikipedia. It has a mechanism to call for article translation from bilingual or multilingual volunteer editors. Any user can post a translation request and the community decides on the translation priority, what article(s) should be translated first, and bilingual or multilingual volunteer editors translate the articles in the order of the decided priority.

The Wikipedia community has a policy for the use of machine translation. Machine translation results of Wikipedia articles should only be used as a reference for human translation and the translations should not be considered as the final content of a translated article for two reasons. Firstly, because of existing copyright issues editors should be careful not to violate the copyright of the original content, as well as the copyright of the machine translation engine, since some machine translation engines assert copyright for their translation results. Secondly, because the quality of direct machine translation of articles is not considered to be up to par with the Wikipedia article quality, machine translation of a Wikipedia article is considered to be merely a good way for getting an idea of the original article in a foreign language, and a good start for creating and editing the article by human editors in different languages. The Wikipedia community complies with a policy that all content including articles, discussions and other multimedia content should be edited and revised by users, edition and revision history with contributor information should be viewed by all users, and any user can revert any content to any status in its history.

15.2.2 Translators and Proofreaders

The Wikipedia translators and proofreaders are able to advertise their language skills on their personal user pages. In the English Wikipedia, users interested in translating and proofreading articles can sign-up as one, or both, through the *Wikipedia Translation* pages. This is to promote their skills as Wikipedia translators, and make them easier to find for users requesting a translation into a particular language or in a particular domain.

Currently, the English Wikipedia includes registered translators to English in 56 languages, and proofreaders in 34 languages. The total number of translators in all available languages is 1325, out of which the French (259), Spanish (256) and German (193) translators are the biggest user groups. Similarly, the French (137), Spanish (99) and German (71) proofreaders are the biggest groups among the total of 568 registered proofreaders in all available languages. However, most languages have fewer than 10 registered translators or proofreaders.

Since Wikipedia allows anonymous editing of articles, the peripheral users account for a much larger base of potential translators within their domain of interest (Bryant et al. 2005). Furthermore, translation communities in other language Wikipedia include translators and proofreaders in multiple language pairs who are not registered in the English Wikipedia. Especially in languages that have only a few registered translators, supporting tools for translation and communication for the peripheral users become essential for reducing the cost of translation and for reaching domain experts in particular fields.

Translation in the domain of "National Parks of the United States" in the English Wikipedia is one example of English to Japanese translation activities in one translation community. Currently, half of the articles are completely translated to the Japanese Wikipedia, but 10 articles out of 59 include non-translated sections of over 2000 words. Many of the articles in the Japanese Wikipedia are direct translations from the English Wikipedia, but in rare cases articles have also been independently created in the Japanese Wikipedia. Especially with translated articles, updating and maintenance of the Japanese articles require active user contribution from the community. In the case where the original article is modified, the change is not reflected in the translated article, especially if the author of the original article is not proficient in the language of the translated article.

Besides the translation communities, region-specific communities exist in Wikipedia. These communities are commonly organized as WikiProjects, which have their own scope and goal defined by the community members. One such example is the *WikiProject:Japan*. The community aims to improve the quality and quantity of articles related to Japan in the English Wikipedia. In order to engage potential contributors to lend their expertise, the community offers recognition for outstanding editors and members of the community, and maintains a list of the most important articles in the domain to be amended.

Members of the community frequently need to translate articles from the Japanese Wikipedia in order to improve existing articles or create new articles in the English Wikipedia. Subsequently, the members often request translation assistance in the community discussion page. An example of an actual discussion about romanization of a name in Japanese is shown in Fig. 15.1.

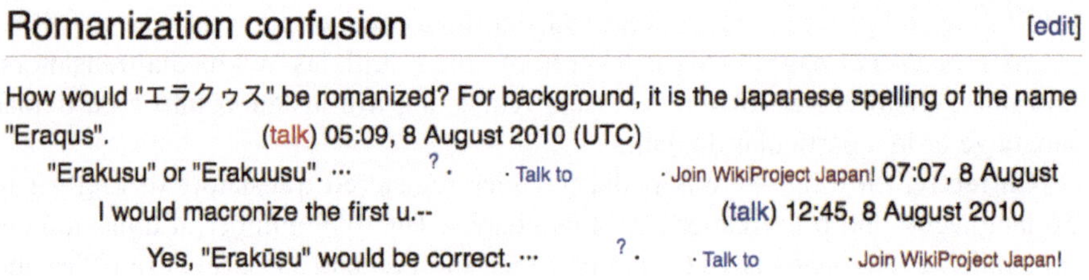

Romanization confusion   [edit]

How would "エラクゥス" be romanized? For background, it is the Japanese spelling of the name "Eraqus".   (talk) 05:09, 8 August 2010 (UTC)

   "Erakusu" or "Erakuusu". ⋯   ? .   · Talk to   · Join WikiProject Japan! 07:07, 8 August

     I would macronize the first u.--   (talk) 12:45, 8 August 2010

       Yes, "Erakūsu" would be correct. ⋯   ? .   · Talk to   · Join WikiProject Japan!

Fig. 15.1 Discussion about resolving the romanization of a name in Japanese

15.2.3 Multi-Language Discussions in Wikipedia

Different language Wikipedia, such as the English Wikipedia, the German Wikipedia, and the Japanese Wikipedia, all have their own central communities. The different language Wikipedia apply local policies and activity plans as well as international ones. An example of a local policy is "flagged revisions", which states that an experienced volunteer editor for Wikipedia signs off any change made to an article by the public before it can go live. It is applied to a few Wikipedia such as the German Wikipedia. A decision to introduce a local policy is made through discussions among the local Wikipedia community members in the corresponding Wikipedia language.

On the other hand, international policies and activity plans also exist. For example, an international Wikipedia conference should be planned through discussions among the international Wikipedia community members. In some cases, a language barrier makes it difficult for non-English speakers to participate in the discussion of international policies or activity plans.

Articles in Wikipedia are created by Wikipedia communities and modifications to the articles are decided via discussions held in the Wikipedia discussion pages. In some cases, especially in articles on foreign topics, we observed discussions among contributors from different countries and with different languages. For example, in the discussion page of the article "Ponyo", a Japanese animation movie, in the English Wikipedia there is an ongoing discussion about "Ponyo is not a goldfish." The argument centres on whether "Ponyo", the main character of the Japanese animation "Ponyo on a Cliff by the Sea", is a goldfish or not. First, an English speaker asserts that "Ponyo is not a goldfish" based on the mannerism in the movie. A Japanese speaker with an opposing view then quotes an interview with the director Hayao Miyazaki, in Japanese, making it difficult for English speakers to understand.

Most of the content in *Wikimedia Commons* ("Commons" for short) is language independent, such as photos. Therefore, the contents are referred from many articles in various language versions of Wikipedia. *The Village Pump* page is used for discussions about the operations, technical issues, and policies of Commons. Though many language versions of the Village Pump page are provided in Commons, particularly the English Village Pump is very active compared to other languages, making it inconvenient to refer to for non-English speakers.

A *help-page for non-Japanese speakers* exists in the Japanese Wikipedia. This page is dedicated to discussion about the Japanese Wikipedia for users that are not proficient in Japanese. The policy for discussions states that messages can be posted in any language, but few Japanese contributors are fluent in other languages besides Japanese and English. Subsequently, messages in multiple languages, including English, Japanese, Korean and French, have been posted on the help-page. However, in this particular example, discussions started in other languages, for example in Korean, tend to receive an answer in Japanese (Fig. 15.2). Hence, users who are not proficient both in Japanese and Korean are excluded from the discussion on the topic in question.

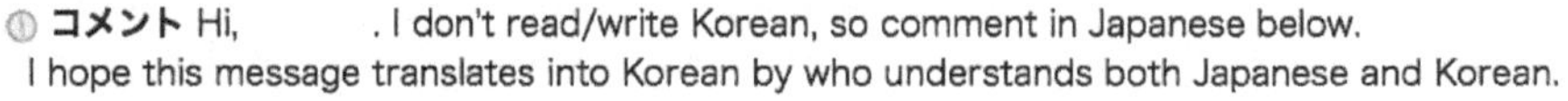

ⓘ コメント Hi,   . I don't read/write Korean, so comment in Japanese below.
I hope this message translates into Korean by who understands both Japanese and Korean.

Fig. 15.2 A reply by a Japanese user to a discussion started by a Korean user

15.3 Collaborative Translation in Wikipedia

One of the problems in the current Wikipedia is the uneven distribution of articles in different languages. The English Wikipedia is currently the largest with almost 3,400,000 articles, followed by the German, French, Polish, Italian and Japanese Wikipedia. Presently, only 33 Wikipedia in different languages have more than 100,000 articles. One reason for the contrast in the number of articles in different language Wikipedia is the lack of active contributors (Ortega et al. 2008). Collaborative translation (Morita and Ishida 2009) activities aim to increase the quality of Wikipedia by translating articles into languages where a corresponding article has not been created.

Traditionally, document translation has been done by native, or close to native level speakers of the source and the target language. Hence, the barrier for entry to traditional translation activities is high, usually requiring years of training in a language and in the translation process. Machine translation has been proposed as a supporting tool to allow people with non-native level language skill to participate in translation activities (Morita and Ishida 2009).

In order for translation projects in Wikipedia to be successful, a large base of bilingual or multilingual users is needed. Désilets et al. (2006) argues that traditional translation practices, such as sequential translation (Schütz and Nübel 1998) or parallel authoring (Harley and Paris 1997), are not appropriate for Wikipedia. For example, a system presented in Kumaran et al. (2008) aims to support the translation communities specifically in the Wiki-context. Collaborative translation tools provided by the Language Grid offer a solution to the problem by enabling community members to participate in translation tasks without high proficiency in the source language of the translated article.

15.3.1 Machine Translation Supported Wiki-to-Wiki Translation

We conducted a Wiki-to-Wiki translation experiment where the participants used machine translation resources provided by the Language Grid as a supporting tool. The participants took either the role of the source language side or the target language side in a collaborative translation scenario (Morita and Ishida 2009). The participants were also provided with a machine translation mediated communication channel where they could communicate and collaborate in their native languages.

One emerging problem with collaborative translation is the excess of context-specific words and common names that are not translated properly with a machine translator. A mistranslation is usually easy to spot in the text, but the meaning is often not easily understood. In a case where a sentence is presented out of context, it can be difficult to determine what the original meaning of the sentence should be with only one mistranslated word.

Translators often turn to domain experts to find out the meaning of a particular word. However, if all the participants do not share a common language, the bilingual users are the main contributors in communication inside the translation group. Participants that lack the language proficiency in one of the languages used are excluded from the conversations held between the bilingual participants.

15.3.2 Machine Translation Mediated Communication

Previous studies on machine translation mediated communication suggest that conversational participants are able to effectively converse through a mediated channel if they can successfully build common ground (Hautasaari 2010, Yamashita et al. 2009, Yamashita and Ishida 2006). Since in our experiment scenario all communication was conducted through a machine translation mediated channel, all members of the translation group were able to participate in the collaborative translation activities, such as correcting a mistranslated word or finding the right spelling for a domain-specific noun.

Table 15.1 Machine translation mediated discussion in collaborative translation

Message Number	Original Language	Message (English Translation)
1	Japanese	I checked translation result and the Japanese word which isn't translated right "jita kyouei" was added to the dictionary.
2	English	Is the meaning "sharing your wealth with others"?
3	Chinese	Chinese was added too. Chinese have adopted literal translation. But general people do not understand completely, so I have added the meaning in a bracket.
4	Japanese	"Jita kyouei" means mutual prosperity of self and others together.
5	English	I added this just as "mutual prosperity". I think this includes the correct meaning.

Table 15.1 includes a typical example of a machine translation mediated discussion in a collaborative translation task. In this example, a Japanese participant

points out a flaw in the machine translated text in Japanese. The English-speaking participant asks for a clarification on the meaning of the word in English. In Message 4, the Japanese user rephrases the word so that the English-speaking user can understand the meaning and correct the English translation accordingly. The Chinese-speaking user adds a clarification to improve the adequacy of the translation in Message 3. The messages in Table 15.1 are translated into English using machine translation and the original language is shown in the second column.

The experiment participants encountered a number of domain-specific words and expressions that were not translated properly with machine translation. In order to determine the meaning of a mistranslated word, the participants had to use external resources, such as consulting other participants, to find the correct translation in each language. After a mistranslation was solved, a correct translation was added to a collaboratively edited domain-specific dictionary.

In the case of a monolingual user, a problem arises if there are no means to find the correct translation through external resources. Often, it is hard to determine whether the closest equivalent or the equivalent in the original language should be used. Usually the bilingual users have to solve these inconsistencies between languages. An example of hard to resolve dictionary entries is illustrated below.

- Yağlı güreş (Turkish wrestling)
- Shima (Ryukyu sumo)
- Sirum (Korean wrestling)
- Shuaijiao (Chinese wrestling)
- Bökh (Mongolian Wrestling)

In addition, the translation group also faced some cultural issues. A native speaker may be familiar with a concept or a meaning of a sentence without it being explicitly stated. However, subtleties are often lost with a non-native speaker or a person not familiar with the culture, history or technical terminology of the domain. An example of such a problem would be the difference in the meaning of "budo" in Japanese and English. "Budo" in English generally means "Japanese martial arts", but in Japanese the meaning is just "martial arts".

To overcome this type of problem, the participants could request a revision of the source sentence from a native speaker. Furthermore, bilingual participants were able to directly ask for a clarification on the subject in hand from the native-speaking participants. However, without machine translation support, only bilingual participants were able to make requests for revision. A typical example of a machine translation mediated discussion on dictionary creation is shown in Table 15.2.

With machine translation support, the monolingual experiment participants were also able to contribute to dictionary creation in their native languages. Moreover, when discussing the correct translation of a word, every participant was able to contribute to the discussion. For example, a Chinese participant could improve the adequacy of a mistranslated word in Chinese for a Japanese-English translation.

Table 15.2 Machine translation mediated discussion in collaborative dictionary creation

Message Number	Original Language	Message (English Translation)
1	Japanese	"Kodo-kan" was added as an translation.
2	English	I think the right form is Kodokan.
3	English	I checked this on Wikipedia and added "Kodokan" for English and Finnish translation.
4	Chinese	I checked the meaning using Google. Added the Chinese translation.
5	English	The entry for "伝講道館" is wrong. The whole word is "日本伝講道館柔道". I will add it as "Japanese Kodokan Judo". Is this correct?
6	Japanese	I agree with him.

In this example, a Japanese user adds a translation to the collaboratively edited dictionary. An English user disagrees with the entry, checks for the correct spelling in Wikipedia and corrects the English and Finnish translations (Messages 2 and 3). A Chinese participant also notifies the group about adding the Chinese entry to the dictionary. In Message 5, an English user corrects the entry further and asks for a confirmation from the group. A Japanese user then confirms the entry as correct and it is added to the final version of the collaboratively created dictionary.

15.4 Multilingual Discussion Support System for Wikipedia

We designed a multilingual discussion support system for Wikipedia translation communities together with Wikimedia Foundation based on the experiment results and the case study on the Wikipedia translation community described above[1]. In the system design, not only social needs of the Wikipedia community, but also technical requirements of the existing Wikipedia system are taken into account.

---

[1] Our approach can be considered as an example of the value sensitive design approach (Friedman et al. 2006).

15.4.1 Technical Requirements

Numerous MediaWiki Extensions are available to add new features or enhance the functionality of the MediaWiki software from the users' point of view. Our goal in the development was that the actual Wikipedia community, which has a great number of users internationally, would accept the multilingual support system. From a technical point of view, as in any system development project, there are some technical requirements raised by the open-source community, the first one being coding conventions. All code should follow the conventions defined by the community. The conventions define indenting and alignment, logical structure, naming rules, and so on.

The second one is performance. Because Wikipedia is viewed by a great number of people every day, in particular a short response time is one of the very critical elements of the system design.

The third is usability. MediaWiki has its own look and feel, which should be consistent throughout the multilingual Wikipedia. Since Wikipedia is viewed by a variety of people of different age and computer skill, usability is one of the key elements to attract users.

The fourth is security. As Wikipedia is one of the most famous web sites around the world, it is the target of lots of cyber attacks. In general, a Wiki-style web site is more likely to attract cyber attacks than a basic non-wiki site, because it allows users to access and change the contents without login requirements.

Lastly, neutrality and independence is important for the Wikipedia community. The community does not depend too much on specific vendors, services or influence of third parties, but employs open source software and services.

15.4.2 System Design

Fig. 15.3 shows the system architecture of the final goal in the development process. From the software point of view, the architecture consists of MediaWiki, the Language Grid, the Language Grid Extension and Multilingual LiquidThreads Extension.

In order to develop a multilingual support system for Wikipedia discussion, in addition to meeting the needs of the community and technical requirements, the system is configured in accordance with the Wikipedia structure. Based on the results of the case study on the Wikipedia community and the analysis of MediaWiki structure, we configured the selected multilingual language resources to reflect both an article page and the related discussion page. Since the Language Grid is a multilingual service infrastructure, the Language Grid services should allow access by any other MediaWiki extensions for general purposes.

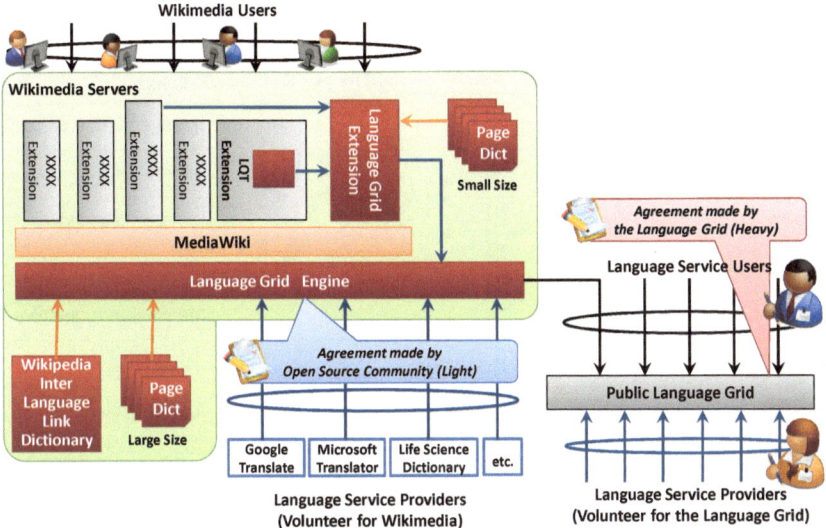

Fig. 15.3 Language Grid Extension for MediaWiki

15.4.3 Language Grid Extension

The Language Grid Extension enables users to select and combine machine translators and multilingual dictionaries registered in the Language Grid as an extension to MediaWiki. After the Language Grid Extension is installed, two new tabs will appear in each article: "Setting" and "Dictionary". "Page Dictionary" enables users to add technical terms or domain-specific words that appear in Wikipedia articles to multilingual dictionaries (Fig. 15.4). The dictionaries created with the Language Grid Extension are categorized by article, and the existing Page Dictionaries are accessible for all users. The Page Dictionary improves the machine translation quality, for example in the discussion page of a related article, with the added domain-specific words.

Using the "Setting" tab, users are able to change the settings for the machine translators and multilingual dictionaries, including settings for the user interface of the Language Grid Extension. In the settings page, users are able to customize their preferred combination of language resources from any services available. Thus, the Language Grid Extension meets the policy of the Wikipedia community to avoid relying heavily on one specific proprietary service.

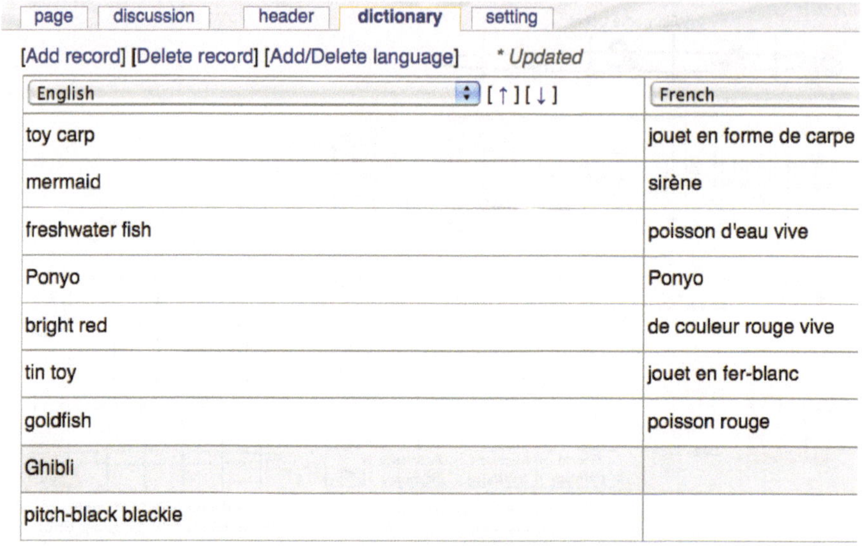

| page | discussion | header | **dictionary** | setting |

[Add record] [Delete record] [Add/Delete language]   *Updated*

English ⬍ [↑][↓]	French
toy carp	jouet en forme de carpe
mermaid	sirène
freshwater fish	poisson d'eau vive
Ponyo	Ponyo
bright red	de couleur rouge vive
tin toy	jouet en fer-blanc
goldfish	poisson rouge
Ghibli	
pitch-black blackie	

Fig. 15.4 Page Dictionary creation with the Language Grid Extension

15.4.4 Multilingual LiquidThreads Extension

The Multilingual LiquidThreads Extension is a multilingual version of the LiquidThreads Extension, which was developed to enhance the usability of the discussion pages in MediaWiki. Messages from the users in MediaWiki's discussion pages are automatically translated by the Language Grid Extension and displayed in the Multilingual LiquidThreads.

The Multilingual LiquidThreads Extension includes a feature for revision control and history. The revision history is accessible to all users as described in the MediaWiki conventions. Human correction of machine translated discussions and a history page for translated messages was added to the Multilingual LiquidThreads Extension in accordance with MediaWiki conventions. Every user is able to improve the quality of any translated message. Furthermore, changes in the translated messages are reflected in the revision history and messages can be reverted to any previous version.

The interface of Multilingual LiquidThreads is illustrated in Fig. 15.5. An actual discussion in Wikipedia Commons attracted both English and Japanese users to contribute. In this example, English-speaking users started a discussion on a Japanese animation character (see Sect. 15.2.4). A Japanese user then contributed to the discussion, in Japanese. In Fig. 15.5, the machine translated version of the Japanese discussion entry is shown. The original language of the message is indicated at the bottom of each message (i.e. "Posted in Japanese").

As described earlier, the language of the messages can be changed to any available language from the page settings. Hence, a Japanese user can read all the messages on the discussion page in Japanese, where the English messages are machine translated to Japanese, and the messages posted in Japanese are shown in their original form. Subsequently, a user not proficient in either Japanese or English would view all the messages in their machine translated form in his or her preferred language, thus enabling any user to participate in the discussion regardless of their language ability.

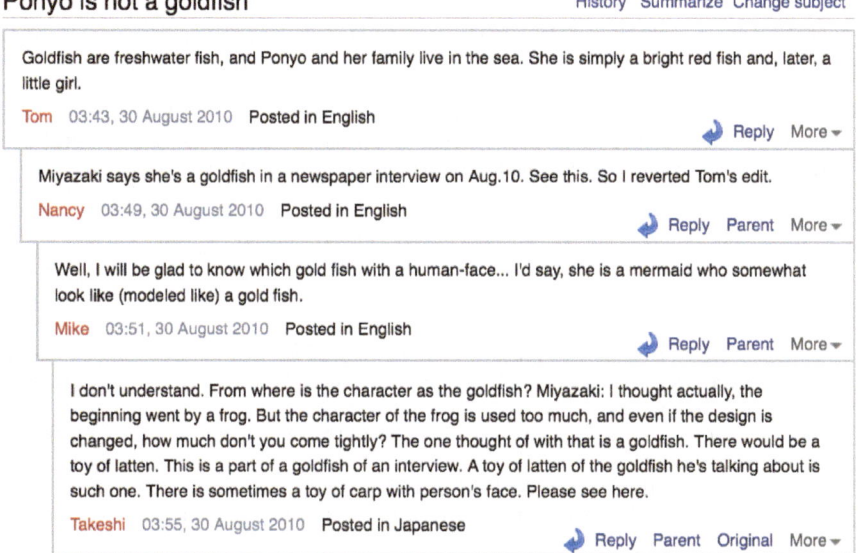

Fig. 15.5 English view of Multilingual LiquidThreads discussion

15.5 Conclusion

Wikipedia has become one of the great success stories in the early 21st century. Contrary to the expectations of many, volunteer Wikipedia contributors, or Wikipedians, continue to lend their expertise and knowledge to further improve the largest free open-content encyclopedia available. The Language Grid Extension was developed to support the Wikipedia translation communities in their work. Based on experiment results and case studies of existing communities, the Language Grid Extension offers a multi-language channel for Wikipedia contributors to communicate and collaborate in their native languages. Furthermore, the Page Dictionary feature in the Language Grid Extension allows users to improve the quality of machine translation through their collaborative efforts.

Wikipedia is a collective intelligence project and the multi-language discussion platform we developed supports the creation of a web of collective intelligence in the Wikipedia translation community. The Language Grid collects many language resources such as machine translators and dictionaries, which end users can combine as services to match their individual requirements. Although all messages in Multilingual LiquidThreads are translated with a machine translator, human users are able to modify the results. The ongoing development process concentrates on meeting the needs and requirements of the actual users, and the open-source community of Wikipedia.

Acknowledgments   We would like to express our gratitude to Erik Möller and the whole Wikimedia Foundation for endorsing and supporting this project. We extend our appreciation also to Andrew Garrett and his colleagues for their remarkable work on LiquidThreads. This research was partially supported by Strategic Information and Communications R&D Promotion Programme from the Japanese Ministry of Internal Affairs and Communications, and Global COE Program on Informatics Education and Research Center for Knowledge-Circulating Society.

References

Bryant SL, Forte A, Bruckman A (2005) Becoming wikipedian: transformation of participation in a collaborative online encyclopedia. 2005 International ACM SIGGROUP Conference on Supporting Group Work: 1-10

Désilets A, Gonzalez S, Paquet S, Stojanovic M (2006) Translation the wiki way. 2006 International Symposium on Wikis: 19-32

Friedman B, Kahn P, Borning A (2006) Value sensitive design and information systems. Zhang P, Galletta D (ed) Human-Computer Interaction and Management Information Systems: Foundations: 348-372

Harley A, Paris C (1997) Multilingual document production: from support for translating to support for authoring. Machine Translation 12 (1-2): 109-129

Hautasaari A (2010) Machine translation effects on group interaction: an intercultural collaboration experiment. 3rd International Conference on Intercultural Collaboration (ICIC 2010): 69-78

Kumaran A, Saravanan K, Maurice S (2008) WikiBABEL: community creation of multilingual data. Babel Wiki Workshop 2008: Cross-language Collaboration, WikiSYM 2008 Conference: 1-11

Morita D, Ishida T (2009) Designing protocols for collaborative translation. International Conference on Principles of Practice in Multi-Agent Systems (PRIMA-09), Lecture Notes in Artificial Intelligence 5925: 17-32

Ortega F, Gonzalez-Barahona JM, Robles G (2008) On the inequality of contributions to wikipedia. 41st Annual Hawaii International Conference on System Sciences: 304

Schütz J, Nübel R (1998) Evaluating language technologies: the MULTIDOC appproach to taming the knowledge soup. Third Conference of the Association for Machine Translation in the Americas on Machine Translation and the Information Soup (AMTA '98): 236-249

Yamashita N, Inaba R, Kuzuoka H, Ishida T (2009) Difficulties in establishing common ground in multiparty groups using machine translation. ACM Conference on Human Factors in Computing Systems (CHI'09): 679-688

Yamashita N, Ishida T (2006) Effects of machine translation on collaborative work. ACM Conference on Computer Supported Collaborative Work (CSCW'06): 515-524

Part VI

Towards Federation of Service Grids

Chapter 16
Pipelining Software and Services for Language Processing

Arif Bramantoro[1], Ulrich Schäfer[2], and Toru Ishida[1]

1 Department of Social Informatics, Kyoto University, Japan, Yoshida-Honmachi, Sakyo-ku, Kyoto 606-8501, Japan, e-mail: arif@ai.soc.i.kyoto-u.ac.jp, ishida@i.kyoto-u.ac.jp

2 Language Technology Lab, German Research Center for Artificial Intelligence, Gmbh Campus D 3 1, Stuhlsatzenhausweg 3, D-66123 Saarbrücken, Germany, e-mail: ulrich.schaefer@dfki.de

Abstract This chapter reports on our experiences with combining two different platforms in natural language processing research, i.e. Heart of Gold and the Language Grid, to provide more language resources available on the Web. Heart of Gold is known as middleware architecture for pipelining deep and shallow natural language processing components. The Language Grid is one of the service grid infrastructures built on top of the Internet to provide pipelined language services. Both of these frameworks provide composite language services and components. Having Heart of Gold integrated in the Language Grid environment contributes to increased interoperability among various language services. The integrated architecture also supports the combination of pipelined language services in the Language Grid and the pipelined natural language processing components in Heart of Gold to provide a better quality of language services available on the Web. Thus, language services with different characteristics can be combined based on the concept of Web service with different treatment of each combination. An evaluation is presented to show that the overhead of the integration is not significant.

16.1 Introduction

To utilize language services more robustly and to preserve precious language resources, we need to integrate multiple infrastructures. Two of the famous ongoing developments of natural language infrastructures are the Language Grid (Ishida 2006) and Heart of Gold (Schäfer 2006).

The Language Grid is a service based collective intelligence framework which enables access to various language services (Murakami and Ishida 2008) in the world based on a single powerful protocol, HTTP. For the Language Grid, the more language services it has the better it is for the availability of composite services. Composite language service means the ability to create a new service by combining existing services.

Heart of Gold is also a framework that tries to accommodate any natural language processing (NLP) tool regardless of the depth of the analysis. The return value of this framework is an XML standoff annotation string which can be further processed by any application. Since Heart of Gold provides a high degree of flexibility for accessing its server as well as defining processing strategies for integrating multiple NLP components, many new applications have been developed utilizing Heart of Gold to gain the benefits of such hybrid analysis results (Schäfer 2007; Schäfer and Spurk 2010).

The language services for NLP provided by the Language Grid are similar to the NLP functions provided by Heart of Gold. However, only a few shallow tools such as ChaSen (Asahara and Matsumoto 2000) and TreeTagger (Schmid 1994) are provided by the Language Grid so far. There are various NLP functions in Heart of Gold which are not provided by the Language Grid, especially the efficient deep parser PET (Callmeier 2000), but also shallow tools such as tokenizers, part-of-speech taggers, morphological analyzers, named entity recognizers, PCFG and dependency parsers, sentence boundary detectors and coreference resolvers, accompanied by language resources for various languages.

On the other hand, functionalities for management of access to distributed language resources are implemented for the Language Grid, but not for Heart of Gold. Companies and research organizations which provide their language resources for the frameworks usually have conditions for use in order to protect the intellectual property rights of their language resources. Therefore, access to language resources must be controlled. Statistics of access to resources should be available to service providers. Thus, the Language Grid and Heart of Gold can complement each other. Integrating them into a single framework will have great benefit for users and service providers of both frameworks.

We have identified three general problems concerning the integration.

- Heart of Gold is a framework based on components, while the Language Grid is a service-oriented framework. We need to survey which architecture is suitable and reliable to accommodate these frameworks.
- The standard interfaces of these two frameworks are not the same. Heart of Gold provides XML annotations as output, while in the Language Grid standard interface, there is no such type for output parameter.
- Both frameworks provide a processing strategy for language resources but in different ways. The Language Grid provides service workflows for pipelining composite language services, while Heart of Gold uses an NLP pipeline by default, but can be customized to more flexible processing strategies by an optional description language for controlling multiple language components.

This article proposes that the Language Grid as one of the service grid frameworks for pipelining services can be enhanced through integration with any pipelining software, for example, Heart of Gold. This will lead to more language services becoming available in the Language Grid environment. The integrated architecture treats Heart of Gold not only as an atomic service in the Language Grid, but is also able to pipeline other services in the Language Grid. In general, having a hybrid architecture in the service grid, it will allow Web services to scale up.

16.2 Hybrid Architecture for Pipelining

While the architecture of the Language Grid is widely discussed in other chapters of this book, we focus in this chapter on Heart of Gold, a middleware that bridges user application and external NLP functionalities. Heart of Gold provides integration between deep and shallow NLP annotations as shown in Fig. 16.1. Deep NLP applies as much linguistic knowledge as possible to analyze natural language sentences (Pollard and Sag 1994).

On the other hand, shallow NLP neglects the use of the whole range of linguistic details, but concentrates on specific aspects. Both shallow and deep NLP may involve statistical as well as rule-based methods for linguistic modeling. It can be shown that combining shallow and deep NLP can improve the analysis results in terms of accuracy and efficiency. The detailed list of NLP tools provided by Heart of Gold can be found in (Schäfer 2007) and on the Heart of Gold website[1].

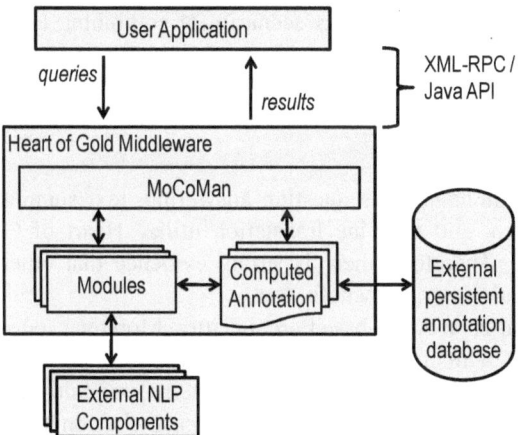

Fig. 16.1 Heart of Gold framework that integrates many NLP functionalities

There are two kinds of interfaces in Heart of Gold. The first interface is between applications and Heart of Gold as a middleware. This interface enables applications to communicate either via Java API (for Java applications) or XML-RPC (for remote applications or applications written in other programming languages). To open a communication to Heart of Gold in this interface, an applica-

---

[1] http://heartofgold.dfki.de

tion creates an instance of the Heart of Gold architecture. The second interface is between external NLP components and Heart of Gold's middleware. In this interface, the components are packed as subclasses of either Module (local Java-based components) or XmlRpcModule (remote, possibly non-Java, components).

The main advantage of using Heart of Gold is the availability of deep NLP for computing deep semantic representations for natural language sentences (sentence semantics). For example, as mentioned in (Schäfer 2007), for the sentence "Tom gave his son a toy" Heart of Gold produces a deep, semantically analyzed result such as *past(give(Tom, his son, toy))*. This deep analysis can be used to create other syntactic variants such as "A toy was given by Tom to his son" or "Tom gave his son the toy". Besides first-order logic-like representation, deep parsing also provides further linguistic information on the fly, such as detailed morphological and syntactic information for words and phrases.

16.2.1 Integration into the Language Grid

To combine the two frameworks, the Language Grid and Heart of Gold, it is necessary to find the most useful and reliable scenarios. A number of alternatives were designed to combine Heart of Gold and the Language Grid. Because of the limited space in this book, we will not present the alternative architectures here. We found that the most promising scenario for combining Heart of Gold and the Language Grid will be by wrapping Heart of Gold as a Web service, so that it can be accessed through the Language Grid.

Here are the characteristics of Heart of Gold that can be considered for realizing a Web service on top of it:

- Many applications such as question answering, text summarization, information extraction, and machine translation utilize Heart of Gold as their NLP analysis tool. Therefore, there is strong evidence that other, Language-Grid-based applications would benefit, too.
- Heart of Gold is an XML-based architecture. Moreover, one of the methods to communicate with its managing module (Module Communication Manager, MoCoMan), either from application or external modules, is XML-RPC. With XML-RPC, any application or module can easily be connected to Heart of Gold even though remotely located on a different server.
- Heart of Gold can provide flexible processing strategies through processing order and information flow between NLP modules, including parallelism and loops. This is comparable to composite Web services (Khalaf et al. 2003).
- Both frameworks, Heart of Gold and the Language Grid, are built on Java technology. However, these two frameworks also support user applications built on different programming languages and platforms. The Language Grid provides Web service technology with its main characteristic of independent interaction between platforms and languages. Heart of Gold also allows user applications

to build on different programming languages and platforms via XML-RPC connection. One advantage of Heart of Gold is the ability to add more language resources via XML-RPC, which increases their interoperability.

Based on the above-mentioned characteristics, the proposed architecture for Heart of Gold and the Language Grid integration is illustrated in Fig. 16.2. The left part of Fig. 16.2 shows the architecture of the Language Grid, while the right part shows that of Heart of Gold. The architecture of the Language Grid consists of four layers, P2P Grid Infrastructure, Atomic Language Services, Composite Language Services, and Intercultural Collaboration Tools.

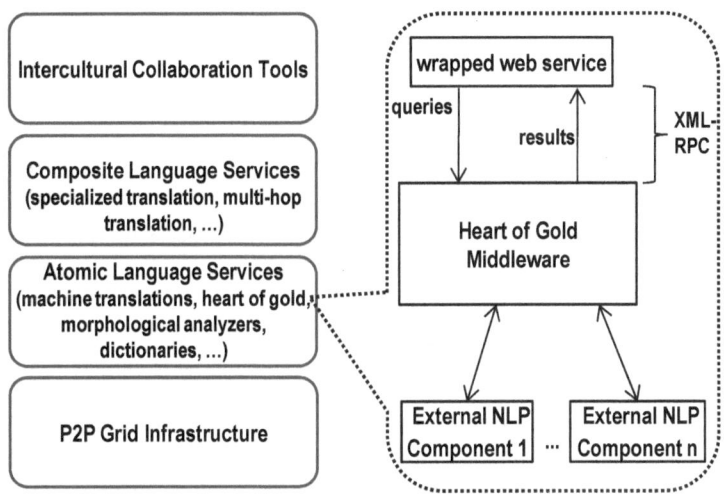

Fig. 16.2 Hybrid architecture for pipelining software and services

We propose that the Language Grid can utilize Heart of Gold by adding it to the Atomic Language Services layer. Although it is not common in the Language Grid to have multiple NLP components in the layer of atomic language services, the standard wrapping technique of the Language Grid requires Heart of Gold to be located in this layer. Consequently, we have to treat Heart of Gold differently in this layer since it contains many NLP functions that behave as composite services. We will discuss the detailed treatment of this layer in the next section.

To realize this scheme, we wrap Heart of Gold as a Web service that implements the Language Grid standard interface. From Heart of Gold's point of view, this Web service acts as an application, whilst from the Language Grid's point of view, this Web service is considered as a wrapped language resource. The wrapped Web service connects to Heart of Gold's middleware via XML-RPC. Therefore, the Heart of Gold server can be located at a different node in the Language Grid.

The NLP functions of Heart of Gold integrated in the Language Grid can be accessed by adjusting the depth value of the Web service parameter. If the user of the Language Grid wants to obtain deeper NLP analyses, the depth value has to be set higher. Likewise, to access shallower NLP functions, the depth parameter can be decreased.

In the original Heart of Gold architecture, there is a multi-session system and database that enables an offline processing mode. This means that the Heart of Gold engine does not have to use online NLP tools for analyzing sentences that had already been entered and analyzed before and were stored in an annotation database (caching via XML database). However, since there is no concept of multi-session and annotation database in services computing, we have to disable these features in the current Heart of Gold service. Heart of Gold service in the Language Grid will have only single sessions and will not store any analyzed results in a database.

16.3 Pipelining Composite Services

It is a common observation in NLP research that to get a higher quality of language processing, we need to pipeline more than one processing tool. Some techniques have been developed both in Heart of Gold and the Language Grid to accommodate this characteristic of language processing.

Heart of Gold allows the user to execute more than one language component. Unless a user defines the smallest depth value, more than one language component is executed. There might a case that the empty result is retrieved from the requested depth. This situation forces Heart of Gold to perform a fall-back strategy returning the result from the previous component. However, we skip the fall-back mechanism since it is not applicable for a Web service mechanism.

The final result of a query in Heart of Gold is retrieved from the deepest component in the sequence. One particular component obtains the output of the previous component (a component with lower depth value in the default strategy). The component can also obtain the output of other components based on the configuration of the pipeline. The default processing strategy is a pipeline; more flexibly, different configurations can be described by using the System Description Language (SDL) extension.

SDL (Krieger 2003) is a specific language initially used for building NLP systems and may be used in Heart of Gold to pipeline sub-architectures of multiple components. SDL uses a declarative specification language to define a flow of information (input and output) and a pipelining process between linguistic processing components. The declarative specification consists of operators, symbolic module names, assignment of these symbolic module names to Java class names, constructor arguments and some other processing options. The basic operators currently available in Heart of Gold are as follows.

- + for *sequence*. A component runs in sequence after the previous component has finished. It takes the previous output as its input. The input to the first component becomes the input of the sequence.

- | for *parallelism*. Multiple components run in parallel by using Java threads. The outputs are then aggregated into a single output object.
- * for *unrestricted iteration*. A component runs in a loop until its output remains unchanged.

A set of component descriptions D in SDL can be recursively formalized based on an initial set C of (atomic) components as follows.

- $c \in C \Rightarrow c \in D$
- $d_1, \ldots, d_k \in D \Rightarrow d_1 + \ldots + d_k \in D$ (sequence; infix operator)
- $d_1, \ldots, d_k \in D \Rightarrow (| d_1, \ldots, d_k) \in D$ (parallelism; prefix operator)
- $d \in D \Rightarrow (* d) \in D$ (unrestricted iteration; prefix operator)

While multiple NLP components in Heart of Gold are pipelined by using SDL, composite services in the Language Grid can be pipelined in BPEL as commonly used in Web service research, but we do not cover them in this article because BPEL doesn't come with any language (resource) specific support.

16.3.1 Use Scenarios for Pipelining of Composite Services

There are two urgent combinations between the multiple language components and services of Heart of Gold service in the Language Grid. Firstly, we need to incorporate multiple components of Heart of Gold into the Language Grid's workflow. For example, there is a specialized Japanese-English translation service in the Language Grid that includes a Japanese morphological analyzer, an English morphological analyzer, a community dictionary and term replacement service. The concrete Web service for English morphological analysis available in the Language Gird is TreeTagger, for English to Japanese translation the service is J-Server, for Japanese morphological analysis it is ChaSen, and for community dictionary service there are Science Dictionary Service and Tourism Dictionary Service run in parallel.

As illustrated in Fig. 16.3, the TreeTagger morphological analyzer from the Language Grid is replaced with the deeper NLP of SProUT morphological analyzer from Heart of Gold service. SProUT in Heart of Gold provides a better quality in the language domain (Bramantoro and Ishida 2009) since it can provide not only morphological analysis but also named entity recognition. This new functionality in the Language Grid's workflow enables users to dynamically select the right community dictionary service during workflow execution.

In this scenario, we show that the location term in the sentence can be detected and tagged by the named entity recognition component (SProUT). When the location term is tagged by SProUT, the workflow execution engine automatically chooses Tourism Dictionary Service instead of Science Dictionary Service. The final result is the same as the existing workflow before combination, but the workflow execution by using Heart of Gold service should be more efficient and task-

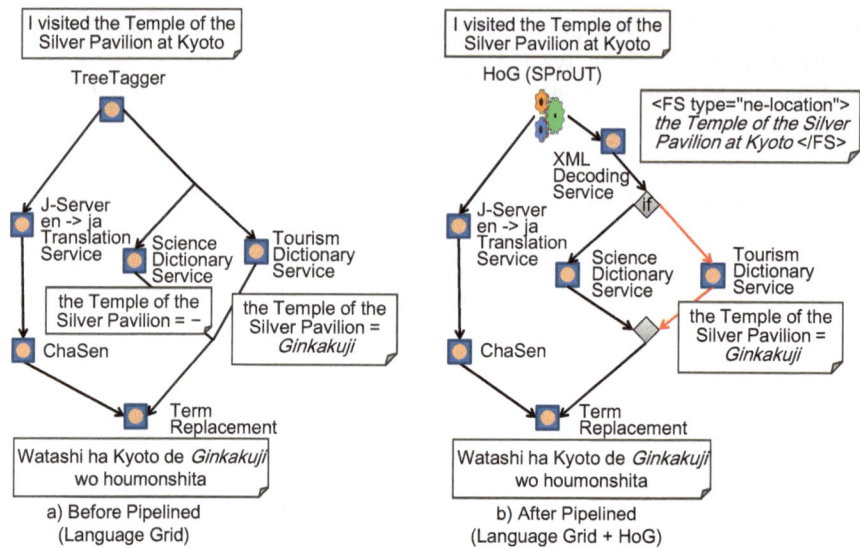

Fig. 16.3 Heart of Gold multiple components in the Language Grid's workflow

oriented since it runs one dictionary service at a time, not all dictionaries in parallel. This scenario is also applicable to other dictionary services in the Language Grid by using the current tag set in the named entity recognition component related to the dictionary service. It is also possible to train a new tag set according to dictionary service entries.

Secondly, we need to incorporate language service(s) of the Language Grid inside the processing flow of Heart of Gold. To do this, it is necessary to realize Service as a Software (SaaS) by wrapping language service(s) in the Language Grid as a Heart of Gold component which has additional parameters of XML output and, therefore, needs a special tool to convert the service output into the XML format. This is useful when we want to try NLP components of Heart of Gold in different languages. For example, ChunkieRMRS in Heart of Gold that can deliver recursive chunks (Skut and Brants 1998) is only available in German and English. Hence, the new deep NLP for Japanese could also be realized by utilizing a Japanese-English translation service from the Language Grid as described in Fig. 16.4 together with its SDL (it is important to note that a composite language service such as a multi-hop translation service can also be wrapped as a language component).

In addition to improving the existing composite services and composite-components scenarios, we also found that having processing flow and workflow combined in a single architecture can create new possible services. One of them is a paraphrasing service. This paraphrasing service can be composed together with a translation service. For example, a translation service from Japanese to English is sometimes difficult to understand for a non-Japanese user. It needs additional features to help the user better understand the translation result. The paraphrasing service based on the deep structure of NLP provided by Heart of Gold could be a

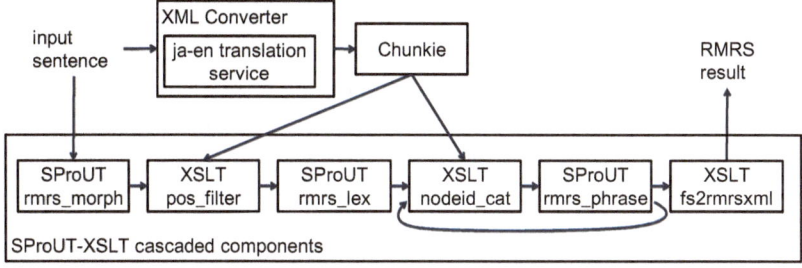

chunkiermrs = (sprout_rmrs_morph + xslt_pos_filter + sprout_rmrs_lex
                + (* xslt_nodeid_cat + sprout_rmrs_phrase) + xslt_fs2rmrsxml)

sprout_rmrs_morph = SproutModulesTextDom("rmrs-morph.cfg")
xslt_pos_filter = XsltModulesDomDom("posfilter.xsl", "annotation_id", "Chunkie")
sprout_rmrs_lex = SproutModulesDomDom("rmrs-lex.cfg")
xslt_nodeid_cat = XsltModulesDomDom("nodeinfo.xsl", "annotation_id", "Chunkie")
sprout_rmrs_phrase = SproutModulesDomDom("rmrs-phrase.cfg")
xslt_fs2rmrsxml = XsltModulesDomDom("fs2rmrsxml.xsl")

Fig. 16.4 Language service inside Heart of Gold's processing flow with its SDL

solution to improve the translation accuracy. For example, when the translation result is "Akita had Tanaka help with homework", the composite deep analyzer in
Heart of Gold service can improve the result by providing deep structure *past
(have, help (Akita, Tanaka, homework))* and then delivers the new sentence
"Tanaka helped Akita's homework". The example scenario of a paraphrasing service
is illustrated in Fig. 16.5 by utilizing the Language Grid's playground, an open
source website that provides easy access and step-by-step creation of various language services in the Language Grid environment (Sakai et al. 2009).

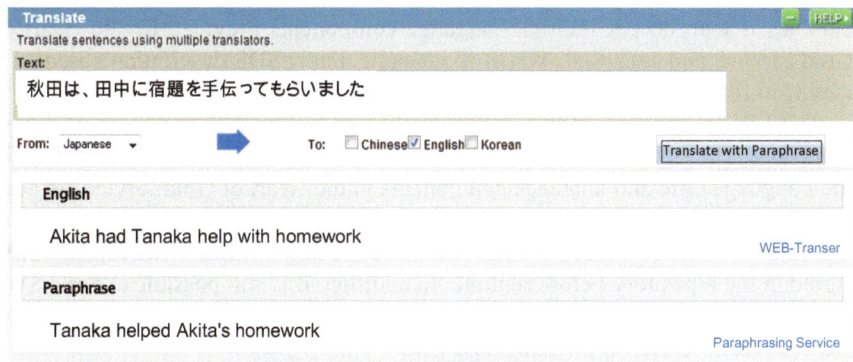

Fig. 16.5 Paraphrasing Service to improve translation accuracy

16.4 Processing Flow and Workflow Pipelining Service

To realize the combinations, we propose a pipeline service and its architecture to integrate the processing flow and workflow as described in Fig. 16.6. This service consists of three components: Processing Flow Analyzer, Workflow Analyzer and SDL Writer. Three repositories are utilized by this service, i.e. Language Component Information, Language Service Information and Workflow Repository. An alternative workflow is automatically created and stored in the workflow repository together with its generated SDL description of incorporated Heart of Gold components. We argue that by declaring the pipeline system as a Web service invocation, the integration between Heart of Gold and the Language Grid becomes more interoperable.

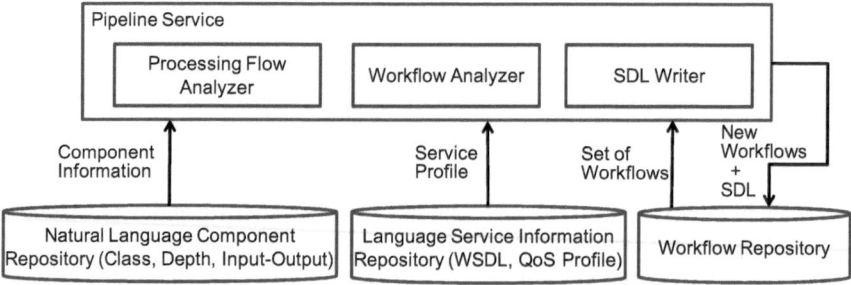

Fig. 16.6 Pipeline service architecture for composite language services and components

The Web-service-triggered SDL Writer can be called either online or offline. Here online means that the service can be merged with other services during service composition. When a user requests a particular task to be performed by composite language services, the pipeline service analyzes an alternative workflow, enriches it with deeper multiple language components provided by the Heart of Gold service, and calls SDL Writer to generate a new SDL description based on a new workflow combination to be delivered to the user.

The SDL Writer can also be called offline to optimize the creation of a new workflow. The offline SDL Writer is called especially when language services in the Language Grid and language components in the Heart of Gold service are added frequently. The advantage of calling the SDL Writer offline is that the processing time of a user request is not affected since the new workflow has already been stored in the repository before runtime. In addition, it is still possible to write SDL from scratch, as the Heart of Gold framework, and store it in the repository of the Heart of Gold service in the Language Grid.

16.4.1 NLP Pipelines: Risks, Challenges, Benefits

In this section, we focus on a general criticism that was formulated some years ago and has often been repeated since then. We will briefly explain it and describe our solution in Heart of Gold and Language Grid.

The criticism is about the appropriateness and correctness of the way NLP pipelines are realized in Heart of Gold and Language Grid instantiations, and also in other approaches such as the LFG-based analysis pipeline in the Powerset division of Microsoft's Bing! search engine (Kaplan 2010).

A typical NLP pipeline for English consists of tokenizer, part-of-speech tagger, named entity recognizer, followed by a shallow and/or deep syntactic parser with optional sentence semantics or dependency structure output. As some components of the pipeline rely on the output of previous components, errors may accumulate. The best PoS taggers typically are only 96% accurate; the case is even worse for named entity recognizers, depending on how close the application domain is to the training domain. Subsequent parsing, which may rely on tagger and NER component output, will add further errors, and so on. A similar problem arises if one follows a more cautious approach by relaxing ambiguity instead of taking a decision by selecting a reading, e.g. of the right PoS tag, in each pipeline stage. Instead of accumulated errors, one ends up with accumulated ambiguities and the problem of how to resolve them in the end.

Our answer to this question is to minimize errors and error propagation in each step as well as eliminating ambiguity as soon as possible. This requires a very detailed and fine-grained, partially also text domain-specific integration of NLP components. Heart of Gold and thus also the Language Grid is exactly the experimental platform to support this kind of integration. Recent boosts in hybrid parsing coverage (roughly from 65% to now more than 85% on scientific paper texts from the ACL Anthology, cf. Schäfer and Spurk 2010) could be achieved by combining the new fine-grained shallow-deep NLP component integration based on the "chart mapping" approach described in Adolphs et al. 2008, with a chart pruning technique described in Cramer and Zhang 2010.

The chart pruning technique is especially suited to achieving full analyses of even very long sentences. Briefly, the idea is to restrict the search space during parsing by setting a maximum number of tasks per chart cell. A priority model based on the generative probabilities of rule applications ensures that it will be unlikely that good readings will be dropped. Another important aspect of this technique is a drastic improvement of parsing speed, especially of long sentences.

Chart mapping on the other hand is based on a rewrite formalism that mediates between token information delivered by shallow pre-processing components and the input (inital chart) expected by a deep linguistic grammar. This formalism has been devised because of the observation that shallow NLP tools, e.g. PoS taggers trained on the Wall street Journal (Penn Treebank) make different assumptions on tokenization than a deep linguistic grammar, e.g. with respect to punctuation. Ignoring these subtle details leads to considerable loss of coverage, as was observed in the initial integration scenarios within Heart of Gold.

Is there an alternative to the NLP pipeline? In our opinion, there is no realistic alternative. It would consist in learning the whole I/O behavior from raw text input to output of a semantic representation just from (manual) annotation. This would be (a) very expensive, and (b) only applicable to restricted domains. One of the great advantages of the NLP pipeline, however, is its greater flexibility and robustness towards different text domains in general.

16.4.2 Pipelining Management Issues

The Web service of Heart of Gold in the Language Grid is registered in the Language Grid service manager. Any language resources registered in the service manager can be monitored for their statistical usage information, such as total number of accesses, users who accessed the resources and access time. A copyright and license manager is also added to the service manager which enables the setting of access control for language resources. Each resource can be limited to specific time (per day, per month, per year). Likewise, each user can be given a limitation on access numbers per day, per month or per year. Moreover, user rights can be allocated to particular users while not to others.

Heart of Gold, on the other hand, does not have specific license, copyright and user allocations for its resources. The copyright and license information of each components are published on its website along with the downloadable code but not along with the resource access restrictions. This means that if there is an access from a user, it is guaranteed that the user understands the information on copyright and license. It is also not possible to grant rights for different users and different resources. When Heart of Gold is integrated into the Language Grid, copyright, license, and user rights management cannot be obtained automatically.

Having Heart of Gold equipped with access management as a service in the Language Grid is nice, but this functionality does not deal with individual NLP components in Heart of Gold service. In fact, individual NLP components in Heart of Gold have different copyrights that may require different access management. For the example of Heart of Gold as an atomic service mentioned at the beginning of this article, user rights can be managed by admitting users based on the most restricted license of NLP components. The problem arises when pipelining a processing flow of multiple components in Heart of Gold with a workflow of composite language services in the Language Grid. This scenario needs individual treatment of NLP components used by the processing flow. We believe that by copying the service profile of individual NLP components in the Language Service Repository from Natural Language Component Repository, the access management can be easily implemented.

16.5 Evaluation

We performed an evaluation to investigate the performance of Heart of Gold service in the Language Grid either accessed as an atomic service or pipelined with other services. The performance, as indicated by the quality of service (QoS) metric of response time, is important since Heart of Gold service is registered in the Language Grid's service manager and will be open to the public. The evaluation had both Heart of Gold's Module Communication Manager (MoCoMan) server, Heart of Gold service and client application running on the same host, although other language services in the Language Grid are each located in their service node.

To evaluate Heart of Gold as atomic service, two components of Heart of Gold were used, TreeTagger and SProUT. TreeTagger is also available in the Language Grid, but not SProUT. Table 16.1 shows experimental results we obtained in the evaluation that compares the execution of Heart of Gold as component (not as a service) and Heart of Gold as atomic service. It is interesting to note that running Heart of Gold as atomic service needs less response time than running Heart of Gold as component, although the standard deviation is rather high. This is due to the characteristics of a Web service that is based on XML and naturally compatible with the access method to Heart of Gold's middleware that is based on XML-RPC. However, the existing NLP service provided by the Language Grid, Tree-Tagger, had the lowest response time. The reason here is specific for this component which relies on TreeTagger's built-in tokenization in the Language Grid, while the Heart of Gold runtime includes the runtime of a global Tokenizer (JTok) plus subsequent transformation to provide a uniform tokenization for different taggers.

Table 16.1 The evaluation of implementing Heart of Gold accessed as atomic service

	Heart of Gold (TreeTagger) as Component	Heart of Gold (TreeTagger) as Atomic Service	TreeTagger in Language Grid	Heart of Gold (SProUT) as Component	Heart of Gold (SProUT) as Atomic Service
Avg. Response Time (sec.)	4.49	4.44	0.24	2.12	1.96
Standard Deviation (sec.)	0.07	0.29	0.08	0.08	0.23
Depth Value	20	20	20	40	40

In this evaluation, we also found that the depth value of an NLP component had no correlation with the response time, although a deeper NLP component might contain more functionalities such as a finite-state tokenizer, gazetteer lookup, unification-based rule interpreter and XSLT transformation. In other words, the shallower and monolithic C-written TreeTagger that contains only a statistical PoS tagger based on a single model could be slower than a deeper, rule-based and Java-written SProUT. It depends on the processing time of each component and how the component is connected to Heart of Gold's middleware, i.e. as internal or external component.

To evaluate Heart of Gold service pipelined together with other services as a composite service, two workflows previously illustrated in Fig. 16.3 were used. We compared the existing workflow of specialized translation service without combining Heart of Gold service and the new workflow using Heart of Gold service. Although it seems that two NLP components used in these two workflows are different, we need to evaluate this scenario to show that the overhead of the integration is trivial.

16.6 Conclusion

In this article, we have proposed an integration of two complex frameworks, Heart of Gold and the Language Grid. We have examined several design alternatives for the integration and chosen the most promising one. To facilitate the use of NLP functions in Heart of Gold, we wrapped Heart of Gold into a Web service in the Language Grid environment. By having a Heart of Gold service in the Language Grid, we can exploit distributed language resources in NLP-based applications. The availability of deep parsers in Heart of Gold allows a translation service to provide high quality translations.

We showed that language resources with different characteristics can be combined based on the concept of service-oriented computing with different combinations. The multiple language components in Heart of Gold can be pipelined with the existing workflow of composite services in the Language Grid environment. On the other hand, the composite language services in the Language Grid can be pipelined in the processing flow of Heart of Gold components. If both Heart of Gold and the Language Grid are considered as service grids because of their multiple language components and composite language services, we can say that the integration of various service grids is possible. In evaluation, we prove that the overhead of the integration is not significant.

The major contributions of this article are (i) the extension of the Language Grid's standard interface to communicate with multiple components as provided by Heart of Gold; (ii) better language accuracy available on the Web by enabling the substitution of language components in Heart of Gold with language services in the Language Grid and vice versa within an integrated pipeline; (iii) interoperability among various language services by creating new combinations of multiple language components of Heart of Gold and composite language services of the Language Grid. We realize that there have been some breakthroughs in Web service research that try to transform software components into more loosely coupled components by using standard internet technology so-called Web services. However, it is hard to find a good reference that provides a real solution for a complex integration task between a huge Web service framework (the Language Grid) and a dynamic, highly customizable software system such as Heart of Gold.

Acknowledgments   This research was partially supported by Strategic Information and Communications R&D Promotion Programme from the Japanese Ministry of Internal Affairs and Communications, and also by Global COE Program on Informatics Education and Research Center for Knowledge-Circulating Society. The work has also been funded under contract 01IW08003 (project TAKE - Technologies for Advanced Knowledge Extraction) by the German Federal Ministry of Education and Research.

References

Adolphs P, Oepen S, Callmeier U, Crysmann B, Flickinger D, Kiefer B (2008) Some fine points of hybrid natural language parsing. The Sixth International Conference on Language Resources and Evaluation (LREC2008)

Asahara M, Matsumoto Y (2000) Extended models and tools for high performance part-of-speech tagger. The International Conference on Computational Linguistics, Saarbrücken, Germany: 21-27

Becker M, Drozdzýnski W, Krieger H-U, Piskorski J, Schäfer U, Xu F (2002) Sprout- shallow processing with typed feature structures and unification. The International Conference on Natural Language Processing, Mumbai, India

Bramantoro A, Ishida T (2009) User-centered QoS in combining web services for interactive domain. The International Conference on Semantics, Knowledge and Grid: 41-48

Bramantoro A, Schäfer U, Ishida T (2010) Towards an integrated architecture for composite language services and components. International Conference on Language Resources and Evaluation (LREC2010): 3506-3511

Bramantoro A, Tanaka M, Murakami Y, Schäfer U, Ishida T (2008) A hybrid integrated architecture for language service composition. The IEEE International Conference on Web Services: 345-352

Business Process Execution Language for Web Services (BPEL), version 1.1. (2003) Retrieved December 5, 2007, from http://www.ibm.com/developerworks/library/ws-bpel/.

Callmeier U (2000) PET-a platform for experimentation with efficient HPSG processing techniques. Natural Language Engineering 6(1): 99-107

Clark J (1999) Xsl transformations (xslt) version 1.0, w3c recommendation. World Wide Web Consortium. Retrieved January 19, 2008, from http://www.w3.org/TR/xslt/.

Copestake A (2003) Report on the design of rmrs. Technical Report D1.1b. University of Cambridge, Cambridge, UK

Cramer B and Zhang Y (2010) Constraining robust constructions for broad-coverage parsing with precision grammars. The 23rd International Conference on Computational Linguistics (COLING-2010): 223-231

Ishida T (2006) Language Grid: an infrastructure for intercultural collaboration. 2006 IEEE/IPSJ Symposium on Applications and the Internet: 96-100

Kaplan R (2010) Semantics on the tail. Keynote Speech Held at the NAACL 2010 Semantic Search Workshop, Los Angeles, CA

Khalaf R, Mukhi NK, Weerawarana S (2003) Service-oriented composition in BPEL4WS. The World Wide Web Conference, Budapest, Hungary

Krieger HU (2003) SDL-a description language for building NLP systems. The HLT-NAACL Workshop on the Software Engineering and Architecture of Language Technology Systems, Edmonton, Canada: 84-91

Murakami, Y., and Ishida, T. (2008). A layered language service architecture for intercultural collaboration. 6th International Conference on Creating, Connecting and Collaborating through Computing (c5 2008): 3-9

Pollard C, Sag IA (1994) Head-driven phrase structure grammar. Chicago, USA: University of Chicago Press

Sakai S, Gotou M, Murakami Y, Morimoto S, Morita D, Tanaka M, Ishida T, Murakami Y (2009) Language grid playground: light weight building blocks for intercultural collaboration. The 2009 International Workshop on Intercultural Collaboration, Palo Alto, California, USA: 297-300

Schäfer U (2006) Middleware for creating and combining multi-dimensional NLP markup. The EACL Workshop on Multi-Dimensional Markup in Natural Language Processing, Trento, Italy: 81-84

Schäfer U (2007) Integrating deep and shallow natural language processing components: representations and hybrid architectures. Dissertation, Faculty of Mathematics and Computer Science, Saarland University, Saarbrücken, Germany

Schäfer U, Spurk C (2010) TAKE scientist's workbench: semantic search and citation-based visual navigation in scholar papers. The Fourth IEEE International Conference on Semantic Computing (ICSC-2010), Pittsburgh, PA, USA: 317-324

Schmid H (1994) Probabilistic part-of-speech tagging using decision trees. The International Conference on New Methods in Language Processing, Manchester, UK

Skut W, Brants T (1998) Chunk tagger: statistical recognition of noun phrases. The ESSLLI Workshop on Automated Acquisition of Syntax and Parsing, Saarbrücken, Germany

Wang H, Huang JZ, Qu Y, Xie J (2004) Web services: problems and future directions. Journal of Web Semantics: Science, Services and Agents on the World Wide Web 1(3): 309-320

Chapter 17
Integrating Smart Classroom and Language Services

Yue Suo[1], Yuanchun Shi[1], and Toru Ishida[2]

1 Department of Computer Science and Technology, Tsinghua University, Beijing 100084, China, e-mail: {suoyue, shiyc}@tsinghua.edu.cn

2 Department of Social Informatics, Kyoto University, Yoshida Honmachi, Sakyoku, Kyoto, 606-8501 Japan, e-mail: ishida@i.kyoto-u.ac.jp

Abstract The real-time interactive virtual classroom with tele-education experience is an important approach in distance learning. However, most current systems fail to meet the new challenges raised by the development of the service-oriented architecture. First, the learning systems should be able to facilitate easier integration of increasingly dedicated services, such as language services on the Internet. Second, the learning systems must open their internal interfaces as web services to other systems, so as to enable deeper integration of these systems and easier deployment. Third, the systems are expected to provide flexible interfaces to support mobile device interaction. To address these issues, we build a prototype system, called Open Smart Classroom, by upgrading the original Smart Classroom into a service-oriented open system. With the help of Language Grid services, two Open Smart Classrooms deployed in Tsinghua University and Kyoto University are connected and experimental co-classes have been successfully held. The results of the user study show that integrating Smart Classroom and language services is an interesting and promising approach to building future multicultural distant learning systems.

17.1 Introduction

The traditional learning mode, in which teachers and students face each other in the same classroom, has unrivalled advantages in terms of cultural effect, over the new generation of web-based learning. Rather than the asynchronous technique of web-based learning in which the teacher publishes learning content statically on the Internet and students obtain static learning materials at different times, traditional learning in a real classroom is a synchronous process, where students in and out of the classroom listen to the live instruction given by the teacher. It is true that the asynchronous approach reduces travel expense and provides more flexible learning schedules; however, it is much less effective in catching the learner's attention and interest. Therefore, how to integrate the advantages of the newly emerging learning modes into the traditional classroom to enhance learning effectiveness is an important issue for building future real or virtual classrooms.

The real-time interactive virtual classroom with tele-education experience is one of the successful attempts. It tries to keep the cultural effect for both local and remote students, and also provides a platform for asynchronous review and feedback. Examples include Tsinghua University's Smart Classroom (Shi et al. 2003), ActiveClass (Ratto et al. 2003), eClass (Abowd 1999), and Interactive workspace (Johanson et al. 2002). However, the development of the service-oriented architecture poses new requirements and challenges to the openness of these systems, as elaborated below:

1) Integrating increasing dedicated services on the Internet. The development of the Internet and Service Oriented Architecture has yielded a large number of dedicated services that can improve existing learning systems. A common mechanism is required for the modules inside the learning systems to invoke outside services. Establishing a service-oriented communication bridge between the inside modules and outside services is a feasible solution, which provides standard interfaces and improves system safety.

2) Opening the internal interfaces of learning systems to facilitate deeper service-oriented integration. In the service-oriented architecture, internal interfaces must be encapsulated as services, in order to facilitate easier deployment and deeper integration. Considering the different infrastructures of these systems, it is reasonable to build a proxy to wrap the services of one system to create services with standard format (e.g. web services), so that different learning systems are able to talk to each other and collaborate with each other seamlessly. This mechanism also enables learning systems and other service-oriented platforms to build deeper integration.

3) Providing better interfaces for mobile device access. Mobile devices, especially smart phones, are becoming more and more popular. Researchers (Nakahara et al. 2005) have shown that easy-to-access mobile devices play an important role in learning. Because of the limited computing capability and size of display, the integration of mobile devices into learning systems requires flexible interfaces that can support mobile device interaction.

Addressing the aforementioned challenges, we present a prototype system called Open Smart Classroom, which is an open classroom-based e-learning system based on the Smart Classroom in Tsinghua University (Shi et al. 2003). Two Open Smart Classrooms have been built and connected to each other. One is in Tsinghua University, and the other is in Kyoto University (Fig. 17.3). Combining the two Smart Classrooms via an open network not only required us to facilitate simple communication (e.g. video/audio/controlling messages), but also to address the intercultural communication issues. Therefore, Open Smart Classroom not only tackles intercommunication in the open network, but also leverages the necessary transformations between these classrooms to fill the gaps between different languages and cultures. We integrate the Language Grid (Ishida 2006), which is a multilingual service-oriented infrastructure on the Internet for intercultural collaboration. To fill the language gap between these classrooms, Language Grid Translation services (Murakami and Ishida 2008) are invoked to translate the teacher's original slides in English into different languages. Moreover, we also adopt Langrid Blackboard (Inaba et al. 2007), an application accessible by both the teacher and students. It organizes the multilingual discussion content, stimulates the students from different classrooms by encouraging discussions with each other, and allows them to give feedback to the teacher simultaneously.

All software modules run on our software infrastructure, called Open Smart Platform (Suo et al. 2009), which is designed as a generic service-oriented software infrastructure for Smart Space (Rosenthal and Stanford 2002). As a learning environment integrated by pervasive computing technologies, Open Smart Classroom could be regarded as a Smart Space, and so benefits from the existing Smart Space technologies. Open Smart Platform not only leverages the communication and coordination of distributed modules, but also facilitates services (both inside and outside) invocation, management, and integration.

One trial co-class has been conducted in our Kyoto-Tsinghua classroom, and interesting and promising results have been collected. In addition to evaluating system performance, we also carefully analyse how the students felt about this form of learning, and how effective the language services were in helping them to understand the learning materials and to hold discussions.

In this chapter, we first introduce the architecture used to integrate Smart Classroom services and other service platforms in Sect. 17.2. Section 17.3 explains the design of Open Smart Classroom. Section 17.4 details the evaluation and user study results. Section 17.5 presents related work and we draw our conclusion in Sect. 17.6.

17.2 Integrating Smart Classroom Services with Service-oriented Platforms

Integrating Smart Classrooms Services with service-oriented platforms requires upgrading the existing Smart Classroom with the service-oriented architecture. To satisfy this demand, we extend Smart Platform, the software infrastructure for Smart Classroom, to yield the service-oriented platform named Open Smart Platform. It allows Smart Classroom and other service-oriented platforms to be successfully integrated with each other, as is elaborated in this section.

17.2.1 Upgrading Smart Platform to Service-oriented Open Smart Platform

Open Smart Platform was developed based on Smart Platform (Xie et al. 2002), a generic software infrastructure developed by Tsinghua University for connecting and coordinating various software and hardware modules in smart space to perform specified tasks. Since most of the modules in smart spaces are parallel working processes and have no centralized control logic, Smart Platform adopts the MAS (Multi-Agent System) model and thus is inherently a multi-agent system. In the run-time environment, Smart Platform consists of three main modules: Agent, Container, and DS (Directory Service). The Agent is the basic encapsulation of the software module. It provides the module with interfaces for communicating with other Agents. One instance of DS lies in the center of Smart Platform and is responsible for agent registration, directory service, and message dispatching. One instance of Container runs on each computing devices as a daemon process, acting as the mediator between the Agents running on the same host and the DS. Pub/sub scheme with the notion of Message Group for instant messaging is the main communication tool for agents; extended streaming and bulk schemes are also provided to obtain better QoS.

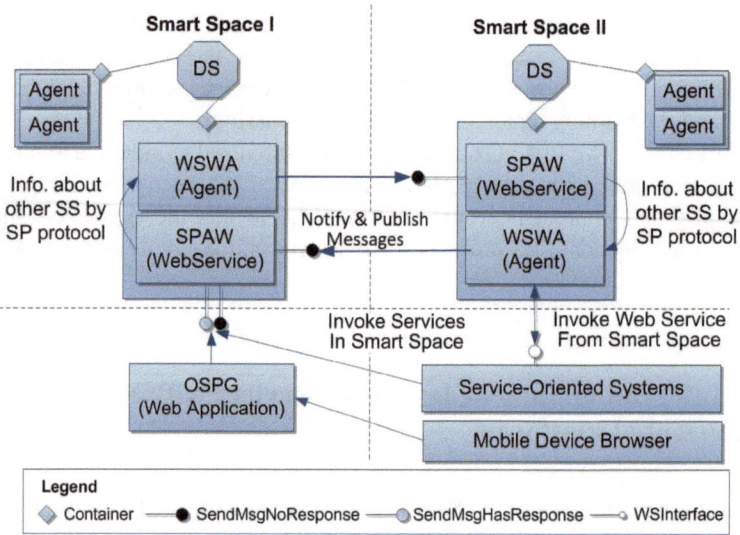

Fig. 17.1 Open Smart Platform runtime architecture.

To make Smart Platform more open to other service-oriented systems and other smart spaces, we built Open Smart Platform by using WSWA, SPAW and OSPG as the access points. They enable service-oriented communication and integration; the architecture is illustrated in Fig. 17.1. WSWA (Web-Service-Wrapper-Agent) is an agent serving as the service proxy to help the agents invoke external web services. It invokes external web services based on the messages received from other agents and returns the response from the external web service to them. SPAW (Smart-Platform-Agent-Web-service) is a web service deployed on Apache Axis and acts as the service adapter; it makes the services inside the smart space accessible to external systems. It receives messages from external systems, transforms the messages into the protocol used in the Smart Platform, creates a SPAW-agent to dispatch the message, and returns the reply from the agent to the external systems. It also allows the developer or administrator to create and deploy workflows, such as BPEL (Business Process Execution Language), which makes it easier to create customized tasks. OSPG (Open-Smart-Platform-Gateway) is a web application serving as the proxy between mobile devices and the smart space. Specifically, the servlet of OSPG generates web pages that suit mobile devices, which use their browsers to interact with the services inside the smart space with the help of SPAW.

WSWA and SPAW are also used to implement message transfer between multiple smart spaces, which extends the original pub/sub coordination mechanism into multiple smart spaces. Thanks to WSWA and SPAW, agents in different smart spaces are able to share the same message groups. It also makes an assembly of connected multiple smart spaces transparent to existing agents, which alleviates the effort needed to update legacy agents for a single smart space to be compatible with connected multiple smart spaces.

17.2.2 Integrating Language Services with Smart Classroom

By introducing WSWA and SPAW, it is easy to integrate the Smart Classroom and language services. The Agents in Smart Classroom are able to invoke dedicated services of other service-oriented platforms via WSWA. At the same time, the interfaces of Agents in Smart Classroom are wrapped into Web services deployed on SPAW, and so can be invoked by other service-oriented platforms. All these invocations are based on the web service standard, and it is reasonable and feasible to provide the developers and administrators with workflow designer tools to create or customize the tasks in Open Smart Classroom.

First, we can integrate Smart Classroom and language services based on the Web Service Orchestration (Fig. 17.2 (a)). In Section 17.3.3, we take one workflow, "Prepare-PPT-Workflow" as example. Created by the third-party workflow tool, "Prepare-PPT-Workflow" integrates several services from Smart Classroom and translation services from Language Grid services. All these services interact at the message level, and feature loose-coupling and easy deployment.

In addition, multiple Smart Classrooms and other service-oriented platforms, such as Language Grid services, are able to realize service collaboration based on the Web Service Choreography (Fig. 17.2 (b)). The Smart Classrooms provide message services, enabling multiple classrooms to exchange the control messages necessary to realize their integration. At the same time, different classrooms invoke different types of language services or workflows in terms of their own preferences. Moreover, the tools (e.g. Langrid Blackboard) provided by the language services collect related information from all classrooms and provide a shared platform on which teachers and students can hold discussions in different languages. The collaboration of these service grids (e.g. Smart Classroom service grid, Language Grid) provides an integrated learning environment such that students in different places with different languages can experience co-classes. The presented Open Smart Classroom demonstrates the significant potential of integrating different service grids to build an enhanced learning environment.

Therefore, with the help of Open Smart Platform, it is highly possible and relatively easy for Smart Classroom service grids and other service-oriented platforms to be integrated together to build enhanced virtual classrooms in an open network.

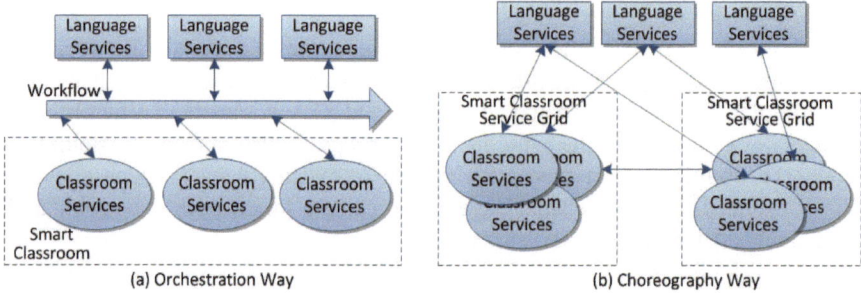

Fig. 17.2 Smart Classroom integrated with language services.

17.3 Open Smart Classroom

Keeping the experiences of a real-time interactive virtual classroom as Smart Classroom does (Shi et al. 2003), Open Smart Classroom emphasizes more the service-oriented collaboration between multiple classrooms to provide a new experience for teachers and students (Fig. 17.3).

17.3.1 Experimental Scenario

The experimental scenario was designed as an international class for Tsinghua in China and Kyoto in Japan. The scenario can be divided into two parts: the first part focuses on the teachers and the second one focuses on the students.

1) Teacher Pierre enters smart classroom in Tsinghua, with an English PPT in his own smart phone. Pierre uploads his PPT file through the Open Smart Classroom Gateway (OSCG) via the web browser on his smart phone. When the file is uploaded successfully, the website redirects to a link that invokes the Prepare-PPT-Workflow of this scenario. The PPT file is automatically translated from English into Chinese and Japanese using a Language Grid Web service. Pierre uses his smart phone to select his uploaded slides and start the presentation. The English and Chinese PPT slideshows are launched on two projectors in Tsinghua, while the English and Japanese versions are copied to Kyoto and displayed on two LCD Screens in Kyoto. As the class proceeds, Pierre uses his smart phone to control the presentation, such as Turn-To-Next-Page, by clicking the link given on the OSCG. The PPT files in English, Japanese and Chinese are turned to the next page synchronously.

2) As Pierre gives his class, Miyata, who is in Kyoto, has some questions about this presentation. To avoid interrupting the presentation, he raises his question in Japanese via Multi-language Chat Agent. Weijun, in China, who sees the question, which has been translated into Chinese, answers his question in Chinese. However, the answer is incorrect. Pierre sees both the question and answer on Langrid Blackboard in English. To avoid misunderstanding, he stops his presentation at an appropriate time, gives the correct answer, and then continues his presentation.

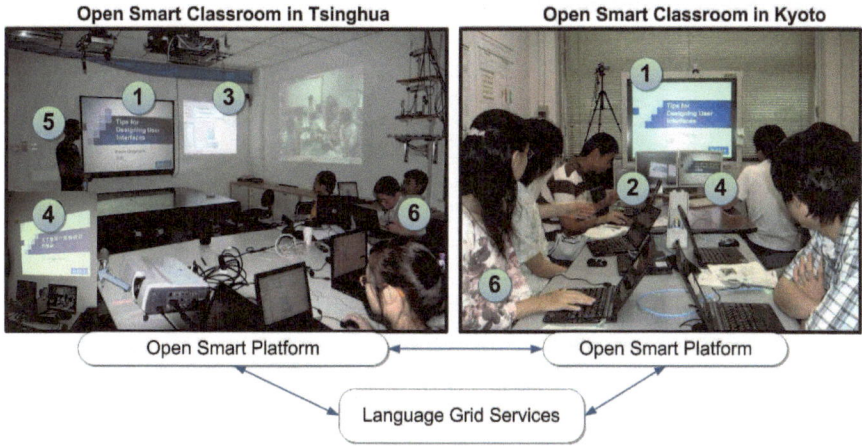

Fig. 17.3 Open Smart Classrooms enhanced by Language Grid services: Two classrooms located in Tsinghua and Kyoto. 1) Synchronized original presentation in English; 2) Live video of the other classroom; 3) Langrid Blackboard helping the students to communicate with each other in different languages, and also giving feedback and questions to the teacher; 4) On-line Chinese/Japanese translated presentation by Language Grid Translation services; 5) The teacher, giving a class in Tsinghua; 6) The students, using Language Grid Blackboard for discussion.

17.3.2 Combined Classrooms' Setup

With the help of Open Smart Platform, Smart Classrooms and language services can be integrated to build enhanced virtual classrooms. In our experiment, two classrooms were established, one in Tsinghua University in China, and the other in Kyoto University in Japan (Fig. 17.3 shows a snapshot of these two classrooms). Fig. 17.4 illustrates the architecture of the runtime environment of combined classrooms collaborating with Language Grid services. Both classrooms run on their own Open Smart Platform, consisting of DS, SPAW, WSWA, OSPG, several

Containers, SameView Agent, PPTController Agent and PPTDisplay Agent. SameView Agent, which enables participants in the two classrooms to see and hear each other, was designed for large-scale deployment over an open network environment (Che et al. 2003). PPTController Agent runs on the Presenter's PC. It translates the slides and dispatches the results to other PPTDisplay Agents; slide display in both classrooms is synchronized. Every participant brings his/her laptop to join in the class, and logs in to the Langrid Blackboard to hold discussions as needed. Langrid Blackboard is a virtual multi-language blackboard. It also acts as a feedback platform for students to post their questions and suggestions to the teacher.

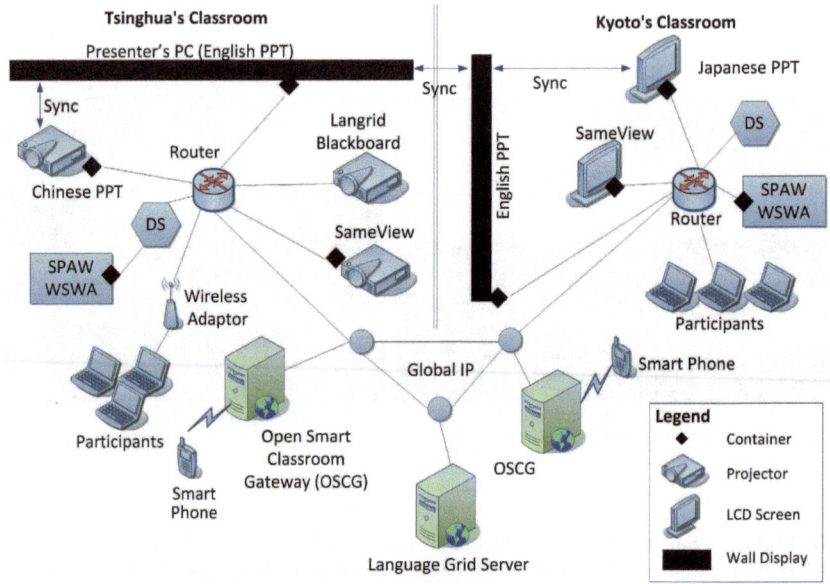

Fig. 17.4 Setup of Combined Classrooms (presenter in Tsinghua).

As Fig. 17.4 illustrates, Language Grid Server provides the language translation services that can be utilized in each classroom. Each classroom has its own Open Smart Classroom Gateway (OSCG) developed based on OSPG (Fig. 17.1). OSCG maintains adapted web pages, which are automatically generated or manually built, to help the mobile devices invoke services in smart space.

17.3.3 Workflow Implementation for Integrating Language Translation Services in Smart Classroom

In the aforementioned scenarios, "Prepare-PPT-Workflow" is responsible for translating the teacher's PPT uploaded from his smart phone into different languages. The "Prepare-PPT-Workflow" was built using the Active-BPEL design tool. It enables administrators to visually create workflows and so avoid tedious and error-prone hand-coding. The Active-BPEL design tool makes it easy to modify the workflow to meet different circumstances and establish new classrooms. We created two types of the "Prepare-PPT-Workflow" in Open Smart Classroom to meet the requirements of different circumstances.

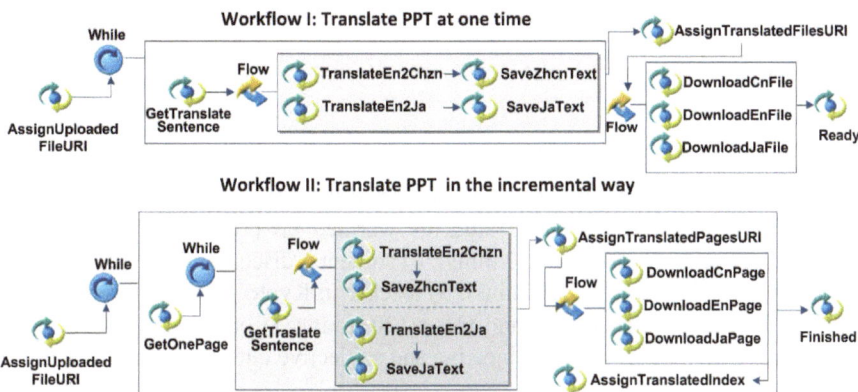

Fig. 17.5 Two implementations of Prepare-PPT-Workflow.

Fig. 17.5 illustrates the two workflows in details: one-time processing (Workflow I) and incremental processing (Workflow II). In one-time processing, the complete PPT file is translated, but the teacher is unable to start the presentation until the translation is completed. In incremental processing, the pages of the PPT file are translated separately and the results are sent to each client, which combine the shared segments into the new PPT file. The teacher can start the presentation when the first few pages have been translated and shared. The latter workflow is more convenient in that it saves the teacher from waiting for the whole translation process to complete, but consumes more total translation time than the former one does.

By integrating different Language Grid translation services, the developers and administrators can easily revise the workflows with Active-BPEL design tools to meet new demands. For example, if the presenter's language changes from English to German, the administrator simply replaces "TranslateEn2Chzn" with "TranslateDe2Chzn". Moreover, Active-BPEL designer can also help the administrator to monitor task status in the classroom. This type of loose-coupled service integration provides flexibility and convenience for the developers and administrators in maintaining the Smart Classrooms.

17.4 Evaluation and User Study

An Open Smart Classroom between Kyoto University and Tsinghua University was established from September, 2006 to December, 2007. To test and validate the work, we evaluated user comprehension and system performance in terms of message transfer.

17.4.1 User Study

The user study mirrored the aforementioned experimental scenarios: 1) the organizers established the environment and described the seminar (15 mins); 2) teacher in Tsinghua uploaded PPT and students warmed up (10 mins); 3) teacher in Tsinghua gave a presentation (30 mins); 4) students' discussion, Q&A, and teacher in Kyoto uploaded PPT (20 mins); 5) teacher in Kyoto gave a presentation (30 mins); 6) students' discussion and Q&A (20 mins); 7) questionnaire (15 mins). The questionnaire consisted of objective and subjective questions.

• Results

For the objective questions, the participants were required to answer a quiz on the two presentations; the results are listed in Table 17.1.

Table 17.1 Objective results of user study

Main Classroom	Students in	Highest Score (%)	Lowest Score (%)	Average Score (%)
Tsinghua	Tsinghua	100	62.5	71.9
	Kyoto	100	37.5	62.5
Kyoto	Tsinghua	80	40	54.3
	Kyoto	100	60	72

The subjective results consist of self-measured English proficiency and comments on Open Smart Classroom. The English proficiency result is illustrated in Table 17.2, which shows that in general the participants in both Tsinghua and Kyoto had some difficulties in understanding the presentation in English.

Table 17.2 Self-assessed English proficiency

Students	Reading[1]	Writing[1]	Listening[1]	Speaking[1]
Tsinghua	3.9	3.4	3.2	3.0
Kyoto	3.2	2.6	2.2	2.0

[1] Ability rating runs from 1 (Beginner) to 5 (Native-like)

Participants were then required to give their comments on Open Smart Classroom. The results for several representative questions are shown in Table 17.3. There are also some other questions, including the operability of Langrid Blackboard, the delay and the quality of the video image and voice. The participants mentioned that Langrid Blackboard had good operability, but it still needs improving to add some label templates to help the participants add comments. During the class, the students in Kyoto felt there was virtually no delay in the video and voice, while the students in Tsinghua felt that there was some slight delay.

At the end of the questionnaire, the students were required to give their overall impression of the whole learning environment. Most participants mentioned that although the system still needs improving, this kind of class gave them a wonderful opportunity to communicate with students in another country, and through the help of the facilitation tools such as Langrid Blackboard and translated PPT, attending this kind of class is quite interesting and motivating.

Table 17.3 Selected subjective results of user study

Question	Students in	Avg.	Max.	Min.	Comments
Q1: How well did the Langrid blackboard help you understand the class?[1]	Tsinghua	2.9	4.0	1.5	*"The function of automatic translation helped me."; "It was easy to understand because they wrote some examples to answer my question about the pictographic characters used in China"; "Not so many labels were created related to the presentation."*
	Kyoto	2.0	4.0	3.0	
Q2: How well did the translated slides help you understand the presentation?[1]	Tsinghua	3.0	4.0	2.0	*"The function of automatic translation helped me."; "It was easy to understand because they wrote some examples as an answer to my question about the pictographic characters used in China"; "Not so many labels were created related to the presentation."*
	Kyoto	3.8	5.0	3.0	
Q3: How well did the Langrid blackboard help you discuss?[1]	Tsinghua	3.4	5.0	3.0	*"I think we could communicate with each other because someone responded when I asked some questions."*
	Kyoto	3.6	4.0	3.0	
Q4: Did you find any problems operating Langrid Blackboard while listening to the presentation at the same time?[2]	Tsinghua	0.43	1.0	0.0	*"I was able to find enough time during the presentation to use Langrid tools."; "It is impossible for me to listen to the presentation while writing in the Black-board at the same time."; "I couldn't concentrate on both tools and presentation because the presenter spoke in English."*
	Kyoto	0.20	1.0	0.0	

[1] The first three questions (Q1- Q3) were rated from 1 (not at all) to 5 (very much).
[2] Q4 question requires a "Yes" (1.0) /"No" (0.0) answer. 4/7 in Tsinghua checked "No"; 4/5 in Kyoto checked "No".

A teacher mentioned that it is very useful to get feedback from the students via Langrid Blackboard. He could stop his presentation at the appropriate time to answer those questions.

• Analysis of the results

During the presentation, most students found that Langrid Blackboard was not very helpful. According to the participants' comments, this was mainly due to two reasons: 1) some students find it hard to operate Langrid Blackboard while listening to the presentation; 2) most participants' attention is focusing on the presentation and translated PPT but not the Langrid Blackboard. Yet Langrid Blackboard still played an important role in providing a platform for the participants to raise questions and give real-time feedback, which is very useful for the teachers.

During the discussion, both participants in Tsinghua and in Kyoto felt that the Langrid Blackboard was quite useful in communicating with each other. Some students reported that it was difficult for them to use Langrid Blackboard while listening to the presentation, but using it during the discussion posed no such problems.

The translated PPTs were not as useful as we expected. The main problem was the poor translation quality, especially for the Chinese version of the Japanese PPT. We believe that translating the PPT will become more useful when the translation service quality improves.

It is true that the objective results show that the students in the local classroom understood the presentation better than those in the remote classroom. However, some remote students still reported getting 100% understanding in the trial. One of the students in the remote classroom reported that although some concepts were not well understood in the presentation, the students in the local classroom explained the concept to him. Hence, using Langrid Blackboard as a supplement to allow the local and remote students to discuss the material with each other is very useful.

17.4.2 System Performance of Message Transfer

We evaluate the performance of message transfer of Open Smart Platform. Open Smart Platform adopts Web Service technologies (WSWA and SPAW) to connect to other Open Smart Platforms. Incorporating Web Service technology brings the advantage that other systems can be easily connected; however, it also imposes an overhead and so impacts system performance.

We conducted a simple experiment to compare the WSWA-SPAW mechanism (in the service-oriented architecture) to the TCP-connection mechanism (non-service-oriented architecture). SenderAgent in Tsinghua's smart space sent a message to the ReceiverAgent in Kyoto's smart space, while the latter returned the same message to the sender. We recorded and compared the time taken to complete the round trip. With the WSWA-SPAW mechanism (WSM), the smart spaces are connected by SPAW and WSWA. With the TCP-connection mechanism (TCPM), Containers in Kyoto were directly connected to DS in Tsinghua through a TCP connection. Fig. 17.6 illustrates the results.

We find that as the message size increases, WSM becomes much slower than TCPM. However, since the size of most of the messages transferred in smart spaces is less than 2 Kbytes, the delay time for one-way message transfer is only about 250ms for WSM, and no complaints about the message delay were reported in the trial. Considering the advantages provided by WSM, we think the sacrifice of performance of WSM is acceptable. Hence we still adopt WSM in Open Smart Platform, regarding it as the feasible solution for connecting two smart spaces.

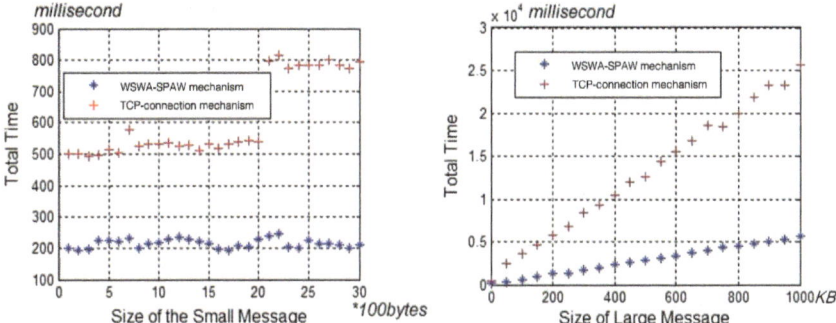

Fig. 17.6 Performance comparison of message transfer between WSWA-SPAW mechanism and TCP-connection mechanism. Note that total time is for round trip message transfer. The message size is only the size of the content in the message, and does not include the message header (SOAP header or Smart Platform header).

17.5 Related Work

Several projects are attempting to improve the experience of traditional classroom-based learning by using Smart Space technologies. Active Class encourages in-class participation using personal wireless devices, where the students give feedback on the class using their own wireless devices. EClass in Georgia Tech is another project with the automated capture of live experiences for later access. Similar to the Smart Classroom project in Kyoto University, its main focus is on capturing the live experiences of the class for later review. Interactive workspace in Stanford explores new possibilities for people to work, discuss, and learn together in technology-rich spaces, which have large displays, wireless, multi-modal devices, and seamless mobile appliance integration. Smart Classroom in Tsinghua University, is similar to Interactive workspace but supports remote students' interaction and communication. None of these projects support multiple classrooms working together, or discuss multicultural learning issues.

Several software infrastructures have been developed for Smart Space. Smart Platform developed by Tsinghua University addresses the communication and coordination of multiple distributed modules in smart space, but fails to take the service-oriented architecture into account or support multiple Smart Platform communication. Similar to Smart Platform, iRos (Johanson et al. 2002) by Stanford is a meta-OS which ties devices together, each of which has its own low-level OS. As an extension of iRos, iCrafter (Ponnekanti et al. 2001) allows users flexibly to interact with services in the Interactive Workspaces. Unfortunately, even with iCrafter, the software infrastructure does not consider the issue of multiple smart space communication. Hyperglue (Peters et al. 2006), which is an extended version of Metaglue (Phillips 1999) in MIT, provides a mechanism of resource management for multiple Smart Spaces. Yet Hyperglue fails to adopt the service-oriented architecture and only supports communication among multiple Hyperglue entities. Gaia (Roman et al. 2002) is a middle infrastructure with resource management and provides user-oriented interfaces for physical spaces populated with network-enabled computing resources. Gaia enables data and applications of users to be abstracted, moved across and mapped to different Smart Spaces. Gaia supports services quite well, however, it does not provide specific interfaces for communication in multiple smart spaces.

17.6 Conclusion

This chapter pointed out new challenges and requirements when developing classroom-based learning systems on the service-oriented architecture. To meet them we developed the Open Smart Classroom by integrating the Open Smart Platform with Language Grid services to enable international and intercultural learning. Open Smart Classroom presages a future learning system, where Smart Classrooms combine with each other in an open network so that students and teachers with different cultural backgrounds and using different languages in different countries can hold classes together.

Open Smart Platform, as an upgrade of Smart Platform, is still a multi-agent system. It provides a sound basis for integrating service-oriented systems with systems in smart spaces.

Enhanced by Language Grid services, Open Smart Classroom provides a novel experience to both the teacher and students and prompts learning in multiple classrooms with different languages. Adopting the service-oriented architecture not only improves the functionality of Smart Classroom, but also facilitates easier deployment and better flexibility. As a prototype learning system, it still has several limitations that need to be overcome, but it has been demonstrated that integrating Smart Classroom with language services is an interesting and promising approach to build distant learning systems, whose impact on multicultural and multi-language communications is worthy of being studied further.

Acknowledgments   We would like to acknowledge the support of the National High-Tech Research and Development Plan of China under Grant No. 2008AA01Z132, National Natural Science Foundation of China under Grant No. 61003005, International Collaborative Research Grants from National Institute of Information and Communications Technology (NICT), Global

COE Program on Informatics Education and Research Center for Knowledge-Circulating Society, and Strategic Information and Communications R&D Promotion Programme from the Japanese Ministry of Internal Affairs and Communications.

References

Abowd GD (1999) Classroom 2000: an experiment with the instrumentation of a living educational environment. IBM Systems Journal 38(4): 508-530

Che Y, Shi R, Shi Y, Xu G (2003) SameView: a large-scale real-time interactive e-learning system based on TORM and AMTP. ICWL 2003: 122-133

Inaba R, Murakami Y, Nadamoto A, Ishida T (2007) Multilingual communication support using the Language Grid. Intercultural Collaboration. Lecture Notes in Computer Science 4568: 118-132

Ishida T (2006) Language Grid: an infrastructure for intercultural collaboration. 2006 IEEE/IPSJ Symposium on Applications and the Internet (SAINT-06): 96-100

Johanson B, Fox A, Winograd T (2002) The interactive workspaces project: experiences with ubiquitous computing rooms. IEEE Pervasive Computing 1(2):71-78

Murakami Y, Ishida T (2008) A layered language service architecture for intercultural collaboration. 6th International Conference on Creating, Connecting and Collaborating through Computing (C5 2008): 3-9

Nakahara J, Hisamatsu S, Yaegashi K, Yamauchi Y (2005). Itree: does the mobile phone encourage learners to be more involved in collaborative learning?. CSCL 2005: 470-478

Peters S, Look G, Quigley K, Shrobe H, Gajos K (2006) Hyperglue: designing high-level agent communication for distributed applications, technical report MIT-CSAIL-TR-2006-017. Laboratory of CS and AI (CSAIL), Massachusetts Institute of Technology

Phillips B (1999) Metaglue: a programming language for multi-agent systems: [M.Eng Thesis]. Massachusetts, USA: Massachusetts Institute of Technology

Ponnekanti SR, Lee B, Fox A, Hanrahan P, Winograd T (2001) ICrafter: a service framework for ubiquitous computing environments. UBICOMP 2001: 56-75

Ratto M, Shapiro RB, Truong TM., Griswold WG (2003) The ActiveClass project: experiments in encouraging classroom participation. CSCL 2003: 477-486

Roman M, Hess CK, Cerqueira R, et al (2002) Gaia: a middleware infrastructure to enable active spaces. IEEE Pervasive Computing 1(4): 74-82

Rosenthal L, Stanford VM (2002) NIST smart space: pervasive computing initiative. IEEE 9th International Workshop on Enabling Technologies: Infrastructure for Collaborative Enterprises (WETICE): 6-11

Shi Y, Xie W, Xu G, et al (2003) The smart classroom: merging technologies for seamless tele-education. IEEE Pervasive Computing 2(2): 47-55

Suo Y, Miyata N, Morikawa H, Ishida T, Shi Y (2009) Open smart classroom: extensible and scalable learning system in smart space using web service technology, IEEE Transactions on Knowledge and Data Engineering 21(6): 814-828

Xie W, Shi Y, Xu G, Mao (2002) Smart platform - a software infrastructure for smart space (SISS). 4th IEEE International Conference on Multimodal Interfaces: 429-434

Chapter 18
Federated Operation Model for Service Grids

Toru Ishida[1], Yohei Murakami[2], Eri Tsunokawa[3], Yoko Kubota[1], and Virach Sornlertlamvanich[4]

1 Department of Social Informatics, Kyoto University, Yoshida Honmachi, Sakyoku, Kyoto, 606-8501 Japan, e-mail: {ishida, yoko}@i.kyoto-u.ac.jp

2 Language Grid Project, NICT, 3-5 Hikaridai, Seikacho, Sorakugun, Kyoto, 619-0289 Japan, e-mail: yohei@nict.go.jp

3 NTT Advanced Technology Corporation, Musashino Center Bldg., 1-19-18 Naka-cho, Musashino-shi, Tokyo, 180-0006 Japan, e-mail: eri.tsunokawa@ntt-at.co.jp

4 National Electronics and Computer Technology Center, 112 Thailand Science Park, Phahonyothin Rd., Klong 1, Klong Luang, Pathumthani, 12120 Thailand, e-mail: virach.sornlertlamvanich@nectec.or.th

Abstract The concept of collective intelligence is contributing significantly to knowledge creation on the Web. While current knowledge creation activities tend to be founded on the approach of assembling content such as texts, images and videos, we propose here the service-oriented approach. We use the term *service grid* to refer to a framework of collective intelligence based on Web services. This chapter provides an institutional design mainly for non-profit service grids that are open to the public. In particular, we deepen the discussion of 1) intellectual property rights, 2) application systems, and 3) federated operations from the perspective of the following stakeholders: *service providers*, *service users* and *service grid operators* respectively. The Language Grid has been operating, based on the proposed institutional framework, since December 2007.

18.1 Introduction

Based on scalable computing environments, we propose a service-oriented approach to developing collective intelligence. This approach requires institutional design to share services among participants. In this chapter, we call the infrastructure to form service-oriented collective intelligence the *service grid*[1]. The service grid has three stakeholders: *service providers*, *service users* and *service grid opera-*

---

[1] Service grid is a generic term meaning a framework where "services are composed to meet the requirements of a user community within constraints specified by the resource provider" (Furmento et al. 2002) (Krauter et al. 2002).

tors. For the institutional design, we should consider the following issues related to each stakeholder:

- How to protect intellectual property rights of service providers and to motivate them to provide services to the service grid. To this end, service providers should be allowed to define for what purpose or purposes their services can be used and to define usage rights accordingly.
- How to encourage a wide variety of activities of service users to increase their use of the provided services. To this end, service users should be allowed to run application systems that employ the services permitted for such use.
- How to reduce the load on service grid operators, while allowing them to globally extend their service grids. To this end, federated operation should be facilitated, where several operators collaboratively operate their service grids by connecting them in a peer-to-peer fashion.

In this chapter, we describe our institutional design for a public service grid typically operated by non-profit organizations such as universities and research institutes. Based on this discussion, we have already developed the *service grid server software* and started the Language Grid that focuses on language services (Ishida 2006). The rest of this chapter describes the concept of service-oriented collective intelligence, the institutional design considering stakeholders including service providers, service users and service grid operators, and our experience in operating the Language Grid.

18.1.1 Service-Oriented Collective Intelligence

To understand service-oriented collective intelligence, we first survey the existing research on *services*. A service is defined as "a time-perishable, intangible experience performed for a customer acting in the role of co-producer" (Fitzsimmons 2005), or as "an activity or series of activities of more or less intangible nature that normally, but not necessarily, take place in interactions between customer and service employees and/or physical resources or goods and/or systems of the service provider, which are provided as solutions to customer problems" (Grönroos 2000). In both definitions, interaction plays a significant role in service provision. Therefore, we have to take account of interaction among service providers and service users in institutional design. Fig. 18.1 shows a common understanding of interaction between service providers and service users. Service providers use their own technologies and resources to respond to service requests from service users, while complying with contracts and service level agreements. To provide services customized to a specific purpose, the service providers need to interact with the service user closely (Spohrer et al. 2007).

The features of services have been changing due to the emergence of the Web. Web services can guarantee the quality of services relatively easily, because Web services remove the physical constraints and human factors from service providers. There are several operation models of Web services such as *hosted service model* and *online broker model*. These operation models allow service providers to provide loosely-coupled and reconfigurable services. In most operation models, service providers can control access to their services to prevent fraudulent use by service users. On the other hand, service users are released from the overhead of operating and maintaining their systems, and can focus on their work that involves using the services.

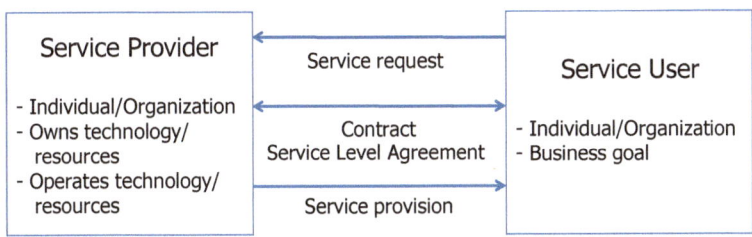

Fig. 18.1 Definition of Service

To simplify the following discussions in this chapter, the main stakeholders are classified into three groups:
- *Service provider* provides all kinds of services to the service grid.
- *Service user* invokes and uses the services provided to the service grid.
- *Service grid operator* is provided with services from the service providers, and allows the service users to invoke and use the provided services.

Service providers and service users are collectively called *service grid users*. A service grid user can act as a service provider as well as a service user. The role of the service grid operator is to stand between service grid users (typically between a service provider and a service user) and support their provision and use of the services. In the following sections, we discuss institutional design in terms of the contracts between a service grid operator and a service grid user.

Note that Web services are classified into *atomic services* and *composite services*. An atomic service means a Web service that enables service grid users to access the provided resources. Such provided resources include data, software, and human resources that are shared in the service grid as atomic services. On the other hand, a composite service means a Web service that is realized by a procedure called *workflow* that invokes atomic services.

To handle the intellectual properties present in the services and resources, the service grid operator may propose a unified license (GPL, Creative Commons etc.) to the service grid users to register their services with the service grid. While a unified license will simplify the operation and promote the use of the service grid, it could cause the service providers to lose some or all of their incentives. Therefore, to better support the service providers, the institutional design of the service grid will not be based on the premise of a unified license.

The operation of the service grid discussed in the rest of this chapter assumes that it is operated publicly mainly by non-profit organizations such as universities and research institutes. It does not assume the case of the service grid in a business firm, where service grid operators can completely or partially control the incentives of service grid users.

18.2 Service Provider

18.2.1 Purpose of the Service Use

From the service provider's standpoint, any discussion of the protection of their intellectual property must address the purpose intended in using their services. In fact, many research institutes and public organizations clearly specify that their services are for *non-profit or research use only*. To reflect such service providers' concerns, we classify the purpose of service use into the following three categories and allow each service provider to permit one or more of the categories:

- *Non-profit use* means 1) use by public institutions and non-profit organizations for their main activities, or 2) use by companies and organizations other than public institutions and non-profit organizations for their *corporate social responsibility* activities.
- *Research use* means the use for research that does not directly contribute to commercial profit.

- *Commercial use* means the use for purposes intended to directly or indirectly contribute to commercial profit.

The above classification can be applied to organizational use as well as personal use. However, when personal use only means private use, personal use can be classified as non-profit use. Note that activities by public institutions and non-profit organizations other than their main activities are excluded, aiming to prohibit service use to obtain funding. Meanwhile, corporate social responsibility activities are included in non-profit use because such activities are often operated in collaboration with public institutions or non-profit organizations.

If a service provider is already selling its service to organizations like local governments, it may not wish to allow non-profit use through the service grid. If service users want to use services, the specified purpose of service use must comply with the terms of use specified by the service provider.

18.2.2 Control of Service Use

When service providers register their services in the service grid, they are required to provide information on copyright and other intellectual property rights of the resources included in their services. In the event that the service provider has been granted a license to the resource by a third party, such information shall also be included. The service provider is required to own the resources or the authority to allow third parties to use the resources. This prevents the service users from accidentally violating the third party's intellectual property rights.

Now, who should register and manage the services in the service grid? If we stand on the premise that the collective intelligence is autonomously formed by the service providers, the service providers should be responsible for the maintenance of their resources, and the process of developing the resources into an atomic service, which we call *wrapping*. The service providers also have to maintain their services and the connection between the services and the service grid. On the other hand, to guarantee the service's quality and safety, the registration and maintenance of services should be done by the operator or with the operator's approval. Therefore, the decision about who should register and manage the services needs to be made considering the trade-off between stimulating the autonomous activities of the service provider and ensuring the quality and safety of the service grid.

Likewise, we need to consider whether to leave the service deregistration process to the service provider or the operator. When focusing on the quality and the safety of the service grid, at least to cover the case of emergencies, the operator needs to be able to deregister a service.

For the service provider, it is desirable that there be flexibility in setting out the terms of use of their services. For example, the possible conditions are as follows:

- Restrictions on the service users who may be licensed to use the services;
- Restrictions on the purpose for which the services may be used;
- Restrictions on the application systems that use the services;
- Restrictions on the number of times that the services may be accessed and the amount of data that may be downloaded from the services.

In general, when the service grid allows the terms of use to be set in detail, it will increase the service provider's satisfaction, while forcing greater overhead on the service users to comply with the detailed terms of use. Moreover, when the service users use a composite service, they need to satisfy all terms of use of every atomic service in the composite service. If we try to assure that automatically, the operator must provide technical measures to ensure that the service users will not violate the terms of use. Therefore, we must trade the service provider's flexibility off against the service user's convenience and the operator's cost.

18.3 Service User

18.3.1 Service Use through Application System

When service users use the service grid for purposes other than personal use, many of them provide services to other users through an *application system*. Here *application system* means, as shown in Fig. 18.2, a system that is provided by a service user that allows users of the system to indirectly access the service grid without being personally authorized by the service grid. In this case, the service user is responsible for ensuring that the application system users comply with the terms of use of each service that is used through the application system.

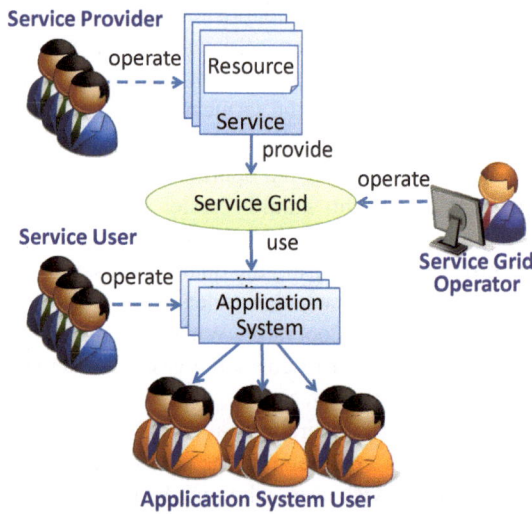

Fig. 18.2 Service Use through Application System

18.3.2 Control of Application System

A service user may operate different types of application systems; for example, one provides a service to the general public through the Web, and another provides a service through a particular terminal in a certain location like a reception counter. This paper focuses on how an application system can control the use of the services and classifies the control of application systems into two types: *under client control* and *under server control*.

- *Under client control* means the status where the users of an application system are under the control of the service user who provides the application system. More specifically, it means the status where the terminals of application system users are under the control of the service user or where the service user is able to identify each application system user. In all cases, the service user who provides the application system must be able to fully grasp at any time the status of use of the application system at each terminal and/or by each user, and have the technical and legal authority to suspend use as necessary.
- *Under server control* means the status where the server on which the application system runs is under the control of the service user, while applica-

tion system users are not under the control of the service user. In this case, the service user must be able to fully grasp at any time the status of use of the application system server and have the technical and legal authority to suspend the server as necessary.

Two examples of the operation of an application system are shown in Fig. 18.3. When an application system provided through the Web can be accessed by users from home without authentication, the status is not *under client control*; however, if the service user controls the Web server, the status is *under server control*. When an application system is provided through a terminal at a reception counter and the terminal is under the control of the service user, the operation is classified as *under client control*.

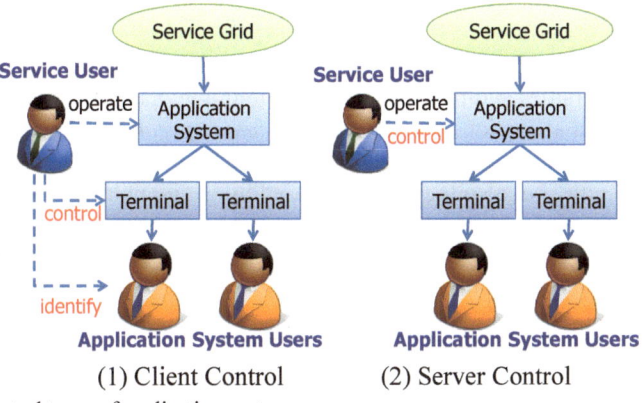

(1) Client Control   (2) Server Control

Fig. 18.3 Control types of application system

The classification aims to allow service users to develop their own application system and select properly the range of services to be offered. Furthermore, the service provider can limit the range of application system users by specifying which type of control the provided service must adopt. For example, when a service provider sells a service to local governments, the service provider may agree to provide the service to patients at a reception counter in a hospital (*under client control*) but may refuse to provide the service to the public through a local government's Web server (*under server control*).

18.3.3 *Return for Service Providers*

Where is the service provider's incentive for providing their services? When the service providers provide their services for free, the service grid operator is required to provide statistical information on the use of the services to the service providers. The statistical information shows who used or is using which service and to what extent. Such information stimulates the interaction between the service providers and the service users. However, the statistical information should not include any transferred data or personal information regarding the senders of data. In case the service providers wish to obtain information on the use of the services other than statistics, the provider should conclude an agreement that establishes the provision of such information with the service user. The service grid operator is not involved in such an agreement.

When service providers provide their services for profit, they will receive fees from the service users by concluding a contract for the payment of such fees. Again, the operator is not involved in such contracts.

18.4 Service Grid Operator

To globally disseminate the service grid, which is centered on non-profit organizations like universities and research institutes, multiple operator organizations need to create/join an affiliation. We call this *federated operation*. The reasons driving federated operation include not only the limited number of users that a single operator can handle, but also the locality caused by geographical conditions and application domains.

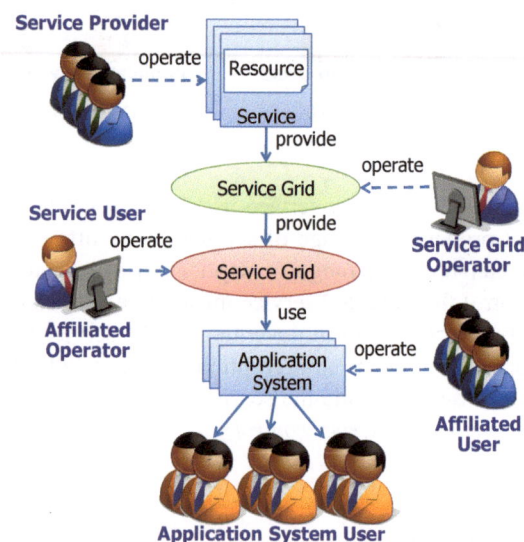

Fig. 18.4 Federated operation of service grid

There are two types of federated operation. One is *centralized affiliation*, where the operators form a federal association to control the terms of affiliation based on mutual agreement. This yields flexibility in deciding affiliation style, but incurs a lot of cost in maintaining the federal association. The other is *decentralized affiliation*, which allows a service grid user to create and become the operator of a new service grid that reuses the agreements set by the first service grid. This type of operation promotes forming peer-to-peer networks by the operators. The type of affiliation is defined by reuse of agreements, but the formation of the peer-to-peer network by the operators is flexible and no maintenance cost is necessary. In the following section, we further discuss decentralized affiliation since it suits non-profit organizations like universities and research institutes.

Let an *affiliated operator* be a service grid user which operates its own service grid that reuses the agreements of the original service grid. Let an *affiliated user* be a user who is licensed to use the affiliated operator's service grid. In such a case, as shown in Fig. 18.4, the affiliated user can use the original service grid, in which the affiliated operator takes the role of a service grid user. That is the key idea of the peer-to-peer federated operation. Even in such case, service providers still have the right to choose whether to allow the affiliated user to use their services or not.

Two service grids in equal partnership are likely to establish a *bidirectional affiliation,* where both operators become users of the other service grid. *Unidirectional affiliation* is also possible. For example, if one service grid provides only basic services and the other provides only applied services, the latter can be a user of the former service grid.

Sometimes it is impossible for different service grids to use exactly the same agreements. A typical problem is the governing law. For international affiliation, a possible idea is to adopt a common law like New York State law, but operators may wish to adopt the governing law of their own locations. In such a case, operators will use the same agreements except for the governing law. In that case, the service providers would need to accept the use of the different governing law to handle the affiliated users in that location.

18.5 Operation of the Language Grid

18.5.1 Language Grid Service Manager

The Language Grid is a service grid for language resources. Its concept was developed in 2005, and the project was launched in April 2006 (Ishida 2006). The fundamental software forming the service grid was developed and has been released by the National Institute of Information and Communications Technology (NICT).

In designing the Language Grid system, it was important to deal with service providers, who had various incentives. For example, some language services may already be sold for profit. If the service grid failed to allow the service provider to receive fees for their services, it would be hard to realize a service grid that truly satisfied service users. Furthermore, since each of the existing dictionaries and language processing software had various types of licenses, the operator could not unify those licenses. Many research institutes that develop language resources can provide their resources as long as they are used only for research. However, if they are used by non-profit organizations for their activities, the research institutes may need to know by who, when, and how much their resources are being used. Such various incentives and conditions form the background of our institutional design prioritizing the intellectual property rights of the service providers. In our operation model (Ishida et al. 2008), language service providers can fully control access to their language services. Language service providers can select users, restrict the total number of accesses per year/month/day, and set the maximum volume of data transfer per access. Providers can set those conditions via the Language Grid Service Manager (see Fig. 18.5). This software provides the registration of services, measurement of service usage frequency, and always monitors the Language Grid.

Fig. 18.5 Language Grid Service Manager

On the other hand, service users wish to use the provided language resources in their various activities. At a school with multi-national students, teachers and parents as well as students will use language services. To allow a large number of people to use the services, the school is required to identify their registered users properly. At the reception counter of a hospital, however, it is difficult to ask patients to register themselves to the reception support system. It is more realistic to identify the terminals to permit service access. In this way, the system must be designed to allow many application system users to use language services in their different environments. To avoid the fraudulent usage of language services, however, service users should not allow the application system users to discover the ID and password of the Language Grid. For example, in the case of an NPO offering medical interpreter services to foreign patients, the NPO is required to enter their Language Grid ID and password in such a way that they do not become public; one solution is to embed the ID and password in their patient support systems.

18.5.2 *Centralized Operation*

The *service grid server software* has been developed and released as open source software. Using this source code, universities and research institutes can operate any kind of service grid. The Department of Social Informatics of Kyoto University started operation of the Language Grid for nonprofit purposes in December 2007. As of September 2010, 132 groups in 18 countries had joined the Language Grid: research institutes include Chinese Academy of Sciences, the National Research Council (CNR), German Research Center for Artificial Intelligence (DFKI), and National Institute of Informatics (NII), universities include Stuttgart University, Princeton University, Tsinghua University and a number of Japanese universities, NPO/NGOs and public sector bodies. Companies have also joined: Nippon Telegraph and Telephone Corporation (NTT), Toshiba, Oki and Google are providing their services without any charge.

We first expected that NPO, NGO and public sectors would become the major users, but universities are using the Language Grid more intensively at this moment; researchers and students who are working on Web analyses, CSCW, and multicultural issues are using language services for attaining their research goals. This trend is natural in the early stage of introducing a new Internet technology. Fig. 18.6 shows the recent statistics of member organizations.

Research institutes, universities, and companies are providing atomic language services such as dictionaries and machine translators. The number of shared language resources now totals 67. Organizations that provided language resources include Chinese Academy of Sciences, Stuttgart, Princeton, Kookmin, and Kyoto Universities, NICT, NII, NTT, Google, Toshiba, Oki, Kodensha, Asian Disaster Reduction Center and a number of public sector groups and NPO/NGOs. When providing atomic language services, providers specify copyright notices and license information in the profiles of the resources. To create composite services that involve the combination of atomic services, many workflows are being written and released. Currently more than 91 services are registered in the Language Grid.

The operation model designed by the authors reflects the intentions of user groups around the world like research institutes and non-profit organizations (Ishida et al. 2008). We were only able to attract such participants because we developed the Language Grid with a strong bias towards formalizing the obligations of all parties. Design of the operation model was conducted in parallel with devel-

opment of the service grid server software. It took more than six months to
achieve consensus on the model. It is probably fair to say that the software was
written to realize the operation model.

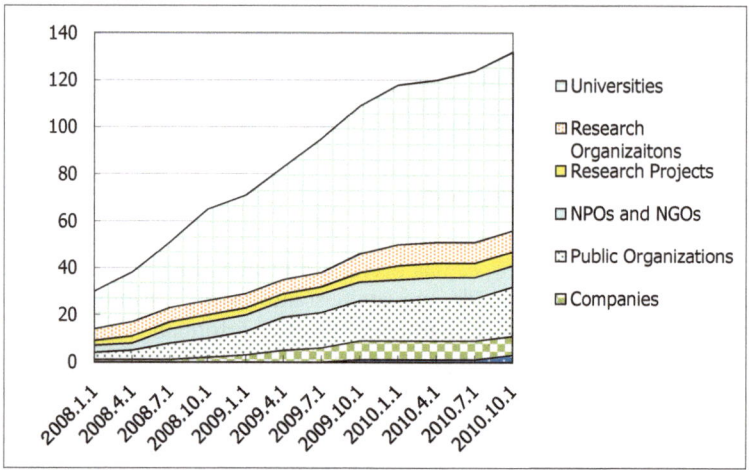

Fig. 18.6 Number of participant organizations

18.5.3 Federated Operation

From operating the Language Grid over two years, we have gained many insights.
One of them is the importance of federated operation. Since the operation center in
Kyoto cannot reach local organizations in other countries, 74 percent of participating organizations are in Japan. Since we need global collaboration, even for solving language issues in local communities, this imbalance should be overcome: the
Language Grid operators need to be dispersed into different organizations globally
and to collaborate with each other. The federated operation model was invented to
realize such collaboration. In fact, the National Electronics and Computer Technology Center (NECTEC) in Thailand launched the Bangkok Operation Center in
October 2010, and is now federated with the Kyoto Operation Center. The Bangkok Operation Center has a plan to provide a collection of atomic services for language processing i.e. LEXiTRON for a Thai-English dictionary, ParSit for English
to Thai machine translation, Vaja for Thai text to speech conversion, and morphological analysis utilities. Those services can be accessed by users of the Kyoto
Operation Center.

So far, we have described the federated operation of the same kind of service
grids. In fact, we had an opportunity to realize the collaboration of different kinds
of service grids. The joint research between Tsinghua University's Smart Classroom and the Language Grid is a typical achievement (Suo et al. 2009). We rebuilt
Tsinghua University's Smart Classroom as a collection of pervasive computing

services. That allowed easier connection between the Smart Classroom and the Language Grid to develop Open Smart Classroom, which connects classrooms in different countries. NECTEC also needs the collaboration of different kinds of service grids provided by neighboring interest groups. These services will soon be extended to cover other media resulting from NECTEC's initiative called the Digitized Thailand Project. The digital contents and applications created from the project will convey the results of digitizing the knowledge assets of the country in terms of local wisdom and practice, cultural heritage, social communication, health care, security and the like. Digitized Thailand on federated service grids is NECTEC's next target to create a collective intelligence for total media integration. Fig. 18.7 shows a possible form of federated operation between Thailand and Japan. As described above, since the basic software of the Language Grid is not specific to language services, it can be applied to collaboration between different service grids with federated operation.

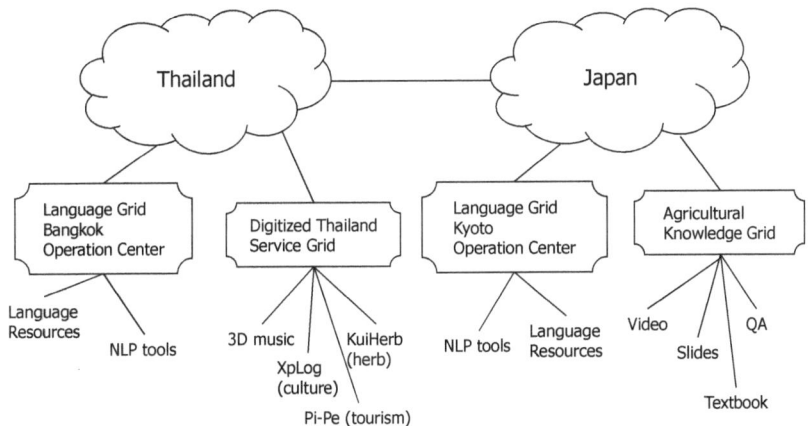

Fig. 18.7 Federation of Service Grids

18.6 Conclusion

In this chapter, we named an infrastructure that forms collective intelligence based on Web services a *service grid*, and designed an institutional framework for a public service grid operated by non-profit organizations such as universities and research institutes. From a consideration of the different standpoints of *service providers*, *service users* and *service grid operators*, which constitute the service grid, we proposed the following framework:

- To protect the intellectual property rights of service providers, the purposes of service use are classified into *non-profit use*, *research use*, and *commercial use*. The service providers can set the terms of service use for each purpose.

- The type of control employed by application systems are classified into *client control* and *server control*. This flexibility allows service users to employ different types of application systems to support their activities.
- To decrease the cost of service grid operators and extend service grid operation globally, the framework allows service grid operators to conduct *federated operation*. The collaboration is realized in a peer-to-peer fashion by introducing the concepts of *affiliated operators* and *affiliated users*.

The institutional design discussed in this chapter is based on our three-year experience of operating the Language Grid. We hope that our experiences will promote the accumulation of knowledge about designing institutional frameworks and contribute to the development of service-oriented collective intelligence.

Acknowledgments   The operation of the Language Grid would not have been successful without the contributions of researchers working on language resources worldwide. We thank Qun Liu, Tu-Bao Ho, Mirna Adriani, Seung-Shik Kang, Christiane D. Fellbaum, Ulrich Heid, Shoko Aizawa, Sadao Kurohashi, Tatsuya Kawahara, Koichi Hashida, Kentaro Torisawa, Hitoshi Isahara, Taku Kudo, Toshiki Muraka and Kazuo Sumita for providing valuable language resources to us. We are also grateful to Shigeo Matsubara, and Hiromitsu Hattori of the Language Grid Kyoto Operation Center, and Pansak Siriruchatapong, Chai Wutiwiwatchai, Thepchai Supnithi and Nattapol Kritsuthikul of the Language Grid Bangkok Operation Center. This work was supported by Kyoto University Global COE Program: Informatics Education and Research Center for Knowledge-Circulating Society, and a Grant-in-Aid for Scientific Research (A) (21240014, 2009-2011) from Japan Society for the Promotion of Science.

References

Fitzsimmons J (2005) Service management: operations, strategy, information technology. McGraw-Hill/Irwin

Furmento N, Lee W, Mayer A, Newhouse S, Darlington J (2002) ICENI: an open grid service architecture implemented with Jini. International Conference on High Performance Networking and Computing:1-10

Grönroos C (2000) Service management and marketing: a customer relationship management approach. John Wiley & Sons

Ishida T (2006) Language grid: an infrastructure for intercultural collaboration. 2006 IEEE/IPSJ Symposium on Applications and the Internet (SAINT-06): 96-100

Ishida T, Nadamoto A, Murakami Y, Inaba R, Shigenobu T, Matsubara S, Hattori H, Kubota Y, Nakaguchi T, Tsunokawa E (2008) A non-profit operation model for the language grid. International Conference on Global Interoperability for Language Resources: 114-121

Krauter K, Buyya R, Maheswaran M (2002) A taxonomy and survey of grid resource management systems for distributed computing. Software: Practice & Experience 32(2): 135-164

Maglio PP, Srinivasan S, Kreulen JT, Spohrer J (2006) Service systems, service scientists, SSME, and innovation. Communications of the ACM 49(7): 81-85

Spohrer J, Maglio PP, Bailey J, Gruhl D (2007) Steps toward a science of service systems. IEEE Computer 40(1): 71-77

Suo Y, Miyata N, Morikawa H, Ishida T, Shi Y (2009) Open smart classroom: extensible and scalable learning system in smart space using web service technology. IEEE Transactions on Knowledge and Data Engineering 21(6): 814-828

Appendix: Service Grid Agreement

This Service Grid Agreement (the "Agreement") is concluded between the Service Grid Operator (the "Operator") and the Service Grid User (the "User"), as identified on the last page of the Agreement.

Article 1 Definitions

1. The "Service Grid" means a software infrastructure designed to accumulate and share Web services. The "Service Grid Software" means the Service Grid Server Software developed by the National Institute of Information and Communications Technology, as well as any of its derivative software. The "Operator's Service Grid" means the Service Grid that is operated by the Operator.
2. The "Operation Entity" means a group or a department within the organization of the Operator that operates the Operator's Service Grid in line with the Agreement. The "User Entity" means a group or a department within the organization of the User that uses the Operator's Service Grid in line with the Agreement.
3. The "Associated User" means a user, including the User, who is licensed to use the Operator's Service Grid by the Operator under the terms of the Agreement herein. The "Affiliated Operator" means an Associated User that operates its own Service Grid under the terms of the Agreement herein, except for the governing law. The "Affiliated User" means a user that is licensed to use the Service Grid by the Affiliated Operator under the terms of the Agreement herein, except for the governing law.
4. The "Resource" means data or software, which is used through the Web services that are accumulated in the Operator's Service Grid. The "Provided Resource" means a Resource that is registered in the Operator's Service Grid by the User.
5. The "Atomic Service" means a Web service that is compliant with the specifications required by the Service Grid Software and that is realized by the procedures that allow the use of the Resources (the "Wrapper"). The "Provided Atomic Service" means an Atomic Service that uses a Provided Resource and that is registered in the Operator's Service Grid by the User.
6. The "Composite Service" means a Web service that is realized by the procedures that invoke Atomic Services (the "Workflow"). The "Provided Composite Service" means a Composite Service that is registered in the Operator's Service Grid by the User. An Atomic Service and a Composite Service are collectively called "Service," and a Provided Atomic Service and a Provided Composite Service are collectively called "Provided Service."
7. The "Terms of Service Use" means the terms and conditions that Associated Users and Affiliated Users must comply with when using Services. "License

Conditions" means the conditions that the Associated Users and the Affiliated Users must comply with when using Resources.

8. The "Application System" means a system that is provided by the User and that allows users of the system to indirectly access Services without knowing the ID and password of the Operator's Service Grid.

9. "Under Client Control" means the status where the terminals of the users of an Application System are under the control of the User who provides the Application System or where the User who provides the Application System is able to identify each user of the Application System. In all cases, the User who provides the Application System must maintain the technical measures to fully grasp at any time the status of use of the Application System at each terminal and/or by each user, and to have the technical and legal authority to suspend the use as necessary.

10. "Under Server Control" means the status where the server used for operating an Application System is under the control of the User who provides the Application System, while the Application System is not Under Client Control. In this case, the User who provides the Application System must maintain the technical measures to fully grasp at any time the status of use of the Application System's server and have the technical and legal authority to suspend the server as necessary.

11. "Non-profit Use" means (i) the use by public institutions and non-profit organizations for their main activities or (ii) the use by companies and organizations other than public institutions and non-profit organizations for their corporate social responsibility activities. "Research Use" means the use for research that does not directly contribute to commercial profit. "Commercial Use" means the use for purposes which aim to directly or indirectly contribute to commercial profit.

12. The "Statistics of Use" means the statistical information on the use of Services by each Associated User and Affiliated User that the Operator records. The Statistics of Use shall not include any transferred data or personal information regarding the senders of data.

Article 2 Conclusion of the Agreement

1. At the time of the conclusion of the Agreement, the User shall complete the blank items on the last page of the Agreement. In the event of a change in any information on the last page, the User shall promptly notify the Operator of such change. The Operator shall have the right to disclose to the public the information provided by the User on the last page of the Agreement.

2. The User shall disclose to the public a summary of the User's activities or research conducted using the Operator's Service Grid; this shall be published on the website of the User or the User Entity.

3. The Operator shall provide the User with the ID and initial password necessary to use the Operator's Service Grid. The User shall securely maintain this

ID and this password. The User shall change the password without delay when instructed to do so by the Operator.

Article 3 Registration of Resources and Services

1. The User allows the use of its Resources and Services to Associated Users and Affiliated Users by registering them in the Operator's Service Grid with the Operator's approval. The User shall have ownership of Provided Resources, Provided Services, and the Wrappers and Workflows that realize the Provided Services, or shall have the authority to allow third parties to use them.
2. The User shall be responsible for the maintenance of its Provided Resources and Provided Services, the development and maintenance of the Wrappers and Workflows, that realize the Provided Services and the maintenance of the connection between the Provided Services and the Operator's Service Grid, and any necessary expenses.
3. The User shall expressly provide the information on copyright and other intellectual property rights of a Provided Resource (in the event that the User is granted license by a third party to the Provided Resource, such information shall be included), the Terms of Service Use, and the License Conditions; the User shall state the above information in the profile of the Provided Resource and Provided Service. The Operator shall take technical measures to allow the Associated Users and the Affiliated Users to check such information before the use of the Provided Service.
4. The User may unregister a Provided Resource and a Provided Service in the Operator's Service Grid at any time, for any reason, without terminating the Agreement and without notice to the Operator. However, the User shall make best efforts to notify the Operator of the unregistration in advance.

Article 4 Service Provision

1. The User may set out the Terms of Service Use of each Provided Service, which include:
    i.   restrictions on users who may be licensed to use the Service (including the permission/prohibition of the use by the Associated User and the Affiliated User);
    ii. restrictions on the purpose for which the Service may be used (including the permission/prohibition of Non-profit Use, Research Use, and Commercial Use);
    iii. restrictions on the type of control adopted for an Application System that uses the Service (including permission/prohibition of the use Under Client Control or Under Server Control);
    iv. restrictions on the number of times that the Service may be accessed and the amount of data that may be downloaded from the Service.

2.   The Operator shall make reasonable efforts to take the technical measures to limit the use of a Provided Service by Associated Users and Affiliated Users in accordance with the Terms of Service Use set out by the User. However, the Operator shall have no obligation regarding the monitoring of compliance with the Terms of Service Use, and have no liabilities for any damages arising from the violation of the Terms of Service Use.

3.   In the case where the User allows Affiliated Users to use a Provided Service, the User shall understand that the Affiliated Users may use the Provided Service under a different governing law.

4.   The User may receive from Associated Users or Affiliated Users fees for its use of a Provided Service, by separately concluding an agreement that establishes the payment of the fees with the Associated Users or the Affiliated Users. In no event will the Operator be involved in such fee agreement, nor have any obligation or liability with respect to such agreement.

5.   The Operator shall take technical measures to provide the User with the Statistics of Use of Provided Services. In the event that the User wishes to obtain information on the use of the Provided Services other than the Statistics of Use, the User shall separately conclude an agreement that establishes the provision of such information with the Associated User and the Affiliated User. In no event will the Operator be involved in such agreement, nor have any obligation or liability with respect to such agreement.

Article 5 Service Use

1.   The User may use Resources and Services in compliance with the License Conditions and the Terms of Service Use.

2.   At every time the User uses Services, the User shall specify the purpose for which the User will use the Services as one of the following: Non-profit Use, Research Use, or Commercial Use.

3.   The User shall understand and agree that the Statistics of Use of the User will be provided to the Service's provider by the Operator.

4.   The User may provide an Application System to an arbitrary third party in a way falling within the conditions of Under Client Control or Under Server Control, in line with the Terms of Service Use. The User shall have the Application System's user comply with the Terms of Service Use and the License Conditions of the Services and Resources that are used through the Application System.

Article 6 Operation of the Service Grid

1.   The Operator may prohibit the Commercial Use of all Services by the User by specifying this on the last page of the Agreement.

2.   The Operator may, at any time, temporarily or permanently, suspend all or any part of the Operator's Service Grid for any operational or technical reasons, or to comply with laws or regulations, by giving notice to all Associated Users.

3. In the event that the Operator wishes to modify the terms of the Agreement, the Operator shall give a one-month prior notice to the User. In the event that the User accepts the modification, or that the one-month period passes without the User giving any response to the Operator, the Agreement shall be modified in accordance with the notice given by the Operator to the User at the end of the one-month period.

4. In the event that the User refuses the modification proposed by the Operator with notification, the Agreement shall be terminated. In the event that the User falls within an Affiliated Operator, the User shall choose either to modify the agreements with all of its Affiliated Users to the same terms proposed by the Operator, or to terminate the Agreement.

5. All notices from the Operator will be given in writing, by e-mail, or on the website of the Operator. The notice may be given on the website of the Operator provided that neither a notice in writing nor by e-mail is practical.

6. The Operator does not warrant any accuracy, security, or usability of Services or the results from the use of Services, and is not liable for any direct or indirect damages arising out of the use of the Operator's Service Grid. The Operator has no liability for any disputes between the User and third parties arising out of or in relation to the use of the Operator's Service Grid.

Article 7 General

1. The Agreement shall be effective as of the date on which both parties sign on the last page of the Agreement and continue in full force and effect until terminated.

2. Each party may terminate the Agreement, at any time, for any reason, with notice to the other party. Upon termination of the Agreement, the Operator shall unregister all Provided Resources and Provided Services from the Operator's Service Grid, and the User shall cease its use of the Operator's Service Grid (including the use of Services and Resources, and the provision of Application Systems).

3. The Agreement shall be governed by, and interpreted in accordance with, the laws of the jurisdiction where the Operator is located. In the event of any dispute between the Operator and the User arising out of or in relation to the Agreement, the parties consent to the exclusive jurisdiction of a court located in the jurisdiction where the defendant in the dispute is located.

[Name of the Operator's Service Grid]   _____

[Service Grid Operator]
Corporate Name of Operator   _____
Corporate Address   _____
Name of Operation Entity   _____
Operation Entity's Address   _____
Operation Entity's Website   _____

Operation Entity's Representative   _____
Operation Entity Representative's E-mail   _____
Operation Entity's Contact E-mail   _____
Authorized Signature   _____
Signed Date   _____

___   Any Commercial Use of the Service by the User is prohibited (Article 6, Paragraph 1.)

[Service Grid User]

Corporate Name of Operator   _____
Corporate Address   _____
Name of User Entity   _____
User Entity's Address   _____
User Entity's Website   _____
User Entity's Representative   _____
User Entity Representative's E-mail   _____
User Entity's Contact E-mail   _____
Authorized Signature   _____
Signed Date   _____

Biography of Authors

Ahlem Ben Hassine got her doctoral degree from Japan Advanced Institute of Science and Technology (JAIST) in 2005. From 2005 to 2008, she was a researcher of National Institute of Information and Communications Technology (NICT), Japan. Currently, she is a faculty member of National School of Computer Science (ENSI), Tunis University, Tunisia. Her research interests include multiagent systems and Web service composition.

Arif Bramantoro holds a master's degree in Information Technology from Monash University, Australia and a bachelor's degree in Informatics from the Bandung Institute of Technology (ITB), Indonesia. He is currently a Ph.D. candidate in Kyoto University, Japan, and planning to complete by March 2011. His research interests include component-and-service based system integration, user oriented Quality of Service and customized-language service composition.

Paul Buitelaar is a senior research fellow and head of the Unit for Natural Language Processing of DERI, a leading research institute in semantic technologies at the National University of Ireland, Galway. Before joining DERI in 2009, he was a senior researcher at the DFKI Language Technology Lab and co-head of the DFKI Competence Center Semantic Web in Saarbruecken, Germany. His main research interests are in language technology for semantic-based information access. He has been a researcher and/or project leader on a number of national and international funded projects, e.g. on concept-based and cross-lingual information retrieval (MuchMore), semantic navigation (VIeWs), ontology-based information extraction and ontology learning (SmartWeb and Theseus-MEDICO), semantic-based multimedia analysis (K-Space), ontology lexicalisation and localisation (Monnet).

Nicoletta Calzolari is Director of Research at the Istituto di Linguistica Computazionale of the CNR in Pisa, Italy, and former Director of the Institute (2003-08). She received an Honorary Doctorate in Philosophy from the University of Copenhagen in 2007. She has promoted internationally the fields of Language Resources and Standardisation and the need for new language resources infrastructures. Her research fields include human language technology, lexical semantics, corpus linguistics, knowledge acquisition, integration and representation. She has coordinated a large number of international and national projects, and is currently coordinating the EC FLaReNet Network. She is a member of ICCL, chair of the Scientific Board of CLARIN, convenor of the ISO Lexicon WG, former vice-president of ELRA, former member of the ACL Exec, and a member of many International Committees and Advisory Boards. She has been General Chair of LREC (since 2004) and of COLING-ACL-2006, and a invited speaker, member of program committees, organiser for numerous international conferences and work-shops, as well as a member of journal editorial/advisory boards. She is Co-editor-in-chief of the Journal Language Resources and Evaluation, Springer.

Heeryon Cho is a researcher at the Department of Interaction Science, Sung-kyunkwan University, Korea. Her research interests include the application of Bayesian networks to context prediction problems, semantic web, intercultural collaboration, and human-computer interaction. She received her B.A. in Mass Communication from Yonsei University, Seoul, Korea in 1995, and received her Ph.D. in informatics from Kyoto University, Kyoto, Japan in 2009.

Thierry Declerck joined the DFKI's Language Technology Lab in June 1996. He first worked within the national projects COSMA (Automated Appointment Sche-duling by E-Mail) and PARADIME (on Information Extraction), the Saarland SHOW-SOG project (automatic hyper-linking and organization of knowledge on the web) and for the European MUMIS project on Multimedia Indexing and Search (2001-2003). He worked at the University of the Saarland from 2002 till 2004 in order to conduct the IST Esperanto and the eContent INTERA projects. At DFKI he has been involved among others in the eTen WINS project (2004-2005), the eContent project LIRICS (2005-2007) and the European NoE "K-Space" (Knowledge Space of semantic inference for automatic annotation and retrieval of multimedia content, 2006-2008). He coordinated the research activities of the EC Integrated Project MUSING, dealing with the Semantic Web for Business Intelli-gence (2006-2010). He was involved in the German project Theseus Medico (till June 2010). He is now contributing to the European project "MONNET" (on Multilingual Ontologies). He taught on various topics at ESSLLI 2004, 2005 and 2007 and he is involved in standardization activities, such as the ISO TC37 com-mittee on the management of language resources.

Ari Hautasaari received a master's degree in Information Processing Science from the University of Oulu, Finland in 2008. He is currently a Ph.D. candidate in Department of Social Informatics, Kyoto University. His research interests include computer-mediated multilingual communication, human-computer interaction and intercultural collaboration.

Yoshihiko Hayashi is a professor in Graduate School of Language and Culture, Osaka University, Japan from 2004. He holds the Ph.D. degree from Waseda Uni-versity, Japan. Before moving to Osaka in 2004, he was a research engineer in NTT Laboratories for almost twenty years, engaged in Japanese-to-English Ma-chine Translation, Japanese Text Revision, Cross-Language Information Retrieval on the Web, Multimedia Indexing utilizing Speech and Language Technologies and Foundation of Information Behavior and Intelligent Information Access. Dur-ing 1994 to 1995, he was a visiting researcher in CSLI (Center for the Study of Language and Information), Stanford University. His research interests include natural language processing, language resources and infrastructures, intelligent information access and computational lexical semantics.

Katsuya Ikenobu holds a bachelor's degree from Faculty of Systems Engineering, Wakayama University, Japan. He is currently a master's student of Graduate School of Systems Engineering, Wakayama University, Japan. His research interests are in Second Life and intercultural collaboration.

Rieko Inaba received B.A., M.S., and Ph.D. in Science from Department of Mathematical and Physical Science, Japan Women's University in 1998, 2000 and 2003 respectively. She worked as a research fellow at the Language Grid Project, Knowledge Creating Communication Research Center in National Institute of Information and Communications Technology from 2005 to 2009. Currently she is a senior lecturer in Department of Social Informatics, Kyoto University, Japan. Her research interests include e-learning technologies, human computer interaction and intercultural collaboration.

Toru Ishida is a professor of Department of Social Informatics, Kyoto University and a leader of the NICT Language Grid Project. Until 1993, he was a research scientist of NTT Laboratories. He spent some time at Department of Computer Science, Columbia University, Institut fuer Informatik, Technische Universitaet Muenchen, Le Laboratoire d'Informatique, Université Pierre et Marie CURIE, and Institute for Advanced Computer Studies of University of Maryland, Shanghai Jiao Tong University, Computer Science and Technology Department of Tsinghua University as a visiting scholar/professor. He is an IEEE fellow from 2002. He studies social informatics and is running research projects related to digital cities and intercultural collaboration.

Jun Koyama is the president of EIP. Co., Ltd., Japan. He is a software expert in Web-based applications and mobile applications. He participated in the open source activities of the Language Grid and Language Grid Toolbox.

Yoko Kubota is a coordinator of Department of Social Informatics, Kyoto University, Japan. Since 2007, she has been a leader of Language Grid Kyoto Operation Center, and a coordinator of Global COE and Field Informatics Core at Department of Social Informatics, Kyoto University. During 1996 to 1999, she was an editing assistant of IEEE Transactions on Pattern Analysis and Machine Intelligence. She was also a core member in the organization committee of many international conferences.

Donghui Lin holds a Ph.D. in Informatics from Department of Social Informatics of Kyoto University, Japan, and an M.E. degree from Department of Computer Science and Engineering of Shanghai Jiao Tong University, China. He is currently a researcher of National Institute of Information and Communications Technology

(NICT), Japan. His research interests include business process modeling and coordination, interorganizational workflow management, Web service composition and service-oriented collective intelligence.

Shigeo Matsubara is an associate professor of Department of Social Informatics, Kyoto University. From 1992 to 2006, he was a research scientist of NTT Communication Science Laboratories, NTT. He received his Ph.D. in Informatics from Kyoto University. During 2002-2003, he was a visiting researcher at University of California, Berkeley. He was also an advisor of NICT Language Grid project from 2006 to 2007. His research focuses on multiagent systems and information economics. He has published in Artificial Intelligence Journal and other academic journals.

Mai Miyabe holds a master's degree from Graduate School of Systems Engineering, Wakayama University, Japan. She is currently a Ph.D. student of Graduate School of Systems Engineering, Wakayama University, Japan, and planning to complete by March 2011. She has developed a multilingual medical reception support system to facilitate reliable communication through conversations between hospital staff and the patient. The system has been introduced in three large general hospitals in Kyoto, Japan. Her research interests include multilingual communication, and human computer interaction.

Monica Monachini is a senior researcher of the Istituto di Linguistica Computazionale "Antonio Zampolli" at the National Research Council (CNR-ILC), Italy from 1986. Her research interest is natural language processing.

Yumiko Mori is the president of NPO Pangaea. She graduated from Saint Mary's College, California, with infant psychology / education major. After experience as a research fellow at Schizophrenia Biology Research Center, Palo Alto, Stanford Univ., she joined Japanese toy maker TOMY in the midst of her doctor's program at Education Dept. of UCLA. She left the company in 1999 to work on the development of the space for children, so that she can demonstrate her own theories that the harmonization among the tool (toy), the space and the human relationships is beneficial for the development of children. She planned and started up R&D Center of Workshops for Children at Okawa Center CAMP (Children Art Museum and Park) located at West-Japan Science City, Kyoto, in April 2001, sponsored by CSK Corporation as part of its social contribution program. She became a visiting researcher of MIT Media Lab in 2002, and started the project Pangaea to create a universal playground in cyberspace, where children across the globe can connect. Pangaea was registered as a certified non-profit organization by Tokyo Prefecture in April 2003.

Daisuke Morita holds a master's degree from Department of Social Informatics, Kyoto University, Japan. He is currently on the R&D staff in NTT Information

Sharing Platform Laboratories, Japan. His research interests include tools for intercultural collaboration and collaborative translation.

Yohei Murakami received his Ph.D. in informatics from Kyoto University in 2006. He is a researcher of National Institute of Information and Communications Technology, Japan. He currently leads the research and development of the Language Grid project, the purpose of which is to share language resources as Web services and enable users to create new services. His research interests lie in services computing and multiagent systems. He founded the Technical Committee on Services Computing in the Institute of Electronics, Information and Communication Engineers in 2009.

Akiyo Nadamoto is an associate professor at Department of Intelligence and Informatics, Konan University, Japan. She holds a Ph.D. in Engineering from Graduate School of Science and Technology, Kobe University, Japan. Until 2007, she was a senior researcher of National Institute of Information and Communications Technology (NICT), Japan. Her research interests include Web computing, database and data engineering.

Takao Nakaguchi received his master's degree from the Kyoto College of Graduate Studies for Informatics in 2006. Currently, he is a senior staff member of NTT Advanced Technology Corporation, Japan. He is a core member in the development and open source activities of the Language Grid Software.

Ulrich Schäfer received his Ph.D. degree from the Faculty of Mathematics and Computer Science, Saarland University, Germany, in 2007. He is a senior engineer and project manager at the German Research Center for Artificial Intelligence (DFKI). Before joining DFKI in 2000, he worked as a software developer and consultant for industrial customers and European institutions. He has also lectured several courses on programming, natural language processing and XML query languages. His research interests include natural language processing software architecture, language understanding, question answering, multilingual information extraction, knowledge representation, knowledge management, semantic web and XML technologies.

Yuanchun Shi is a professor of the Department of Computer Science, the director of HCI & Media Integration Institute, Tsinghua University and the director of Pervasive Computing Division of Tsinghua National Lab of Information Science and Technology. Her research interests include pervasive computing, human computer interaction, distributed multimedia processing and e-learning. She has been guiding the Smart Classroom Project and SEMIC Project which are experimental Smart Space systems for pervasive computing. Prof. Shi received her Ph.D., M.S. and B.S. in Computer Science from Tsinghua University. She was a senior visiting scholar at MIT AI Lab in 2001.

Aguri Shigeno is the chair of Center for Multicultural Society Kyoto, which is a nonprofit organization founded in 1998 to provide a medical interpreter dispatching service to four designated hospitals in Kyoto since 2003, in collaboration with Kyoto City and Kyoto City International Foundation. She led the Center for Multicultural Society Kyoto to win the Award for Encouragement from the Minister of State for Special Missions, Japan with the commendation of the promoter of barrier-free universal design in 2009.

Tomohiro Shigenobu received his master and doctoral degrees in Graduate School of Systems Engineering, Wakayama University, Japan in 2003 and 2006 respectively. Currently, he is a researcher of National Institute of Information and Communications Technology (NICT), Japan. His research interests include human computer interaction and tools for intercultural collaboration.

Claudia Soria is a researcher at the Istituto di Linguistica Computazionale of the CNR in Pisa, Italy. Her research interest is natural language processing.

Virach Sornlertlamvanich received his bachelor's and master's degrees in Engineering from Kyoto University in 1984 and 1986 respectively, and doctoral degree in Computer Science from Tokyo Institute of Technology in 1998. Currently, he is a principal researcher of National Electronics and Computer Technology Center (NECTEC), Thailand. His research interests include natural language processing and information technology.

Yue Suo received his B.Eng. and Ph.D. degree in computer science and technology from Tsinghua University, China in 2005 and 2009, respectively. He is currently a Post-Doctoral Researcher in the Key Laboratory of Pervasive Computing of Ministry of Education, Department of Computer Science and Technology, Tsinghua University. He worked as a visiting student in Kyoto University, Japan (in 2006 and 2007) and the Extreme-Blue internship in IBM China Research Lab (in 2008). His research interests include software infrastructure for Smart Spaces, context-awareness modeling, and intercultural learning.

Toshiyuki Takasaki is a vice president of NPO Pangaea and a part-time researcher in the Department of Social Informatics, Kyoto University. He received his B.A. at the Department of Precision Mechanical Engineering, the University of Tokyo in 1999, and M.A. at the Graduate School of Frontier Sciences, the University of Tokyo in 2001. His research interests include intercultural collaboration and field informatics.

Masahiro Tanaka earned a Ph.D. from Department of Social Informatics of Kyoto University. He is a researcher of National Institute of Information and Communications Technology (NICT), Japan. He is currently working on services computing, focusing on runtime execution management of Web services. His achievements in runtime execution framework for composite Web services have been published at major international conferences in services computing. He also has experience on development of infrastructures for Web service composition and service-based applications.

Rie Tanaka holds a master's degree from Department of Social Informatics, Kyoto University, Japan. She is currently on the research staff in C&C Innovation Research Laboratories, NEC Corporation. Her research interests include multiagent systems, context-based translation and so on.

Eri Tsunokawa is on the staff of NTT Advanced Technology Corporation, Japan. She is in charge of the PR publishing in NTT Cyber Communications Laboratory Group. During 2006 to 2010, she was a coordinator of the Language Grid Project. She was also an editor of the Language Grid Newsletter from 2007 to 2010.

Naomi Yamashita is a researcher in NTT Communication Science Laboratories. She received her B. Eng. and M. Eng. degrees in applied mathematics and physics and a Ph.D. degree in Informatics from Kyoto University in 1999, 2001 and 2006, respectively. She currently conducts research in Computer Supported Collaborative Work and Human Computer Interaction. In particular, her main focus is in multilingual communication and video mediated communication. She examines these issues using a variety of quantitative and qualitative analysis methods.

Alvin W. Yeo is the Director of the Centre of Excellence for Rural Informatics and an Associate Professor at the Faculty of Computer Science and Information Technology, Universiti Malaysia Sarawak (UNIMAS). He has expertise in the area of Information and Communications Technology for Rural Development (ICT4RD). He has published in The Encyclopaedia of Developing Regional Communities with ICT, evaluated Malaysian federal-funded ICT4RD initiatives, and worked with United Nations Economic and Social Commission for the Asia Pacific (UNESCAP). He has been involved in the eBario Project which garnered numerous awards including the Commonwealth CAPAM Innovation award which beat 112 international submissions worldwide. In addition to ICT4RD research, he is also active in Human Computer Interaction research, specifically in software internationalisation, multimodal interaction, gaze-based systems, and the use of ICTs for the preservation of indigenous languages. He currently heads the Sarawak Language Technology (SaLT) Research Group, is involved in numerous national projects, and two European Union projects. He earned his PhD from the Computer Science Department, University of Waikato, New Zealand.

Takashi Yoshino is an associate professor of Wakayama University, Japan from 2004. He received his Ph.D. from Tohoku University in 2001. He has joined the Language Grid Project, and has developed various types of multilingual communication support systems: a multilingual annotated chat communication system, a multilingual chat communication in Second Life, an all-for-one-type multilingual conference support system, a travel information-gathering system for foreign travelers, a Web-based multilingual utterance collection system, a Web-based multilingual parallel corpus collection support system, and so on. His research interests include computer supported collaborative work.